SYNERGY
of
INFLUENCE

SYNERGY *of* INFLUENCE

Leadership, Law Enforcement, *and the* Media

TODD R. SCHMADERER

Copyright © 2024 Todd R. Schmaderer. All rights reserved.

Published and Managed by Latifron Strategic Communications, LLC.

Author Photos by Hodges House
Jacket Design by Andrea Reider
Jacket Front Cover Art Image (Latifron, Title and Author Name) by Mindstir Media
Printed in the U.S.A.
Production by Total Printing Systems, Newton, Illinois
eBook Conversion by Total Printing Systems
Copy Editing by Joanna Booth
Line Editing by Jessica Filippi
Website Design by Kenny Beyer Design
Digital Marketing by Data Axle

No part of this book may be reproduced or transmitted in any form whatsoever, electronic, or mechanical, including photocopying, recording, or by any informational storage or retrieval system without the expressed written, dated and signed permission from the publisher and author.

ISBN (print): 979-8-218-54056-2
ISBN (e-book): 979-8-218-54057-9
ISBN (paperback): 979-8-218-54729-5

LIMITS OF LIABILITY/DISCLAIMER OF WARRANTY:
The information in this book is for educational and informational purposes only. It should not be taken as professional advice. The author and publisher make no representations or warranties regarding the accuracy or completeness of the information provided and will not be held liable for any errors or omissions. The opinions expressed in this book are those of the author and do not reflect the official policy or position of any agency or organization. Readers should seek professional advice as appropriate.

Any memoirs reflect the author's personal experiences and memories. Names and identifying details may have been changed to protect the privacy of individuals. The events and conversations described have been recounted to the best of the author's memory, though some details may have been altered or condensed for narrative purposes. The views and opinions expressed are solely those of the author and are not intended to harm or defame any person, living or dead.

The testimonials in this book are real, but the results may vary. Your results may be different.

Table of Contents

Acknowledgments	vii
Dedication & Foreword	xi
Introduction	1
CHAPTER ONE: Societal Monumental Events and Their Impact on Collective Consciousness	5
CHAPTER TWO: Omaha's National Crime Events—Unveiling the Impact	41
CHAPTER THREE: Law Enforcement Media Ecosystem	59
CHAPTER FOUR: Law Enforcement—Baseline Media Strategy	75
CHAPTER FIVE: Law Enforcement—Critical Media Strategy (A)	101
CHAPTER SIX: Law Enforcement Critical Media Strategy (B) – Mastering Policing Press Conferences	127
CHAPTER SEVEN: Brand Damage Control in Officer-Involved Shootings	155
CHAPTER EIGHT: Race, Police, and Media—Unraveling the Puzzle	177
CHAPTER NINE: Media Self-Rule and Its Effects on Law Enforcement	215
CHAPTER TEN: Freedom of Information Act and Leaks: Navigating the Maze of Information Access	239
CHAPTER ELEVEN: Media Case Study—The Enigma of Serial Killer Dr. Anthony Garcia	255
CHAPTER TWELVE: Final Thoughts—Chief's Perspicacity	287
ADDENDUM ONE: Kerrie Orozco's Writings (Chapter 1)	301
ADDENDUM TWO: Omaha World Herald Verbatim Transcripts (Chapter 1)	305
ADDENDUM THREE: Society of Professional Journalists Code of Ethics: A Guide for Media Integrity	315
ADDENDUM FOUR: Omaha Police Department Organizational Chart	317
Answers to Chapter-End Questions	319
References	333
Glossary	345
About the Author	355

Acknowledgements

UNO: I want to acknowledge with profound respect the University of Nebraska at Omaha, School of Criminology and Criminal Justice. Led by Dr. Gaylene Armstrong Ph.D. UNO's School of Criminology and Criminal Justice is a national leader in criminology, criminal justice, research, and education. UNO Criminal Justice Program Rankings in the United States:

- BS (Bachelor of Science) #17
- MS (Master of Science) consistently in the top #10
- Ph D (Doctorate) #13

As a leader in the academic world of criminal justice, UNO has the vision to understand the evolving dynamics in the law enforcement spectrum. The changing dynamics of law enforcement is ripe for new curriculum and the motivation to write *Synergy of Influence* was to advance the profession of policing in America.

Dr. Mark Foxall PhD - Dr. Foxall is a prominent faculty member of UNO's School of Criminology and Criminal Justice and deserves special acknowledgement. Dr. Foxall and I have met for lunch over the last twelve years during my time as Chief of Police with the Omaha Police Department. He has been a tremendous resource with his executive perspective on a plethora of high-level policing subjects.

When I approached Dr. Foxall about the need for a fresh new criminal justice perspective on leadership, the media, and law enforcement, he was eager to the vision. His guidance, insight, vision, and academic prowess was paramount in the architecture of *Synergy of Influence*.

SYNERGY *of* INFLUENCE

Dr. Foxall, Ph D

"With great respect, thank you, Dr. Foxall,"
— Omaha Police Chief Todd Schmaderer

Dedication

Synergy of Influence : Leadership, Law Enforcement, and Media *is dedicated to the professional men and women of the Omaha Police Department, the citizens of Omaha, and all crime victims and their families. My twelve plus years as chief have been gratifying because of the dedicated, professional, and impressive employees of the OPD. The nature of their work takes them to "dangerous and eerie" places, but they do it because they love the City of Omaha.*

The citizens of Omaha have made my time as chief successful and rewarding. Together we have accomplished many goals. Omaha is a far better city today than it was a decade ago because of our community partnerships, for which I am extremely humbled. Omaha is a tremendous city to be chief of police.

Crime victims and their families will always hold a soft spot for me. We did our best, sometimes to the detriment of our own well-being, to try and bring justice and closure. For all the cases we are still working on, the OPD will not stop. There are crime victim's family members I have grown to respect so much, I will ask about their cases until I am done being chief, even though some of the victims preceded me as chief. There is a hole in us until we can get closure for the families.

To all the above, I salute you.

And to my love, our four children, my parents and my brother,
and our parents. Thank you for the ongoing support, love and extreme patience
to make this entire journey possible. I am forever grateful for each of you.

Foreword

In the realm of law enforcement and criminal justice, few individuals have the depth of experience and academic foundation that Chief Todd Schmaderer brings to the table. As a colleague and observer of his career spanning twenty-eight years at the Omaha Police Department, I have witnessed his evolution from a dedicated officer to the Chief of Police, a role he has held with distinction for twelve years.

This book, under Chief Schmaderer's authorship, is a reflection of his profound understanding and insights into law enforcement. During his tenure, he has navigated an array of challenges: from intricate, protracted investigations and managing sensitive community relations to handling high-profile incidents and officer-involved shootings. These experiences have not only tested but also honed his leadership and managerial skills, always with an emphasis on maintaining transparency and effective communication with the media and the community.

Chief Schmaderer's approach to sensitive law enforcement issues, shared in this book, offers a rare and candid glimpse into the inner workings of a major metropolitan police department. His experiences, articulated here, are invaluable for police executive staff, academics, and students alike. They provide a comprehensive understanding of not just media strategy in policing but also the intricate decision-making processes that guide a police leader.

Through a series of case studies, this book allows readers to follow critical incidents from their inception to resolution, offering insights into the strategic planning, accountability, and transparency that are crucial in minimizing the use of deadly force. Chief Schmaderer's focus on public relations, especially regarding officer-involved shootings, highlights the complexities and necessities of managing these critical events.

As one of the longest-serving chiefs in the history of the Omaha Police Department, Chief Schmaderer has not only brought stability to the department but also fostered a culture of community policing, innovation, and technological advancement. His ability to maintain positive relationships within the department and with external stakeholders has been pivotal in his successful tenure.

This book is more than a chronicle of Chief Schmaderer's remarkable career; it is an indispensable resource for understanding the evolving dynamics of law enforcement in the twenty-first century. It provides a window into the strategic thinking and leadership required to effectively manage a major metropolitan police department in an era of complex challenges and rapid change.

I am confident that readers, whether they are criminal justice practitioners, scholars, or students, will find Chief Schmaderer's insights and experiences both enlightening and inspiring. His contributions to this field are not only significant in terms of practical knowledge but also in shaping the future of policing strategy and community relations.

Dr. Mark Foxall, PhD
University of Nebraska at Omaha, School of Criminology and Criminal Justice

Introduction

Synergy of Influence is a first edition book on the complex interplay between leadership, law enforcement and the media. The book provides a pathway for law enforcement to influence at a maximum through the American press with leadership principles and media insight woven throughout. The book's photos provide a powerful foundation for the author's perspective. **Synergy of Influence** provides upfront experience for readers on a myriad of law enforcement topics, such as race, serial killers, and media misconduct, with a focus on the complex media interplay.

There are law enforcement/media seminars and practical media training where law enforcement is given the opportunity to learn how to interact with the media. However, they severely lack the leadership depth, grasp of complex subjects, and press insight requisite for a deep appreciation of the instruction.

Synergy of Influence takes a "deep dive" into the complex interplay between law enforcement and the media with insight on matters never talked about before. Law enforcement agencies are mandated to have transparency through an effective media strategy. A proper law enforcement media strategy is just as important in today's policing as the investigative process and tactics. This book will provide a baseline media strategy as well as a law enforcement critical media strategy for readers.

Special chapters on:

- Societal Monumental Events and Their Impact on Collective Conscious
- Omaha's National Crime Events – Unveiling the Impact
- Race, Police & Media: Unraveling the Puzzle
- Media Self-Rule, and Its Effects on Law Enforcement
- Brand Damage Control in Officer-involved Shootings (OISs)
- FOIA and Leaks: Navigating the Maze of Information Access
- and a Media Case Study: The Enigma of Serial Killer Anthony Garcia gives readers a jolt of the momentous role of the American press and law enforcement.
- Final Thoughts- Chief's Perspicacity

The author is a twelve year plus police chief for a major city in the United States and provides the insight and strategy necessary for law enforcement agencies today. The average tenure for a major city chief of police is about three years. The chief remains in charge of the Omaha Police Department today.

A well-thought-out media communications strategy must be timely, transparent, factual, and influential. Gone are the days where the law enforcement executive has the luxury of focusing solely on the inside operations of the agency. Yes, the agency executive will always oversee major operations and strategic decisions, but the greatest attribute of the role has morphed into that of a compelling influencer and communicator. The media is a law enforcement agency's conduit for communicating with the public.

Ferguson Missouri 2014

On August 9, 2014, the Ferguson Police Department, a suburb of Saint Louis, Missouri located within Saint Louis County, with an estimated population of 20,631, had an officer-involved shooting (OIS) (fergusoncity.com). The OIS involved a young African American male — eighteen-year-old Michael Brown Jr. — who died of his injuries. The Ferguson Officer, Darren Wilson, was white, and the incident garnered heavy national media interest (U.S. Department of Justice 2014).

For five days, the department released no information. On the sixth day, they released the name of the officer and a video of Michael Brown shoplifting and being aggressive inside a convenience store, just prior to the OIS. The department did not release much else. The incident had racial overtones, as the deceased was Black and the officer was White. In an extension of the racial overtones, the body of Michael Brown laid dead in the street for four hours with no justification put forth by the police.

The Ferguson community was pained over Michael's body being on display for so long. The city went into civil unrest, in part because there was no explanation for the OIS of Michael Brown (Associated Press 2019).

The nation was left to wonder what occurred: Was it self-defense by the officer or skewed judgment from the officer because of racial bias? Early on the public was left to guess or assume, as agency leaders did not communicate with the public through the press. True to form, the information void was left to be filled with unknowns and ad hoc facts of the case. Witnesses said Michael Brown had his hands up or said "don't shoot," but later an FBI investigation exposed that there was no evidence Michael Brown had done so (History.com Aug 2009).

In the days and months following Michael Brown's death, rioting and violent demonstrations took place in Ferguson and quickly spread across the country. The violence was covered extensively by the national media. The Ferguson Police Department's lack of transparency and inability to quickly provide answers in a highly emotional environment has greatly damaged law enforcement's public image. Is it possible

INTRODUCTION

all of this could have been avoided with a timely, effective press conference by the Ferguson chief of police? Would the aftermath have been different if the public had been made aware of the Ferguson officer's version of events? Was this a missed opportunity for meaningful police reform, shadowed by emotion, fear, and agendas?

Law enforcement executives across the country were holding their collective breath as the high-tension atmosphere surrounding race and law enforcement was peaking. The next law enforcement shooting of a Black citizen under dubious circumstances would only pour gasoline on an already high-tension fire. Michael Brown's death unearthed the anger over a history of police shootings of African American males in our country and posed a very real ti nder box scenario.

Seventeen days after the officer involved shooting death of Michael Brown, Omaha, Nebraska, had such an incident. The well renowned television show *COPS* was in Omaha filming OPD for a series of episodes when an officer-involved shooting (OIS) of an African American male took place. The Black male died from his police gunshot injuries.

The suspect was in the process of robbing a Wendy's restaurant and had what turned out to be only a pellet gun as his weapon. The sound employee for the *COPS* television show, Bryce Dion, was struck by friendly police gunfire and died at the scene as well. All eyes were now on Omaha, Nebraska's largest city with nearly 500,000 population (visitomaha.com). The initial portrait to the nation was an African American male killed by white officers while carrying only a pellet gun. Furthering the portrait, a *COPS* TV employee was killed in the same incident in which over thirty rounds were fired by police!

A horrific early impression of a tragic police encounter— and if five days were to pass without effective communication from Omaha police, can the reader imagine the righteous anger and overflow of emotion that would have occurred? Would riots reignite across the country as demands for transparency and accountability hit a boiling point? Would Omaha, Nebraska, become the next Ferguson, Missouri, as the country was in a heightened state of negative police sentiment?

What followed was a stark contrast between how Ferguson police and Omaha police handled the aftermath. The very next day, Omaha police held a press conference to inform the public of what happened, confirming only facts known to them at the time. Transparency, professionalism, and a tone of empathy allowed the facts of the case to shine through.

Instead of a vacuum where supposition filled the information gaps as in the Michael Brown shooting, an understanding of what took place and why was demonstrated by the evidence at hand. Subsequently, Omaha police received minimal public backlash during an emotionally charged atmosphere. OPD had an effective critical media strategy, eliminating information voids and ad hoc narratives.

The lack of a timely and transparent account by Ferguson Police is unfortunately not an aberration, as over and over again, porous communication following a police shooting has caused national reverberations. There is a new reality for law enforcement executives, where the public demands and rightfully expects a timely account of what took place. The public demands their law enforcement to effectively communicate daily and most especially during critical events.

Sure, Omaha police had the opportunity of learning what not to do from Ferguson's media debacle, but it allowed Omaha police to show the nation what a successful critical media strategy looks like. In the aftermath, OPD was praised for transparency and communication with the media. It gave the nation a reason to trust OPD and see it as a professional organization.

A well-researched and implemented communications strategy with the media is just as important as the initial police response and the follow-up investigation. All law enforcement agencies must have an informed baseline and critical media strategy. It is paramount for today's law enforcement!

CHAPTER ONE

Societal Monumental Events and Their Impact on Collective Consciousness

Introduction

There are rare moments in history when the populace recalls precisely where they were and what they were doing during a particular event. They are defining moments that have historical significance. These are called societal monumental events, and they can be described as occurrences so impactful that they change the course of history—and even the collective thoughts or consciousness of a population. A collective consciousness is the shared morals, beliefs, and ideas that operate as a unifying force within society (Open Sociology Education Dictionary, n.d.).

In this chapter, we will dive into the concept of monumental events that have significant impacts on society. We will look at a range of examples, from events that have moved nations to those that have touched individuals, and we will consider why these moments hold such weight.

We will also explore the idea of collective consciousness—the shared sense of understanding and significance that emerges among a group of people. Through real-world illustrations, you will see how this consciousness is formed and how it can shift over time.

Additionally, we will introduce the concept of media ecology, examining how different forms of media contribute to the way events are perceived and remembered. The role of the press in documenting and disseminating the narratives of these events will be a focal point, as we will distinguish between the coverage of national and local happenings.

The death of Kerrie Orozco, a police officer whose passing had a profound effect on her community and beyond, will be analyzed as a case study to demonstrate these concepts in action. We will evaluate the media's role in covering her story and its impact on society's collective consciousness.

Lastly, we will define what constitutes a signature occurrence—events that are distinctive and noteworthy—and offer examples that underscore their relevance.

By the end of this chapter, you should have a clear understanding of how monumental events shape our world and our perceptions, and a range of factors that influence their legacy.

READER REFLECTION
In 2016, San Francisco 49ers quarterback Colin Kaepernick began kneeling for the national anthem as a form of protest against police brutality and social injustices. Many others followed. In a one-page paper, describe the circumstances behind the change in society's collective consciousness in deciding whether to stand for the national anthem.

Collective Consciousness

Laws that socialize what is "right and wrong" in a society are examples of parts of the collective consciousness. One example would be a state's ban on the death penalty. The society (state) has collectively determined the death penalty is unjust or immoral, and their votes enacted the ban. Other societies have legalized THC, as the collective consciousness in their society does not view it as an immoral act (Wallace, R. M. et al. 2007, 10).

"The Star-Spangled Banner" is the national anthem of the United States. Spectators standing for the national anthem is a demonstration of collective consciousness, as patriotism and solidarity have been reinforced. It takes a major shake-up to alter collective consciousness. Until 2016, it was common to see everyone stand for the anthem; now, some Americans kneel rather than stand.

There are three defining characteristics of a societal monumental event.

1. The occurrence will be embedded in the collective consciousness of a society. Society could be a nation, state, or city.
2. The occurrence will be so colossal that most of the populace can recall where they were and what they were doing when the event happened.
3. The occurrence is covered extensively by the media when it occurs, every step of the way after, and on anniversary memorials for years after, possibly forever.

A societal monumental event is different from an individual monumental event. The latter captures the consciousness of an individual and/or the individual's inner circle. It does not capture the collective consciousness of an entire society. In fact, there may be no media coverage of the event at all because it is individualized.

An example of an individual monumental event is the birth of a child, a marriage, or a death in the family. The media is in no rush to report on individual monumental happenings unless the individual is famous and their status in society makes the occurrence of public interest. If the death in a family is a murder, there may be heavy news coverage, but the reporting of the event will not change the collective consciousness of a society.

Practically everyone knows where they were and what they were doing when the buildings of the World Trade Center were hit by two planes during the September 11, 2001, terrorist attack. The previous generation recalls where they were and what they were doing when President John F. Kennedy was shot and killed. Society's collective consciousness was forever altered after the two phenomena occurred. Each occurrence was a monumental event for American society. Each event is wrought with remembrance memorials with accompanying television and documentary coverage, keeping the event alive in society's collective consciousness.

Media Ecology

Media ecology is the study of the media and how it affects the human environment through perception, understanding, and feelings. Media ecology research was at an all-time high during the two catastrophic events of 9/11 and the assassination of JFK. From the moment the planes hit the Twin Towers, the media went into overdrive to give blanket coverage of the American tragedy. America found itself at war, and the media was set to cover it from start to finish.

The role of the media during and after a monumental event is to cover the event copiously in sequence so the populace understands what has occurred. The media coverage must capture the impact to humanity of the societal monumental event, thus shaping the collective consciousness of a society.

9/11

The collapse of the World Trade Center buildings on 9/11, after being struck by terrorist-hijacked commercial planes, was symbolic of the loss of security in America's collective consciousness. When the Twin Towers collapsed, 2,753 people died. Despite America's impressive military prowess and the large geographical distance from terrorist countries, Americans understood after 9/11 that they were not immune to large-scale terrorist attacks.

That societal monumental event marks only the second time the United States has been attacked by a foreign adversary and where a large number of Americans died. The other was Pearl Harbor on December 7, 1941, where the Japanese air-bombed the United States naval base in Honolulu, Hawaii, killing 2,403 sailors, soldiers, and civilians. Pearl Harbor was a societal monumental event and secured America's entrance into World War II.

The overwhelming vote count in favor of holding the perpetrators of 9/11 accountable is evidence of its impact on the collective consciousness of the American populace. The Authorization for Use of Military Force (AUMF) became law just one week later. The AUMF gave the president of the United States the authority to use all "necessary and appropriate force" against those who were determined to be behind the terrorist attacks.

The AUMF initially passed in the United States Senate on September 14, 2001, with a vote of 98-0. It then passed in the United States Congress by a vote of 420-1 on the same day and was signed into law on September 18, 2001, just seventeen days after the terrorist attacks. The collective consciousness of the American populace imposed its will through the AUMF votes.

The media was on the front lines, so Americans and the world could see all the events unfold. For the first time in history, America watched on live television as their first bombs were dropped on Iraq. The term used to describe the very beginning of the invasion of Iraq was "shock and awe." The world was able to see the invasion's progress all the way to the toppling of Iraq and Saddam Hussein. The media gave us all a front-row seat, documenting the historical time in America.

The World Trade Center had also been attacked previously in 1993 when an explosion carved out nearly an 100 foot crater several stories deep and several more high. That first attack killed six people and wounded many others, but it was not prominent enough to change the collective consciousness of society and be considered a societal monumental event. However, many feel it should have been a wake-up call for America.

President John F. Kennedy's Assassination

After President Kennedy was assassinated on November 22, 1963, the press corps started a presidential watch. This is when major news correspondents travel wherever the president goes, presumably so the press never misses a national moment involving the president. The press had missed President Kennedy's assassination.

All decent footage of President Kennedy's assassination came from a private citizen named Abraham Zapruder. He was filming as President Kennedy's motorcade

SOCIETAL MONUMENTAL EVENTS

passed through Dealey Plaza in Dallas, Texas, on November 22, 1963, and the footage is referred to as the Zapruder film. The only media footage covering the day President Kennedy died is of before or after the shots were fired at the motorcade, killing President Kennedy.

The collective consciousness of society was changed forever with the assassination of President Kennedy. It showed that even the president of the United States of America, a symbol of our country's strength, can be killed, and therefore America's prowess can be penetrated.

This was not the first time an American president had been assassinated. The assassination of President Abraham Lincoln on April 14th, 1985, however, did not carry the same impact on society's collective consciousness as President Kennedy's. There was no mass media covering President Lincoln when he died, nor did he have the Secret Service as we knew it when President Kennedy died. There was no television or rapid mass media capabilities during President Lincoln's assassination. As such, the collective consciousness of America was not altered when President Lincoln was killed.

In contrast, President Kennedy's assassination struck at the core of America's prowess and power, penetrated the Secret Service protectors of the president, and showed all Americans its vulnerability through mass media coverage.

READER REFLECTION
On July 13, 2024, former President of the United States (POTUS), Donald J. Trump, was shot by Thomas Mathew Crooks at a rally in Butler, Pennsylvania. Trump was campaigning in Butler as the Republican Presidential candidate. Trump was shot in the ear from a rifle shot as Crooks positioned himself on the roof of an industrial building. The incident was captured on live television, and the world was witness to the historic assassination attempt. Former POTUS Trump turned his head, and the bullet struck his ear instead of its trajectory toward his head, in what would have been a fatal shot. Trump was quickly covered by Secret Service agents before emerging with a bloody ear dripping down his face, pumping his fist to the crowd. If former POTUS Trump would have been assassinated on the campaign trail, would it have been considered a societal monumental event and why?

SYNERGY *of* INFLUENCE

Officer Kerrie Orozco (1985–2015)
Official Omaha Police Photo

The death of Omaha Police Officer Kerrie Orozco in the line of duty was a societal monumental event for the populace of the Omaha, Nebraska, metropolitan area. All Omaha officers knew where they were and what they were doing when word reached them that Kerrie had been shot.

The Omaha community—including Council Bluffs, Iowa, to the east, right across the river—rallied behind Kerrie and solidified our unity. As is distinctive about such events, the press played a vital role in covering the devastation the community endured.

I could argue that Omaha has had three or four societal monumental events in the past fifteen years. It has had two serial killers and a mass killing.

Officer Orozco's death in 2015 was not the first time an officer had been killed. Every ten years or so, Omaha loses an officer in the line of duty.

Officer Jason "Tye" Pratt was killed by gunfire twelve years prior to Kerrie. He had been searching for a wanted person, and the suspect shot him after being discovered hiding in bushes. Eight years prior to Jason Pratt, Omaha Police Officer James B. Wilson Jr. was killed by gunfire while conducting a traffic stop. Both Wilson and Pratt served as a collective conscious reminder for Omaha society of the dangers police officers face and that Omaha's community is not immune to tragedy.

Kerrie's death stands out as the top collective-consciousness-altering event for Omaha. It reminded our collective consciousness that evil exists, and that Omaha's guardians can be killed. Terrible things can happen to admirable people, and it is a challenge to fathom that.

There was something about Kerrie's murder that really hit Omaha hard; harder than ever before. Perhaps it was the newborn baby she left behind. Perhaps it was her charisma or because she was the first female Omaha police officer killed in the line of duty. I do not fully know the answer, but the media ecosystem surrounding Kerrie's murder was ferocious, for good reason, and her death qualifies as a societal monumental event for the Omaha area populace.

For any readers not from Omaha, what is your city's defining moment? Is it a natural disaster like Hurricane Katrina or a mass killing that affected the collective consciousness of your city?

Every major city will have a defining moment. Kerrie's death was Omaha's.

The Day That Shook Omaha

- Detail the events of the day Officer Orozco was killed, emphasizing the immediate response from law enforcement and the community.
- Discuss Officer Orozco's background and her significance to the Omaha Police Department (OPD) and the local community.

This chapter starts with the story of the day Kerrie Orozco was murdered. The story sets the stage for an understanding of the relationship between law enforcement and the media. It is also a heartbreaking segment that allows readers to understand the gravity of societal monumental events and the effect they have on a society's collective consciousness.

The Day Officer Orozco Was Killed

Main Participants

The firsthand accounts of those who were present for Kerrie's death have never been told before, but each of the main participants has agreed to be interviewed: OPD Sergeant Jeff Kopietz, OPD Officer Jeff Shada, trauma surgeon Dr. Mike Wagner, Pastor Greg Ashley, trauma nurse Anne Monroe, and me (OPD Chief Todd Schmaderer). I want to personally thank each one of them for agonizing, crying, and being completely open to talking about their roles and wounds associated with May 20, 2015.

We all felt it was imperative to preserve Kerrie's memory and share our collective pain over that day. The accounts are being archived in this textbook for all future readers and students.

The interviews were emotional; there were tears as we went back to the god-awful day. Some lasted way longer than expected as we got caught up in the sentiment of revisiting. All of us are haunted by the events, and until now, we have been emotionally unable to talk about it.

We decided to open our wounds to impart the real essence of the dangers and reality of police work. We are all keenly aware that Kerrie's death is embedded in the collective consciousness of the Omaha area and feel the essence of the day and the trauma of the aftermath need to be preserved. The heavy emotional toll is synonymous with other societal monumental events across other major cities and is important for readers to feel.

READER REFLECTION:
Law enforcement leaders must consider the following:
- **How can a traumatic occurrence be broken down into digestible pieces for the public through the media?**
- **What parts of the event are too traumatic to share for public consumption while maintaining an important level of transparency?**
- **What is the best approach to making the unknown known?**
- **How will law enforcement utilize the media as the best resource for reaching the public?**

These are questions law enforcement leaders must ask themselves and then create a media strategy to address.

The Dreaded Call

I recall every moment of May 20, 2015, from the second I received the dreaded phone call. It was a sunny and comfortable day in Omaha. I was walking into my office as chief of OPD when I answered a cell phone call from one of my commanders around 12:59 pm.

The commander's tone was direct, yet somber, with no unnecessary words: "There has been an officer-involved shooting, and an officer has been shot, in bad condition."

There was no mistaking a dire situation from the tone of his voice and the direct nature of his words. I matched his tone and asked only vital questions: "Who is the officer?"

His answer: "It is Kerrie Orozco."

The following are my questions and the answers on the phone call related to the incident:

Chief: "How bad is her injury?"
Answer: "It is bad."

SOCIETAL MONUMENTAL EVENTS

Chief: "Is it life-threatening?"

Answer: "Very much."

Chief: "Are there any other officers hurt?"

Answer: "Not physically."

Chief: "Status of the suspect?"

Answer: "He is near death from police officer gunfire."

Chief: "Do you know who shot him?"

Answer: "Yes, Sergeant Jeff Kopietz."

Chief: "Are there any suspects at large?"

Answer: "None."

These were the final questions I asked before giving directions and expediting to the scene:

Chief: "Do we know who the suspect is?"

Answer: "We believe it is Marcus Wheeler."

Chief: "Do we know the race of the suspect?"

Answer: "He is Black."

The question of race is important, as ethnicity is a factor in media coverage. I will save further explanation until Chapter Eight, where the subject of race, police, and the media is thoroughly discussed.

Eerie Drive to the Scene

Putting my emotions aside, I divided up duties to each of my deputy chiefs and jogged to the garage to get my vehicle—designated as Car-1 within OPD. I wanted to go to the scene and be there before Kerrie was transported by Omaha Fire Department (OFD) paramedics. I also wanted to check on my officers, get a layout of the incident, talk to my commanders, verify the criminal investigation was intact, and ensure the media portion was addressed. I knew the media machine would be in overdrive.

As it turned out, the symbolism of the chief coming to the scene was powerful. OPD and the community needed to see the chief on the news at the unspeakable scene. It was imperative that OPD and the community saw and felt high-level leadership during Omaha's collective conscious event.

The drive to where Officer Kerrie Orozco was shot—the area of 30th and Martin Avenue in northeast Omaha—was surreal. Car-1 was expedited with lights and sirens, yet everything I observed was in eerie slow motion.

Police patrol cars blocked off major cross streets so the ambulance could proceed expediently to Creighton University Medical Center without worrying about other traffic. It was a life-or-death motorcade, set up on the fly to try and get Kerrie to the hospital rapidly and maybe save her life.

The officers blocking streets were standing outside their patrol cars and all had the same despondent look on their faces. The officers knew Kerrie's gunshot injury was devastating and a miracle was needed. Word spreads fast in police work as the bond among officers is sky-high.

OPD did everything in its power to ensure Kerrie got the chance for doctors to save her life. The men and women of OPD sprang into action for one of their own, and I will be forever proud of them for that.

Arrival at the Scene

People were gathering in droves, held back only by a sense of respect and the yellow crime scene tape. The media was rabid and everywhere, even though a media staging area had been established. A media staging area is a cordoned-off location for the press that is closer than the public but still safely away from the crime scene. The media knows it is set up for them and it ensures all the media are captive to hear any updates OPD will issue at the scene.

The moment I arrived at 30th and Martin Ave, a galley of reporters, reacted. They wanted to get camera footage of the chief at the scene. Reporters spun in my direction for coverage, and the reporters out of position ran to get an angle for a camera shot. It was at this moment that it registered that leadership was going to be front and center for the entire Omaha community, the state of Nebraska, and the nation.

A number of factors made this a critical moment. There was an immensely important investigation needing to be conducted, grieving officers, an injured officer near death, a suspect near death from police gunfire, and a community in fear—the kind of fear that only surfaces when something horrendous occurs and there are unknowns. *Unknowns* lead to a sensation of helplessness. Unknowns block the grieving process as everyone is stymied trying to come to grips with what occurred.

I knew the unknowns of this day were going to have to be unraveled and the only way to reach a million-population metropolitan area was going to be through the media.

The media is always a willing conduit, but this was different. The media is composed of people, and they were in shock as well. Just like everyone else, the reporters wanted to know how the injured officer was doing. They wanted to tell the world what occurred and unravel the unknowns for the community. In pursuit of that mission, the press would take anything they could get early on, from any source, to put it out to the public.

I must positively acknowledge the Omaha press corps. They verified all information put out and were professional to the core. Nonetheless, there was maximum tension and heaviness in the air.

I wanted to allow myself to feel and hurt when I got to the scene, but I knew it would consume me, so I was forced to push that aside and out of my subconscious. Just like all the officers who responded to work on the investigation, we had to *detach*. My focus was entirely on the duties of being chief of police, and the grieving process was going to have to wait until my chief duties were complete.

As it turned out, that would not be until the day after Kerrie's funeral. The press played a gargantuan role in how OPD walked Omaha through this tragedy. The singular emotion that the community needed to see from the chief of police was professional composure.

I got my briefing from the commanders on the scene.

Marcus Wheeler, twenty-six, was sought by our Fugitive Unit, as he was the suspect in a previous shooting. Wheeler was one of Omaha's most wanted. He had a violent past and an active felony assault warrant for the shooting. A judge had issued a warrant for his arrest.

Wheeler fired his gun at two Fugitive Unit officers, and one of his rounds struck Kerrie. She was left in critical condition and taken to the hospital by the OFD. Wheeler was shot in return by the Fugitive Unit supervisor and was also in critical condition, being taken to the same hospital to which Kerrie was en route.

Wheeler is a textbook example of why the working conditions in the Fugitive Unit are so treacherous. He was a man in his prime: 6'3", 188 pounds, and highly capable. He was also determined not to be caught by law enforcement. A 9mm with a fifty round drum magazine was found at the scene. The details of the encounter will be further expanded later in the chapter.

The Happiest Day Turns into a Nightmare

The morning of Kerrie's death was an upbeat, special day. It was the last day of work for Kerrie, as she was set to take maternity leave to be with her newborn daughter. Olivia Ruth had been born prematurely and was in the intensive care unit for infants. To maximize her time with her newborn, Kerrie elected to save her maternity leave until her daughter was able to come home.

The members of the Fugitive Unit described Kerrie as jovial and in a joking mood on the morning of her death. She was beyond excited to have her daughter with her the next day at home. It had been the happiest day.

The Fugitive Unit had been investigating where Wheeler might be, and team leader Sergeant Jeff Kopietz left the office to conduct surveillance on a house Wheeler had been known to stay at. As the Sergeant was leaving, Kerrie joked with him, "I'm gone for twelve weeks, so you better not leave." No one knew at the time that it would be the last time Sergeant Kopietz would talk to Kerrie. It was around 11:00 a.m.

Sergeant Kopietz set up a residence near 30th and Martin Avenue and conducted surveillance on the house. Wheeler was suspected of living there with a female. In previous surveillance of the house, Wheeler had never been spotted, but the female had been trailed as she had left the house to learn her movements and see if she would lead to Wheeler. Up to that day, all surveillance for him had been a strikeout, as he had never been seen.

Another Fugitive Unit Officer, Bob Laney, a seasoned veteran of OPD and the Fugitive Unit, came to assist Sergeant Kopietz. Laney was set up near the house, but away from Sergeant Kopietz. A maintenance man showed up at the house and was let in. The plan was to wait until the maintenance man left and pull him over to find out if he had seen Wheeler in the house. The maintenance man left, and Laney saw a guy walking from the house as if he had left through the back door. The man looked a lot like Marcus Wheeler.

Laney took a hard right to catch up to the person. He saw Wheeler and yelled out his name. Without hesitation and not saying a word, Wheeler started firing his gun at Officer Laney, striking his unmarked police car.

Laney was unable to fire back at Wheeler because of the distance and the high chance of an errant round. It would have been futile to return fire at this time, as Wheeler had run off after firing his gun. Laney got on the radio and said, "Shots fired," alerting the other members of the Fugitive Unit. Laney and Kopietz were on a channel reserved for the Fugitive Unit only, so no other police officers heard the "shots fired."

Fugitive Unit Officers Jeff Shada and Kerrie Orozco heard the radio and started heading to the area. Sergeant Kopietz pulled up to the female's house to get into position to help Laney. Once he got out of his unmarked vehicle, the female resident of the house came outside and immediately started screaming at him. Sergeant Kopietz believes it was to distract him from Wheeler. The fatal encounter was seconds away.

The Fatal Encounter

Given Wheeler's criminal history and weaponry to hand, I believe he was predisposed to shooting it out with the police. Wheeler had it in his mind that he was not going back to jail. Mentally and physically, he was equipped with a high-capacity magazine, prepared to fight to his death to get away. He had just finished firing rounds at an Omaha police officer (Laney) and was feeling full of extra bravado.

SOCIETAL MONUMENTAL EVENTS

Wheeler saw Sergeant Kopietz and, from approximately 18 yards away, crouched down, and started firing rounds at Kopietz before running away again; he still failed to say a single word. During Wheeler's encounter with the Omaha police, he fired his weapon nine times at Omaha police officers.

Sergeant Kopietz immediately exchanged gunfire with Wheeler, striking him as he ran off. Sergeant Kopietz knew one of his rounds hit Wheeler, as the man flinched in a way indicative of taking a round. Wheeler kept running and found a location behind some bushes where he was preparing to continue firing at Kopietz or any police officer who arrived.

Wheeler and Kopietz were in a life-or-death gun battle. To be clear, this was a gun battle Wheeler had little chance of winning. Sergeant Kopietz was a twenty-four-year OPD veteran and is one of the longest-serving Special Weapons and Tactics (SWAT) team members in the history of OPD. He had served over six hundred warrants as a SWAT team operator and had over a thousand SWAT deployments.

It is my professional belief that even if Wheeler had had the foresight to know who he had just fired upon, he would have done it anyway. Wheeler was on a bravado high after just firing at Officer Laney. Sergeant Kopietz would later tell me that Wheeler had a look of shock on his face as if he had expected Kopietz to retreat.

Surprising Wheeler, Sergeant Kopietz did not retreat. Instead, he started firing his service weapon at him. Kopietz was in a vastly different set of circumstances than Officer Laney and could return gunfire at the fugitive. It was at this moment that Wheeler realized he was no longer in charge and no longer the bully.

Officers Shada and Orozco Arrive

Even though Wheeler was hit, he continued to run and did not give up. Sergeant Kopietz felt that the initial round that struck Wheeler had been fatal, but adrenaline and a bad mindset were keeping him going. Wheeler ran behind homes and crouched down behind the bushes there, preparing to fire again.

Sergeant Kopietz ran after him and was joined by officers Jeff Shada and Kerrie Orozco who courageously entered the "hot zone" to help Kopietz.

Wheeler fired again at Kopietz and he, in return, ended the encounter with his gunfire, striking Wheeler to incapacitation. There were no more threatening movements from Wheeler, but he needed to be checked just to be sure.

Kopietz was unaware that Officers Shada and Orozco were behind him, and he only realized it when he heard Kerrie say, "I've been hit." Those were Kerrie's last words. Wheeler's round had entered her jugular notch area. The notch is the V indentation at the bottom of the throat and top of the upper chest, just above the ballistic vest line.

SYNERGY *of* INFLUENCE

Omaha Police Photo: Marcus Wheeler's Gun

**Official Omaha Police Photo:
Sergeant Jeff Kopietz retired in February 2021**

SOCIETAL MONUMENTAL EVENTS

Personal Photo: Sergeant Jeff Kopietz being honored by the United States Department of Justice for his heroism.

Officer Shada pulled Kerrie out of the gunfire funnel and behind the cover of a house.

Sergeant Kopietz went over to assist, and he believed the injury to be a round to the shoulder. He went back after Wheeler. In actuality, the bullet had traveled through her chest and body before lodging in the back ballistic vest panel. The round lost inertia and dropped while going through the body, and then the vest caught it on the back side.

Jeff Shada had been my partner for a year, eighteen years prior to this day. Jeff and I had worked as a two-officer car in North Omaha. We made countless arrests and took hundreds of 911 calls during our time together. I know from firsthand experience he was a top-of-the-line officer.

Shada was also a long time- serving SWAT team officer and knew he needed to get Kerrie out of the gunfire funnel. Shada instantly began tending to Kerrie's injury.

I recently talked with Jeff Shada, and, like the others who were deeply involved in the incident, he had been emotionally unable to talk about it until now. For him, the moment Kerrie was shot was still tender and fresh in his mind. He said Kerrie was trying to talk but could not and at first Shada could not find her injury.

He would ask her "Where are you hit?" but she could not speak even though she was trying. Kerrie was awake, but the look on her face was the "worst look I've ever seen," Shada later described. Her eyes were pleading for help, and she was reaching toward her upper chest.

SYNERGY *of* INFLUENCE

Omaha Police Photo: Kerrie's ballistic vest and gun belt, removed at the scene to perform life saving measures. The bullet that struck Kerrie was found in the back ballistic vest panel. The bullet entered Kerrie's body just above the vest line and then lost inertia, so it dropped and was caught by the back panel.

Officer Jeff Shada

**Officer Shada retired in May 2023
Official Omaha Police Photo**

SOCIETAL MONUMENTAL EVENTS

**Personal Photo: Jeff Shada (left) and Chief Todd Schmaderer
at his retirement party in May of 2023.**

He believed that Kerrie knew she was going to die; the look on her face spoke for her. It was panic and forced belief that the worst may very well happen. A day that had started out as "upbeat" and "joyful" had turned into a nightmare.

Shada found the entry wound from the bullet and started to put pressure on it.

Kerrie's mouth was moving; she tried to speak but to no avail. All communication was through her eyes, and Shada is haunted by what happened next. He was drastically working on stabilizing and assessing Kerrie when he saw the "light go out in her eyes." In the grass yard of a house, around the corner from the gunfire funnel, Kerrie went unconscious and unresponsive.

Shada paused and, at the worst possible time, the female who lived at the surveillance residence started to yell, "That b---- got what she deserved!"

The female was arrested by other responding officers at this time. As chief, I note that even at this critically emotional time, the OPD officers professionally detained the yelling female.

To this day, the memory of that female interrupting at this critical juncture remains a point of distress for Shada. The only way he can suppress the memory is to focus on the community who supported us in our time of need. He fondly remembers the funeral procession of thousands who gathered along the procession route to support

OPD. It is a memory that trumps the agony of the words the female yelled; a memory where all the good in the world outweighs the bad.

Radio Transmission and Medical Personnel Page

The radio transmission that took place next, from the 911 dispatcher, brings chills down the body. In law enforcement, it is the ultimate distress signal.

"Help an officer 30th and Martin Avenue! Help an officer 30th and Martin Avenue! Help an officer 30th and Martin Avenue! Officer down!"

All OPD has just been alerted to the situation, and Omaha police officers started expediting from across the city. For the officers on the original scene, the sound of the sirens coming to help is indomitable and reassuring. A male officer can be heard shouting over the police dispatch radio, "Get a squad here now!" The male officer was Jeff Shada as he was tending to Kerrie.

For tactical reasons, OPD never releases the number of officers working on a given day and shift. The number of law enforcement personnel expediting the "officer down" call is spectacular and commensurate with the distress signal. Once a commander determines there are enough police officers on the scene, the expediting officers are given the directive to stand down. Many Omaha citizens commented to me that they knew something was going on because of the police cars coming from everywhere with lights and sirens.

Anne Monroe

Anne Monroe was a trauma nurse on duty at the hospital that day. She works in a similar role in another state now but vividly recalls May 20, 2015.

Her pager went off: "Code-99, officer down, CPR in progress." She had just been paged to Omaha's societal monumental event, and her memory of that day is now forever etched. Anne had been a critical flight nurse for the marines and was used to elevated levels of trauma. Unfortunately, she has now added this event to her memory bank of horrifying moments.

Anne recalls running to the trauma room from another part of the hospital. When she arrived, Wheeler was in the trauma bay right next to Kerrie and was being aggressively worked on by other medical professionals. She proceeded past him and entered Kerrie's room, where she started assisting with the CPR.

Health Care Accountability and Portability Act (HIPAA) laws are still in play, so the medical treatment for Kerrie and Wheeler cannot be discussed. Anne was able to say that Kerrie received the best medical care, and that Dr. Mike Wagner gave her the "best chance to live" any doctor could give. The moment Kerrie was pronounced deceased will resonate forever.

As Anne worked on Kerrie, she could tell that she had recently given birth. That knowledge colored her emotions and recall of the day.

Kerrie's injury was a penetrating wound where major veins connect. Her chances of survival were nil. The outcome meant that a young mother, who had been working a challenging job, would never see her child grow up. The day still resonates with Anne as strongly as her worst military memory. The effect of Kerrie's monumental event stretches further than her family and co-workers. It has affected veteran medical personnel and the community.

The second that Dr. Wagner declared her time of death; Kerrie entered the collective consciousness of the whole Omaha area.

Voices from the Front Line

Survivor's Guilt

The incident has been an emotional marathon for Sergeant Kopietz and Officer Jeff Shada. For Shada, that manifests as a wish that the round had hit him. It was a thought that made him emotional during our interview.

For Kopietz, a tactician, and an asset to all young police officers in how to mentally prepare in advance of a fatal encounter, it comes as constant reminders. To this day, Kopietz is still momentarily taken aback when he sees the time of day at 12:58 p.m.—the moment Kerrie was shot.

Shada sees Kerrie's eyes pleading with him when television coverage of her comes on. The local media continues to cover her legacy on anniversaries of her death and memorial events. They do it professionally, but Shada relives it every time.

Both men are retired from OPD now. Both suffer from survivor's guilt. Sergeant Kopietz feels guilty because he is convinced that Wheeler's bullet was intended for him in a continuation of their gunfight. Shada's guilt is due to the agony of not being able to save her and having to see the "light in her eyes go out."

Both men fondly and proudly recall how the community picked up the whole department during the funeral procession for Kerrie. The pain of being up close and personal with Omaha's defining moment has haunted each of them in their own way. There was comfort, however, in the uplifting memory of the Omaha area community showing its support for the police department after Kerrie's death. The media showed their support for the community through their coverage of the monumental event.

Creighton University Medical Center

Paramedics performed CPR on both the officer and the suspect as they were rushed to the Creighton University Medical Center shortly after 1:00 p.m.

When Sergeant Kopietz caught up to Wheeler, he was lying face up and gurgling, gun still in his hand. He was not consciously moving it as a threat, so the gun was secured by Kopietz. Notification for the location was given so the paramedics could tend to him. Wheeler did not say anything; it is likely he was physically unable to, as he was dying.

On my drive to the hospital, the side streets were still blocked off. Car-1 is a black Ford Explorer and is unmarked, meaning it is not identifiable as a police vehicle. The emergency lights are discreetly placed in the front grill above the bumper. However, the media knows Car-1, and the press had converged on Creighton Hospital. They were set up outside on the public right of way, where they could see the ambulances and officers arriving at the emergency room (ER).

The press was looking for a statement, photo, or anything they could get. They would have to wait for another hour or so when a live press conference would be given. Right then, my top priority was checking on my officers, Kerrie, and her family.

Trauma Bay and Meeting Dr. Wagner

I was met by hospital security and two OPD officers. They took me directly to the ER trauma bay, and I passed by the OPD officers who had lined the hallway in tears, yet none of them uttered a word. I nodded at my officers and verbally thanked them as I walked by. They stood up straighter and acknowledged me as well. At this moment, the officers felt the chief was one of them.

At the trauma room entrance, I was met by Dr. Mike Wagner, the attending trauma surgeon that day. Dr. Wagner was clearly in emotional pain and guided me to the trauma bay where Kerrie lay dead. Dr. Wagner explained all the lifesaving measures he had taken and showed me where Kerrie had been shot. He pulled a white linen cloth down so I could see her injury. That moment was cataclysmic, and that word does not even come close to how I felt. Dr. Wagner explained the destructiveness of her injury, as the bullet entered her chest where major veins connect. I was numb but took in every word Dr. Wagner said.

To this day, when I see Kerrie on the news, my mind flashes to the image of her body with the gunshot wound and remnants of trauma equipment left behind. Over time, the flash has gotten shorter.

Dr. Wagner told me that Kerrie had recently given birth. I could easily discern that saying this bothered Dr. Wagner. He implied that he knew this from her body's condition. I acknowledged his statement but could not emotionally handle telling him I already knew she had a newborn. For some reason, I did not feel it was the time to hit him with the reality that it had been her last day at work before going on maternity leave.

Dr. Wagner had a strong presence about him. His bearing and medical acumen stood out on a first impression. He was professional but human, and I could tell he wanted to ensure I was aware of all the lifesaving measures he had undertaken to try and save Kerrie. In my mind, I never questioned Dr. Wagner. As a longtime law enforcement officer, I could sense that from the way Dr. Wagner carried himself that his explanations and words shone like those of a high-level professional. I knew Kerrie's injury was just too catastrophic, or Dr. Wagner and his team would have saved her.

Molasses at the Speed of Light

Dr. Mike Wagner and I became friends the day Kerrie died. We formed a bond in the worst of circumstances; each one appreciating the role of the other and recognizing the gravity of what we went through together. I contacted Mike for an interview about that day since I think his perspective and emotions while trying to save Kerrie were salient to the topic. When I contacted him about the request, he indicated that his sentiments about the incident were rough. He had not been able to bring himself to talk about the impact of that day until now.

Dr. Wagner and I were in similar positions but with vastly dissimilar roles. They were similar in the sense we had to detach from our emotions to focus on our roles at hand. Mike used a phrase called "molasses at the speed of light" to describe his role on May 20, 2015.

He had received the same page as nurse Anne Monroe, so he was keenly aware an officer was on the way in critical condition. For thirty minutes, Dr. Wagner and his team worked on Kerrie trying to save her life. He described those thirty minutes as "molasses at the speed of light," meaning that the time during the process of trying to save her went by at the "speed of light" but were experienced as if time stood still like "molasses." I have heard star athletes use this term before. To the average eye, the athlete is going a mile a minute, but to the athlete, the play is in slow motion. Dr. Mike Wagner experienced this time distortion while working on Kerrie.

After thirty minutes, it was a painfully brutal moment when Dr. Wagner had to declare Kerrie's death. It was a moment that everyone in the room will remember forever. Shortly thereafter, I arrived at Creighton and was met by Dr. Wagner, who took me to Kerrie and relayed all the medical procedures he had performed.

Another trauma surgeon worked on Marcus Wheeler in the trauma bay next door. There had been an aggressive attempt to save him as well. The medical personnel of Creighton Medical Center are true professionals and give it their all for every patient. It is interwoven in their medical oaths and personal moral compasses.

Dr. Wagner made sure to point out that Marcus Wheeler had an eight-year-old daughter at the time and a family that loved him. He had had to notify Wheeler's family as well as Kerrie's about the death of their loved one. He pointed out how he was hurt by the initial response of Wheeler's family, who expressed that the medical team could have done more for Marcus.

The corridors outside the trauma rooms were filled with officers, and there was heavy tension in the air because a police officer was being worked on in the trauma bay right next door to the man who shot her. However, what occurred inside the trauma bays for both Kerrie and Marcus was nothing less than an aggressive attempt to save both their lives.

As a law enforcement professional for twenty-eight years, I have learned that no one is *all* bad. Everyone has redeeming qualities. Even the worst figures in the history of the world have people who love them. Every year there is a memorial put up for Marcus Wheeler on the anniversary of his death at the location where he was shot by OPD. He has an innocent family that misses him greatly. It is important to always remember that.

The last message Dr. Wagner relayed was that he was emotionally stretched by that day as he was faced with the reality of both sides leaving loved ones behind. He had to deliver the news to the Wheeler family and then to the Orozco family. I was by his side during the delivery of the news to Ellen (Kerrie's mom) and Hector (Kerrie's husband). Mike and I were fortunate to have some unexpected company to help us during this dreadful time, through a mutual friend, Pastor Greg Ashley.

Pastor Ashley

In a strange twist of fate, a good friend of mine, Pastor Greg Ashley, had an appointment with me at my office at the time Kerrie was shot, so he came to the ER to offer his assistance and support. At the time of Kerrie's death, Pastor Greg Ashley had been a pastor at Saint John MBC in North Omaha for fourteen years. His appearance was a godsend for both Dr. Wagner and me.

When Pastor Ashley arrived, I saw Dr. Wagner collapse into a hug with him. I had no idea the two of them had known each other, but they were close. Dr. Wagner had worked on Pastor Ashley's daughter, who had been injured in a severe car accident, so their bond had formed over time as the pastor's daughter recovered.

Pastor Ashley and I became friends shortly after I was appointed as chief. He and Chief Bishop Tyler came to meet with me to discuss police-community relations. The three of us came to an understanding after the meeting but with guarded skepticism.

SOCIETAL MONUMENTAL EVENTS

About a month after the meeting, Omaha police experienced a headline-shattering corruption scandal where four officers were publicly fired.

READER NOTE
Readers will learn about the events surrounding corruption as well as other national crime events in Omaha over the last decade. Each one is used as a real-world learning example for this book in Chapter Two.

The day before the scandal broke, Pastor Ashley and I had talked. I had indicated to him but had not told him my decision about the officers involved; that I would make a *just* finding based on the evidence. One hour after my press conference, Pastor Ashley and other North Omaha pastors held a press conference supporting my decision to terminate the officers. There were three men who came to an understanding in my office that day and from then on had no skepticism about each other. Pastor Ashley and I have been friends ever since.

Pastor, Doctor, and the Chief

Dr. Wagner, Pastor Ashley, and I went to deliver the grim news no one ever wants to—to tell the family their loved one has died. Pastor Ashley would prove to have an iconic delivery when talking to those in dire need. Hector Orozco was in a room near the trauma bay and was understandably distraught. Pastor Ashley was able to provide the perfect combination of words and took him in to see Kerrie, where Hector could say his goodbye. Saying goodbye in person is a powerful need, and Pastor Ashley knew Hector needed to do that.

Dr. Wagner and I then went to deliver the news to Kerrie's mom, Ellen Holtz. I vividly recall meeting her for the first time under the worst conditions imaginable. Dr. Wagner delivered the news that her daughter had died from her gunshot injuries. There really is no good way to say it, other than to take a gulp and let it out.

I spoke next. I offered my words of sympathy and condolence as best I could. Ellen's reaction was commensurate with what just occurred; it is forever etched in Dr. Wagner's and my memory. The rest of our time with Ellen is confidential, just as I promised her it would be the day Kerrie died.

I am forever grateful to Dr. Wagner and Pastor Ashley. I needed them, and their presence was the perfect balance. No doctor, chief, or pastor ever wants to be in this situation, but we did it together, and the shared experience bonded us forever. The three of us still support and depend on each other. Every year on May 20 we still talk and text to reminisce and to check up on each other.

Personal Photo: Dr. Mike Wagner, Pastor Greg Ashley, and Omaha Chief Todd Schmaderer

Leaving the room, I choked up but gathered myself. I did not want to let the penetrating emotion get in the way of my job.

I headed to speak to my officers gathered at the hospital. Pastor Ashley came with me. No chief of police ever wants to be in the situation of presiding over a death in the line of duty. The officers intuitively knew that Kerrie had died, but it still had to be officially announced. Word spread like wildfire. I knew it would be among such a close-knit police agency.

Once again, Pastor Ashley had follow-up words to mine that proved to be therapeutic. His delivery of words carries a great amount of synergy and is very soothing.

I then turned my attention to the community. A live press conference was needed to let the community and the world know that a brave officer had died in the line of duty. The media portion of any large event is of paramount importance, and all of us at the hospital were completely drained. However, as professionals, it was now time to tell the Omaha community, on live television, that one of their guardians had died. Omaha had been waiting for an update, as the media had been providing live coverage ever since the ambulance took Kerrie to the hospital.

I have seen too many good police departments around the country focus on an impeccably detailed investigation that could survive all courtroom scrutiny but fail to address the aftermath of the media messaging. Today's chiefs of police need to be adept at inserting the media portion into the layers of a large event, the police response, the investigation, and crime scene work.

SOCIETAL MONUMENTAL EVENTS

Live Press Conference

Let us look at all the stakeholders for the live press conference at Creighton Hospital, which took place two hours after Kerrie died. The community wanted to know if the unthinkable had happened to one of their protectors. They also wanted to know that OPD had a professional response, as a white police officer had been killed by an African American male, who in turn was killed by a white police sergeant.

The OPD has 1200 employees, so I was speaking to my officers and staff, who loved Kerrie. I was introducing Kerrie to the broader world at this time. I was speaking on behalf of all law enforcement, and, of course, I was speaking to Kerrie's family and friends, who would be watching.

I knew the live press conference would have ramifications for the community at large and OPD. It would directly start the healing process for both and be designed to ensure that the bond between the community and the OPD was intact. It was also the start of the grieving process for the Omaha metropolitan area. My words were carried live and printed verbatim on the front page of the *Omaha World Herald*, Omaha's major newspaper.

Other Media

Countless interviews and media inquiries followed. In addition, there was a second live press conference the following day that went into the details behind her death and the officer-involved shooting that followed. This press conference was *clinical*; it was designed to impart the evidence and the chronological order of events. It was a press conference similar in fashion to those for other large policing events, except the circumstances kicked up the meaning and media coverage substantially.

Kerrie's death made the national news on all the major networks, including major cable networks. Over the years, so many interviews and so much media coverage have been dedicated to Kerrie's death that I have lost track. All the press coverage has been very professional and respectful of the family. Even though the event has been covered in abundance, the behind-the-scenes details included in this textbook are only now being shared for the first time.

Kerrie's Funeral and Procession

Kerrie's funeral was carried live by all news stations as befitting a societal monumental event. I had the privilege of being a speaker and eulogizer. I took this opportunity to highlight who Kerrie was and tout her legacy of breaking down barriers. It was also an opportunity to thank the community for supporting OPD in our

SYNERGY *of* INFLUENCE

Photo courtesy of the Omaha World Herald: Orozco Funeral Procession

Photo courtesy of the Omaha World Herald: Orozco Funeral Procession

SOCIETAL MONUMENTAL EVENTS

Photo courtesy of the Omaha World Herald: Officer Kerrie Orozco's funeral procession was miles long through two states (Nebraska and Iowa); over one hundred police vehicles were in the procession from across the country. Citizens from both states lined the streets in the thousands to pay their respect to a fallen hero.

Personal photo: A portrait of the view all Omaha police officers saw during the funeral procession. It was no wonder the community's support resonated deeply with the officers.

lowest moment and highlighting the dangers and nobility of OPD and police work in general.

The people of Omaha and Council Bluffs, Iowa, where Kerrie was from, lined the streets in support and held banners for the funeral procession. Over one hundred police vehicles from around the country were part of the procession for miles. It was the most amazing sight I have ever seen as chief. The community and Kerrie's family were fantastic, just as she was! I broke down days after the funeral, as my emotions up to that point had been purposefully suppressed so I could focus on being chief. Eventually, they had to come out. There is no way to bottle up so many emotions without an eventual eruption. In my mind, that was the perfect time to let it all out.

A Tribute to Kerrie—From the Chief's Perspective

Kerrie was a popular, twenty-nine-year-old police officer, having been a seven-year veteran of OPD. I was the Training Academy Commander when Kerrie was hired and, from day one, I saw her grow into a seasoned veteran. She was professional, knowledgeable, and the consummate community police officer.

At the time of her death, she was working in the Fugitive Unit, a tight-knit group of highly skilled officers—because they had to be. They went after the most dangerous criminals in Omaha, tracking them down and bringing them to justice. The Fugitive Unit has dangerous working conditions, so each team member must be massively capable and able to work in unison. Kerrie, who was very physically tough, fit right in.

She was also respected for her physical prowess. Kerrie was a three-time boxer in the annual Guns & Hoses community charitable event, where OPD squares off against the OFD. Her fights were classics, and her personality shone through as she fought valiantly against an OFD boxer who boxed like a professional. Kerrie more than held her own and secured a victory in the final bout.

She was community-minded and a remarkable ambassador for OPD. OPD officers volunteer at the Police Athletic Community Engagement (PACE) program to break down barriers for underserved youth in our community. When Kerrie volunteered, she was simply "Coach Kerrie" to kids—and happened to be an Omaha police officer. Her impact was so widespread that the death galvanized the community.

Kerrie Holtz married Hector Orozco Lopez in April 2011, becoming Kerrie Orozco. She had two stepchildren, Natalia, and Santiago. Her daughter, Olivia Ruth, was born prematurely on February 17, 2015, and was in the neonatal intensive care unit at the time of her mom's death. Olivia Ruth was set to go home the day after Kerrie was

SOCIETAL MONUMENTAL EVENTS

killed. Kerrie had returned to work in the interim period to save her leave time to use when her daughter arrived home.

Kerrie was an influential powerhouse in every facet of her life as a mom, wife, daughter, and co-worker, and she still had time for the community. After her death, the local legacy she started as an officer continues to this day. Her legacy of breaking down barriers resonates in Omaha's underserved community and in every neighborhood.

The community has never forgotten Kerrie, since the Kerrie Orozco Park, a baseball field for youth, was built in her honor Every year, on the anniversary of her death, her memory lives on. In 2025, the ten-year anniversary of her death will commence, and the remembrance events will be mammoth.

Despite the circumstances, I am proud the entire country got to know Kerrie. She will live on forever through her legacy of community and breaking down barriers. Kerrie's mom, husband, and daughter are living reminders of her character, sacrifice, and strength in the Omaha community. The fabric of who Kerrie was is embedded in the collective consciousness of Omaha.

Kerrie's Mom, Kerrie's Writings, and Kerrie's Husband

Kerrie's mom, Ellen Holtz, has been a rock through all this and is a highly impressive person. I have spoken with Ellen many times over the years. We see each other at commemorative events for Kerrie and during police recruit graduations, where the top recruit is given the Kerrie Orozco Award.

Omaha Police Photo: Kerrie as a coach at Pace.

SYNERGY *of* INFLUENCE

Personal Photo: Ellen Holtz, Hector Orozco, Olivia Ruth, and Chief Schmaderer at the Horses of Honor celebration. Kerrie and all the fallen Omaha police officers had a dedicated horse made for them with personalized artwork.

Personal Photo: Ellen Holtz and I at the groundbreaking for the new Kerrie Orozco baseball Field.

SOCIETAL MONUMENTAL EVENTS

Sadly, the first time I met Ellen was in the trauma room where Kerrie died. Ellen and I have never talked about our first meeting, as we would rather focus on positive memories.

Ellen knows her daughter is in the collective consciousness of the Omaha community and has made the sacrifice to attend remembrance and honoring events for Kerrie for the last eight years.

I reached out to Kerrie's mom for this textbook. I wanted readers to feel and appreciate the overwhelming emotion present on the day Kerrie died. Ellen has given approval for this segment, as have all the people whose names are referenced. Kerrie's husband, Hector Orozco, has also given his blessing on this segment of Chapter One.

Kerrie's mom has shared with me writings her daughter authored as a child and adult. The writings embody Kerrie in her own words, and we both felt the content should be included in this book because of the impact they were sure to have. Kerrie's writing has never been shared publicly before and can be found in Addendum 1. There are three of Kerrie's own pieces of writing in the addendum, and the work entitled "It Could Have Been Me" is of particular interest for this chapter.

Hector Orozco is a hulk of a man, inside and out. He displays a physically strong exterior, along with an inner strength that is stately. Hector and I talked about the textbook, as I wanted his approval for this segment so readers could feel and understand the heavy emotional toll of his loss.

There is no playbook for what Hector has been through. He misses Kerrie terribly to this day, and his daughter, Olivia Ruth, was only three months old when her mom died. Hector and Kerrie's plans for raising Olivia together were shattered, leaving the sole responsibility for the little girl to Hector. Yes, Hector has received help, and Olivia has mighty female role models—one being her grandmother Ellen—but the toll on Hector is unique.

Olivia is now nine years old and thoroughly entrenched in grade school. Hector worries if he has done a respectable job of being the sole parent. By all accounts, he has excelled, but he is understandably pensive about his sole parenting role.

When Olivia was first starting preschool, she would come home and ask her dad, "Where is my mommy?" Olivia would see other preschoolers being picked up from school by their moms and she would wonder why she does not have a "mommy."

Hector has done his best to explain the hard circumstances that Olivia was faced with as a three-month-old. As a nine-year-old now, Olivia is proud of her mom. Her eyes light up at her mention because Hector has imparted how special Kerrie was, how much Kerrie loved Olivia, and how much the community loves her mom.

Olivia had many questions about her mom. No doubt she will continue to have questions, but Hector has answered them and filled in the gaps with stories of who her mom was in an admirable way. Olivia is a healthy and happy little girl; for Hector, this means the world, even as he misses Kerrie tremendously every day.

Societal Monumental Events and Media Strategy

At any moment, a police chief and a police department may be thrust into the national spotlight for a myriad of large events: the death of an officer, the presence of a serial killer, and instances of severe police misconduct are some examples. An understanding of the media ecosystem is imperative for law enforcement agencies to succeed and properly relay their messages.

See Addendum 2—From Chief Schmaderer's remarks. Addendum 2 provides the verbatim transcript of the chief's speech from the hospital press conference. The *Omaha World Herald* **used them, word for word, on the front page the day after Kerrie was killed. The following day, after the hospital press conference, another press conference was held at OPD headquarters. The transcript of this conference was also published verbatim by the** *Omaha World Herald*.

Major City Societal Monumental Events

Can you think of any other societal monumental events?
    Here are a few from across the country. In each instance, the occurrence became embedded in the collective consciousness of the society through the two main characteristics: heavy news coverage and the trauma of the event.

- 1974–1991: Wichita Kansas "BTK" Serial Killer
- 1999: Columbine High School Massacre
- 2013: Boston Marathon Bombing
- 2015: Charleston, South Carolina Church Shooting
- 2016: Orlando Nightclub Shooting
- 2017: Las Vegas Mass Shooting
- 2022: Uvalde, Texas School Shooting

READER REFLECTION
1. Pick one from the above examples and draft a one-page paper on the event and why it qualifies as a societal monumental event. Remember to include how the three characteristics of these events are manifested.
2. Identify a societal monumental event that is not listed above and draft a one-page paper as to why it qualifies as such.

Signature Occurrence

Signature occurrences are different from societal monumental events. A signature occurrence is an event where everyone in society knows what happened. It has received in-depth media coverage, but the collective consciousness of society has not been altered by the signature event. There may be remembrance events or there may not be. If there is a remembrance event on the occurrence's anniversary, the media does not provide coverage with vigor.

A signature occurrence is one step below a societal monumental event. It may not qualify a societal monumental event in one city, but in another city it might. It all depends on the society that is affected and how. For example, a high-profile murder in New York City will not likely change the collective consciousness of the populace, since too many major happenings occur there. However, if a high-profile murder occurs in a city with a population of five thousand, it very well may become the city's societal monumental event.

In another example, if four kids die in a car accident after being hit by a drunk driver, it would be considered a signature occurrence in Omaha. The event would not garner the attention of the collective consciousness of a city with half a million in population. On the other hand, if the accident took place in a town of one thousand people, it very well may become the city's societal monumental event.

Conclusion

Chapter One delved into the profound impact of societal monumental events, drawing on both local and national examples to illustrate their significance. Kerrie Orozco's tragic murder emerged as Omaha's societal monumental event, while 9/11 served as an iconic example of such events on a national scale. Readers gained insights into the distinction between individual and societal monumental events, recognizing that the latter holds the power to permeate the collective consciousness of an entire community or nation.

The vital role of the media in shaping the perception and response to societal monumental events was discussed. News coverage plays a pivotal role in disseminating information, providing context, and fostering a shared understanding of the event's gravity. As a result, these events have far-reaching impacts that extend beyond their immediate occurrences.

Chapter One also introduced the concept of signature occurrences, shedding light on events that, while extensively covered by the media, do not fundamentally alter the collective consciousness of society. The distinction was emphasized through examples that underscored the significance of community size and dynamics in determining the lasting impact of an event on the public psyche.

Throughout the chapter, readers gained an understanding of the complex interplay between events, media coverage, and societal perception. Societal monumental events serve as pivotal moments that demand reflection and remembrance, leaving indelible marks on the fabric of communities and nations alike. The chapter's exploration aimed to foster a deeper appreciation for the transformative power of events that resonate with individuals on a profound level, shaping their perspectives and priorities for years to come.

In Chapter Two: Omaha's National Crime Events, we introduce several high-profile crime and policing events that have thrust Omaha, Nebraska, into the national spotlight. These will provide a grounding for your knowledge as you read the textbook.

8/22/13
"It could have been me"—by Kerrie Orozko, 27 years old
Kerrie Oke
It could have been me. I have children, I'm young, I'm beautiful inside and out. I sometimes drive home alone late at night after work. I have hobbies, dreams, and goals for myself and my family. All of the story hasn't been released yet, but I could fit right into the victim's shoes. Except someone thoughtlessly took the victim's life.

They haven't caught the suspect(s), YET. I don't know who they are, I don't know anything about them. I don't know how old the person responsible is. I don't know what race, sex, nationality, or gender this person is. I don't know their ideology. I don't think any of that matters. I don't know the background of this person, yet I don't think that any sort of messed up childhood, adulthood, addiction, abuse, or anything should excuse this kind of behavior.

Even if I couldn't compare myself to the victim, any victim of a horrific crime such as this doesn't deserve to be killed in a senseless matter. No parent, child, friend, or family member should have to deal with the pain and questions of why after such a horrible ordeal.

The world is headed into a dangerous and scary direction. The price of life is worth far much less than it ever has been. Loved ones are being killed for money, drugs, possessions, greed, respect, publicity, for the name of the 'hood,' and even out of boredom. We no longer have a common sense of belonging or responsibility to each other.

Sometimes I think our 'freedoms' are used as an excuse to do whatever we want and demonize whoever dare question us. We've put personal choice above common sense. We support those who don't feel the need or satisfaction to work for themselves and build something.

It could have been me. It could have been you. It could have been anyone in that spot at the same time under the same circumstances. But instead of pointing the finger at the person(s) responsible, we will divide ourselves and fight over silly things should never play a role in the case. People will lay blame on the victim for working late, the gun for shooting her, the parents that didn't raise the person(s) responsible the "right" way. The mental health system will bear blame, the criminal justice system will feel the burn if the person was let out early. All the while, the pain will be felt by the victim's family, friends, husband, and children.

When will we learn?

Again, they haven't caught the suspect(s), YET. When that day comes, let's put all of the conversation about whose fault it is stay on the suspect. There is no excuse for this action. Let's join together and let them know, we know it's their fault and they will pay for their crime.

Questions for Discussion and Review

Attempt to answer the following questions before looking up the answers at the back of the book.

1. What is media ecology?
2. What is the function of a presidential watch for the press?
3. How was the media a vital aspect in Officer Kerrie Orozco's' death?
4. Describe what is a societal monumental event.
5. What is considered a society for the purposes of Chapter One?
6. What are the three characteristics of a societal monumental event?
7. What is an individual monumental event?
8. What is a signature occurrence?
9. Give two examples for each of the following: a societal monumental event, an individual monumental event, and a signature occurrence in society.

CHAPTER TWO

Omaha's National Crime Events

Over the Last Decade

As readers traverse through this book, they will come across several high-profile crime and policing events that have thrust Omaha, Nebraska, into the national spotlight. The events are highlighted in this chapter, providing a foundation of knowledge to help readers understand the synergy of influence between leadership, law enforcement, and the media.

The stories are recounted in chronological order over the last decade, starting with 2013. Knowledge of these events will aid readers' learning experience, as they are used as real-world examples throughout the book. The story of Kerrie Orozco was narrated in Chapter One—Societal Monumental Events and Their Impact on Collective Consciousness. Kerrie's death was a top national news story and is referenced in some chapters that follow as well.

In addition, behind-the-scenes information about these events is revealed to enhance the feel of the times and spotlight the executive law enforcement decisions. The best learning takes place when concepts are combined with real-world insight and examples.

Public Corruption Scandal

Public corruption involves the breach of public trust and abuse of position by federal, state, or local government officials (Cornell Law School, Legal Information Institute, n.d.). In 2013, the city of Omaha suffered from dilapidated community relations and trust. I was appointed chief of police in August of 2012. The two greatest challenges during the national police chief's search were the high volume of shootings in the city and the need for better community relations. The 33rd and Seward scandal was the first of many high-profile challenges.

The corruption scandal is referred to as "33rd and Seward" because the incident in question was brought to light from a citizen's video recorded at the intersection of

Courtesy of the Omaha World Herald.

33rd and Seward. On March 21, 2013, the video showed an officer taking down a suspect from behind, by his neck, and a large contingent of officers arriving on the scene to help. There is a struggle with the man on the ground, and another man runs into a nearby house and is chased by a contingent of the officers. The officers enter the house; a female in a wheelchair is knocked over, and the officers emerge with two more arrests. There were three arrests in total: the man taken to the ground outside and two men from inside of the house, out of the video's view.

The video originally struck concern in the community for the officer's use of force. The citizens involved in the incident were all Black, and the officers were predominately white. There was considerable and understandable pressure for Omaha's "rookie" chief of police to account for his officers' actions.

The video was sent to a local news reporter, and the news station covered it as headline news for days. The other stations originally did not cover it. However, as the community became enraged by the video and the political environment heated up in Omaha, the other stations and the city's major newspaper picked up on it, and it became an inferno in Omaha.

The environment overall sentiment in Omaha surrounding 33rd and Seward was intense and filled with politics, racial overtones, and my first real test as chief. The calamity itself took place in the middle of a mayoral election and led the conversations in Omaha for weeks. Incumbent Mayor Jim Suttle, who appointed me as chief of police, was facing off against challenger Jean Stothert. The Omaha community was jittery as it waited for my findings to see how the new chief would deal with the scandal.

Seven months prior to 33rd and Seward, I faced protests at my swearing-in ceremony for chief. Clearly, the jury was still out on how I would lead, and the community was eager to find out. After all, I was a forty-year-old white chief of police who was tasked with improving community relations.

There was heavy skepticism and drama in the city as everyone was awaiting the results of the internal investigation surrounding 33rd and Seward. The Omaha community was tired of the lack of progress on violent crimes and lackluster community relations. Dark clouds loom over cities that have tense police–community relations. In 2013, Omaha was considered a "dark cloud" community.

The 33rd and Seward scandal was the first time the Omaha Police Department (OPD) had faced an organized public corruption scandal. Of course, over its history, an agency the size of Omaha had individual officers commit crimes and engage in unprofessional acts that embarrassed the police department. What makes this case different is the organized nature of the corruption.

When corruption is organized, it is a sure sign that a dangerous subculture has formed. Organized corruption must be dealt with swiftly and firmly. The core of the problem subculture must be eradicated, or it will spread. When corruption exists within a law enforcement agency, it will never garner community support to reduce violent crime.

What the community did not know

What the community did not know is that the officers who ran into the house and made two arrests took a cell phone (sim card) from the occupants inside. The presumption is that the cell phone was recording their actions inside the house, where some force was used by the police. The first-line supervisor on the scene, a sergeant, facilitated a cover-up. The sergeant involved in this case put together a plan for the officers to lie to internal affairs and cover up the theft of the cell phone. The cover-up was uncovered, and six officers were fired for conspiring to deceive internal affairs.

READER NOTE
A sergeant is a first-line supervisor who commands eight to thirteen officers. The sergeant is responsible for responding to scenes in the field that require a supervisor or during times when officers need guidance. They conduct a roll call every day, give out shift assignments, and are responsible for relaying messages from senior command about policies and procedures. Sergeants are "gatekeepers" of information, as they have direct contact with the officers. In a large police agency, they can be responsible for setting a negative tone and, in this case, a dangerous subculture within the crew.

I had been a deputy chief for two years prior to 2013, overseeing the Uniform Patrol Bureau. Basically, I oversaw any officer in a uniform. I was skeptical of a few complaints our department had received about missing cell phones, with the allegations that police officers had taken the phones in order to lie to internal affairs. The citizen complaints came from the same work area covered by the officers involved in the 33rd and Seward cover-up.

Now that I am chief, the cell phone incident at 33rd[d] and Seward makes the hairs stand up on the back of my neck. My senior commanders and I were at odds over how to handle the situation, as it was virgin territory. I elected to threaten the use of a polygraph in internal affairs for all the officers involved in the incident. The threat of the polygraph, which was not a threat but a reality if the truth did not come out, cracked a few of the officers involved. The officers' attorneys reached out to *talk*, and the truth became known. Case closed. I learned what took place and how it was organized.

Corruption needs to be aggressively rooted out. The termination of six officers, who were fired for conspiring to deceive internal affairs, spoke for itself. One of the terminated employees cried on the way out of OPD after his internal affairs interview, saying, "If I had only been a man, none of this would have ever happened."

Corruption is ultra-dangerous to a law enforcement agency because of the potential for a "spreading effect." Some officers are not ready to take a hard line on wrongdoing and may elect to just avoid those officers in the future. An agency with a strong professional culture will ferret out corruption instantly. I am proud to say OPD has grown into that agency.

The handling of the corruption scandal received high community marks. It was the first time accountability had taken place on such a swift and grand level. Because it occurred during a mayoral election, both candidates praised the action taken by

OPD. The incumbent mayor, Jim Suttle, saw his poll ratings go up in the aftermath. Despite this, Jim Suttle would go on to lose the election.

Mayor Stothert and I have worked together for over eleven years, during her three terms as mayor. She has been a steadfast supporter of public safety, and now presides over one of the safest major cities in the country for its size. Her practice of mayoral governance should be considered a national example of how to lead and prioritize public safety.

Law Enforcement Media Ecosystem

Two live press conferences (PPCs) were held in relation to the 33rd and Seward event. One was to announce my findings, and the other was to let the public know that we would get to the bottom of it. The signature occurrence was covered nationally after the first four terminations were announced at a live press conference; two more terminations took place later as the internal affairs investigation concluded. Within the Omaha media market, the coverage was robust. It was the subject of talk shows, community meetings, nightly news, and pundits who weighed in.

The incident received national attention for being infamous as well. I would receive a lot of hate mail, with the best one being a dunce cap made just for me. In addition, I was doxed by the infamous national hacker group Anonymous, and encryption software had to be installed on my computer to minimize any future hacks. The Anonymous group also posted a video giving out my phone number to the public. As a result, I received many threatening phone calls and correspondence that would last for weeks. Police corruption strikes at the heart of society and can unearth strong emotions.

> **READER NOTE**
> **Anonymous is a decentralized international activist and hacktivist movement primarily known for cyberattacks against government institutions and government agencies. (Huddleston 2022)**

Peyton Benson

On January 15, 2014, a beautiful five-year-old girl, Peyton Benson, was killed while she was eating breakfast. She was caught up in gang crossfire and killed by a high-powered rifle's bullet that traveled through the house and struck her. The bullet was not intended for Peyton.

I was out of town at the time, in Kansas City for work, and immediately drove back to Omaha. I went directly to my office to coordinate, receive a detailed briefing, and deliver a live press conference that evening.

Peyton's death galvanized a community and led to the takedown of an entire gang.

Though extremely tragic and painful, Peyton's death was not in vain because it brought the Omaha community together. People from all walks of life in Omaha questioned how this could happen. A massive amount of police resources were assigned to this case, and the motivation to solve it was unsurpassed.

The investigation into Peyton's death probably utilized the largest contingent of Omaha detectives in an investigation during my time as chief. The investigation into the serial killer Anthony Garcia was also large, but it entailed many other agencies.

Every day I checked on the status of Peyton's case, hoping we were making progress so I could tell her mom. Very early on in the investigation, OPD Gang Unit Detectives identified some suspects. Detectives were able to use social media (Facebook) and cell phones to track down her killers from there.

Law Enforcement Media Ecosystem

The signature occurrence was covered extensively in the Omaha media market. Peyton's death received national attention, first when she died and then again when the perpetrators were arrested. The news coverage continued through the sentencing of the arrests and on the anniversaries of the tragedy.

COPS TV Show Officer-Involved Shooting

In the Introduction, the tragedy behind the iconic TV show *COPS* was touched on via a comparison to the officer-involved shooting (OIS) of Michael Brown in Ferguson Missouri.

On August 26, 2014, I received word that Bryce Dion, thirty-eight, the soundman for the *COPS* on-scene filming crew, had been shot and killed during a robbery. Bryce was friends with the Omaha police officers he rode and filmed with. The Omaha officers and the *COPS* videographer, Bryce's co-worker for the show, still stay in touch to reminisce and to pay respect.

I traveled to Boston with the officer crew he filmed with for his funeral, where his family allowed me to speak. We all liked Bryce. His loss was painful for all involved. Bryce had an amazing family. The incident was a national news story during a period in policing that was very intense, following the police shooting of Michael Brown in Ferguson, Missouri, and the civil unrest that resulted.

There were many media intangibles at play in this signature occurrence. For starters, it was the first time a member of the *COPS* team had been killed in the line of duty, and it's a television show that represents live policing. The show first screened in 1989 and is still on air today in some media markets. Its theme song, "Bad Boys," is well known and forever linked to the television show.

The suspect in the robbery was a Black male, Cortez Washington, thirty-two, armed with a pellet gun that looked like a real gun. Further compounding the issue, the suspect pointed and fired at the officers as if he had a real gun. The pellet gun made a noise when fired. It's understandable that the officers under stress mistook it for a real gun.

The atmosphere of policing, at the time of the *COPS* incident, was a tinderbox. The *COPS* officer-involved shooting occurred less than a month after Ferguson. National police watchdog groups and nationally known police activists were watching every move the Omaha Police made in the aftermath of the incident.

As the officers ran into the Wendy's restaurant, two went to the east side, and the third officer went to the west side. Bryce Dion and the cameraman were riding with the two officers who entered the restaurant from the east. They both followed. The soundman, Bryce, got caught up in the entrance vestibule, while the cameraman made it to the eating area for patrons.

The suspect began firing his pellet gun at the officers and started to run out of the vestibule where Bryce was crouched down. The officers returned fire. In the crossfire, Bryce was shot in the side as he crouched down, where the ballistic vest is most vulnerable to openings.

The officers fired over thirty rounds, lending to a brief theory by some of the public that the officers may have been showing off or being reckless. The grand jury and the court of appeals in the civil legislation all sided with the city of Omaha and its officers/agents. Most of the rounds were fired as Washington exited the restaurant and turned around toward the officers in the parking lot. The officers fired from inside the Wendy's at the suspect in the parking lot. He was hit several times and died from his gunshot wounds.

A live press conference was held the day following the incident. A well-planned critical media strategy was in place to prevent the many intangibles from distracting from the real issue at hand: the officers had no other choice but to return gunfire from someone who was pointing at them and shooting.

Law Enforcement Media Ecosystem

Extensive national news coverage was given to the event, and it was also covered robustly in the local media. The coverage continued through every stage (original incident, press conference, civil court proceedings, and court rulings) until ceasing a few years ago as the final court actions ended. However, Bryce's memory has not ended for his family or OPD.

Serial Killer Dr. Anthony Garcia

Anthony Garcia killed four people in a five-year time span as revenge for being expelled from Creighton Medical School. He harbored revenge and returned to Omaha from

SYNERGY *of* INFLUENCE

Omaha Police photo: Still photo from the COPS cameraman video. The cameraman was able to hold his camera up over the tables in the eating area and capture the incident. Two OPD officers are confronting Washington who jumps the counter and acts like he is shooting his pellet gun at the officers.

Omaha Police crime scene photo of Washington's pellet gun.

other states in 2008 and 2013 to kill two people each time. Dr. Thomas Hunter and Dr. Roger Brumback signed Garcia's official removal from Creighton Medical School and were the focus of his revenge killings.

In 2008, fifty-seven-year-old Shirley Sherman and eleven-year-old Thomas Hunter, the son of prominent Creighton University Medical Center doctors, were brutally killed in Dr. Hunter's home. Shirley was the matriarch of her family and deeply loved. She happened to be working at the Hunter house on the day of the killings as their housekeeper. The brutal nature of the killings by a knife in the middle of the day shocked and panicked the community of Omaha. For five years, a cloud hung over the Dundee neighborhood and the Hunter and Sherman families.

I oversaw the OPD's training academy at the time. I had zero role in the 2008 investigation, but I was always intrigued by the mystery about what occurred and who did it. For five years, the eerie nature of the murders was perpetuated by the mystery of who did it. I felt bad for the innocent parents of Thomas Hunter. The scrutiny and rumors that followed while grieving the death of their son must have been excruciating. When I took over as chief in August of 2012, I asked for a detailed briefing on the case and turned the pressure up on our Cold Case Unit to solve it.

In 2013, I was a part of an interview panel for a prominent community group as we were searching for an executive director, when I had to step out for an emergency phone call. The call was from a commander informing me of the death of a Creighton doctor and his wife, Roger and Mary Brumback, in their house. My fledgling thought was to presuppose this was a murder-suicide, end of story. However, the call took on a whole new meaning, as the deaths bore the same killing signature as Shirley Sherman's and Thomas Hunter's murder from 2008. It was unmistakable. Omaha had a serial killer, and the killer had waited five years to strike again.

A task force was formed to catch the killer and bring peace back to Omaha. Garcia was arrested for the four murders on July 15, 2013. Garcia was convicted of all four murders and was sentenced to death. He is currently on death row in a Nebraska penitentiary.

READER NOTE
In Chapter Eleven, this case is featured as a case study with a behind-the-scenes look at the leadership and media surrounding the case. Five-year-old Peyton Benson and eleven-year-old Thomas Hunter's murders were motivating beyond belief. All murders of innocent lives are heart-wrenching, but the murder of a child will never leave you.

Law Enforcement Media Ecosystem

The national media covered the case during the formation of the task force and during the arrest of Garcia. The case involved a serial killer doctor, whose crimes occurred outside of the hospital, a child killer, and a demented sense of revenge; it seemed made for a media bonanza. The Omaha media market covered the case in depth and with great precision.

The national show *Dateline NBC* would go on to air a show about the serial killings called "The Haunting." It would also be the subject of multiple crime TV documentaries and a book called *Pathological: The Murderous Rage of Dr. Anthony Garcia*. The long-running television show *Law and Order* did an episode based on the case, and the case was featured on *America's Most Wanted*.

Serial Killer Nikko Jenkins

Less than two months after the task force captured serial killer Dr. Anthony Garcia after a ten-year search, homicide detectives asked to brief me on four homicides. Four people of different races were killed with a shotgun on different days and locations. There was no mistaking it; Omaha now had another serial killer! We were all emotionally drained from the Garcia serial killer investigation that had taken months, but now we had to buckle down and fight through it again.

> **READER NOTE**
> **It is rare for a killer to cross racial lines. Nikko Jenkins did so by killing two Hispanic men, a Black man, and a white female. The cold-blooded nature of his shotgun killings, coupled with the crossing of racial lines, made for a rare killer who was on a killing spree before being caught by the OPD.**

Nikko Jenkins would eventually be caught by Omaha police, even though he vowed not to be taken alive. When push came to shove, when faced by OPD, he surrendered. His shotgun of choice was found where he was staying with blood DNA from some of the victims still on it.

Controversy swirled because prior to the murders, Nikko Jenkins spent years in prison solitary confinement before being released from solitary onto the public, in an abrupt and without warning manner. Imagine, Nikko was so dangerous in prison he had to be held in solitary confinement and then be released onto the public, as if he is no longer dangerous. Nikko was a colorful character because of his loud outbursts and tattooed face, no doubt heightening his sickening celebrity.

During his time in prison, Nikko wrote letters to players in his case such as the prosecutor, media executives, others, and myself. He had impeccable handwriting and was an adequate scribe. This is the first time I have acknowledged getting letters from Nikko, as I did not ever want to give him any credence! I never responded or admitted to receiving his letter, including not participating in a news story where others acknowledged getting letters from Nikko. I trust it bothered Nikko greatly that I brushed him aside and would never dignify the letter with a response.

Coincidentally, Nikko and Garcia had jail cells near each other while awaiting trial. I inquired once about whether they talked, and I was told that Dr. Garcia is considered very odd by the other inmates and does not talk to anyone. Nikko, on the other hand, talks to everyone and never misses an opportunity to manipulate. You would be surprised how many people fall for his charm.

Garcia and Jenkins, both serial killers who operated with a different modus operandi in 2013, represent two of the five serial killers the state of Nebraska has had in its history. They are on death row, awaiting their fate. There are eleven death row inmates in Nebraska. It is a rare occurrence to be sentenced to death in Nebraska and be placed on death row.

Law Enforcement Media Ecosystem

The media coverage was monstrously intense in the Omaha media market, and Nikko's crimes and arrest were covered nationally. Nikko was a colorful person who tried to get local media attention. Nikko would say he committed the murders at the command of Apophis, an ancient serpent god. He would mutilate himself in solitary confinement as a means of getting attention.

In my professional assessment, Nikko feels he is charismatic and thrives on being the focus of attention. He is a cold-blooded killer who has no remorse or feelings for others. If Nikko was ever to get out of prison, I believe he would start killing again. Nikko is used to the prison system, as he has spent much of his life incarcerated. The greatest punishment for him is to receive no attention; he loves the media spotlight and is forever trying to "up" his last outburst to get back the media's attention.

Personal photo: Letter Chief Schmaderer received from Nikko Jenkins written from his jail cell.

Target Active Shooter

On January 31, 2023, at 10:45 a.m., one of my deputy chiefs, Steve Cerveny, came running into my office, saying there was an active shooter at a Target store in the western part of the city. A lone white male gunman in his thirties entered the Target store and started shooting his AR-15 rifle. Twenty-eight calls were received by our 911 center reporting the active shooter at Target.

I knew that once the threat was neutralized, Omaha was instantly going to be front and center for a national news day—maybe more than one day if there were citizens killed.

Omaha was fortunate. The suspect was firing an AR-15 and had over three hundred rounds, but he did not hit anyone. The suspect was shot to death in the head by the first-responding Omaha police officers.

There was a lot of speculation about whether this was a "suicide by cop." I can share with readers that the Target subject suffered from schizophrenia and had a history of mental health issues. He also had previous run-ins with the law and had his guns confiscated in the past.

It is entirely possible, from my professional viewpoint, that he had two voices going on in his head, both competing for relevance. He was heavily armed, so he was at least prepared with equipment to commit a mass killing. He posed outside of Target, possibly waiting for law enforcement to arrive before going back into the store. I surmise he was waiting to shoot at officers or be shot by officers. He went back inside after realizing we would not be there in thirty seconds like in the movies.

He was making his way to the rear of the store, where there were people, when he was confronted by Omaha officers. He may have been caught off guard. It is hard to say what voice the shooter was listening to at this point. Was he headed to the back of the store to shoot people? Ultimately, he refused commands by officers to put the gun down and was shot once in the head. He yelled at officers right before that he would kill them, and started to raise his AR-15 rifle slightly.

Curious as to what a chief of police does when the call comes in on an active shooter?

After all, the chief is a CEO, with the highest-level office to run the agency. My attire is a suit most days unless I know I have a media or large crowd event and need to wear my police uniform.

I expedited to Target from my office downtown, followed by Deputy Chief Steve Cerveny. We coordinated our response on the drive, knowing the shooter might have escaped to a nearby business or that there may be more than one shooter. We both donned our ballistic vests over our shirts and ties and grabbed our extra-round magazines for our guns. Steve and I were ready to divert and confront the gunman if he escaped the sea of officers responding to Target, as we knew that, coming from downtown, many officers would be much closer than us.

Omaha Police photo: Active shooter waiting for law enforcement outside of the Target store.

When we arrived at Target, the place was littered with police cars from OPD and surrounding jurisdictions. It was an impressive sight. We had learned on the way that the gunman had been killed, but neither of us knew what we would see upon entering Target and were mentally prepared to see dead bodies. A commander took us through the crime scene, and I can't tell you how happy I was to find out that the only person dead was the gunman. No one else was hit by his gunfire. It is strange, though, I must say, to be looking at a man lying face down in his own coagulating blood and feel a sense of relief. It could have been so much worse.

As I was looking over the crime scene and the dead gunman, there were still some citizens inside the store emerging from their hiding places. I will never forget a young boy, probably around five years of age, holding his mom's hand, scared and crying profusely. His mom comforted him by pointing out all the police officers there to protect him and saying that he was now safe. The mom was very impressive as she suppressed all her emotions for her son, but I could tell she was terrified. People from all walks of life are affected by mass shootings in our country. The way of life in our country has forever been changed by the active shooter dynamic that plays out repeatedly in America.

Law Enforcement Media Ecosystem

NBC National News, *Good Morning America*, and other national news programs covered the event. There was extensive local coverage where the on-scene presser was held live, breaking into regular television programming. The event was the talk of Omaha for sure. I have had many citizens recount where they were and what they did when word started to spread of an active shooter. Stores and schools all went into lockdown until Omaha was given the all-clear to reopen.

> **READER NOTE**
> **I am not using the name of the active shooter in this book. There is no reason to glorify his actions or give the incentive of fame to a prospective active shooter in society. The on-scene presser will be discussed in Chapter Six.**

Officer-Involved Shooting (OIS)

Protests erupted in Omaha after a white OPD officer fatally shot a Black man during a traffic stop in November 2022. Kenneth Jones, thirty-five, died from his gunshot injuries. The incident took place months after citywide protests and unrest in Omaha, following the George Floyd criminal death in Minneapolis.

Two white police officers had initiated a traffic stop on a vehicle where Kenneth Jones was in the back seat. The officers could see Jones moving around and acting strangely. They issued numerous verbal commands for the occupants of the vehicle to show their hands. The driver and the passenger immediately complied, but Jones would not. The officers pulled Jones out of the car, and a struggle ensued. One of the officers could feel a gun with Jones's hand on it. Jones made a move with the gun and was shot and killed (Kesslen 2020).

Despite the officer being cleared by a grand jury, it was a tense time in Omaha, and the incident made national news with renewed protests and calls for releasing the officer's body-worn camera (BWC) footage. Racial overtones were present, and the city of Omaha was still in shock over the protest events in the city in the aftermath of George Floyd's death.

Law Enforcement Media Ecosystem

The OIS death received national attention. A live press conference (PPC) was held at Omaha Police Headquarters to provide a chronological account of what took place. I stated at the press conference that the officers had been justified in the fatal OIS, in accordance with the policy of the police department. The BWC was not released, and still photos were used at the press conference. The protests stopped after the live press conference by OPD.

Protest and Civil Unrest in Omaha

Following George Floyd's videoed criminal death in Minneapolis, Omaha, like other major cities across the country, experienced protests and civil unrest. In Omaha, thousands of people gathered at 72nd and Dodge Street—the city's largest intersection—where, for two nights in a row, clashes with the police took place.

A citywide curfew was put into emergency effect. All officers were ordered to work twelve-hour shifts and don riot gear. After the second night, the decision was made to call in the Nebraska National Guard to assist. That was a call I will never forget. After years of building up community relations, it was a low moment to ask for the National Guard.

Nebraska Governor Pete Ricketts approved the decision for the Nebraska National Guard to come to Omaha. The city of Lincoln, Nebraska, followed suit in asking for the National Guard as well.

Compounding Omaha's problem was the shooting death of a Black man, James Scurlock, by a white bar owner, Jake Gardner. I was in the mobile command post when

SYNERGY *of* INFLUENCE

**Omaha Police Facebook photo: Protests
outside of Omaha Police Headquarters.**

Personal photo: Deputy Chief Scott Gray (left) and myself
(Chief Schmaderer) with the Nebraska National Guard on night three
of the civil unrest. The building to the left is Omaha Police Headquarters.

I heard the shooting come out. I knew instantly it was going to pour gasoline and an already hot fire. There was a video of the incident with two very different viewpoints.

Many white citizens of Omaha saw a case of self-defense by Jake Gardner, while many Black Omaha citizens saw the white bar owner as the aggressor. The county attorney made the determination of no charges. The case had such twists and turns that a grand jury was convened, and Jake Gardner was to stand trial. Gardner killed himself before that could happen.

READER NOTE
The second night of the protest was the longest night in the history of Omaha. The civil unrest was intense, and, in a never disclosed fact, OPD headquarters was nearly overrun by protestors that night. Luckily, police department commanders were able to use resources to stave off the mob's entry into headquarters. An arrest for throwing a Molotov cocktail near central headquarters was made that night.

I have never been so proud of OPD as I was during the 2020 civil unrest. The officers stood strongly and professionally, for days, against a crowd throwing rocks, urine, and other objects at them.

Law Enforcement Media Ecosystem

National media coverage was given across the country to the civil unrest not only in Omaha but in other major cities as well. Locally, four live press conferences were held for four days in a row by Omaha Mayor Jean Stothert, Governor Ricketts, and me. The media coverage was intense; it received the focus of the entire Omaha metropolitan area, as the city was in partial shut-down mode from the coronavirus. I was told by a local veteran media person that the viewership ratings were sky-high in the one-million-person Omaha metro area as a result.

READER NOTE
The Scurlock and Gardner fatal encounter will be discussed further in Chapter Eight—Race and Police Media.

Zachary Bearheels

Mr. Bearheels died after an encounter with Omaha Police in June 2017. Bearheels suffered from mental illness and had not committed a crime. As OPD officers took him into custody, he was tasered twelve times and punched in the head. He later died as officers were taking him into custody. The rear cruiser camera caught the incident on video, and the four officers were fired.

Three officers got their jobs back after an arbitration hearing. One officer was charged with a felony for his role with the Taser. The officer was acquitted at trial, but an arbitrator upheld his termination. The officers who returned to OPD after the arbitration have since been productive members of the OPD.

Law Enforcement Media Ecosystem

This incident happened before 2020, or it is conceivable that Mr. Bearheels' death would have received even more attention. The incident received local attention and national attention for the treatment of Native Americans. Mr. Bearheels was a Native American from the Rosebud Sioux and Kiowa Apache tribes and lived in Oklahoma. He happened to be passing through Omaha (Lakota Times 2017).

In a little-known personal twist, my longtime girlfriend is Native American, and her sister is heavily involved in securing grant funding for native tribes across the country. Her father owns a major manufacturing business on the Gulf Coast. They are from the Iowa tribe near Rulo and Falls City, Nebraska, which is in the corner of the state and only minutes from Missouri and Kansas. The Iowa Tribe of Kansas and Nebraska encompasses parts of each state (https://iowatribeofkansasandnebraska.com).

There is continued scrutiny of the OPD to this day over the death of Mr. Bearheels. If I could make an observation, it seems there are more racial undertones to the scrutiny now since the nations' 2020 civil unrest than there were when the incident occurred in 2017. An annual march occurs every year in honor of Mr. Bearheels' remembrance.

Conclusion

The cases outlined in this chapter were chosen to provide a foundation of knowledge about occurrences in Omaha and to cover a range of situations. There were instances of police corruption, OISs, and mass civil unrest. Note the way the cases were dealt with by the police, the media, and the courts. All three provide an understanding of how leadership, law enforcement, and the media interact.

Chapter Three—The Law Enforcement Media Ecosystem delves into the intricate media landscape that envelops law enforcement operations in the United States. This chapter not only explores the multifaceted role of the media within society but also delves into comprehending the dynamics of a media market. Moreover, it provides a comprehensive insight into how law enforcement agencies can strategically equip themselves to effectively navigate this distinctive media landscape.

CHAPTER THREE

Law Enforcement Media Ecosystem

Introduction

The media ecosystem theory refers to an environment with an explicit concern for the media's evolution, effects, and forms. It is a theory about the complex interplay between humans, technology, media, and the environment.

Media ecosystems are complex combinations of print, broadcast, digital, and social media that work together to create a self-referential information environment. The definition used for this textbook is more succinct. The media is made up of many mediums (TV, cable, social media, print), and the mediums compete around an environment found to be of interest to society. Topics that have garnered a strong interest in American society over the last decade include crime, law enforcement scandals, and racial issues (The Technology and Social Change Project, n.d.).

Why Study Media Ecosystems?

Studying the spread of information (and sometimes disinformation) can help advance an agenda and help political parties, activists, law enforcement executives, school superintendents, athletes, and actors present their own messages or agendas (Center for Media Literacy).

A successful law enforcement agency in the new era of policing needs to have a foundation in baseline media theory and an understanding of how they will work with the media. The press is a necessity for presenting a message in a manner the law enforcement agency wants the public to perceive it.

It is vital to have a strategy for overseeing the serious incidents that inevitably arise when dealing with a large population. Large collections of people result in critical matters arise for law enforcement to manage. This is called *population certainty*. It is not a matter of if but when. Successful law enforcement agencies therefore need to have a critical media strategy.

After engaging with this chapter, you will have the ability to:

- Explore the intricate media ecosystem
- Analyze the diverse roles of the media in society
- Comprehend the nuances of the police media ecosystem
- Examine the essential functions of the press information office
- Recognize the significance of law enforcement training and certification
- Recognize the significance of misconduct in media interactions
- Gain insight into the media aspect of George Floyd's death
- Grasp the concept of a media market and its implications.

The Role of the Media

The media is more than just a source of information; it is a powerful force in shaping how we see the world. From TV and radio to the vast realm of the internet and social media, these platforms touch every aspect of our lives (Democracy and Me).

Think of the media as your personal news curator, offering a variety of channels—whether it is the traditional evening news or scrolling through online articles. The depth and duration of media coverage gives us clues about what is considered important in the world around us (Vedantu).

But it is not just about news; the media can sway our thoughts and beliefs, from voting decisions to personal views on key issues. Remember the impact of media coverage on the 9/11 events? That's just one instance. Media narratives shape our opinions on everything from gun control and immigration to local community projects. The media is a powerful player in driving social change and influencing our views on everything from fashion trends to political movements (Yeung, D., 2018).

The Media as Watchdog

Think of the media as democracy's guard dog—always alert, always watching. In a world where a free press is essential, the media keeps an eye on those in power. It is not just about reporting news; it is about keeping politicians and public officials in check. Major newspapers like the *New York Times* and the *Washington Post* are at the forefront of exposing corruption and wrongdoing.

These papers have teams dedicated to digging deep into stories, a stark contrast to the quick, two-minute segments on local TV. National programs like *60 Minutes* go even further, investigating stories worldwide. But it is often the major city papers that keep local governments on their toes.

Take the Watergate Scandal, for example. It was *The Washington Post* that unraveled this complex web of deceit, leading to President Nixon's resignation.

LAW ENFORCEMENT MEDIA ECOSYSTEM

On June 17, 1972, several burglars were arrested in the office of the Democratic National Committee, located in the Watergate complex of buildings in Washington, DC. The prowlers, connected to President Richard Nixon's reelection campaign, had been caught wiretapping phones and stealing documents. Nixon took aggressive steps to cover up the crimes, but when *Washington Post* reporters Bob Woodward and Carl Bernstein revealed his role in the conspiracy, Nixon resigned on August 9, 1974.

And closer to home, the *Omaha World Herald* has been instrumental in uncovering corruption. An audit of the Omaha schools' pension plan showed a 1.2 billion shortfall on questionable investments, and an Omaha city council vice president was exposed for being under federal investigation and eventually indicted on public corruption allegations.

These newspapers are struggling financially in the internet age. If they fail, our democracy's watchdog loses its bark, and that could lead to more unchecked power and corruption at the local level. These reporters are the ones probing and questioning—imagine if that just stopped.

READER REFLECTION
A) **Pick a major city and identify its major newspaper.**
B) **Identify an example of public corruption or government resource mismanagement the newspaper has uncovered.**

Another part of newspapers' watchdog roles is probing and reporting on local political candidates so readers can be informed voters. These profiles will uncover questionable backgrounds and the essence of the political candidate's platform. Imagine if this service to the local voting populace was lost or diminished because of internet competition and the need to access quick news.

The Media Needs to Attract Viewers and Readers

An essential caveat to the role of the media must be acknowledged: while its primary function is to deliver news, the inherently competitive nature of the industry dictates that this news is presented in a way that attracts viewers and readers. Media outlets often engage in sensationalizing content within the bounds they deem acceptable, carefully crafting events and topics in news stories to captivate the largest possible audience. This competitive landscape pits each media entity against the others, with the urgency to be the first to report breaking news seen as a crucial market advantage. The industry imperative is clear: to stay competitive, attracting and retaining viewers and readers is essential.

According to the National Bureau of Economic Research's "Media Competition and News Diets," survival in this cutthroat environment is challenging. Not all companies operating in the press can maintain profitability; those that fail to compete effectively face closure. A case in point is the McClatchy newspaper chain, which filed for bankruptcy and owned major newspapers across fourteen states, including the *Kansas City Star* and the *Miami Herald* (Hall, 2020).

This phenomenon is not limited to major chains; it is also evident at the local level. In Omaha, for instance, longstanding media companies like *The Reader* and *El Perico* ceased operations in 2023, reflecting a broader trend of closures and turnovers in news sources across major cities.

Misleading headlines and overhyped news promos are common tactics used to attract audiences, often leading to discrepancies between headlines and the actual content of articles. This competitive rush extends to television and internet news outlets as well. While the primary role of the press is to inform, the pressure to present news in the most engaging and rapid manner is undeniable. This drive for speed and sensationalism, however, can lead to errors and misrepresentations in reporting. Professional news organizations strive to uphold journalistic integrity and guidelines to minimize such inaccuracies, but the challenge remains a significant aspect of modern journalism.

Law Enforcement Media Ecosystem

The law enforcement media ecosystem is intense—only lower in intensity than the White House Press Corp itself. Big city mayors, pro athletes, and movie stars can relate, but the point is simple: media coverage is intense during large events and constant during the rest of the time in policing and law enforcement in general. Large police departments have an enormous daily media presence, and this demands the study of the police media ecosystem.

> **READER PERSPECTIVE**
> **A) Consider the following question: Do major city police departments have a journalist assigned specifically to cover the agency? The answer will be found later in the chapter.**

Policing Matters, Society, and News Coverage

Policing matters have consistently been at the forefront of news coverage, from the historic race riots in the 1960s to the widespread civil unrest in 2020 following George Floyd's tragic death at the hands of the police.

LAW ENFORCEMENT MEDIA ECOSYSTEM

This next section explores social, and police matters over time in relation to their news coverage. It is easy to understand why law enforcement is wrought with lofty media intensity and scrutiny when serious issues such as a society's sense of peace and security, taxpayer dollars, social issues, and even life and death are involved. It is important to note that as policing advances, the rest of society tends to follow.

Policing was front and center in the 1960s as the push for equality was on the front lines. The 1960s saw the most serious and widespread race riots in the history of the United States. Major riots occurred in Birmingham, Alabama, in 1963; New York City in 1964; Watts in Los Angeles, California, in 1965; and Chicago, Illinois, in 1966 (encyclopedia.com; Olzak et al., 1996; Myers, D.J., 1997).

Personal Photo: Omaha's 1960s Race Riots

READER NOTE
My dad, Richard Schmaderer, is circled in the photo of Omaha's 1960s Race Riots above. He worked for OPD for thirty-four years and retired as a sergeant. My brother, Brian Schmaderer, is currently an OPD lieutenant.

The 1960s race riots were instrumental in producing social advances in America. Consider that, in modern times, the civil unrest the country saw in 2020 was the result of the disproportionate balance of policing Black citizens versus white citizens. So, what social change will come from 2020?

Major corporations promised a more diverse representation of society in hiring, leadership, and board of director positions. Policing advanced as well, with many departments scrambling to catch up to the social progression.

The progression toward best practices in policing took on a whole new energy, especially for major city departments affected by the 2020 civil unrest. Omaha police enacted a "duty to intervene" clause into the use-of-force continuum for officers. This means that if an officer witnesses another officer use excessive force, they must intervene to stop it and then report it. Other major city police agencies enacted more guidelines, and the initiative to lower deadly citizen encounters with the police was forged.

In Chapter Seven, Brand Damager/Officer-Involved Shootings, the quest to lower deadly police encounters is dissected and broadened. The reader will see that even post-2020, the number of deadly encounters with the police is still on the rise.

However, it is important to note that social change and police interest go hand in hand. Media attention in relation to police actions is to be expected. Police agencies, therefore, must prepare for it. The following information describes the roles and functions of various institutions concerning the media and law enforcement ecosystem.

Press Information Office

To cope with the ever-present police media interest, all major city police departments have press information offices to deal with the daily media inquiries from reporters. Reporters are assigned to cover the police departments. Reporters are not assigned to Google, or Facebook, or Tesla, yet there is one assigned to Omaha police department (OPD). Several are assigned to the New York City, Los Angeles, and Chicago police departments. In fact, many major city police departments hold daily or weekly press briefings.

Every morning at OPD, a reporter will sift through the previous night's police reports, looking for a crumb of a story. A politician got arrested, there was an accident, or an interesting crime story occurred. Omaha once had a wayward female trespass into the city's zoo to pet the tigers. It became a huge story because the tiger bit some of the person's fingers off. The reader can see why the possibility of finding such a gem of a story in the police reports might make searching through them compelling (KETV.com).

There are several requests on a daily basis for sound bites and interviews on individual crimes that have occurred and on crime's broader meaning to society. If the crime involves a child, or a school, or has a unique twist, it will get media attention. For example, an elderly lady was punched in the entryway of a church, and this local Omaha incident received national attention. The assaulter then proceeded to rob the elderly lady and steal from the church collection basket. This was a mere misdemeanor crime, but it had a unique twist or two, driving it to the national news scene (Fox News, 2015).

Population Certainty

Police involvement with the media is inevitable. Population certainty implies that anytime a large mass of humans is concentrated and they interact, newsworthy events will manifest. Police work happens to be the best source of constant newsworthy stories. The police are first responders in the most interesting situations, and since they create a log or report of the event, it creates a tremendous pond in which reporters can fish in for a story.

"If it bleeds, it leads" is a real phenomenon. If law enforcement responds to crimes, accidents, and rescues—i.e., there is a chance someone could be hurt—the reader can be sure that the media will be there to cover it. OPD has led the state of Nebraska for the biggest news stories for seven years out of the last decade. Serial killers, police protests and civil unrest, police scandals, OISs, and police discipline all carry a compelling media dynamic and have been top news stories, all coming out of the OPD.

Law Enforcement Media Training

A law enforcement agency's media training sets the culture for a "peer" relationship with the media up and down the rank structure. Law enforcement agency executives need to instill the training from the top down, as at any time a command officer may be required to give an on-scene interview. Some instances that can be handled by the commanding officer at the scene are fatal traffic accidents, robberies, and pursuits where an arrest is made and there are no injuries. These are situations that do not require handling by the press information officer (PIO).

Law enforcement media training can be layered:

- Entry-level training for new recruits on the media
- More advanced training for first-line supervisors
- Intense training for the PIO and upper-level commanders

A department that instills media training into its culture and training curriculum is more likely to understand the importance of the media in policing. As with any training, the idea is to instill confidence, protocols, and a culture that embraces dealing with the media (Parrish 1993, 24).

Being Visible as an Agency

All law enforcement agencies provide training in the art of policing, investigating, collecting evidence, interviewing suspects, managing a variety of calls, and understanding the laws of arrest. Very few agencies are progressive to another component that needs to be added to the list: managing the media. The media intensity surrounding policing in America is real. One of the purposes of the book is to advance the law enforcement learning curve on interacting with the media.

How do citizens know if their local police or sheriff's department is a good one? There is no national championship, no award or trophy bestowed on the top law enforcement agencies. It is up to the individual police agency to highlight their progress and success to the public. While law enforcement agencies can also use their own social media to highlight their successes, the media is a vital tool in displaying an agency's progress, successes, and goals to the broader public.

A police agency cannot rely solely on their own social media platform to highlight their successes. The public does not follow the police agency's social media enough to make it the sole method of getting their message out to the public. OPD has 131,000 followers on Facebook—for a city with half a million population and a metropolitan area of 1.1 million.

Getting your own police agency's message out is not only important for that department but for policing in general. Bear in mind that the fallout from a negative police encounter occurring anywhere in the country will be applied to local law enforcement agencies as well. OPD and many other major city departments were faced with civil unrest because of the death of George Floyd at the hands of the Minneapolis police.

When the George Floyd video splashed from Minneapolis, every department in the country had to address it. In Omaha, my executive team attempted to get out in front of the situation by crafting a statement denouncing what we saw. We strived to be the first major city to put out a statement because, in our minds, we had witnessed a crime. We instinctively knew it was going to cause major upheaval. In addition, when Minneapolis police officer Derek Chauvin was convicted of murdering George Floyd, OPD prepared a statement because the death was a societal monumental event affecting all law enforcement agencies.

This was the same with the video of Memphis police's Scorpion Unit assaulting and beating Mr. Tyre Nichols to death. In my opinion, what we all witnessed was criminal activity. Even though it had not occurred in Omaha, it was of such interest to the nation that law enforcement agencies around the country needed to have a plan to address it.

> As an agency, we want to express our sadness and offer our condolences to the family of Mr. Tyre Nichols. I want to commend the Memphis Police Chief and

District Attorney for taking swift, decisive actions regarding the involved officers. Criminal activity by police officers can never be tolerated. Not in Memphis. Not in Omaha. Not anywhere. The five Memphis officers have undermined the trust that communities place in law enforcement across the country. We denounce their actions. The Omaha Police Department is dedicated to upholding the trust placed in it by the community. Further, we are committed to transparency, accountability, and the prominent level of integrity that our citizens demand.

—Omaha Police Department Media Release

George Floyd

George Floyd, a forty-six-year-old Black man, was killed during his arrest by the Minneapolis Police Department in Minnesota, a city comparable in size to Omaha, Nebraska. Both cities have similar police force sizes, but Minneapolis has faced challenges with hiring and retention since the incident. The media coverage of George Floyd's death was intense, igniting a national movement against police brutality, with demands for justice and police reform reverberating across the country.

Major cities, including Omaha, experienced civil unrest and large-scale protests. One positive outcome was witnessing police departments nationwide denouncing the actions of the officers involved in Floyd's death, with Omaha Police being among the first to support the swift termination of the Minneapolis officers by the city's chief.

The heart-wrenching video of George Floyd's last moments, with white Officer Derek Chauvin kneeling on his neck while other officers stood by, further fueled the public's outrage. Floyd's repeated pleas that he could not breathe were ignored, and the crowd's pleas for intervention went unheeded.

Both George Floyd and Derek Chauvin have now become symbolic figures, representing the historical struggle between law enforcement and Black communities in America. Their images are recognizable across the nation and the world, serving as powerful reminders of the need for change and reform in policing practices.

What led to George Floyd's arrest?

On May 25, 2020, a store clerk in Minneapolis suspected Floyd of using a counterfeit twenty-dollar bill and phoned the police. Upon the arrival of Minneapolis officers, Floyd was placed under arrest and handcuffed in the conventional manner behind his back. Distressed and panicked over the restraint, he resisted getting into the back of the police cruiser.

Subsequently, Floyd was brought to the ground, face down, and restrained by the officers. The crowd could see Officer Chauvin, while the other officers attending to Floyd were obstructed by the police cruiser. In a chilling and callous rendition, Chauvin calmly disregarded both Floyd's pleas and the concerns of the onlooking crowd for over nine agonizing minutes. At one point, Floyd even cried out for his mother, and the world witnessed his excruciating and heart-wrenching murder unfold on television.

It is important to note that George Floyd was not violent toward the Minneapolis police; he was noncompliant. Police officers often face noncompliant situations, but the brutal and unnecessary death of George Floyd challenged the very essence of policing in our country.

Beyond the incident, who was George Floyd?

Born in Fayetteville, North Carolina, Floyd was an individual with a past in sports, having played basketball and football during his high school and college years. While he had a history of eight convictions between 1997 and 2005, it is pertinent to mention that this fact was irrelevant to his arrest and tragic treatment. In 2007, he was incarcerated for a home invasion and later paroled in 2013. Following his parole, he focused on mentoring and rebuilding his life, even engaging in antiviolence videos. Floyd relocated to Minneapolis in 2014, where he worked until he lost his employment as a trucker and security guard due to COVID-19.

Floyd's family sued, and the City of Minneapolis avoided trial and settled for a $27 million payout to the family. Officer Derek Chauvin was convicted on two counts of murder and one count of manslaughter. He is currently in prison serving a 22.5-year sentence.

On April 13, 2023, the Minneapolis City Council settled two civil cases against former officer Derek Chauvin for $9 million. Both lawsuits allege that Chauvin used excessive force three years before George Floyd's murder, including on one person who was fourteen years old at the time.

The tragedy of George Floyd's homicide will be touched on at various points in this book. It can be argued that his death was a monumental societal event for the country. It is safe to say his death has taken a place in the collective consciousness of the nation and was a catalyst for policing advances. In the aftermath of George Floyd's murder, the country experienced widespread civil unrest, protests, and calls for reform. The subject of race was front and center in the aftermath (Cheung 2020; Ellison 2021; *New York Times* 2020).

The OPD was one of the first police departments in the country to put out a statement after the video of George Floyd's death went viral. Many other cities followed.

OPD Statement

"The officers' actions are not consistent with the training and protocol of our profession. We commend Minneapolis Police Chief Medaria Arradondo for his decisive actions and leadership. The Omaha Police Department works tirelessly to build and maintain trust with our community. Although the incident did not happen locally, it can damage the relationships between law enforcement and communities across the country. As law enforcement officers, we hold ourselves to the higher standard, and when those standards are not upheld, leaders must unite and support corrective measures."

Omaha Police Media Release [May 27th, 2020]

Omaha Police responding to the death of George Floyd in Minneapolis.

"We are deeply disturbed by what we have seen. While not all evidence is out, there is video. The actions of the officers were clearly inconsistent with the actions and training of our profession," Schmaderer said. "It is a sobering reminder of how bad policing can undermine what we do. Even though it did not occur here, it can cause damage here and across the country." Omaha Police Media Release

Omaha Police Press Release after the conviction of Minneapolis Officer Derek Chauvin.

"In May 2020, it was apparent to my senior command staff and I that Mr. Chauvin was guilty, and his actions were reprehensible. Today, the jury's verdict validates those sentiments and holds Mr. Chauvin accountable for his actions. Let us use this moment as an opportunity to find common ground for police and communities across this country as justice was served. Omaha has made great strides when the community and OPD have worked together. OPD would like to use this moment to further commit to our community." Omaha Police Media Release

Law Enforcement Drives the News

Law enforcement officials are public employees, paid by taxpayers and entrusted with impressive authority and responsibility. When they make mistakes, fail to follow policy, commit a crime, or engage in controversial events, the media scrutiny will be an inferno. It is unsurprising that this inspires heavy attention from the press.

Police officers have tremendous power: the authority to deprive a person of their freedom, take a person's property (for example, towing a car), or take a person's life under extreme circumstances. When these events occur, the media will be all over it. When you also consider that America has been historically flawed in policing our citizens of color, then the media intensity will get even hotter.

Indeed, the names of George Floyd, Brianna Taylor, Michael Brown, and Tyre Nichols are household names because of their deaths during police actions. The Black Lives Matter movement was formed nationwide in the aftermath of police-related incidents. Former San Francisco 49ers quarterback Colin Kaepernick knelt during the national anthem to protest police incidents involving African Americans in our country. Kneeling during the anthem spread nationwide and was the subject of many spirited debates and arguments (Washington Post 2020). Real or perceived law enforcement misconduct receives heavy media and social justice attention.

The advent of the body-worn camera, a plethora of private surveillance cameras, and neighborhood door cameras has amplified media interest and scrutiny even further. It was predictable that this would results in more police encounters being caught on camera for the media to use. It was also predictable that with 660,288 police officers in the United States, mistakes were going to be caught on camera (Korhonen 2023).

Law enforcement's use of force is a hard-to-understand dynamic and tends to look bad. The public is not versed in policing procedures, which is understandable. Most citizens know their own careers and do not have time to dive into the procedures of other professions. It was unsurprising that the level of police scrutiny will increase as the media encounters increased video footage of law enforcement in action.

Some law enforcement encounters may look bad but still be within policy, some will be considered totally justified by the public, and some will be perceived as criminal by the public. This was a predictable outcome and one of the reasons OPD elected to become one of the first major city police departments to implement full BWC deployment for its officers. OPD desired, in 2015, to be ahead of the body-worn-camera curve, so there could be an independent archive of what took place.

We live in a country with a history of policing challenges. It is to be expected that the press and social issues would clash and, that with the advent of all the video footage being aired by news agencies, the clashes would become more intense. In short, the law enforcement ecosystem is teeming with aggression, and the plethora of videos showing the police in action has only increased the media's aggression. How an agency manages the media will set the tone for how they are viewed by the populace being served.

LAW ENFORCEMENT MEDIA ECOSYSTEM

READER ASSIGNMENT
A police encounter is caught on video and goes viral. The video shows an officer using excessive force on an arrestee in public. The arrestee is now in the hospital. Issue a press release as if you are the law enforcement agency's PIO.

Media Markets

A media market is defined as a region where a group of consumers has access to the same marketing material. Typically, media markets relate to radio, television, and print media such as newspapers and magazines; they are typically the coverage area for a station or newspaper. The internet is another media market, and it can be worldwide.

The area where the populace can watch the local news is considered the coverage area (Lorette 2024). There are 210 designated media market areas covering the United States, and they are usually defined by their metropolitan area. The top ten media markets in America are as follows:

1. New York, NY
2. Los Angeles, CA
3. Chicago, IL
4. Philadelphia, PA
5. Dallas–Fort Worth, TX
6. San Francisco–Oakland–San Jose, CA
7. Atlanta, GA
8. Houston, TX
9. Washington (Hagerstown), DC–MD
10. Boston (Manchester), MA

(Ground Truth, n.d.)

In every media market, there exists a special driver of the news for viewers and readers. For example, Australia will open the news with shark sightings for the safety of tourists and local beachgoers. For New York City (NYC), coverage will be related to more national news and NYC politics. The Las Vegas media market is geared toward the locals; seldom is their talk of the famous Las Vegas "Strip." Washington, DC is ripe with politics for coverage, and Los Angeles has plenty of movie stars to augment the national and local issues of the day.

When considering the Omaha market, the heavy driver is Nebraska football. The state of Nebraska does not have a pro sports team, so the University of Nebraska football team is our celebrity and pro fix. It is the biggest driver of sales and interest in the state.

READER ASSIGNMENT
Research the Anchorage, Alaska, media market and draft a one-page paper on the main driver of the news.

After football, the main news coverage focuses on city government and OPD due to the "if it bleeds, it leads" phenomenon. It is important for law enforcement executives to know what sells in their communities so there is a gauge of where the pressure will come from. As an example, if homicides and shootings are high in a city—as they are in many major cities—the chief of police had better make it a priority to reduce those kinds of crime.

Commission on the Accreditation of Law Enforcement Agencies (CALEA)

This chapter has dealt with how vital it is to use the media and a police department's own press teams to ensure an appropriate narrative is established. This helps maintain an image of the police department. The additional action a department can take to secure a good reputation is to ensure they are accredited properly.

The Commission on the Accreditation of Law Enforcement Agencies (CALEA) is the closest symbol to a professional trophy for a law enforcement agency. CALEA accreditation programs provide public safety agencies with an opportunity to voluntarily meet an established set of professional standards. The standards require comprehensive and uniformly written directives that clearly define authority, performance, and responsibilities. There are approximately 18,000 law enforcement agencies in the United States, of which 838 are accredited (CALEA, n.d.).

As can be clearly seen from the data, not all law enforcement agencies will meet the highest standards. In fact, a terribly small number do, given the policing environment in America. OPD has been CALEA certified at the highest achievable level, Gold Standard, for more than a decade. In contrast, many major cities are not located on the CALEA certification list in 2020 (CALEA, n.d.).

Conclusion

The media ecosystem is a dynamic interplay of various mediums competing to capture the interests of society. Its principal role lies in shaping public opinions and attitudes. The press serves as a crucial source of information, keeping the public informed about the world we inhabit. Additionally, it operates as a watchdog in a democratic society, holding public officials accountable. However, the media's competitive nature drives them to present news in ways that attract the most viewers, emphasizing the need to be the first to report a story or make it "eye-catching" for readers.

The police media ecosystem stands apart, particularly for large law enforcement agencies like major city police departments, where daily media presence is intense and necessitates thorough examination. Policing matters have consistently been at the forefront of news coverage, from the historic race riots in the 1960s to the widespread civil unrest in 2020, following George Floyd's tragic death at the hands of the police.

The relationship between the media and law enforcement is a critical aspect that requires careful consideration, given its significant impact on public perception. Understanding and effectively managing the media's role is crucial for law enforcement agencies to build public trust and communicate their efforts and successes accurately. As the media landscape continues to evolve, law enforcement executives must adapt their strategies to navigate this challenging landscape effectively.

Law enforcement agencies recognize the significance of managing media inquiries by establishing dedicated press information offices. Media training has become essential in today's police media ecosystem, enabling agencies to navigate media interactions effectively. Moreover, instances of police misconduct can trigger an overwhelming response from the media.

In the United States, there are 210 distinct media markets, each defined by a group of consumers with access to the same marketing material. These markets encompass radio, television, print (newspapers), and the widespread internet medium. While the internet operates on a global scale, each media market maintains a unique local flavor that influences news coverage.

In addition to excelling in criminal investigations, responding to emergency calls, and conducting interviews and interrogations, law enforcement agencies must now master the intricacies of the police media ecosystem. This aspect has historically been overlooked, hindering agencies from leveraging the media to advance their societal mission effectively.

Questions for Discussion and Review

Attempt to answer the following questions before looking up the answers at the back of the book.

1. Define what a media ecosystem is and its significance today.
2. Explore and discuss the role of the media in shaping public opinions and attitudes about various subjects.
3. Examine the concept of the media acting as a watchdog in a democratic free press society.
4. Describe the unique characteristics and dynamics of a law enforcement media ecosystem.
5. Discuss the importance of media training for law enforcement agencies and its impact on public perception.
6. Analyze why instances of police misconduct in one city can have implications for law enforcement agencies in other cities.
7. Explore how CALEA accreditation can set a law enforcement agency apart and enhance its standing in the community.
8. Assess the impact of George Floyd's murder on policing practices and reform efforts in the United States.
9. Identify the ranking of Atlanta, Georgia, in the list of top ten media markets in America.
10. Compare and contrast the historical effects of the 1960s race riots and the nationwide civil unrest in 2020.
11. Investigate the reasons behind the extensive media attention given to cases of police misconduct.
12. Explain the concept of a media market and how it influences news coverage and consumer access to information.

CHAPTER FOUR

Law Enforcement— Baseline Media Strategy

Introduction

In Chapter Four, we delve into the intricate dynamics of law enforcement's engagement with the media, introducing the concept of a baseline media strategy tailored specifically for law enforcement agencies. This chapter aims to equip readers with a comprehensive understanding of both traditional and new media landscapes, highlighting their significance in law enforcement contexts. You will learn to distinguish and define various media forms, understand the diverse types of relationships law enforcement can foster with media entities, and identify the most effective strategies for such collaborations.

We will explore the key tenets of a baseline media strategy, including establishing and measuring an agency's public image and understanding the crucial role and responsibilities of a press information office and its officers. Additionally, the chapter underscores the importance of adaptability within media strategies, the effective use of social media, the operational function of "tip lines," and the value of media insights for law enforcement leaders. Finally, we will discuss strategies for leveraging national shows to enhance a law enforcement agency's message, ensuring a well-rounded approach to media relations in the context of law enforcement.

Law Enforcement Baseline Media Strategy

To deal with the issues covered in Chapter Three, every law enforcement agency needs a baseline media strategy for standard operations and a critical media strategy for major incidents. A law enforcement agency's interface with the press is vital to disseminating information and establishing public trust in a community.

Clear communication through the media establishes trust and legitimacy for a law enforcement agency with its stakeholders and the community. In today's age of "new media," rumor, speculation, and false information can confuse a community. A well-formed baseline media strategy for a law enforcement agency can quickly, legitimately, and transparently unravel the confusion through known facts and timely updates of verified fresh information (Dizikes 2018)

The communications landscape in our society is fast flowing. The speed at which news reaches society is at an all-time high. With social media, news and rumors can go viral and spread rapidly; as 86 percent of Americans get their news from a smartphone, computer, or tablet, latest information is no fa rther than our pockets (Shearer 2021).

How does a law enforcement agency deal with the rapid expansion of information through multiple channels and sources? The agency needs to have a baseline media strategy to establish itself as the sole and trusted source of information when it relates to the agency or a crime in the community.

For the purposes of this book, the following definitions of new media and traditional media apply (Swasy 2015):

New media is used to describe various digital communication sources such as the internet and social media. Challenges arise as information spreads virally through digital and social media. Law enforcement agencies must be prepared to intervene in the digital and social media landscape to correct any speculation or untruths (OUP 2022).

Traditional media refers to the use of radio, television, or print to receive and report on the news. This is still a necessary means of receiving and reporting on the news, and it comes with professional journalists who try to abide by a journalism code of ethics, making this a more reliable source of information than new media. An individual posting a rumor on the internet or social media is not bound by the same code of ethics (Law Insider, n.d.; Madrid 2023).

A law enforcement agency can work with traditional media to quell untrue assumptions and salacious rhetoric when it relates to a law enforcement function that has gone viral. Note that the Pew Research Center (Kennedy et al. 2022) found that 69 percent of respondents had trust in the police versus 46 percent placing their trust in journalists. Nevertheless, it has been my experience that traditional media and journalists are trustworthy with their sources and the information they put out as news, minus a few exceptions.

Law Enforcement—Baseline Media Strategy is the foundation for the day-to-day media operations of a law enforcement agency. It is the minimum or starting point for managing all aspects of the media. As a foundation, it can be stacked upon during critical media times that a law enforcement agency may face. The baseline strategy is an agency's normal conditions or day-to-day media operational practice. (Fritsvold , n.d.).

Law Enforcement—Critical Media Strategy is a plan of action for media communications when a crisis, critical event, or critical time period is upon the law enforcement agency. A critical event may be an OIS, a barricaded gunman with hostages, or a major homicide investigation, such as when a child is murdered. A critical period is a prolonged state of media emergency because of the circumstances. Two examples of such critical time periods occurred in 2020 for major city police agencies: the COVID-19 pandemic and the post–George Floyd civil unrest.

A serial killer investigation, lasting months, or years, would also fall under a prolonged state of media emergency. Law Enforcement—Critical Media Strategy is the subject of Chapter Five and Chapter Six. See Chapter Eleven for a media case study on a serial killer, where a critical communications strategy is on full display.

With meticulously designed baseline media and critical media strategies, a law enforcement agency will be able to respond professionally to day-to-day media inquiries and communications as well as seamlessly transitioning to cope with critical events when circumstances apply. Too many agencies struggle with the nuances of a baseline strategy and are left unprepared for the media during a critical incident.

Relationship Between Law Enforcement and Media

The previous section introduced the types of media environments that law enforcement will encounter. In this section, we look at the relationship between law enforcement and the media. There are three kinds of relationships law enforcement agencies can have with the press: 1) enemy, 2) peer, or 3) ally.

Journalism is a noble profession, and the journalists themselves are in professional careers. Journalists and their parent organizations should be treated with the respect, dignity, and collegiality one would expect in a peer relationship. The respect given will be reciprocated, on most occasions, setting a tone for a professional police agency. There are pitfalls for police agencies when the culture of interacting with the media is that of considering them an enemy or an ally.

Media as the Enemy

In extreme manifestations of this type of enemy relationship, a law enforcement agency feels intimidated. It does not fully understand the new era of policing and accountability with the media, and the dynamic morphs into an adversarial culture where the media and law enforcement agencies are at odds. With this type of backdrop, the police agency views the media as the enemy. The acrimonious relationship between the two organizations causes the agency to want to avoid the media; instead, the media is an afterthought and a burden to the agency.

The media-as-the-enemy culture stretches from the top of the law enforcement agency all the way down to the officers. The public will see the agency's acrimony toward the media, and the agency's image will suffer. The chief, sheriff, superintendent, director, or agency in charge needs to set the tone for interacting with the media and constantly impart it to create the culture of the agency. Viewing the media as the enemy will leave an agency behind. It is an archaic outlook, but it is still present in law enforcement agencies today.

The Ferguson Police Department, in 2015, viewed the press as the enemy. It was as if they were afraid of the media. Following the Michael Brown shooting, the agency waited several days to make a statement, and the outcome was a disaster. Street rumors and suppositions filled in the blanks of the communication void, such as the disproven "his hands were up" account of the shooting. This attitude of treating the media as the enemy damaged the image of the Ferguson Police Department and accelerated the civil unrest in the city.

It also damaged the image of policing as a profession, as what happens in one city is often generalized to other police agencies in other cities. The natural assumption by the populace was that all police agencies lack transparency just like the Ferguson, Missouri, police did. In short, the heavy national news coverage allowed all communities across the nation to see the shortcomings and lack of transparency by Ferguson police. In the aftermath, it was natural for a society to question their own police agency. In 2015, Ferguson police created doubt about all police agencies.

The Federal Bureau of Investigation (FBI) is another organization that frequently views the media as the enemy. The FBI has its reasons for this view, and the structure and nature of the FBI's work make its practices less transferrable to other law enforcement agencies. The FBI's stance is to never comment on an ongoing investigation. This might seem reasonable on the surface, given the size and worldwide imprint of the FBI—but is it?

There are ways of commenting by only providing known facts so that a discussion of an investigation can take place without "blowing off" the media. The direction, steps, time frames, and the agencies involved in the investigation are usually aspects that can be discussed with the media without harming the case. The public today demands it. Let us take the following scenario as an example: If a local police department engages in an OIS of a citizen, telling the media which law enforcement agency is investigating the occurrence can build public trust if the investigating agency is not the agency involved in the shooting.

The FBI is unique in this regard and will foreseeably not change anytime soon. The FBI is a national agency, and its strict adherence to the rule of "will not comment" on investigations makes for a streamlined and universal approach for all their substations. The FBI's approach to the media simply would not work for police agencies, as there are too many local stakeholders on which local police departments rely. The FBI, as a national agency with international attaché substations, simply does not need to conform to community partnerships in the manner municipal police prefer.

For local law enforcement agencies, public safety suffers when the media is avoided and viewed as the enemy. It is essential for a police agency to communicate with the media and relay public safety concerns. It is also essential to be able to communicate with them during critical times.

Try to think of any successful working relationship when there is acrimony. The common mindset of law enforcement that "the media needs us more than we need them" is also problematic. The new reality for law enforcement, and especially police work, is that it relies on the media just as much as the media relies on the police for news stories. A symbiotic relationship exists.

The success of a law enforcement agency in today's policing environment is predicated on a successful media culture. Yes, law enforcement agencies still need to be adept at responding to crimes, engaging in the investigative process, and creating a crime reduction plan, but the only way the public will gain confidence in a police agency is through an adept media plan.

Media as a Peer

The definition of a peer is "a person who is equal to another in abilities, qualifications, age, background and social status" (dictionary.com, n.d.). Law enforcement and the press are separate and distinct but socially equal in status. In basic criminal justice, there are three branches—police, courts, and corrections—which are interrelated as peers. In my estimation, in today's policing there are now four interrelated branches: police, courts, corrections, and the media.

Journalists and reporters are professionals in their field, and most possess a degree in journalism. As such, the media needs to be viewed as a peer. Law enforcement agencies should help the media where they can and try to be collegial and respectful. Most times the press will offer the agency the same courtesy in return.

A journalism major is a practical field of study that educates students to research, report, and communicate objectively for print, web, or broadcast. Increasingly these days, law enforcement is seeing citizen journalists, bloggers, social media reporters, and the like. Even so, police agencies have day-to-day contact with professional journalists or reporters that work for a city's major newspaper or in the television broadcast realm. To advance your agency's mission, it is imperative to have a culture of cooperation with the media (American Press Institute 2023).

The necessity of assisting the media with stories, providing interviews, and understanding the press is here to stay, therefore law enforcement agencies should strive to participate and assist their media duties. The media can be leveraged to communicate the law enforcement agency's message and agenda, while at the same time as professional to the public.

After Ferguson, police agencies started changing their relationship with the media and began treating them as peers. Not long after, post–George Floyd, there was a tidal

SYNERGY *of* INFLUENCE

wave of police agencies transforming and realizing the media's importance. Police agencies were starving for the media as a peer; so much so, that many agencies began stretching the relationship too far into the realm of allies.

The OPD made the cultural shift from enemy to peer with the media in late 2012. The circumstances involved the police department responding to a situation where a domestic violence incident turned into a hostage situation. The suspect was holding a gun to a child on the front porch before being shot by the police.

There had been an ongoing internal struggle within the OPD, between commanders who wanted to continue with their approach of treating the media as the enemy versus those who wanted a new paradigm where they treated the media as a peer. The hostage situation with the child provided an opportunity to chart a new course for the OPD, and the OPD took it.

The OIS was captured on a police cruiser camera (police body cameras were not prevalent yet). State law prescribes how Nebraska's video evidence should be released, and when someone dies in police custody, it is to be released after grand jury proceedings. The cruiser camera video could not be released to the public. However, a still photo from the cruiser video could be released to show the threat to the child's life. Three-quarters of the senior commanders were adamant that OPD should not release the still photo and maintain the policy we had always followed by staying quiet. The argument against releasing the photo was that the situation was a slippery slope: if OPD let the media in, the agency would be heavily subjected to unnecessary criticism.

Omaha Police photo: Police cruiser camera still photo (2012)

LAW ENFORCEMENT—BASELINE MEDIA STRATEGY

A minority of the commanders felt it was time the OPD became more transparent and released the photo. In fact, the argument was in favor of transparency whether it justified the OPD's actions or not. It was time to start a new paradigm of transparency with the community. A further incentive was the struggle OPD was having with police-and-community relations. A fresh approach was needed, and transparency could help to improve public trust.

The release of the still photo was met with complimentary reviews by the public. The era of greater transparency and police accountability was forged within the OPD. Police agency transformations need to start somewhere. The release of the photo was the catalyst used to transform the culture of the OPD from having an enemy relationship to having a peer relationship with the media. It also signaled OPD's desire to be a transparent partner with our community.

Societal signature events are prime opportunities to make dramatic culture shifts and should be viewed as gifts on this front. The law enforcement agency can further instill the culture by revising policy and training to reflect the new paradigm.

Media as an Ally

The definition of an *ally* (noun) is a state formerly cooperating with another agency; as a verb, to ally is to combine resources for mutual benefit. When police agencies move away from seeing the media as the enemy, too often they go to the other extreme and view the media as an ally, or even as a branch of the law enforcement agency.

The media is not an ally. Journalists are professional peers with whom police agencies work in the policing profession. An ally implies one step closer than a peer and denotes trust. There will always be investigative and professional reasons for confidentiality in police work. Allies know the investigative secrets and will maintain them. The media, on the other hand, would—in fact, must—report on them.

Formal agreements exist between law enforcement agencies that mutually benefit each other. For example, between violent crime task forces where federal and city police combine resources to mutually benefit each other through arresting violent offenders and reducing crime. Where does the media come into play on the task force? They do not. The media does not benefit from violent crime reduction. The media is not an ally for crime reduction, as that is not part of their charge or mission. The media's mission is to report on the occurrence of violent crime, not reduce it.

> **READER REFLECTION**
> **The media is not responsible for reducing crime, as the media's operational imperative is to report on singular incidents of crimes of**

interest and the overall landscape of crime in society. Does this mean the media has zero responsibility for public safety?

Can the reader give an example of when the onus is on the media to ensure public safety?

Police agencies have been burned by thinking that the media shares their goals. Usually, a reporter gains the trust of an agency decision-maker, and too much information is then divulged to the reporter. The reporter has an obligation to report on the information. The goal of the police agency is then compromised. For example, if a police agency has a large-scale warrant sweep about to commence, it is not advantageous for the police if the media reports the date and time of the warrant sweep. The media, however, would simply be doing their job in reporting that information.

The police have reasons to withhold information. The media does not. Imagine, for example, releasing information about a unique murder weapon to the media in a situation where only the killer knows the weapon. The media will print or air the information when they come across it, damaging the integrity of the police investigation.

The media is a trustworthy profession with professional journalists who play a vital role in society. The goals and purpose of the media do not totally align with law enforcement, so a healthy respect and some distance is needed. In this regard, law enforcement agencies should view the media as a peer rather than an ally.

Union contracts and laws protect an employee's right to privacy. As a result, police discipline cannot be shared with the media. If the press learns about any details of discipline, they will report on it. In addition, victims have a right to privacy where no arrests have been made. It would be unprofessional if the media were given access to a person's natural death investigation if it showed the person in a compromising position or situation. The media reporting the charred body of Kobe Bryant is a high-profile example of such a situation. The media should never have had access to the crime scene or been given the photos by the deputies.

Media communications books often talk about treating the media as an ally. The idea of allyship is promoted, yet mass communications and media strategy articles are mostly focused on corporations or for-profit businesses. This is one of the first books on media insight and strategy specific to law enforcement agencies. It makes sense for the private sector to declare the media as an ally, especially when the corporation is attempting to do damage control. For law enforcement agencies, viewing the media as a peer is more suitable.

In summary, for police agencies, there are three ways to view the media: as an enemy, peer, or an ally. Viewing the media as a peer is a middle path between the two extremes and is in line with police agencies' objectives. As a peer, avoid yelling at a journalist and go to their supervisor if necessary. Also, as a peer, if you can help them, do so if it does not hurt your mission. For example, if a journalist asks for the homicide clearance rate for the department, give it to them with context if needed. Do not make them look it up for themselves or file a Freedom of Information Act (FOIA) request. Be a respectful peer who understands the media is an everyday facet of policing in today's law enforcement environment.

Omaha Police Organizational Chart

It is important for readers to understand the basic organizational structure of a law enforcement agency. Depending on the size of the agency, the complexity of the organizational chart increases. The larger the agency, the more complex the rank structure and organizational structure become.

The Omaha Police Department (OPD) has a standard rank structure and is used as a sample organizational chart (see Addendum five).

- *Chief of Police (1).* The head of the law enforcement agency. The head of the agency could be a sheriff, commissioner, superintendent, or agent in charge.
- *Deputy Chief of Police (5).* There are five bureaus within the OPD, and each is run by a deputy chief.
- *Captain (11).* Senior staff members who oversee a precinct or section.
- *Lieutenant (35).* Midlevel managers who will oversee a unit, such as homicide or traffic, or an entire shift for the Uniform Patrol Bureau.
- *Sergeant (103).* First-line supervisors who oversee eight to twelve officers, or four to eight detectives.
- *Officer (751).* Entry-level sworn personnel in uniform, plainclothes, or detectives.

Baseline Media Strategy and Philosophy

Law enforcement agencies should consider using an overall approach to the media that is broken down into two distinct strategies. The first is a baseline media strategy, which serves as the foundation for general media inquiries and the handling of the day-to-day media interactions in which law enforcement agencies typically engage.

The second is a critical media strategy that is adopted when a critical event or incident occurs. The baseline media strategy is always still present as a foundation, and when the critical event is over, the agency will transition back to the baseline media strategy.

My philosophy is to have a flexible media strategy for the OPD. The baseline media strategy can bend and is subject to review and analysis for change. In short, it is pliable. The same goes for OPD's critical media strategy. OPD builds on top of the foundation and adapts our critical media strategy when the circumstances arise.

Law enforcement has many variables, and a static media plan is not able to bend and flex to the ever-changing environment in which law enforcement agencies operate. It is for this reason that I developed the two-strategy approach with a baseline media strategy as a foundation from which an agency can escalate to a critical media strategy when needed.

The baseline media strategy has five components.

Baseline Media Strategy

1. Day-to-day media
2. Highlight a law enforcement agency's accomplishments and address needs
3. Define a law enforcement agency's image
4. Define measures of success
5. Troubleshooting

Component 1: Day-to-Day Media

The daily media pressure on a major law enforcement agency is constant. A baseline media strategy is designed to assist the press in their coverage of crime, the community, and the agency. OPD views the press as a peer and will make every attempt to manage all media requests. The day-to-day operations are managed by the press information office and the press information officer (PIO). The PIO attends senior staff briefings on Monday, Wednesday, and Friday to go over all the media inquiries and stories. The press information office and PIO are a staple of any baseline media strategy. The PIO answers directly to the chief of police.

Press Information Office: A press information office is imperative for a law enforcement agency so that it can implement a baseline media strategy and address the daily media concerns for the agency. Federal law enforcement agencies such as the FBI, Drug Enforcement Agency (DEA), or Homeland Security and all major city police or sheriff's agencies also have press information offices. Note, however, that federal law enforcement entities do not face the daily media inquiries and pressure major city, county, or state law enforcement agencies endure.

Depending on the size of the police agency, a typical press information office will vary in size. A major city or a metropolitan area of over a million, like Omaha, Minneapolis, and Kansas City, will have three to six officers or civilians working in the press information office. Smaller departments may have one or two—or none—depending on their size. A city the size of Los Angeles, Chicago, Houston, or New York will have a large contingent of officers and civilians working in its law enforcement agency's press information office. The name of the unit will not always be a press information office. It can have various titles, but the function is the same.

A new wave of thinking calls for major law enforcement agencies to have a strategic communications advisor who oversees a Strategic Communications Office. The director of strategic communications oversees the press information office, large public events, internal communications, and customer support and creative services (recruitment graphic designs, visual productions, print shop, and marketing as examples) (Pal et al. 2023).

The head of the press information office is usually a commander. OPD assigns an officer with the rank of lieutenant, which is a mid-level commander, to oversee its press information office. Some agencies will use a commander of higher rank, while other agencies will hire a non-sworn civilian PIO to run the unit. It is a matter of preference; law enforcement agencies will prefer a civilian—such as a former news reporter—to oversee the office and be the primary PIO.

The blueprint for OPD has always been to pick a sworn command officer as the PIO. The individual chosen is well versed in policing, well spoken, and has the right demeanor for the public. The commander also understands the role and responsibility of being a law enforcement agency insider. The selection for the PIO position needs to come with a good understanding of how the individual will manage the insider role. Not all civilians are prepared for or accustomed to the confidentiality skills needed for the position. In addition, not all civilian PIOs understand the policies and procedures of the agency enough to be prepared on day one to head a press information office.

Civilian PIOs can be a successful choice; however, the learning curve to understanding policing is extremely steep. Civilian PIOs brought into an agency can suffer from a lack of "buy-in" from sworn police officers if the officers know the person's background is not in policing. The PIO will be an insider to the department's inner workings and major crime investigations, so buy-in or acceptance is important.

The OPD press information office has five employees: a lieutenant PIO and three officers, plus a civilian press person for all our social media needs. The press office manages daily media inquiries and coordinates with the department's subject matter experts for answers and interviews. The lieutenant PIO is a primary spokesperson for the agency on major matters unless a deputy chief or the chief of police manages it directly. It all depends on the severity of the critical incident.

Within OPD, if an officer is shot, the chief of police will manage the media interview. The PIO may manage a bank robbery. A deputy chief may oversee a crime series story. The K-9 commander may give a smaller interview and demonstrate the effectiveness of the K-9 Unit in searching for drugs in schools. The Bomb Unit supervisor will participate in stories centered around the unit.

It is imperative that the commander or civilian in charge of the press officer answers directly to the chief of police.

What Makes a Good PIO?

The selection of the right person for PIO is paramount. The position requires a unique set of skills, and the person will help define the image of the police department. The chief of police and the PIO are the most publicly recognizable members of the department.

Traits to look for in the department PIOs are a calming demeanor, humility, trustworthiness, and believability for the public.

In addition to the PIO, law enforcement agencies can have media stars from other departments; these are personnel who work well with the media and seek opportunities to collaborate with them. When a law enforcement agency has non-press-office personnel who are comfortable with the media, they should use them. Omaha police have had a Bomb Unit commander, the department's firearm coordinator, and a precinct captain who have excelled in this way. The public loved them, as they were charismatic and knowledgeable, and if they were on the scene, then the public got the impression that all was going to be fine. Police agencies should identify personnel who work well with the media and use them often.

Component 2: Highlight a law enforcement agency's accomplishments and address needs

The second component of the baseline media strategy is to highlight the law enforcement agency's accomplishments. Law enforcement agencies also have varying needs and require a flexible strategy.

The press information office receives operating needs from the chief and deputy chiefs and will spearhead the directives. For example, when the OPD recently received the gold standard in CALEA certifications, it was important to tout this honor in the community as a macro accomplishment. OPD also promotes accomplishments in crime reduction and community partnerships. The strategy is to make the community aware of any macro accomplishments and project a positive public image.

On a micro level, OPD recognizes the importance of publicly acknowledging the challenging work of our employees. Graduations, promotions, medals of honor, and service honor awards are publicly highlighted through diverse media channels within the agency and the community. The promotion of these accomplishments has a strong morale component, and it humanizes the officers to the public and reinforces a positive culture internally and publicly. I have heard chiefs describe it as "currency" for when things go wrong. In my mind, it is an appropriate function for the culture of an agency.

LAW ENFORCEMENT—BASELINE MEDIA STRATEGY

The needs of a law enforcement agency vary depending on the size of the agency and the environments surrounding the agency. For example, the Chicago police department is going to have more PIO/media demands than that of a law enforcement agency with 200 hundred employees. One need that all law enforcement agencies are facing right now is due to a national staffing crisis. The term "staffing" has recently been adopted, due to the significant decrease in application numbers for the career, while concurrently, the retention of active sworn officers/employees has also greatly decreased. In combination, law enforcement agencies across the country are in a staffing crisis.

Another use (need) of the baseline media strategy for OPD is to recruit, advertise, and push the department out as a top-notch employer. I use the national staffing crisis as an example of the way to address needs because it is currently a "professional complication." Following the 2020 civil unrest across the country, law enforcement agencies faced a legitimacy crisis as the "defund the police" movement swept the nation. There will be other needs following the staffing crisis, so the baseline media strategy must be flexible to address whatever needs arise.

READER ASSIGNMENT
Following the staffing crisis, what could be the next need that law enforcement should address? Draft a one-page paper explaining your forecasted need.

Component 3: Define the Law Enforcement Agency's Image

The third component of a baseline media strategy is to define the image of the law enforcement agency. The image-building process is imperative to the public's perception of the law enforcement agency. When a new coach takes over a "fix it" sports program—one that has not been winning—the coach will talk about building a process toward getting wins, such as recruiting, conditioning, and administration support. Conversely, a coach who takes over a successful program—one that has been winning—will talk about the successes that got them there and how they will keep it going, for example, the fans, support from the administration, coaching, and valuable players.

In 2012, OPD sought to redefine the agency's image to present ourselves as professional and as community partners. The image restructure was needed due to some high-profile mishaps and mistakes by OPD in the past. As a result of those blunders, police–community relations suffered, so OPD sought to project the ideal image of a professional community policing department. To illustrate, see Chapter Two—Omaha's National Crime Events: Unveiling the Impact, which describes a major police corruption scandal. That scandal damaged the OPD's image as professionals. The Omaha

SYNERGY *of* INFLUENCE

police image, or brand in the corporate world, needed to improve to convince the public they should partner with OPD to reduce crime and improve the quality of life in the community.

A baseline media strategy was implemented to push the ideal image of OPD, to set a standard for the public, and to create a culture for the department. The first step of our baseline media strategy was to instill an image of professionalism and community policing.

OPD commanders demanded professionalism from all officers in every instance. The philosophy was that there is a professional way to interact at a traffic stop, there is a professional way for an officer to make an arrest, there is a professional way to use force if it is needed, and a professional way to utilize deadly force when the circumstances leave no other option.

Community policing was sold internally to the officers through training and culture imposition. Externally, to the community, OPD's baseline media strategy included constant messaging that highlighted OPD as a community partner. This mission was instilled over and over through the media. OPD highlighted community events, a newfound transparency with the media as a *peer*, and constant mission talking points of professionalism and community policing. Over the course of time, OPD became known as a professional community policing law enforcement agency.

Component 4: Define Measures for Success

The fourth component is about defining a law enforcement agency's measure of success. It is imperative for the law enforcement executive (chief, sheriff, superintendent, or agency in charge) to define the measure of success for their agency and repeat it consistently. If they do not, law enforcement critics will use the media to negatively define an agency's success and highlight agency failures.

Three vital statistics plagued the image of OPD in 2012:

1) There was an epidemic number of shootings in Omaha.
2) OPD could not solve homicides as our homicide clearance rate was dismally low.
3) Omaha police had too many OISs.

In combination, all three vital statistics were damaging OPD's image in the eyes of the public, causing the community to lose trust in us.

As an agency, we elected to use the number of shootings in the city, the agency's homicide clearance rate, and the number of OISs as measures of OPD's success. The agency was now tethered to the three markers, and it was up to us to improve their metrics. Any improvement in these markers would show progress toward OPD collaborating with the community. If there was an increase in one of the measures, OPD would double our efforts with the community and refine our policing approach.

The inner workings of the agency were reorganized to address the three markers as a priority. As an illustration, gang and gun violence accounted for 95 percent of our shootings in the city, so OPD enacted an increase in size and streamlined efficiencies for the Gang Unit. OPD added an extra crew and implemented a more modern approach to investigating homicides to reduce shootings and improve the homicide clearance rate. It was decided that the gang unit and the felony assault and homicide units would now work jointly on gang shootings and homicides. OISs were made a priority through a change in culture; the focus shifted to full BWC deployment, Tasers for a less lethal option, and mental health training, giving OPD a better format to de-escalate those in a mental health episode.

OPD referred to the three measures as the city's "vital signs" to make it more compelling for the press to follow and report on. A law enforcement agency can define, promote, and highlight its barometers for success in any manner desired, but it is imperative for the law enforcement agency to define the measures appropriately. If a city is ravaged by gun violence, declaring that cracking down on parking violations downtown is a priority will be met with skepticism.

The three Omaha police graphics in the following figure illustrate the progression of shootings, homicide clearance rate, and OISs in the city of Omaha over a ten-year period.

As shown in the graphs, a successful community partnership and internal policing strategy improved Omaha's vitals. The OPD was able to successfully instill its barometers of success. The Omaha press corps routinely reported on OPD's successes for the long haul and on the instances of spikes in violence. Over the course of years, OPD's image revamp was complete. The brand was transformed from a non-professional agency struggling with police–community relations to a professional police department where community partners are valued.

Each barometer chosen by OPD reflected a problem in the community, and a strong community partnership was needed to improve the measures. The vast increase in homicide clearances was achievable only with strong police–community relations. The OPD needed the trust of the community, for people to come forward as witnesses, so they could arrest the shooting suspects.

The increase in the homicide clearance rate reflects strong police–community relations; a decrease would have shown a need to re-engage the community. Of note, in my professional opinion, the greatest singular barometer of a city's police–community relations are its homicide clearance rate; the higher the number of homicide clearances, the greater the police–community relations. A city with a low homicide clearance rate will often suffer from poor police–community relations.

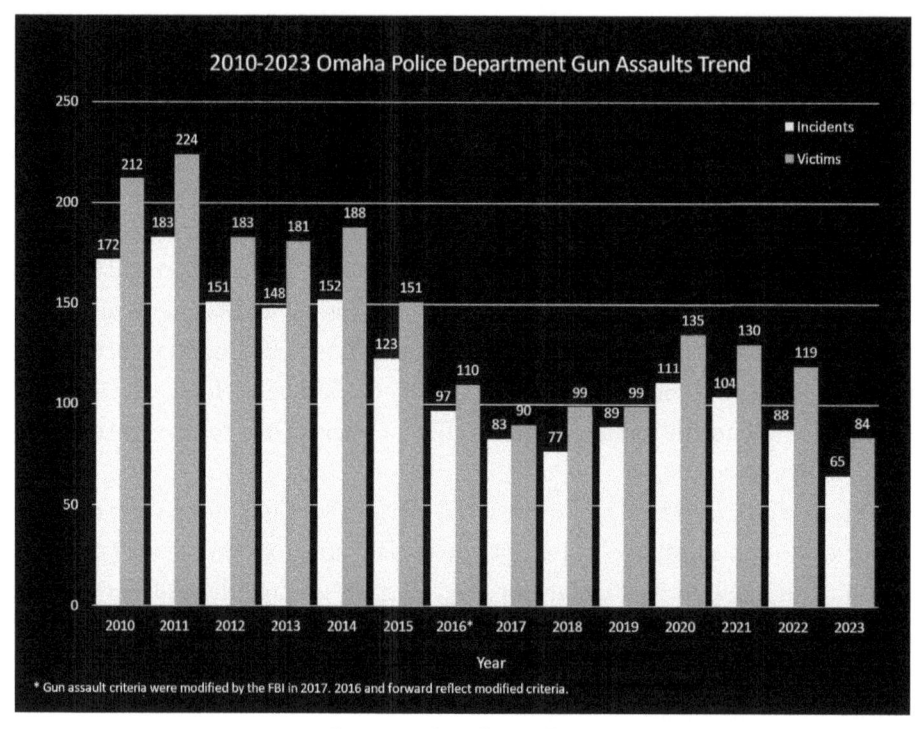

SYNERGY of INFLUENCE

2010-2023 Omaha Police Department Gun Assaults Trend

Year	Incidents	Victims
2010	172	212
2011	183	224
2012	151	183
2013	148	181
2014	152	188
2015	123	151
2016*	97	110
2017	83	90
2018	77	99
2019	89	99
2020	111	135
2021	104	130
2022	88	119
2023	65	84

* Gun assault criteria were modified by the FBI in 2017. 2016 and forward reflect modified criteria.

Source: Omaha Police

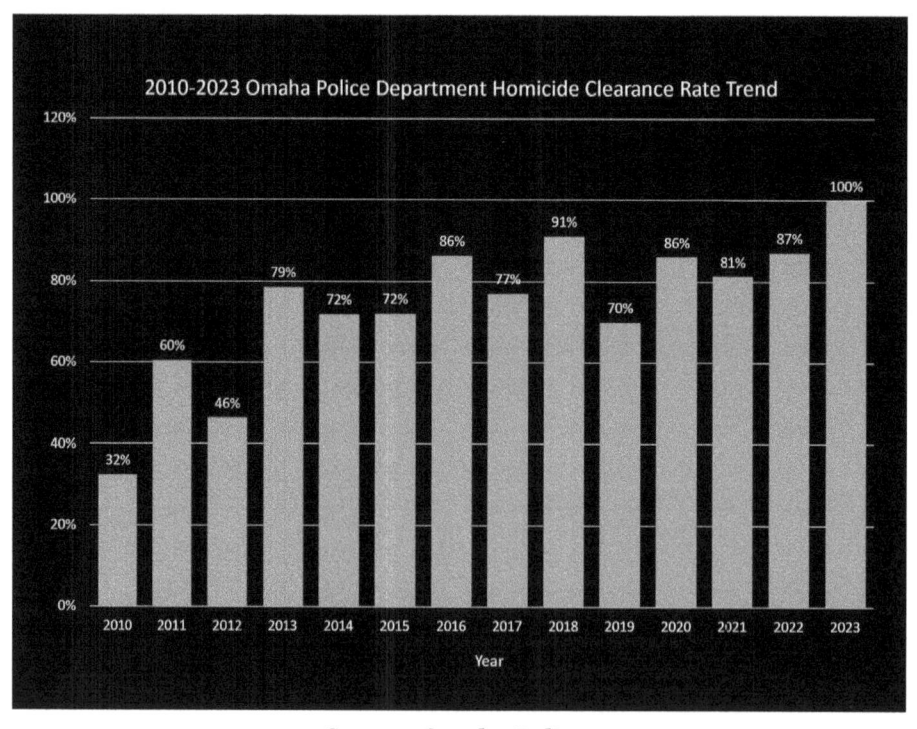

2010-2023 Omaha Police Department Homicide Clearance Rate Trend

Year	Clearance Rate
2010	32%
2011	60%
2012	46%
2013	79%
2014	72%
2015	72%
2016	86%
2017	77%
2018	91%
2019	70%
2020	86%
2021	81%
2022	87%
2023	100%

Source: Omaha Police

LAW ENFORCEMENT—BASELINE MEDIA STRATEGY

2010-2023 Omaha Police Department Officer Involved Shootings Trend

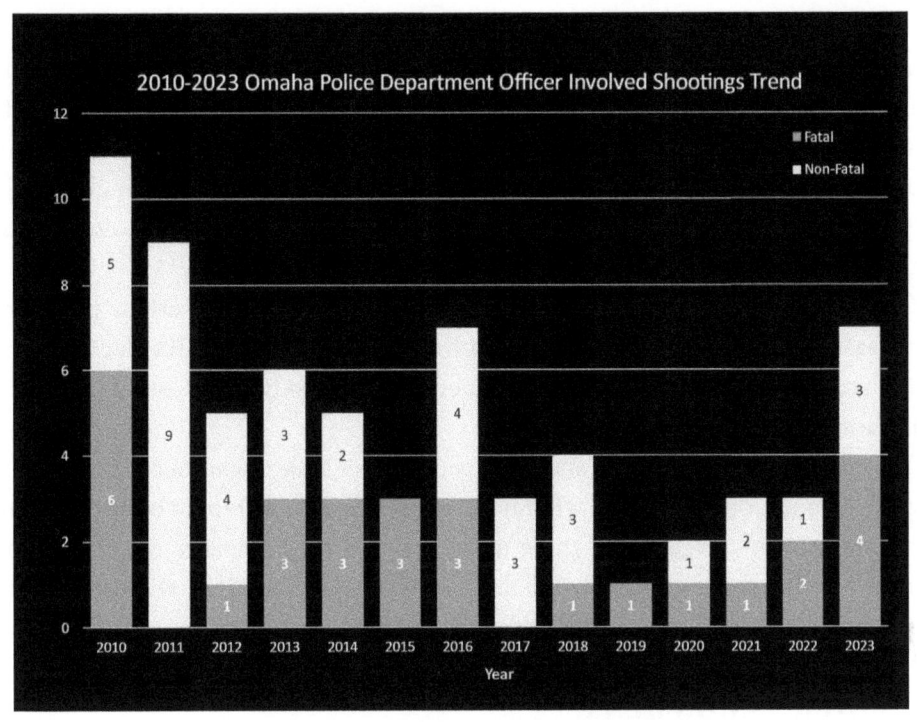

Year	Fatal	Non-Fatal
2010	6	5
2011	9	—
2012	1	4
2013	3	3
2014	3	2
2015	3	—
2016	3	4
2017	3	—
2018	—	3
2019	1	—
2020	1	1
2021	1	2
2022	2	1
2023	4	3

Source: Omaha Police (2010 to May 2023)

Over the last four decades, the national homicide clearance rates have decreased from 71 percent in 1980 to an all-time low of about 50 percent in 2020 (Westervelt 2023.) The homicide clearance rate drop has occurred despite vast advancements in DNA and crime scene technologies. Many major city police chiefs feel the drop is also commensurate with a drop in police–community relations. As police–community relations improve, so will the homicide clearance rates.

A considerable number of shootings occurring in a city can cause a ripple effect of damage that both the community and the police need to address. The ripple effect plays out in affecting whether businesses want to take root in the city or opt for a safer community. It continues as the level of trauma in a community in the aftermath of a shooting leads to more trauma. The police need witnesses to come forward on shootings, as traditional crime scene investigations (CSI) will not often lead to the shooter. The police need the community to have wraparound services for the juveniles and adults most at risk of being victims and suspects of shootings. As such, the number of shootings in a city is a good indicator of the strength of the city's police–community relations.

OISs account for the most prevalent *image damage* to a law enforcement agency. Community relations suffer each time. It is imperative that action is taken to reduce the overall number of OISs in a city. Historically, the more a city embraces its police, the fewer OISs will occur over time. How to reduce the layered and complex issue of OISs in a city and how to engage the media in the aftermath of an officer-involved shooting is the subject of Chapter Seven: Brand Damage Control in Officer-Involved Shootings.

Every city has a unique set of problems. These problems can be used to define the measures for success. If a city suffers from drug overdoses, the amount of drug seizures a year can be used to gauge success. The Ferguson Police Department in 2015 might tout a revamped culture, measured by new de-escalation and cultural competency training for its officers.

Other departments may set the number of uses of force applications per year as their measure of success. If the number of times an officer uses force declines when making arrests, then success has been achieved. Conversely, if the number goes up, modifications need to be made.

The measures of success have statistical gauges, so it is clear whether success is being achieved. In addition, the media will find it more palatable to report on the measures when they know in advance that these measures have been prioritized by the agency. The media loves a statistical chart to define the terrain of a city. They will use the graph and supply interviews to support the rise or fall of the numbers.

READER ASSIGNMENT
Research one of the following cities, Anchorage, Alaska; Honolulu, Hawaii; or Billings, Montana to define three barometers of success for the city's law enforcement agency. The three barometers should be based on the law enforcement problems facing the city. Draft a two-to-three-page paper on the city's three barometers of success while using a law enforcement baseline media strategy.

In summary, a police agency must define its measures for success, or critics will supply them through the media. In today's policing ecosystem, law enforcement agencies must take it upon themselves to have a baseline media strategy to advocate for their successes. The public deserves to know if their police department is acting professionally and addressing critical crime needs. The only way to achieve these goals is through a well-thought-out baseline media plan.

In the absence of a baseline media plan, an agency's destiny is in the hands of others. One inevitable mistake by a law enforcement agency will be used by critics of the police to define your entire organization. Policing is complex with extremely diverse variables; it is inevitable mistakes will be made. A baseline media strategy will help an agency manage expectations so occasional mistakes do not define the agency. Rather, the agency's image should be defined by statistical measures of success.

Component 5: Troubleshooting

A hallmark of a flexible baseline media strategy is the ability to troubleshoot. In law enforcement, diverting and troubleshooting as something comes up is an expected function. For example, an officer might shoot an animal, and now animal rights activists are pressuring the agency for a response. Or a critical event or incident might trigger the law enforcement agency to escalate into their critical media strategy.

Social Media

Social media is used throughout all five components of the baseline media strategy and deserves its own section as a vital aspect of a media strategy. Social media is a gold mine for bettering the image of a law enforcement agency and for highlighting your personnel. Social media is also used to troubleshoot and push an agency's agenda. The PIO oversees the social media aspect of a police agency, and there should be a dedicated employee (sworn officer or civilian) assigned strictly to the agency's social media needs on a full-time or part-time basis. Social media is an excellent channel for pushing out touching stories, thanking the community, acknowledging officers, and recruiting. The OPD opened a TikTok account during a time when the department was in a staffing crisis in 2021. The TikTok account was used as a recruitment tool as part of a police officer hiring campaign. The OPD account went from zero to 130,000 followers in one week!

Use social media metrics to glean what stories get the most reactions and from where your supporters and antipolice comments are coming. Law enforcement agency leaders should know how many members are on the agency's Facebook and X (formerly Twitter) pages. How many people visit your department's website? These metrics are powerful in understanding how best to get your agency's message out to the public and shape the police agency's brand.

For large law enforcement agencies, it may be useful to have a cadre of trusted social media personnel spread throughout your organization. The trusted and trained group can post on X or another medium and generate a ton of support for the agency. The most popular tweeters from OPD are a K-9 officer and an officer who is a pilot within our air support (helicopter) unit. The K-9 officer has content where their K-9 dog appears to be tweeting, and the public loves it. The air support officer gives the public a view of things from the sky and is highly popular among the community.

Social Media Guidelines

Social media can also be a gigantic source of image damage for a police department, especially a major city department with over a thousand employees. The risk comes in the form of officers posting on their personal social media during off times. Officers are passionate about their careers, and, over the last decade, policing has been a hot-button issue for the nation and has a social media life of its own. It is crucial to have set policies and procedures that govern the personal social media accounts of police department employees.

No policy can govern free speech while an employee is off duty. However, an employer can govern what is said in the purview of an officer employed by an agency. The onus is on the police agency, and it has a right to control its own message. OPD has over a thousand employees. They cannot all speak for the department. As such, a policy can control whether an officer can identify themselves on social media as a police officer. For example, Omaha officers cannot identify themselves as Omaha police officers on social media if they are going to voice opinions on policing matters. The chief of police is charged with defining the public statements of OPD, not the one-thousand-plus employees, who may have contrary messages.

READER REFLECTION
Imagine how important it is for the NYPD to have a policy on who can speak for the agency. The NYPD has approximately thirty-six thousand officers and nineteen thousand civilian employees (NYC.gov).

A situation arose for the Omaha police where an officer, identified as OPD on social media, made controversial comments regarding the Black Lives Matter organization. The social media post caused a tremendous amount of public relations damage to the agency. In the subset world of social media, it was a wildfire. The department had to step in and issue a statement to rein in the social-media firestorm.

All executives must control the message coming from their organization, whether it is a large police department or a Fortune 500 company. Social media has made this facet of leadership much harder. Failure to control the messaging of the agency will inevitably catch up with the executive in a negative way. Proper policy and procedures will govern the need for the hardline executives to deal with this situation.

Tip Lines

Tip lines fall into the category of Component 1: Day-to-Day Media and sometimes Component 5: Troubleshooting. Law enforcement agencies need to have a tip line conduit for the public, and it needs to be advertised. Tip lines exist for mass shooters, Crime Stoppers, school bullying, and Amber Alerts for abducted children.

Police commanders should also understand the use of media scrolls at the bottom of the television screen. Scrolls can be highly effective for crimes in progress and missing endangered persons. All a commander needs to do is ask the media to scroll the information if it meets the agency's threshold for use. Using it too much will defeat its effectiveness. Some examples of a television scroll would be used to alert the public of an active killer at a store to keep the public away or to augment an Amber Alert for an abducted child.

READER REFLECTION
The FBI's ten most wanted list of fugitives is often referred to as the most famous of tip lines. (FBI.gov)

We have all heard the tones on our televisions or cell phones when an Amber Alert goes off. Chills go down your spine. Amber Alerts are highly effective because of the impact they have on people's emotions. However, it is best to use a television scroll and social media to push out the details on the abducted child first, since it is immediate. Amber Alerts can take a while as the system is a pre-social-media boon.

Media Insight for Law Enforcement

Most law enforcement professionals do not have a background in the media but accessing it has become just as important to police work as police procedures. There are advantages to be gained by police agencies and especially law enforcement executives in the media realm. Law enforcement leaders simply need to ask the right questions. Newly appointed chiefs, superintendents, agents in charge, or newly elected sheriffs should schedule a meeting with the news directors in their media market. Veteran law enforcement executives should periodically check in with their news director peers.

Some questions that the law enforcement executive should ask the news directors include:

- How many physical paper subscribers do you have?
- How many online subscribers?
- What are your nightly television viewer numbers and ratings?

The news directors will typically divulge the data, and this information is used to determine what station or medium will be utilized to broadcast the law enforcement agency's message for the most impact. Most times a mass press release to all media market news agencies will take place. However, there will be times when a law enforcement agency works with only one media source. For the biggest impact on the public, use the media source that gets the most viewers or readers.

There are three major television stations in the Omaha market and one major newspaper. As the agency executive, I have knowledge of the volume of viewers KETV, WOWT, and KMTV get on their nightly news broadcasts. As such, the home of our weekly Crime Stoppers segments remains the station that gets the most viewers; more viewers mean a higher chance of catching the most offenders. The data also helps to prioritize the department's messaging as to where the most impact will be garnered.

Asking the right questions also made me aware of how many physical paper and online subscribers the *Omaha World Herald* (OWH) garnered every year. The OWH has been used by OPD for many exclusives over the years to reach a bigger audience. In addition, the paper's journalists could do deep dives into important matters, giving the public a robust understanding of the subject at hand.

There is often a news dynamic that plays out, depending on what station or paper breaks the story. If the OWH broke the story, the television stations would pick it up and do their own story. The story would then get repeated coverage. Yet, if a television station broke the story, the other television stations would not always follow, and the OWH would rarely pick it up second. A law enforcement executive can advance their messaging when armed with media insight into statistics such as viewers and subscribers as well as the interplay among different media.

Additional Media Insight Tips

Law enforcement leaders should ask the news directors what subjects get the most viewers and sell the most papers. In Omaha, it was Nebraska University football, the governor, the mayor, public schools, the chief of police, congress/senate, and local government. If there is a scandal occupying the media with the school system, then the spotlight is off a police agency for the time. When the Nebraska football coach was fired in 2021, the news story was huge, and this would have been an opportune time to release negative information about a personnel matter or an embarrassing act of an officer. The PIO should have a strong understanding of using this kind of timing to the agency's advantage.

It also does not hurt to have strong media insight and savvy. Never release three good law enforcement stories in one day. Release stories that make the agency look impressive one at a time for a slow drip into the public's mind. Conversely, if there is more than one image damager, an agency should release them all in one day, peeling the bandage off all at once instead of over multiple occasions. It is useful to release the image damagers during a big news day. No one remembers the second news story of the day on 9/11.

Lastly, for some reason, Friday afternoon is the least attention time for the news, so consider releasing bad news then.

LAW ENFORCEMENT—BASELINE MEDIA STRATEGY

National TV Shows and Movies

National investigative shows will reach out to major law enforcement agencies regularly for episode ideas. Being featured on *Dateline NBC* because your agency caught a serial killer is not a bad move. A national audience seeing how adept your agency is can be a boon. OPD worked with *Dateline NBC* on several shows where killers were caught. The first one was an episode called "Haunting," featuring the OPD catching serial killer Dr. Anthony Garcia. "Scorned" was another episode that featured OPD, where Cari Farver's bizarre murder tale was told. *Dateline NBC* liked working with OPD and has done three other episodes since. It has been good publicity for the image of the department.

Personal photo: Chief Schmaderer and famous *Dateline NBC* host Keith Morrison

Conversely, the OPD invited the long-running television show *COPS* to ride and film officers in the course of their duties. The show was real, and the camera and sound person wore ballistic vests and shadowed the officers. A release had to be signed, holding the city non-liable if they get injured, as the *COPS* personnel are not under the direction of the officers they film.

The movie industry likes police drama plots, so police agency heads will be asked to film movies in their city utilizing officers or featuring them in background roles. It can be good for morale, and consideration should be given. The OPD turns down a substantial number of television crime shows because there are so many, and the existing workload is already high. Cable networks will ask major city police departments almost weekly if they can feature a crime or an investigation.

As for the movies, Omaha police have historically been accommodating since the requests come only once every few years. Historically, it has been a morale booster, but it is important to make sure the movie is designed to reflect well on the agency. Cameo appearances can boost the morale of the officers, and letting officers take part is viewed as a positive thing. If the law enforcement agency executive elects to do a cameo, make sure it is in good taste and reflects an image worthy of being seen by the public. The movie *Going for Two* is set to be released in late 2024. I have a cameo appearance as a criminal who gets arrested. It is hoped that the satire for the movie will be viewed as positive humor for the community and for OPD.

Omaha Police Photo: Omaha Police Headquarters has been the set of movie scenes over the years. The experience has been positive for morale and community relations. The above photo is from OPD headquarters right before a high-speed car chase scene in a movie.

Conclusion

Chapter Four covered the need for law enforcement agencies to have a baseline media strategy. There are three relationships a law enforcement agency can have with the media: enemy, peer, or ally. A culture of viewing the media as a peer will advance the objectives of a law enforcement agency through a balanced approach to the media.

There are five components of a baseline media strategy taught in this book. In addition, the baseline media strategy is a foundation, and a law enforcement agency can escalate to its critical media strategy if needed.

LAW ENFORCEMENT—BASELINE MEDIA STRATEGY

Baseline Media Strategy

1. Day-to-day media
2. Highlight a law enforcement agency's accomplishments and address needs
3. Define a law enforcement agency image
4. Define measures of success
5. Troubleshooting

A press information office is imperative to the handling of the day-to-day interactions with the media. A good PIO will have a calming demeanor, humility, trustworthiness, and believability for the public. Social media plays a vital role within an agency's press information office, as do tip lines.

Law enforcement agency leaders should seek media insight from news directors and be savvy when releasing information to the public through the media. Law enforcement executives should consider national television shows that will highlight the agency's successes. An occasional movie where the law enforcement agency is featured positively should also be considered for officer morale and community positivity.

Chapter Five, Law Enforcement—Critical Media Strategy (A) covers the critical communications every law enforcement agency should be prepared to encounter. The chapter will provide a backdrop of real-world examples while educating readers on the best way to address the media during a critical law enforcement incident.

Questions for Reflection

Attempt to answer the following questions before looking up the answers at the back of the book.

1. What sets "new media" apart from traditional media in terms of communication modes and platforms?
2. Elaborate on the significance of traditional media for law enforcement agencies. How does it serve as a vital conduit for disseminating critical information?
3. Enumerate the three distinct manners in which a law enforcement agency can establish and navigate its relationship with the media.
4. Shed light on why the "peer" rapport with the media is the most coveted for law enforcement agencies. Expound on the benefits of this dynamic.
5. Analyze the dynamics of media relationships—enemy, peer, or ally—within the context of private businesses and nonprofits. Justify the suitability of each approach based on their goals and interactions.

6. Detail the five fundamental components encapsulated within a law enforcement baseline media strategy.
7. Illustrate the necessity of utilizing quantifiable measures of success when engaging with both the media and the public as part of law enforcement agencies' communication strategy.
8. Profile the traits that define an effective public information officer. How do attributes like composure, humility, trustworthiness, and credibility enhance the PIO's capacity to transparently communicate with diverse audiences?
9. Assess the veracity of this statement: A law enforcement executive should universally decline all invitations to participate in national TV shows and movie productions due to potential negative effects on the agency's image.
10. Provide an instance where the implementation of a media scroll by a law enforcement agency is warranted. Elaborate on the scenarios where this real-time information dissemination tool proves indispensable in ensuring public awareness and safety during evolving emergencies.

CHAPTER FIVE

Law Enforcement— Critical Media Strategy (A)

Introduction

In this comprehensive exploration of law enforcement's interaction with the media, we delve into strategies to not only influence the press to an agency's advantage but also to foster trust in law enforcement. The core of this chapter focuses on understanding and implementing a critical media strategy, specifically designed to guide law enforcement through the complexities of media relations during critical events.

We will examine how to effectively navigate press conferences and media engagements in challenging situations, offering real-life examples, and citing national incidents to provide a deeper insight into various scenarios and their media implications. Recognizing the dynamic nature of critical events, this text emphasizes the importance of tailoring media approaches to specific periods and adapting messaging to meet diverse audience expectations.

Special attention is given to managing the media during sensitive situations such as lawsuits and incidents involving law enforcement. The text will guide readers through strategies to distance a law enforcement agency from potential controversies and to identify common pitfalls and controversies to avoid. We also discuss the preferred demeanor and tone for law enforcement executives during critical events, emphasizing confidence, empathy, and transparency. Utilizing media platforms effectively, understanding the strategic use of news embargoes and exclusives, and differentiating between "off the record" and "background" interactions with the press are crucial skills this text aims to impart. By the end of this exploration, readers will have a nuanced understanding of media engagement strategies that uphold the integrity and public perception of law enforcement agencies.

In Chapter Four: Law Enforcement—Baseline Media Strategy, we covered how to manage the day-to-day media, highlight accomplishments, and address the needs of a law enforcement agency. In addition, the baseline media strategy is used to define the image of a law enforcement agency, define the agency's barometers for success, and to troubleshoot.

Chapter Five: Law Enforcement—Critical Media Strategy (A) adds to the foundation of the baseline media strategy to cover critical events in a society.

As a reminder, the definition of critical media strategy is a plan of action for media communications when a critical event or period is upon a law enforcement agency. A critical event is anything that requires an enhanced method of communication from the law enforcement agency because of the sensitive or impactful trauma of the event. A critical event will encompass societal monumental events, signature occurrences, and other happenings that create a critical communication need.

Some examples of critical events are the following: a building collapse with victims, an OIS, a child murder, a hostage situation, an active shooter, a high-speed police pursuit resulting in a death, anything extremely life-threatening for individuals, or a mass casualty. A critical event could also be a case of police misconduct caught on video or a need for the law enforcement agency to distance itself from a controversial statement. A statement on behalf of a law enforcement agency denouncing the actions against George Floyd would be considered a critical event, as it requires a critical media strategy statement given the ramifications for all law enforcement agencies.

A critical period for law enforcement could be a pandemic, civil unrest for days as in 2020, or a serial rapist or a serial killer who remains uncaught for weeks, months, years, or decades. The critical event will last for a prolonged time. The critical nature of the period and critical event forces the law enforcement agency to implement its critical media strategy.

All large city law enforcement executives know it is only a matter of time before their agency is faced with a critical event, necessitating the need to implement a critical media strategy. In this book, this is referred to as population certainty. Anytime there is a population of half a million or more in a metropolitan area, law enforcement will certainly be responding to life and death matters regularly. However, a critical event could happen anywhere, including a town of five hundred citizens. All law enforcement agencies need to have critical media strategies and be cognizant of how to utilize the media as a conduit to the community.

National Critical Events

A police chief, sheriff, or superintendent can suddenly become a widely recognized figure due to their involvement in a critical incident. A notable instance of this was during the 1992 Los Angeles riots, a significant event in policing history for the preceding generation. These riots erupted following the highly publicized arrest of Rodney King, where officers were videotaped using excessive force, striking King multiple

LAW ENFORCEMENT—CRITICAL MEDIA STRATEGY (A)

times with their batons. This incident propelled Chief Daryl Gates of the Los Angeles Police Department (LAPD) into the national spotlight. Both King and Gates are now deceased (Krbechek and Bates 2017; Serrano 1991).

The nation recognized both men as synonymous with the riots. This is similar to the link between George Floyd and former Minneapolis police officer Derek Chauvin. Critical policing events have pitted the landscape of America for decades.

Another figure who was thrust into the national spotlight was Chief Charles Moose of the Montgomery County Police Department. His agency oversaw the DC Sniper serial murders in 2002. Moose authored the book *Three Weeks in October: The Manhunt for the Serial Sniper* following the critical event. He died in 2021.

READER ASSIGNMENT
Research the DC Serial Sniper and draft a three-to-four-page paper describing the critical event. The first page should be a summary of the critical event. The following pages should evaluate the critical media strategy during the prolonged event. Would you have done anything differently?

When George Floyd was killed by a police officer, the Minneapolis chief of police, Medaria Arradondo, was thrust into the national spotlight. Chief Arredondo retired from the Minneapolis Police Department in 2022 (Barr and Guilfoil 2022).

In 2020, every major city chief of police in the country was thrust into the spotlight for several days. In the aftermath of George Floyd's murder, civil unrest was a plight for urban areas across the county. In a similar fashion to a lot of major cities, the National Guard was called in to assist OPD in restoring order. In Omaha, the governor, mayor, and chief of police held live press conferences for four days in a row. Each one of the press conferences was a critical communication, over a prolonged time period, and an example of how OPD enacted our critical media strategy.

Know Your Audience

When delivering critical media communication, you need to know your audience to achieve the appropriate context, tone, and demeanor. Press conferences are a staple of critical communications, strategy, and insight. They are an opportunity for the law enforcement executive to speak directly to the audience, affected community, and stakeholders. The detriment to an agency's reputation from a poorly managed investigation or derelict police action can be salvaged by a professional press conference. Conversely, the attention given to heroic and professional police actions can be diverted if the law enforcement executive is not adept at public speaking on a large stage. As such, Chapter Six: Law Enforcement Critical Media Strategy (B)—Mastering Police Press Conferences is devoted to press conferences, giving readers a guide to follow with copious insight.

Consider that your audience could be the family of the victim, society, the suspect himself, and potentially the entire nation. Knowing the audience is necessary for any critical police communication. The following examples are of three high-profile incidents where Omaha press conferences encountered dissimilar audiences. Note that the audience and circumstance will govern your tone, demeanor, and message each time. The examples are intended to illustrate the importance of understanding and knowing your audience.

CASE STUDY: PEYTON BENSON

(See Chapter Two for the details on Peyton Benson's signature occurrence death)

Peyton Benson was a little girl—five years old—who was struck by gunfire as a bullet pierced her house and killed her while she was eating breakfast. The bullet was not intended for Peyton. It was gunfire for a rival gang. The elements of this critical event were grief at the senseless death of a child, despair about the gang and gun violence in the city, and apprehension as, on the day of the incident, the suspects were not in custody (Gorman 2014; KETV 2014). A press conference was held in the primetime evening hours, as Peyton's death was an important event for the Omaha community. As expected, the media carried the press conference live, and it lasted over half an hour.

The audience OPD was addressing at Peyton's press conference was the community, who were in grief and weary of the violence; Peyton's family; police investigators; and the assailants, who were unknown and still at large. A somber tone was appropriate when announcing Peyton's death, but it changed to a determined stance when addressing the assailants. OPD knew the gang members had not intended to kill Peyton and there were several who knew what had happened. The goal was to let the assailants know their best option was to turn themselves in. It was inevitable that they would be caught.

OPD surmised that the gang members involved in the gun violence, who had mistakenly taken Peyton's life, would likely be holed up somewhere watching the press conference together. True to form, a hotel was used as a gathering point and *hold-up* after the incident. Omaha police gang detectives had a lead on their whereabouts from some intelligence they had gathered.

The following is an extract of Chief Schmaderer's communication. It addresses the suspects who killed Peyton:

LAW ENFORCEMENT—CRITICAL MEDIA STRATEGY (A)

"I want to take a moment to talk to the assailants in this case who were involved in the gunfire that struck and killed Payton Benson. You know who you are, and law enforcement will find out who you are. It may not have been your bullet that struck this little girl. So, do the right thing and do yourself a favor in the process. Come down and talk to law enforcement and tell us what you know."—Chief Schmaderer

A tone of controlled and tempered anger was prudent when discussing the gang and gun violence in the city. This event took place in 2014, and Omaha has since decreased gang and gun violence by almost half. The relevant message for the community was that this level of violence would not be tolerated.

This case study is a useful example of how to deal with a critical situation, how to tailor a press conference to address the issue, and how to know your audience in relation to tempering the message appropriately.

Peyton's death ended up being a catalyst to unite the city and a turning point for reducing gang violence. The resolve of the police department and the community was at its highest point. The assailants did not turn themselves in but were caught by OPD and went to prison.

CASE STUDY: OMAHA 2020—CIVIL UNREST AND PROTESTS

(See Chapter Two for details on Omaha's 2020 Civil Unrest and Protests)

During the 2020 civil unrest in Omaha, OPD hosted press conferences as part of our critical media strategy. The press conferences included the governor, mayor, and chief of police. They were held in the late afternoon and carried live by Omaha's local press. On some days, there was also national press in attendance. It was crucial to know the audience we were speaking to, to tailor the correct tone and demeanor during this critical and prolonged event in Omaha. The unrest and large protests lasted five days.

> **READER REFLECTION**
> **The civil unrest and protests of 2020 took place during the COVID-19 pandemic. In Omaha, businesses were mostly closed because of the pandemic, and people were encouraged to remain in their homes to avoid human contact. In addition, a citywide curfew was in effect at 8:00 p.m. every night due to the civil unrest. Given the restraints placed on their lives due to the pandemic and the curfew, the audience of the press conferences was exasperated. At a typical press conference for a signature occurrence or societal monumental event, over 100,000**

viewers would be watching the press conference live in Omaha, but due to these unique circumstances, there were more in this case.

For class discussion, how many more audience members were created because of the pandemic and the curfew?

The audience for the press conferences about the 2020 civil unrest in Omaha was widespread and diverse; it included the community, protestors, watchdog groups, national civil rights organizations, and Omaha police officers forced into working twelve-hour shifts. In addition, surrounding law enforcement agencies who assisted OPD were also likely to be interested in what was communicated by the lead agency, as were politicians from local, state, and national venues. Lastly, the medical community could not be dismissed as audience members, as the civil unrest took place during the heart of the COVID-19 pandemic.

For the community, the press conference was used to relay information such as why the city was under a curfew, how many injuries and deaths were sustained in the unrest, and when and why the Nebraska National Guard had been called in. But most of all, it was an opportunity to demonstrate that we understood and supported the protest. OPD was disheartened and appalled by the death of George Floyd.

For the protestors, the message was that we would professionally ensure their rights to protest, even if the Omaha Police is where their anger was directed. The press conference was also used as a time to clearly lay out what would not be tolerated during the protests, such as breaking of property, violence, and curfew violations.

The message from the press conferences over the five days of civil unrest was carried and amplified by an editorial from Omaha's preeminent major newspaper, the *Omaha World Herald* (OWH).

An *editorial* is the opinion of the management of a major newspaper or broadcast news station on a major event. Editorials are important because they shape minds and opinions. During major events, they carry a tremendous amount of weight. It is rare for an editorial to be featured on the front page of a major newspaper. They are usually somewhere in the middle or at the end of a major section of the paper. On this occasion, the message was of utmost importance, the OWH gave it front-page placement (Hoffenberg 2022).

This case study is a prime example of how law enforcement executives can set the tone for a community during societal monumental events, signature occurrences, and critical events. Note Chief Schmaderer's words for the community in the editorial (*Omaha World Herald* 2020).

The press conference also presented a prime opportunity for *making a point*. Note, however, that it is important that the point is valid, relevant, and does not come across as someone going on their *soapbox*. The conditions faced by the officers needed to be

LAW ENFORCEMENT—CRITICAL MEDIA STRATEGY (A)

Courtesy of the Omaha World Herald

addressed to the audience. Omaha police officers and our assisting agencies were working twelve hours a day, seven days in a row. Officers were subjected to violence with rocks, debris, and eggs thrown at them. Urine was sprayed at officers via squirt guns, and the insults levied were nonstop and demoralizing.

Through it all, OPD maintained its professionalism, which deserves heavy respect. As a reminder, Omaha police were not the genesis of the unrest; it stemmed from the Minneapolis police murder of George Floyd. Omaha officers and the surrounding law enforcement assisting Omaha Police were tired and completely disrespected, so the press conference was an opportunity to give them the support of the chief of police.

For four days straight, live press conferences were held, and the media asked a ton of questions. Some of the questions asked were about the health and condition of the Omaha police horses. The horses are used in large crowd-control events and so are police chemical munition deployments, so the horses have some exposure. The health and the condition of the protestors was also a common question. How much overtime the unrest was costing the city was also a recurring question. Amid all the many questions asked, there was *not one question* from the Omaha media about how the officers were doing.

On the fourth day of press conferences, a reporter threw out the overtime question again. A point needed to be made in defense of the officers since concern for their well-being had become noticeably absent. The officers were the ones being subjected to twelve-hour days, debris, rocks, and urine, in the scorching summer of Omaha. The media corps needed a reminder. As conduits for the Omaha metropolitan community, there were many citizens who wanted to know how the officers were holding up. The media was taken to task for not asking how the officers were doing, to make a point.

Omaha Police Chief Todd Schmaderer had some tough words for the media covering the protests and riots in his city. When asked about the impact on his overtime budget, he said the following (Law Officer 2020):

"Look, I have stood up here for four press conferences, and I have explained how the officers have worked twelve hours a day. And I have explained how this is terribly hard on them. But I have never had one question yet . . . not one question asking me how the officers are doing," Chief Schmaderer said.

The chief went on to say the officers were tired but determined to protect the city and the chief expected more out of the Omaha press corps. He had expected at least one question of concern for the officers. After he had "made his point," he chose to leave the press conference.

When facing the press, those speaking can see the reporters' body language and faces, and you can gain great insight from that. When chastised for not asking about the well-being of the officers, most of the reporters put their heads down in shame, one intimated it was going to be his next question, and another mumbled that they were sorry.

That was an unexpected, defining moment for Omaha officers. It was a unifying statement where they knew Omaha police command had their backs. Omaha police senior commanders were present from the chief rank on down, every night of the protests, and the officers could sense the support. The public denouncement of the Omaha press corps, who on this occasion had been insensitive and misguided, brought on an uplifting and proud feeling for the officers.

CASE STUDY: ZACHARY BEARHEELS

(See Chapter Two for details on the 2017 Zachary Bearheels critical event)

Zachary Bearheels suffered from mental illness and died in an encounter with OPD in 2017. In the press conference that followed, the audience was the community, Bearheels's family, the Native American community, national watchdog groups, law enforcement, and the mental health community.

Omaha police senior command was extremely critical of the use of force, and it resulted in officer terminations. Nonetheless, it was apparent to us that we had failed in assisting a person in a mental health crisis.

When an agency fails, makes a mistake, or has handled a matter per policy, it is important to come out and explain your analysis. Many times, prior to Bearheels's death, the public statements were about how officers were justified, saved lives, had no other choice, or had acted valiantly, in the aftermath of officer-involved incidents. This time, the police encounter could have been managed significantly better and was not representative of the professionalism of Omaha police. It was imperative to *own* the mistake (*Omaha World Herald* 2017).

The press conference was used to *own* or accept responsibility for our mishandling and to set a path for community reunification. We laid out the steps OPD would take to ensure we improved our handling of those in mental crisis to the community. In addition, a call was made for help from the mental health community in partnering with OPD to improve the overall conditions of mental health treatment in Omaha. The OPD was bearing too much responsibility for those in mental crisis; the mental health community needed to step up.

The public responds well to ownership and transparency of wrongdoing. What other choice is there? Yet it is amazing to see justifications and excuses espoused repeatedly. Never underestimate the intelligence of the community. If you are seeing the mistake, others are too.

"IN MAN'S DEATH, WE FAILED"

Photo courtesy of the *Omaha World Herald*, June 10, 2017
https://omaha.com/eedition/sunrise/articles/
article 363eef23-3b34-5586-864db4f5a70483ac.html

The Omaha community found out about the unjustified death of Mr. Bearheels via OPD. We were not responding to a secret video from the public. Omaha police broke the story on our own accord and owned up to our failures involving the Bearheels incident.

Actions After the Press Conference

When an agency owns up to a failure, it is imperative to have follow-up measures to ensure it does not happen again. In response to Mr. Bearheels's death, Omaha Police implemented new training for how to handle and communicate with those in a mental crisis; we changed policy and made it mandatory for a supervisor to be on the scene when four or more officers are present; and lastly, we took measures to increase the number of veteran officers on the force by starting a lateral transfer program. This set of changes follows our understanding that, as a rule, at least three changes are needed to adequately make progress on a persistent problem.

One of the officers involved was arrested for assault on Mr. Bearheels, and the media covered the trial intently. The jury acquitted the officer. The arrested officer was fired, and three other officers were terminated. All four officers appealed to an arbitrator to seek reinstatement of employment. All terminated officers have this right per their agency's collective bargaining agreement.

The arbitrator upheld the termination of the arrested, tried, and then-acquitted officer. The arbitrator reinstated the other three officers, with one incurring heavy discipline. Robust media coverage followed the arbitrator's decision to uphold one termination but allow the other three officers to return to OPD.

As a side note, the three officers who returned to OPD have successfully reintegrated and are productive members of the force.

Not everything can be in a chief's control. Police arbitrations are complex. The chief of police does not have the final word on an officer's employment. The officer has a right to appeal to a neutral third-party arbitrator, and that arbitrator's decision is then final. Oftentimes, the chief of police will have higher standards than the arbitrator and an officer will be reinstated. A police arbitration study found that arbitrators overturned or reduced chief of police discipline in 52 percent of the cases nationwide.

In cases where an officer is terminated, the arbitration system has overturned the termination 46 percent of the time and has reinstated the officer. The arbitrator's standards are now considered past practice to follow within the police agency. This dynamic makes it problematic for police chiefs to set a culture in line with what the community wants and deserves (Vanderbilt Law School 2021).

Law Enforcement Critical Media Strategy

The three case studies provided examples of how a critical media strategy can work and what a law enforcement agency can do in response to a critical event. It is important that a law enforcement agency has a baseline media strategy and a critical media strategy to escalate to when a societal monumental event, significant occurrence, or a critical event occurs. This next section provides further information about critical media strategies.

The critical media strategy has two distinct phases: the evaluation phase and the transition phase.

Law Enforcement Critical Media Strategy

1) Evaluation Phase
   - **Evaluate the event or occurrence**
   - **Determine the mode of media communication**
2) Transition Phase
   - **Evaluate whether it is appropriate to transition back to the baseline media strategy**

1) Evaluation Phase

The evaluation phase of the law enforcement critical media strategy is, as the name suggests, where evaluations and decisions are made. The critical media strategy takes into consideration that all critical events will vary, and the method of media communication must be adapted to match the event's needs. In the evaluation phase, a determination is made on whether the law enforcement agency is facing a critical event. If it is determined that a critical event is indeed upon the law enforcement agency, the next step is to determine the mode of media communication.

The determination is dependent on the law enforcement agency. Not all agencies will view the threshold for a critical incident the same. Some agencies will determine whether a critical incident is upon them and enact their critical media strategy, while another agency may determine it is not a critical event and the agency's baseline media strategy will suffice in managing the media component.

READER ASSIGNMENT
Place yourself in the command structure of a law enforcement agency. Determine if the following examples are worthy of elevating to a critical media strategy or if a baseline media strategy will suffice. There are no right or wrong answers; it is your justification that is relevant. Each example should have one to two paragraphs describing why it is or is not a critical event.

1. A homicide has occurred in the overnight shift of the city.
2. A viral video has surfaced that shows the law enforcement agency in a bad light.
3. An active shooter has killed three people and has been shot by law enforcement.
4. A traffic accident occurs with no Injuries, but there are four cars involved.
5. A hostage situation has occurred.

Determine the mode of media communication (evaluation phase)

Once it has been determined the event is critical in nature, the agency then escalates into the critical media strategy phase. The evaluation is used to determine the mode of media communication. Some common options are a press conference (on-scene or at a set location), a written press release, an on-scene interview, or a regular one-on-one interview with a news outlet. Some agencies elect to use pre-recorded videos for OISs or other critical events.

LAW ENFORCEMENT—CRITICAL MEDIA STRATEGY (A)

The mode of media communication chosen is based on the law enforcement agency's preference. What is important to the critical media strategy is the evaluation and analysis conducted by the agency. As an example, in Omaha's 2020 civil unrest, it was determined that four live press conferences—one a day for four days—was the appropriate way to communicate with the community about the unrest in the city. In the case of Peyton Benson's death, a live press conference was appropriate for the evening of the critical event. In an example later in this chapter, OPD released a statement distancing the agency from a controversial Omaha Police Officers Association (OPD officers' union) position.

2) Transition Phase

In the transition phase, the law enforcement agency needs to evaluate the ongoing media needs of the critical incident. The evaluation needs to determine when the agency should return to its day-to-day baseline media strategy. The determination will depend on the preference of the agency and the dynamics of the critical event.

During the 2020 Omaha civil unrest, OPD did not return to its normal baseline media strategy until after the curfew was lifted in the city. After Peyton Benson's death, OPD returned to its baseline media strategy the next day, following the live press conference. In the case of serial killer Anthony Garcia (see Chapter Two for details), OPD remained in its critical media strategy for months after the second set of murders, until Garcia' arrest. However, note that OPD was in their critical media strategy only for communication about the serial killer case. For all other media, our baseline media communication was used during this time.

In summation, the benefit of the critical media strategy is the constant evaluation and its flexible nature. Critical events can take on a different status depending on the agency in charge. A murder in a small town may cause the agency to stay in its critical media strategy until it is solved. In Omaha, the murder may not even rise to the level of transitioning out of our baseline media strategy. In addition, critical events are never the same. Each one has unique qualities where evaluation and determination can take place on the strategy to use for communicating with the media. The requirements of flexibility and constant evaluation during a critical event are the hallmarks of a successful critical media strategy.

Special Considerations

Large population bases will come with many special considerations involving critical event communications. The integrity and image of a police agency hang in the balance during these special considerations.

Let's cover the following special considerations in terms of critical media strategies: lawsuits, animal shootings by police, how to distance your agency from controversy, how to avoid traps, preventing overuse of the emotional tone, use of the media to make a social or community statement, news embargo, background versus "off the record," and news exclusives.

Lawsuits

The OPD has 1,200 employees, the NYPD has 55,000, the Kansas City Police 2,000, and New Orleans Police 1,400. All law enforcement agencies will be faced with lawsuits; some will come from the outside, and some will come from your employees. It is a fact.

The agency will not be able to respond to specifics early on when the lawsuit hits the media. The media has a computer program that will alert them to lawsuits of interest, and anytime the city, mayor, or chief's name is used in print across the world. The early advantage of a lawsuit goes to who files it, as anything can be alleged in a lawsuit. Lawsuits can be used for devious purposes as well because it is a legal way to slander someone. In short, in a lawsuit, you can say rumors, salacious notions, and more—without having to prove it (Dershowitz 2019).

A police agency's first response to a lawsuit should be a statement of conviction and the plan to vigorously defend itself, and there should be no further comment to respect the court process. For instance, if the American Civil Liberties Union (ACLU) sues your department for excessive force, your PIO can respond, "The agency takes all cases of excessive force seriously and in this instance plans to defend ourselves in court. Out of respect for the court process, the city has no further comment at this time."

Or they could say that in this incident the department has issued disciplinary action. In short, give a clear global statement that the department takes police use of force seriously, state the position of the agency in the individual case at hand, and then say that, out of respect for the court process, nothing further can be said at this time.

Never defend the details of the allegation, just the macro assertion. It is the same with internal lawsuits where an employee may sue the department for being terminated. The agency's response is "We take personnel matters seriously and respect the employees right to sue, but we respectfully disagree and will strongly defend ourselves in court." Never get baited into addressing details of the incident. Also, keep in mind every situation is different, so your response will be based on the evidence from the internal investigation. Never blindly defend an officer. Ensure the matter is investigated and the facts are known.

LAW ENFORCEMENT—CRITICAL MEDIA STRATEGY (A)

Animal Shootings by Police

While always not foreseen, police agencies will sometimes be forced to kill dangerous animals. It is going to happen. If a dangerous animal is placing humans in peril of severe injury or death, law enforcement must act. The animal could be a vicious dog or a mountain lion. It is certain that animal activists and the media will take exception and express interest in the incident. Sometimes bad humans are hard to love; animals, on the other hand, are easy to love, creating an instant human interest story evoking many emotions.

OPD has had to shoot vicious dogs and a mountain lion or three. Every now and then, one of the shootings will wake up animal rights groups. If the animal is attacking someone, the message is clear from the agency; law enforcement stepped in to protect themselves or others. That is easy to understand. When the animal is not actively hurting someone, the situation takes on a whole new depth.

In one case, there was a mountain lion sitting in a populated area of Omaha on the doorstep of a nonprofit organization. The animal was not posing an immediate danger to patrons, as no people were present. The question at hand was, how would the mountain lion react if a patron decided to exit or tried to enter the building?

Would the mountain lion come back to the business if allowed to be left alone? Why is the mountain lion out of its habitat? Is the animal injured or sick? The mere nature of an alpha animal that is capable of killing a human in a populated entrance to a nonprofit is concerning for public safety.

In the real-life example, the mountain lion was shot by the police from a distance. Aggressive social media protests flooded in. "Why did you have to shoot the mountain lion? You should have used a tranquilizer gun." The vitriolic nature of the comments was shocking, and the energy level of conviction behind the social media comments was impressive.

In this example, the officers conversed with the Humane Society for Animals as well as the local zoo and were given advice to shoot the animal. The animal's presence in a populated area was too unusual to forecast its next move, according to the experts. Therefore, OPD had to make the safest decision for the general population based on guidance from animal experts.

OPD's critical media strategy was to note that the appropriate animal authorities were contacted and that officers carried out their professional advice. In the press release, OPD provided an explanation of the unusual and unpredictable actions of the mountain lion, in combination with the notion that the mountain lion may have decided to return. OPD also noted that the unusual location of the mountain lion upped the unpredictable nature of the situation.

The press release noted that our policy was to follow the experts' (zoo and humane society officials) advice. A general disclaimer was also put out, noting that this is not an enjoyable part of our duties and that we respect animals fully. Lastly, OPD had to dispel the notion that we carry tranquilizer guns. Tranquilizer guns are not always effective and accurate to shoot. In addition, the tranquilizer takes a few minutes to take effect, and the animal can become aggressive and dangerous during the time lag. In this instance, the experts had advised against the use of tranquilizer guns.

Communication with the press was critical in this example. What appeared to be something the public would understand, turned out not to be. The public wanted to know why we had shot the mountain lion and were angry at OPD. The press statements we made were important to understanding the backdrop of the situation and preserving OPD's reputation.

Kobus

In another example, one of the OPD's service dogs was shot and killed in the line of duty. A suspect barricaded himself in a house with a gun, and a standoff was ensured. The suspect shot at law enforcement at the scene, so the situation was dangerous. While the suspect was barricaded inside the house, a single shot was heard. As a result, a police robot was sent in equipped with a video camera. The video from the robot could see the suspect not moving for a prolonged period of time. Was the suspect injured or dead? It was unsafe to send in a human officer to check, so Omaha Police sent in service K-9 Kobus. The suspect woke and shot Kobus, a nine-year-old Belgian Malinois, who died from the gunshot.

The outpouring of support was indicative of Omaha being an animal-loving city.

Questions and scrutiny also surrounded the incident: Why was Kobus sent in? Why wasn't Kobus wearing a ballistic vest for dogs? K-9 Kobus's death in the line of duty brought out OPD's critical media strategy.

OPD wanted to honor Kobus for the ultimate sacrifice, yet not go so far that the public felt uneasy because it is an animal and not a human. A funeral ceremony was held for Kobus, with a focus on Kobus's handler, an Omaha police officer, and how much Kobus meant to the family of the officer. Kobus lived with the officer's family.

Answers were also provided for the questions from the public. It was announced that Kobus would not wear a ballistic vest. Indeed, Kobus and the other Omaha police dogs get agitated wearing the vests. The OPD received donated money for K-9 ballistic vests, which we had to discreetly ask permission to use in another way to benefit the Omaha Police K-9 unit. The community also pitched in to purchase a statue of Kobus, which sits in front of the Omaha Police K-9 offices.

LAW ENFORCEMENT—CRITICAL MEDIA STRATEGY (A)

Photo courtesy of DotKom Studios: Kobus was placed on the Officer Down memorial page.

How to Distance Your Agency from Controversy

There will be times when a police agency needs to distance itself from controversy. On March 13, 2020, a critical incident occurred that gained a lot of attention. Breonna Taylor, a twenty-six-year-old Black woman, was fatally shot in her Louisville, Kentucky apartment when at least seven police officers forced entry into the apartment as part of an investigation into drug-dealing operations (CNN 2022b). The officers were serving a *no-knock* search warrant. A no-knock search warrant is where the officers force their way through the door without giving verbal notice to the occupants inside. It is designed to use the element of surprise for officer safety and so narcotics cannot be flushed down the toilet or destroyed.

The incident received national attention from the media and forced changes in how law enforcement serves search warrants.

When policing controversy hits other cities, it can extrapolate to other law enforcement agencies. In the case at hand, OPD had to do damage control by outlining our search warrant practice and emphasizing that no-knock warrants are rare, not the preferred path, but sometimes a necessity where our robust training takes over.

Another example of OPD distancing itself from controversy was in 2014. The Omaha Police Officers Association (OPOA), the Omaha police officer union, released a toddler in video and drew national fire in response. A diapered child, who was African American, was shown on video saying, "Shut up, bitch" and other choice statements while the adults in the video laughed. The OPOA posted it on their social media and commented on the "cycle of violence and thuggery" that the community faces.

The video and the OPOA's portrayal caused a divide in our community. As the head of the law enforcement agency, it is critical to denounce division. The statement used to denounce division was, "I strongly disagree with any postings that may cause a divide in our community or an obstacle to police-community relations," and it also reinforced that the Union does not speak for the OPD. It is imperative to show unity with the community and repair divisions.

Photo courtesy of the Omaha Police Officers Association

Avoid traps

The media will forever attempt to get a police agency to pit against another agency. Never take the bait. Unless it causes division in your agency or the police misconduct is of a severe nature in another city, refrains from commenting. Because of the severity of the incidents, Omaha Police did denounce George Floyd's and Tyre Nichols's deaths at the hands of the Detroit Police Department.

There have been five times as many controversial police shootings or suspects dying in police custody, but those incidents did not impact Omaha. Weighing in on other agencies invites them to do the same and is not a professional way to lead. Avoid falling for the media's trap on commenting. Take care of your house. If you make a comment about your neighbor's house, they will throw rocks at yours.

Publicly Kneeling

Another trap many police chiefs fell prey to was publicly kneeling in the wrong setting during the 2020 protests. There is nothing wrong with kneeling for the cause at hand;

however, the kneeling will be on the front page of the paper, and your officers will see the photo. Make sure if you elect to kneel, the parties you are kneeling with are not the ones throwing objects or spraying urine on your officers. That is a tough image for the officers to get over.

Show support for the cause when it is righteous, and make sure the public knows of your gesture of support. In Omaha, during the 2020 civil unrest, the chief noted at a press conference that it was heart-wrenching and difficult for my officers, as we also agree police brutality must end. The message showed support, understanding, and empathy for the cause without kneeling via a demand from a potentially hostile crowd toward the officers.

Overly Emotional Tone

Be wary of your tone. There are differing thoughts on overly emotional communications by elected officials, but for law enforcement executives, who are responsible for investigating the issue and controlling its future occurrence, being *overly emotional* gets in the way. Overly emotional reactions can take the form of crying, lashing out at the media in anger, or being overcome with feelings to the extent that you must leave the situation.

Crying or heavy tears do legitimately happen. Former President Barack Obama welled up over yet another mass shooting in America. During one of Peyton Benson's public events, after her somber death, many elected officials cried when it was their time to talk. This display shows the public how much emotion they have for the subject and that they care. But for a police chief, it is different. As chief, your job is to catch the perpetrators and let your actions speak. Hurt and sadness can be shown, but crying is not what the public wants to see from the person leading the investigation. If you want to cry behind the scenes, that is all right.

There have been many law enforcement executives over the years who lost their cool with the media and yelled or went on a tirade. It is a bad look. It looks unprofessional. One can make their point without yelling and looking out of control.

Use the Media to Make a Social or Community Statement

The press conference is a prime pulpit to deliver social and community statements, especially during live broadcasts, because they are not edited. For live press conferences, issue the overriding commentary and then get into a timeline of events, before closing with final thoughts that tie into the opening commentary.

During the Peyton Benson press conference, the message was, "This level of violence will not be tolerated in our society." For the Zachary Bearheels press conference, it was, "The police cannot be the sole entity responsible for addressing mental illness in society."

During the 2020 civil unrest period in Omaha, one of the press conferences was used to announce the citywide curfew time of 8:00 p.m. A side reason behind the 8:00 p.m. curfew was that it gave enough time for the Malcolm X Foundation to hold their rally. The Malcolm X Foundation was a signature voice in Omaha that needed to be heard. During the days of the protests, it seemed the protestors were mostly young and white. This was a time to hear from influential African Americans in Omaha, so the curfew time needed to be late enough to accommodate the Malcolm X Foundation rally. Over a thousand attended, and not one single problem occurred because of the power and effectiveness of the Malcolm X Foundation of Omaha.

News Embargo

Embargoed information in journalism is an agreement by a source that the information or news provided cannot be published until a certain date or after certain conditions have been met (PRLab, n.d.).

The following are some examples of embargoed material:

- statistics
- an announcement
- details of a critical event
- indictment information
- press release about the termination of a police officer

For example, if a major arrest is going to be made, the information can be given to a media outlet beforehand so they can prepare their stories in advance. In return, the promise is in place as to when the story can be released. A police agency is helping the media because it takes time to prepare complete stories. Law enforcement agencies that view the media as a "peer" should consider embargoed information to foster good partnership with the media.

Major city newspapers are most suited for an embargo arrangement because the paper can provide the most depth to a story. The embargo gives the journalist adequate time to be accurate and thorough. Embargoes also prevent leaks, because if the press does not have the story, they will try to appeal to sources to get it.

Journalists are highly unlikely to burn a chief or mayor on an embargo agreement. For starters, it benefits the media organization. Second, it would ruin all future working arrangements as peers. Third, embargoes are industry standards, and by not honoring that, a journalist would run afoul of their own standards.

Exclusives

Exclusives are when a law enforcement agency gives a story to only one media entity (Gallo 2023). It could be a major newspaper or one of the television stations. This is a widespread practice to be used strategically. For instance, if a television station has given your agency good coverage, the PIO could reward them with an exclusive.

Exclusives provide for optimal coverage of an incident, and, if given to the major newspaper, the television stations will follow with the story. OPD has used exclusives to ensure that an important subject is covered in depth. Every year, OPD does an "exclusive" end-of-the-year homicide recap with a major newspaper.

OPD gave an exclusive to the *Omaha World Herald* in the aftermath of the 2020 civil unrest. The exclusive was given to the city's major paper so it could present a deep dive into the catalysts and circumstances that ignited the civil unrest in Omaha. Omaha police have used exclusives to get a complex matter out to the public and to reward a news station for thorough coverage of policing events.

Off the Record versus Background

"Off the record" means that, theoretically, the information the source shares with the reporter cannot be used in any way. When information is given to a reporter on "background," it means a reporter can use the information but cannot name or quote the source directly. Reporters prefer to have their source on background versus off the record. Information that is off the record is a place to start for the reporter, but then they will need to verify it somewhere else to use that information (Keller 2011).

Be wary, however. *Off the record* only truly means off the record if the reporter agrees to it. There are situations where there is no mutual understanding, and the reporter elects to use the source's name. For example, the reporter may have received a text from their source where they say the information "off the record" and then proceeded to give the information before the reporter could text back and agree to the "off the record" stipulation. Always, get an agreement to be "off the record' or "on background" with the reporter, preferably in writing.

On background is a good way to correct errors the reporter may have in their story. It is also a way to get the reporter to look down a certain path. Going on background with a reporter should only be done when there is an established relationship and history with the reporter. There must be some trust.

OPD has gone on background with a few trusted reporters. The story they were running was so off base, it would have been a waste of their time to spend months figuring it out, so using this approach helped the reporter. On another occasion, it was beneficial to the department to be "on background" because it provided context to a story someone was trying to make up to the reporter.

"Off the record" is clean if it is in writing. Text messages are acceptable, and a verbal agreement is good too, but be sure the reporter is trustworthy. "On background" can be a way to have a peer relationship with a reporter. If the reporter is going to find out about something anyway, sometimes, in a collegial working atmosphere, it is best to help them get there.

Issuing Statements on Critical Events

Critical events occur across the country, and sometimes they may require a statement to be issued on behalf of the law enforcement agency or executive. As a rule of thumb, ensure the event is large enough to weigh in, and do not make a habit of critiquing other police departments.

The homicide of George Floyd and the highly publicized death of Memphis resident Tyre Nichols are two national policing events that required a statement (see Chapter Two for the actual press releases). Both incidents were so egregious that they mandated a public statement from agency executives across the country. Each case had the potential to negatively impact local police–community relations.

The key to issuing a statement on a large critical event is the understanding of a few basic concepts:

1) <u>Avoid redundancy</u>: Others will be issuing statements as well, so try to avoid redundancy. The mayor, governor, district attorney, other politicians, FBI, and US attorney may also be weighing in, if the matter has widespread reach.
2) <u>Be concise</u>: The statement must stand out and be concise, as typically the media will show the comment next to the law enforcement executive's photo.
3) <u>Avoid background information</u>: Avoid giving background information in the statement; the media story will cover that aspect in their reporting.

As an example, in Omaha, the United States Attorney for Nebraska issued indictments in 2023 for the Omaha city council vice president, two former OPD police officers, and a fourth person for a multitude of federal crimes. The story was obviously *huge* in the Omaha media market. The US Attorney, FBI, the Omaha mayor, and the Omaha city council president all issued statements. My statement as Omaha police chief took into consideration the basic concepts of issuing a statement.

LAW ENFORCEMENT—CRITICAL MEDIA STRATEGY (A)

Statements from Mayor Stothert, City Council President Festersen, and Chief Schmaderer:

Omaha Mayor Jean Stothert: "Councilman Palermo should immediately resign from the Omaha City Council. He has violated the trust of the citizens he was elected to represent and damaged public confidence in the City Council."

City Council President Pete Festersen: "This is a matter of great concern . . . I can assure citizens that the City Council will continue to serve them . . . as Councilmember Palermo avails himself of due process . . ."

Omaha Police Chief Todd Schmaderer: "I am appalled, but unfortunately not shocked at the content of the federal indictments. As the federal investigation continues, there is a possibility more arrests will be made."

All suspects are considered innocent until proven guilty in a court of law

Conclusion

Chapter Five: Critical Media Strategies (A), delved into the vital concept of critical communications for law enforcement. Across the nation, critical events have consistently posed significant challenges to policing. Large population bases will inevitably experience critical events at regular intervals. It is of utmost importance, therefore, for every law enforcement agency to have a well-defined critical media strategy in place.

Understanding your audience is a vital consideration that sets the tone and essence of critical communication. The law enforcement critical media strategy encompasses two phases: the evaluation phase and the transition phase.

Law Enforcement Critical Media Strategy

1) Evaluation Phase
   - **Evaluate the event or occurrence**
   - **Determine the mode of media communication**
2) Transition Phase
   - **Evaluate whether it is appropriate to transition back to the baseline media strategy**

A defining characteristic of the critical media strategy lies in its flexibility and the evaluation phase, recognizing that each critical event is unique and demands a tailored approach.

Special considerations come into play when crafting a critical media strategy, such as dealing with lawsuits, incidents of animal shootings by police, methods to distance an agency from controversy, avoiding media traps, addressing an overly emotional tone, and utilizing the media to make impactful social or community statements. Additionally, news embargoes and exclusives are valuable components of any effective critical media strategy. Furthermore, it is essential for law enforcement professionals to comprehend the distinctions between "off the record" and "on background" communications.

Questions for Discussion and Review

Attempt to answer the following questions before looking up the answers at the back of the book.

1. True or False: Law enforcement controversy and large occurrences have only recently become national news.
2. True or False: The audience will govern your tone, demeanor, and message in critical communications. How important is it to consider the audience when crafting a message?
3. Describe the two phases of the critical media strategy, the evaluation phase and the transition phase. Why is it crucial to have a well-defined strategy in place to address critical events?
4. True or False: Law enforcement agencies should not admit fault for legal reasons. Discuss the implications of admitting fault and the importance of transparency in critical communications.
5. Describe a time when a press conference can be used to make a social or community statement. How can law enforcement executives effectively utilize press conferences to convey important messages to the public?
6. Describe what is meant by "distancing your agency from controversy." Why is it important for law enforcement agencies to proactively address and mitigate controversies that may arise?
7. True or False: Law enforcement agencies should regularly comment with the local media on other cities' policing events. Discuss the potential risks and benefits of commenting on other agencies' actions.
8. Explain what a news embargo is and how it can be beneficial for both law enforcement agencies and the media.

LAW ENFORCEMENT—CRITICAL MEDIA STRATEGY (A)

9. Explain what a news exclusive is and how law enforcement agencies strategically use it.
10. Describe what "off the record" means and discuss the importance of establishing clear agreements with reporters when providing information.
11. Describe what "on background" means and discuss situations where law enforcement executives may choose to provide information on background.
12. True or False: The reporter must agree that the communication is "off the record." Why is mutual understanding and agreement crucial when engaging in off-the-record communications?

CHAPTER SIX

Law Enforcement Critical Media Strategy (B)—Mastering Policing Press Conferences

In this chapter, we are continuing to look at the importance of a critical media strategy for law enforcement and look specifically at mastering the policing press conference (PPC). Three primary components will be covered: on-scene pressers, PPC preplanning, and the PPC itself.

By the end of this chapter, you will have grasped the significance of press conferences in a critical media strategy, comprehending their role in influencing public perception and disseminating essential information. You will know how to distinguish between on-scene pressers and PPCs as well as understand their respective contexts, purposes, and nuances. You will also have familiarized yourself with the fundamental guidelines governing on-scene pressers, enabling you to conduct them effectively and professionally.

To further your practical knowledge, you will be taught how to demonstrate proficiency in conducting on-scene pressers by employing the provided comprehensive guide, how to follow the pre planning guide for PPCs, and how to ensure a well-organized approach to handling media interactions in critically sensitive situations. You will identify suitable venues for hosting PPCs as well as acquaint yourself with the rules and best practices governing PPCs to ensure ethical and effective communication with the media. You will engage in an interactive pick-the-headline game exercise, honing your ability to craft influential headlines that capture the essence of the information being conveyed.

This chapter will help you gain a comprehensive understanding of the key elements that constitute a successful PPC, including the TTRUST acronym, which serves as a guiding framework. You will implement the PPC formula, enabling you to effectively structure and deliver your message during such events, and learn and appreciate the five essential authentications necessary to build trust and credibility when communicating crucial information to the public. Finally, you will enhance your level of preparation and confidence by engaging in practice sessions involving simulated scenarios, allowing you to refine your skills in a safe and controlled environment.

By accomplishing these objectives, you will be well equipped to conduct successful PPCs that effectively serve your critical media strategy and ensure influential, transparent, and trustworthy communication with the public.

Press Conferences

A press conference is an organized event where individuals, organizations, or governments invite members of the media to disseminate information, make announcements, or respond to journalists' questions in a formal setting.

These conferences serve as a platform for direct communication with the press—and, by extension, the public—allowing the hosting party to control the message, provide clarifications, and engage in real time with the media's inquiries. They enable a structured interaction between the speakers and journalists, ensuring that the intended message reaches a wide audience through various media outlets. Therefore, they require a high level of coordination and mastery of the content (Public Disclosure Commission, n.d.).

In this book, we will be using the term *policing press conference* (PPC) rather than just a standard *press conference*. This is because a law enforcement press conference has unique characteristics separate from a standard one. Standard press conferences are used across a wide variety of genres, such as corporation announcements or political events. A PPC has the characteristics of transparency, public safety, and community trust at its forefront, making it a unique production. As a result, it is infused with specialized insight. A regular press conference does not have the pertinent need for specialized insight (Community Tool Box, n.d.).

Regular press conferences and PPCs are both *productions*. They require preplanning, set preparation, and practice. A production also has an audience. For the law enforcement executive, the audience is the community, which is the agency's primary stakeholder. However, as seen in Chapter Five: Law Enforcement—Critical Media Strategy (A), there are many audiences, and knowing which audience the agency is speaking to is important.

A law enforcement agency should consider using a PPC for critical events, signature occurrences, or societal monumental events. Its purpose is to relay obligatory, exigent, and transparent information to the public. It also provides an opportunity to relay the cultural awareness and moral culture of the agency, since police–community relations are at the forefront of an agency's media strategy.

The PPC warrants its own specialized chapter because it is a major component of a law enforcement agency's critical media strategy.

LAW ENFORCEMENT CRITICAL MEDIA STRATEGY (B)

A law enforcement agency's performance during a PPC can leave the public feeling confident in the agency and leader. Conversely, a poorly conducted PPC can do severe damage to the image of the agency and its leader, damaging police–community relations. This chapter will cover three key factors in depth:

1) On-scene pressers
2) PPC preplanning
3) The PPC itself

While many speech and press conference guides, checklists, formulas, and reference materials have already been published, this book is the first to infuse strategic insight into the press conference production, and that is why I refer to it as a PPC. A PPC can be conducted by any law enforcement agency, and it is specifically tailored to law enforcement.

Nonetheless, there is bound to be some overlap or similarities with regular press conference guides, checklists, and formulas. What is unique to press conferences conducted by law enforcement is the content, gravity, focus on police–community relations, and the essential need for transparency (within reason). The formulas and guidelines in this textbook are based on over a decade of experience as chief of police. During my career, I have conducted nearly one hundred press conferences and hundreds of public speaking engagements.

Of the nearly one hundred press conferences, around twenty-five have been on live television, where the normal show broadcasting was suspended for the presser. The rest were either held on Facebook Live through the media or filmed for later media use.

I am a firm believer that the law enforcement PPC is critical in establishing and maintaining public trust in a community. In appropriate situations, the law enforcement executive must embrace the moment and show leadership through the PPC. Accompanying the formulas and guidelines in this chapter is insight based on real-world experiences.

1) On-scene Pressers

The on-scene presser is unique to law enforcement. When tech companies, politicians, or public schools give press conferences, it is rarely at the scene of a tragedy. Some critical incidents, however, are so central to their communities that an on-scene presser must take place.

Press conferences take a considerable amount of time to set up. The difference between an on-scene presser and a PPC is the preparation time for the production and location of the presser. Timing is essential to highlight transparency and to alert the public of critical events. The law enforcement agency can always follow up the next day or days later with a PPC to impart further details and instill a sense of community.

Law enforcement executives should know that significant delays in relaying information to the public will cause community mistrust. Time and transparency go together. It is therefore prudent to alert the public at the scene of a critical event and inform them more information will be forthcoming after a thorough investigation is completed.

On-scene pressers should be held at the scene of critical events. The presser itself will offer limited details, but it is critical for police–community relations to share a generic account of what took place. This is also a moral and just thing to do, given the severity of critical events.

When a critical event occurs, the public expects their law enforcement agency to be on top of it. When Officer Kerrie Orozco was killed in the line of duty, an on-scene presser was held at the hospital. Then, a PPC followed at OPD headquarters the next day. At other times, a detailed press release can follow the on-scene press conference.

Law enforcement agencies can follow either procedure. It all depends on the critical event at hand. The incidents below provide some examples of who should do the on-scene presser and when. It is impossible to forecast every possible critical event, which is why flexibility and evaluation are vital components of the law enforcement critical media strategy.

Officer Casualties

When an officer is killed, shot, or seriously injured in the line of duty, OPD will hold an on-scene presser and follow up with a detailed press release or comprehensive PPC the next day. The on-scene presser is presented by the chief, as it is a time when the law enforcement executive should be front and center for the community and the agency's employees.

Active Shooters

In an active-shooter or active-killer scenario, an on-scene presser is needed to alert the public and to report what has taken place. The critical incident warrants the law enforcement executive to be at the scene and give the on-scene presser.

Note: The term *active killer* has replaced *active shooter* in police terminology. The term has evolved into *active killer* because some mass murderers use other means of killing—for example, a truck to plow into a crowd. Not all mass killers shoot guns. However, most active killers are active shooters. For the purposes of this book, the terms active shooter and active killer are interchangeable (Omaha Police Policy and Procedure Manual 2024).

LAW ENFORCEMENT CRITICAL MEDIA STRATEGY (B)

Officer-Involved Shootings

When there is an OIS, a high-level law enforcement agency commander should give the on-scene presser. The public needs to know that a very serious event has taken place and that a full-scale investigation into the matter has commenced. At OPD, a deputy chief will conduct the on-scene presser with full PIO assistance. The agency executive should wait to speak on the matter when the investigation is complete—or near complete—enough to speak on the officer's actions. Depending on the details of the OIS, a press conference production (PCP) or a detailed press release will follow the investigation.

Officer-Involved Death (Not an Officer-Involved Shooting)

There will be times when an officer is involved in a death that is not an OIS. Perhaps a citizen dies during the arrest-and-apprehension phase and no gun was fired. Or an officer is in a high-speed chase and a citizen dies.

The on-scene presser should be done in the same manner as one for an OIS; it should be conducted by a deputy chief or another high-level commander. Depending on the public outcry about the situation, the law enforcement executive may have to issue a statement in advance of their follow-up PPC.

Bank Robbery or Barricaded Gunman Situation

In these situations, the PIO or field commander can hold an on-scene presser. The follow-up will be based on how the incident unfolds.

On-Scene Presser Guidelines

When giving an on-scene presser, consider the following guidelines and specialized insight:

Preparation

Media Staging Area: A media staging area should be set up near the scene. This is a place where the reporters can gather to receive information from the police agency.

Fifteen-Minute Warning: The PIO will give the media a fifteen-minute warning when the law enforcement representative is about to enter the staging area and speak. This allows the media time to go live if they choose and prepare the public.

Approach to the Media Staging Area: The law enforcement executive should walk to the staging area with confidence and consider placing the command staff behind the law enforcement executive while they speak. It gives a powerful impression that the matter is serious and being fully addressed.

Note: The media will want to *mic up* the law enforcement executive before the on-scene presser. It is my preference not to allow it. To mic up means to affix a microphone on the law enforcement executive. It is not needed, as the media and public will be able to hear the law enforcement executive. The media will film the process of placing a microphone on the executive live. The viewing audience does not see the behind-the-scenes preparation of news anchors, so they don't need to see the behind-the-scenes mic up of the law enforcement executive. It only distracts from the message and the production.

Content

On-Scene Presser Opening Statement: The presser should be opened with the purpose of giving the community an update on the critical event that has just taken place. The law enforcement leader should then provide the basics of what is known at that time.

Early Assessment: The law enforcement executive may give an early assessment but should never say anything that must be walked back later if the investigation proves otherwise. During the Target store active shooter on-scene example provided in Chapter Two, I did give an early assessment of law enforcement's response.

Basic Information: Gather basic information from the commanders on the scene. Only use verifiable information known at that time. There will always be certain information early on that can be verified for use. For on-scene pressers, there is little time to prepare, so a focus on verifiable facts is prudent.

Original 911 Call and Time: The 911 call time and officer arrival time can be easily verified at the scene for release. The 911 call will show what originally brought law enforcement to the scene.

Officer and Suspect Condition: The current condition of the suspect or any injured civilians and officers will be known.

Never report on any piece of the investigation unless it can be confirmed. The commanders on the scene will know the general medical status of those involved. Medical status is an updatable fact as well.

Never confirm any injured or deceased officer(s), suspect(s), or civilian(s) at the scene. The law enforcement agency will want to inform the next of kin before releasing names to the public.

Investigating Agency: The law enforcement agency will know who is investigating the critical event. This is a good piece of information to relay to the public for transparency. At OPD, a Critical Incident Investigative Team (CIIT) will conduct OIS investigations, assisted by two outside law enforcement agencies. The two outside law enforcement agencies provide for the mitigation of conflicts of interest, transparency, and community trust. Other law enforcement agencies have a sole investigating agency separate and distinct from the agency involved, providing for the ultimate elimination of any conflict of interest for community confidence.

Body Camera or Other Video: Most of the time, the law enforcement executive will know if video is available as part of the investigation. It is a positive step toward transparency to let the public know an impartial piece of evidence is available. The law enforcement executive should review the video, if possible, before the on-scene presser.

Danger to the Public: The law enforcement executive should relay if the critical event is over and if there is no further danger to the public. Conversely, if the suspect(s) is still at large and there is a danger to the public, the law enforcement executive must convey that information.

Other Verifiable Information: If there is information that is verifiable and not subject to further investigation, it is fine to inform the public. In the Target active shooter on-scene presser (see Addendum 1 for details), OPD knew the suspect had fired rounds inside the store. There was value in relaying the information to the public. The Target store active shooter on-scene presser is used below as a learning example.

Concluding

Question and Answer: The law enforcement executive may take questions or not. It is up to the agency leader. Either way, the law enforcement executive should end the on-scene presser on their terms.

Where to Call with Witness Information: A good way to end the on-scene presser, before thanking the media, is to give a phone number or tip-line the public can use to contact law enforcement with information about the incident.

Closing: Thank the media and advise them that the law enforcement agency will keep them apprised of new developments on an ongoing basis.

Case Studies – Reader Activity

There are two on-scene press conferences attached as case studies. E-book learners can click right on the URL to access them, and hard-copy textbook learners will need to go to the URL online.

Activity 6.1: You are given transcripts of on-scene pressers and segments of PPCs. Identify the elements of the communication and note what was included and what was omitted. Use the On-Scene Presser Guidelines to identify the components of an on-scene presser.

Case Study 1: Omaha, Target Store Active Shooter—January 2023

Please refer to Chapter Two for the details of the Target active shooter incident.

A white male gunman in his thirties entered an Omaha Target store and began shooting. Omaha was fortunate that the suspect did not hit anyone, even though he was firing an AR-15 and had over three hundred rounds. The suspect was confronted by the first responding officers and was shot dead by police.

Law Enforcement Media Ecosystem

NBC National News, *Good Morning America*, and other national news outlets covered the event. There was extensive local coverage, and the on-scene presser was held live, breaking into regular television programming.

Transcript 1: Omaha Target Active Shooter

The following is a transcript of the introduction to the on-site presser:

> We have a live camera as they await a press conference by Omaha Police Chief Todd Schmaderer. It's been a very busy day. Of course, just last night, there was an OIS at the Dino storage center. That was at 53rd and Center. The police chief gave a briefing to media last night, right around midnight. So here we are about to hear from the police chief twice within a matter of 13 hours.
>
> What we do know, before we hear officially from police at this hour, is that there were shots fired at Target, just around noon today. Nobody was transported from the scene, that's the good news. It does not mean there were not any victims, however. Here is the police chief, Todd Schmaderer, walking up right now to address the media. Let's listen in.

Questions

1. **What does the media relay about the situation?**
2. **What information do they have?**
3. **What do they not know?**

LAW ENFORCEMENT CRITICAL MEDIA STRATEGY (B)

The following is a transcript is of the communication to the media by Police Chief Todd Schmaderer:

Good afternoon, everyone.

I want to give a quick update on what took place at Target.

At 11:59, calls started coming in to our 911 center about an active shooter within Target, 178th and Center.

That initiated a heavy local, federal, and state response. You saw the police officers here, everybody in the city responded to this call if they were able to.

The first arriving officers went into the building, confronted the suspect, and shot him dead.

The suspect is a white male. I'm going to estimate that he's in his thirties. He had an AR-15 rifle with him and plenty of ammunition.

There's evidence to suggest, with shell casings, that he entered the Target and was firing rounds.

It's unknown at this time if he was firing at anybody.

We did a search for any victims, customers, workers because there were some people hiding in there.

We could not find anybody that has been hurt. We did a second sweep just to really ensure it, and we're in the process of a third.

At this point in time, we don't have any workers or customers or any civilians hurt, other than the suspect who is dead by gunshot through Omaha police.

We will continually update the media on this situation that's unfolding; the investigation is just starting. We did receive, I know, at this point, at least twenty-nine 911 calls for the active shooter response.

My initial take is, when I came out here, and heard this coming, that this is what you want. When you have an active shooter in your city, you want a massive response like this. So, I want to thank all the surrounding agencies, federal, county, state, and I want to thank the Omaha police officers who responded to this matter as well.

I'm going to turn this over to Neal Bonacci for a minute, and we will continually update the media on this particular matter. Thank you very much. (KETV NewsWatch7 2023)

Questions

1. **What information does the chief of police relay to the media?**
2. **How many components can you identify from the On-Scene Presser Guidelines?**

Omaha Police photo: Omaha police chief giving an on-scene presser flanked by Omaha police deputy chiefs

3. **What information does the media have at this stage?**
4. **What do they still not know?**

The full version of on-scene presser is available at the following link on the Live 5 News website: https://www.live5news.com/2023/01/31/shooting-reported-omaha-target-policesaid-they-killed-suspect/

The following transcript is the information conveyed by Sergeant Neal Bonacci, Public Information Officer:

So, I want to give you some information about how witnesses can contact the Omaha Police Department with any information that they possibly have. We have set up a call center within our department down in our headquarters through our telephone report squad.

They can call 402-444-4877 and they will get in touch with somebody they can provide whatever information whatever vital information they need to further this investigation. As Chief Schmaderer said, we will continually update the media on this situation that will come from the Omaha Police Department public information office, specifically from me or one of my officers.

Again, we'll continue to follow up on it, ok?

Questions

1. **What information does press officer Lieutenant Neal Bonacci relay to the media?**

LAW ENFORCEMENT CRITICAL MEDIA STRATEGY (B)

Omaha Police photo: Lieutenant Neal Bonacci, Omaha police, Press Information Officer took over the on-scene presser after the chief spoke to the media.

2. What information does the media have at this stage?
3. What do they still not know?

The Full Version of Live 5 News Coverage (WOWT Omaha) is available at the following link: https://www.live5news.com/2023/01/31/shooting-reported-omaha-target-policesaid-they-killed-suspect/

In this case study, you have been able to explore how a police department can interact professionally with the media, provide enough information to reduce any communication vacuum, and engage with the media to ensure their message is heard by the public.

Transcript 2: Omaha, Dino's Storage, Two Officers Shot, Suspect Dead by Police Gunfire—January 2023

Transcript of the On-scene Presser:

The location, which is the Dino's storage above 53rd and Center.

Staff members let them in. When they came in, they encountered a white male in his late 30s; a struggle ensued, between the two officers and the white male in the late 30s.

Gunfire was exchanged. Two officers were transported to Nebraska Medicine with lower extremity gunshot wounds. I am told they are in stable condition. I will go down and see for myself right after this.

The suspect is dead. He is in the scene; we are starting the investigation now.

The Omaha Police Department in conjunction with the state patrol and Douglas County Sheriff's Department all conduct this investigation. We will have more information for you tomorrow as soon as we can process the scene.

This is really the best I can give you at the moment. I appreciate everybody coming out here and relaying what I have to say.

Any questions at all, I'll try to answer them but we're real limited at this time.

Reporter: So both officers are alert and awake and that's from your understanding?

Chief: They're alert, they're awake and they're in good condition from what I'm told.

Reporter: Were both officers taken by ambulance?

Chief: So, one officer was taken by ambulance; one officer was transported by another officer.

Alright, everybody. Thank you very much. Have a good night. (Transcript source: *Omaha World Herald*, January 31, 2023)

Questions

1. **What information does the chief of police relay to the media?**
2. **How many components can you identify from the On-Scene Presser Guidelines?**
3. **What information does the media have at this stage?**
4. **What do they still not know?**

2) PPC (Policing Press Conference) Preplanning

The majority of PPCs should be preplanned and held at a set location. All major law enforcement agencies have a media room for PPCs. Unless designated to be held at the mayor's office, the governor's mansion, or the local FBI office, the PPC should be held at the law enforcement agency's media room.

PPCs are the perfect medium to display mastery of a critical event. When a PPC takes place in a timely manner, within a few days of a major incident, it can be very effective at controlling the narrative, while keeping rumors and innuendo at bay.

When delivered correctly, a PPC can be the ultimate form of transparency. The PPC is a direct conduit to the community, and with a question-and-answer segment, it can be the perfect format for transparency. A PPC that does not include a question-and-answer segment has fallen woefully short of the law enforcement agency's transparency standard.

LAW ENFORCEMENT CRITICAL MEDIA STRATEGY (B)

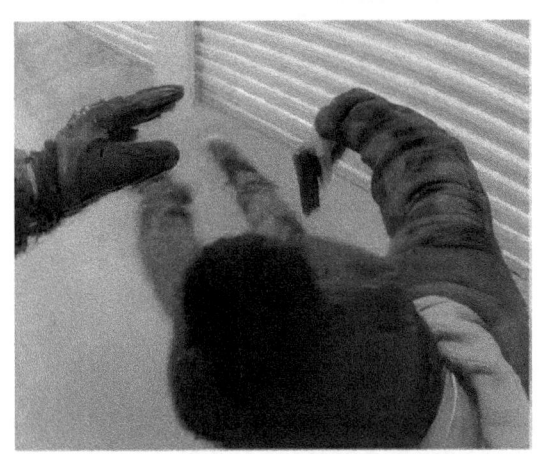

Omaha Police photos: Body worn camera still photos of Dino's storage suspect running and holding a gun. Omaha police officers Nick Lanning and Joshua Moore were shot in the Dino's Storage incident before returning fire and killing the suspect.

When to Hold a PPC

The timing of a PPC is determined by the law enforcement agency itself. The timing depends on the agency and on the specific critical event. You will have determined the mode of media interface between the agency and the media in the evaluation phase of the critical media strategy.

At OPD, a PPC will be held when the matter is of a serious public safety concern, outside of normal high-profile crime.

The recommendation is that a PPC is reserved for only big-time critical events. An agency that does too many PPCs will run the risk of diluting their effectiveness. The following are examples of critical events where OPD elected to hold a PPC:

- To announce the discovery of a public corruption scandal
- To announce that a task force has been formed to track down a serial killer
- To announce the arrest of the serial killer
- To discuss gun violence in the city after a five-year-old was killed by errant gunfire
- To relay the findings of OISs of community concern
- To announce the death of an officer in the line of duty

Pre-PPC Executive Preparation

Once you've decided to deliver a PPC, you need to be well prepared to make it successful. The agency leader conducting the press conference must have a complete understanding and mastery of the critical incident at hand. Even though one person does most of the PPC talking, it is a team effort. The best analogy to understand the effort that goes into this production is to see the person doing the PPC as akin to a professional golfer. All the audience sees is the golfer, but behind the scenes are the caddy, coach, and agent, who form the "team." In a law enforcement agency, the team is the PIO, investigators, and senior commanders. The golfer at critical event PPCs is the law enforcement executive.

Within OPD, the chief gets several briefings on the critical incident investigation, and then there is one large briefing near the end of the investigation. Along the way, the chief can delegate aspects that need to be completed. The large briefing at the end consists of a step-by-step time line of events from start to finish.

Mastery of the critical incident is vital. There is no way to deliver a proper PPC if the presenter does not have a total grasp of the critical event. PPC newcomers should first practice their delivery before attempting to do it live. Go to the press room, walk up to the podium, and deliver the presentation. A mock run will be beneficial in shaking off nerves, as the first live sight of twenty reporters and fifteen cameras pointed right at you can be nerve-racking.

At the end of the mock press conference, the *team* of investigators, PIO, and senior commanders should grill the presenter with questions to simulate the reporters. Newcomers to press conferences will find the mock question-and-answer session to be of great value. Failure to prepare is preparing to fail.

LAW ENFORCEMENT CRITICAL MEDIA STRATEGY (B)

PPC Room Preparations and Setup

Time and Place: Decide on the time and place of the press conference and relay it to the media via a press release.

Professional Backdrop and Equipment Check: In the law enforcement agency's media room, have a professional backdrop. Double-check the microphone, sound system, and screens for any videos that might be played.

Below is an example of OPD's backdrop. OPD purchased the backdrop to enhance the image of the department. The picture below is the new backdrop. Small changes and preparation add up to portray a professional appeal to the public.

Omaha Police photo: New OPD backdrop

Media Packet: Prepare a media packet with information such as the suspect's name and criminal history, officer name and seniority, and official agency photo of the officer, deputy, trooper, or agent. Any photos or displays used during the press conference should be included. Some agencies will provide a timeline of events, which shows transparency and thoroughness.

Choreography: Choreograph every step of the PPC, especially if there are videos, props, or still photos being used. In addition, make sure to cover where members participating in the PPC are to stand and the order of speakers. For major PPCs involving an employee investigation, OPD will have the deputy chiefs on stage with the chief of police to show consensus and uniformity. A law enforcement agency's PIO will not be on stage but will coordinate the media, before, during, and after the PPC.

PPC Media Rules

The public expects the law enforcement executive to be in charge of a situation, and this also includes keeping the media in line during PPCs. Controlling the media and managing how the PPC progresses is an absolute must! The following PPC media rules will help set the stage for a controlled media environment.

Credentialed Media only: Only credentialed or accredited reporters will be allowed into the media room. Allowing members of the public to attend the PPC is a recipe for chaos. There are plenty of examples where a member of the public has disrupted a non-credential media briefing.

For example, in a press conference in Omaha, an elected official was getting ready for a press conference on a matter that attracted activists. The elected official saw a strategic benefit and allowed an activist into the press conference. It was not a PPC. Once the press conference started, the activist started yelling disruptive statements and, essentially, derailed the press conference.

Start on Time: The PPC will start at the scheduled time, and the law enforcement agency will not wait for the media to show up or set up their equipment. A PPC is often held on live television, and the media will inform the public of when the PPC is set to commence. Delaying the start because the media or law enforcement executive is not ready distracts from the production and bearing of the law enforcement agency. In short, start at the time set by the law enforcement agency, and don't be late if at all avoidable.

No Questions Until Called Upon: No member of the press can ask a question until called upon. This should be relayed to the media by the PIO beforehand. It is a good idea, prior to taking any questions from reporters, to reiterate the rules during the PPC. The reporters present will understand that the public has just heard the rules, making it a challenge for the reporter to break them, without being outed.

Microphone: When the law enforcement executive calls on a reporter for a question, a microphone will be walked over to the reporter so the public audience can hear the questions. The viewing audience cannot hear the reporters' questions unless a microphone is present. During some of my early PPCs, a common constructive criticism was that the viewing public could not hear the reporters' questions.

Name and Media Organization: The reporter must give their name and media organization prior to asking a question. If they forget to do so, the law enforcement executive should stop them and have them state this information. Reporters will not push back on this fundamental requirement. It is their chance to say their name and plug their news station. This simple rule has a way of preventing the reporter from blurting out questions out of order. It helps to curtail media frenzy outbursts of questions.

Reporter List: Use a list of reporters to call on. Always allow the local reports to go first over the national reporters. When the national reporters leave, the local ones will be left behind, and it will assist in a good peer relationship. The order of your reporter call-on list can be strategic. At OPD, it has been used to reward a reporter or quietly scold one by putting them last based on some of their past actions.

LAW ENFORCEMENT CRITICAL MEDIA STRATEGY (B)

Use First Names: Consider calling the local reporters by their first names. They are peers, and it shows a working relationship and a personal side during a very intense critical event.

Next Question Approach: If a reporter is getting out of line, put them in their place professionally and go to the next question. Plan in advance which reporter will ask the next question, as moving on quickly will end the skirmish with the other reporter. During intense subject matter PPCs, reporters may push the limit. Being able to move past the reporter to a new one helps to control the media room. The public will see the exchange and appreciate the professional "next question" approach.

Pick-the-Headline Game

The pick-the-headline game is an exercise used in my early days as chief of police. The whole premise is to try to steer the media into our preferred headline. It is a game my deputy chiefs and PIO used at the time to sharpen our message. The game is just how it sounds: pick the headline. In essence, we were picking or supplying the headline we wanted to read. If OPD's message was delivered in an effective production in the PPC, the media would use the headline we picked. The headline must always be the true terrain of the critical event and supported by all the evidence.

My team and I would sit around a conference table and determine the best headline; we would then highlight the statement in the PPC. There are several ways to highlight the statement. The presenter can pause for dramatic effect, then state the headline statement. At other times, a successful technique consisted of leaning into the podium for dramatic effect and then saying the headline statement. On some occasions, forecasting a question from the media can elicit a prepared statement that is the headliner.

The pick-the-headline game is advisable for law enforcement personnel new to PPCs. It is a way to stay focused on the message at hand and relay it to the community. In addition, when it works and the headline is successfully steered, an agency's media confidence will skyrocket. Below are a couple of real-world examples where the headline was chosen by OPD based on the evidence gathered during the investigation.

Example 1: *COPS* Television Show, Officer-Involved Shooting

At the completion of the OIS investigation, the evidence was clear that the officers had no other choice but to shoot the suspect. The suspect was pointing a pellet gun at them and shooting it like it was a real gun. It even sounded real. During the PPC, there was a pause and a lean forward on the podium before the headline statement was made: the Officers had no choice but to respond with gunfire in return. OPD successfully

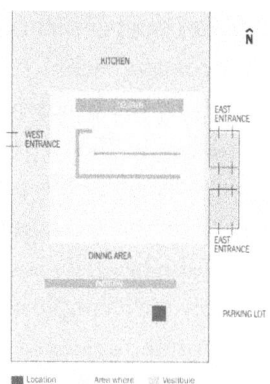

Courtesy of the Omaha World Herald
COPS TV Show Press Conference; https://www.youtube.com/watch?v=pun2K52TO1s&ab_channel=KMTV3NewsNow
Article about the press conference and a link to the video:
ThroughlineGroup.com https://www.throughlinegroup.com/2014/09/02/a-perfect-example-of-a-great-press-conference/

LAW ENFORCEMENT CRITICAL MEDIA STRATEGY (B)

controlled a message in a critical event that was ripe for rumors and innuendo. Evidence must control the message; facts over speculation must prevail.

Example 2: Serial Killer Nikko Jenkins

As soon as he got out of prison, serial killer Nikko Jenkins went on a rampage, killing four people. Nikko had spent almost his entire time in prison in solitary confinement, up until the day he was released. OPD's press conference announcing his arrest was of value, steering the media to an appropriate headline based on Nikko's incarceration history: "Why was he let out early?" See Chapter Two for more details on the serial killer Nikko Jenkins's case.

Reader Activity

Out of the two example case studies listed above, select one and watch the PPC video. After you have watched it, assess the following:

1. Identify the components of the press conference.
2. Note how the pick-the-headline game was enacted.

3) The PPC Itself

The following templates are invaluable in assisting the law enforcement presenter in a PPC.

TTTRUS is an acronym developed over a decade of practice and provides the basic tenets of a PPC.

T = Truth. Always be truthful and provide accurate information. The truth is a hallmark of the PPC. The first time a lie is told, all credibility is lost. The information provided must be vetted and accurate. Do not take liberties with the information provided.

T = Transparency. Transparency is a hallmark of community policing. It is a necessity for positive police–community relations. It is a unique aspect of a PPC, not always found in other press conferences.

T = Timeliness and Tone. The timing of the PPC press conference must be as soon as possible after a critical event. Transparency requires a timely press conference. If, for some reason, certain information cannot be disclosed, tell the media why. The presenter's tone will change based on the audience of the critical event PPC, and the tone can change several times during the PPC or on-scene presser. For the presser after

Photo courtesy of Omaha World Herald, Front Page, September 5, 2013
https://omaha.com/complete-coverage-nikko-jenkins-convicted-of-4-murders-sentenced-to-death/collection_48429228-a038-11e5-9263-8bc352525845.html#3

LAW ENFORCEMENT CRITICAL MEDIA STRATEGY (B)

Kerrie Orozco's death, the tone went from somber, to a clinical delivery of the facts, to some anger.

R = Research. The PPC presenter should know the subject matter and the critical event inside and out. A PPC is the law enforcement agency's opportunity to enhance the image of the agency. As such, it is imperative that the presenter has a mastery of the critical incident.

U = Understand or Know Your Audience. Knowing your audience is essential to the message and tone of the PPC. Knowing your audience was covered in Chapter Four: Law Enforcement—Baseline Media Strategy.

S = Stay on Topic. The media will try to push the presenter off topic during the question-and-answer portion of the PPC. The PPC presenter should bring all discussion back to the subject at hand: the critical event. For example, if the press conference is for an active-killer critical event, don't take questions about an officer who was terminated a week ago.

PPC Formula

The prescribed formula I use for a PPC has been developed over my career. Some law enforcement agencies have replaced PPCs with video presentations. My preference is to augment the PPC with a video but not allow the prepared video to be the entire PPC.

If a law enforcement agency is not confident in its PPC skills, the prepared video can suffice. Always remember that the public wants to see the law enforcement agency executive front and center and taking live questions from reporters. Video presentations can come across as a way to avoid pressure.

> **READER NOTE**
> **Below is a link for a video used by Omaha Police in 2024 where two officers were justified in shooting two people, and those two people died. The chief of police opened the PPC and then played the video. The chief made a further statement after the video and then went into the question-and-answer portion. Readers can find the entire press conference on the internet; for learning purposes, the video link is attached. Please note the production of the video and the work that went into the video for the PPC.**
> **https://www.youtube.com/watch?v=gwU1PmYmVMU&pp=ygUT-b21haGEgcG9saWNlIHZpZGVvIA%3D%3D**

SYNERGY *of* INFLUENCE

READER ASSIGNMENT
The San Luis Obispo chief of police oversaw an incredibly well done video in the aftermath of an officer being killed in the line of duty in June of 2023. Locate the video online and discuss it among the class. Warning: it is a graphic video.

If there is video of the critical incident, and local and state laws allow for it, include the video. In cases of OISs, always augment the video with still photos of the critical event. Still photos slow the critical incident down so the public can see what the officer saw. Oftentimes, the video moves fast, and it is hard for the public to see the critical moment. The still photos below show the critical time in which OPD officers elected to fire their duty weapons in self-defense. It is hard to see this moment based on the officer's BWC video alone.

Template for the Contents of a PPC

- A) Purpose of the PPC
- B) Opening statement
- C) Timeline of events
- D) The executive's findings
- E) Solutions moving forward
- F) Rules for the Q&A
- G) Closing press conference statement

A) Purpose of the press conference: The purpose of the PPC is provided as a very simple statement explaining why it is taking place. It is also an opportunity to lay out the order of the PPC. The order of the PPC can be the speaker order or the sections the presenter will cover. For example, "The purpose of this press conference is to give the public an accounting of the OIS incident from yesterday at Wendy's restaurant."

After the purpose statement, follow with the order of remarks. Clearly state that you will give an opening statement, followed by a timeline of events, then take questions from the media, and then issue a closing statement. This part of the proceedings is also a good time to announce any condolences in situations where there has been a loss of life.

It is tasteful and professional to give condolences to the suspect's family if the suspect has died as well. It does not have to be as enthusiastic as those reserved for innocent lives lost or an officer who dies. In Kerrie Orozco's PPC, deepest condolences were given to her family, followed by condolences to the family of the suspect.

LAW ENFORCEMENT CRITICAL MEDIA STRATEGY (B)

Omaha Police photo: In the police body camera still photo, the suspect spins quickly with his gun pointed at the officer as the officer approaches the car on the passenger side.

Omaha Police photo: In the Omaha police body camera still photo, the suspect is unarmed. The still photo clarifies why the OPD officer fired his service weapon. From the BWC alone, it is hard to pinpoint the exact moment when the veteran officer clearly felt threatened.

B) Opening statement: The opening statement is a message from the law enforcement executive. The statement should consist of broad commentary appropriate for the critical event. Some examples of OPD opening statements have been to talk about the dangers of police work, police–community relations, the state of mental health in our city, or the goal of the department during the 2020 civil unrest, which was to provide a safe environment for everyone to exercise their First Amendment rights. This is the law enforcement leader's moment to show their leadership.

C) Timeline of events: The timeline of events is a chronological order description of the critical event. This segment can be read verbatim. While it is refreshing for the audience if there are moments when the presenter does not read and speaks right to the camera, the timeline of events is a clinical accounting of a critical event. The details will be immense, and it is designed for transparency. The public needs to feel the transparency and the thoroughness of the investigation. The timeline helps to show a mastery of the incident.

D) The executive's findings: The executive's findings are the law enforcement agency leader's assessment of the critical event. For example:

- "My officers are justified."
- "The officers were left with no other choice."
- "Deadly force was in accordance with policy."
- "In this matter, we failed."
- "The use of force was not in accordance with policy."

There are many possible outcomes. The media will often use the law enforcement agency executive's findings as their headline, so ensure the findings are said in a manner to garner their attention.

E) Solutions moving forward: Solutions moving forward is where the next steps to prevent the situation from happening again are communicated. For example, say there is a situation where a civilian has died because a suspect's vehicle crashed into their car during a high-speed pursuit. The solutions moving forward in this case could be policy changes that could prevent a repeat of the event, such as pursuit training for the agency.

The law enforcement executive should be solution-driven; if a problem exists, correct it. A rule of thumb is to relay at least three ways the agency plans to prevent the problem from occurring again.

F) Rules for the Q&A: It is imperative to ensure control over the PPC. Reading the media rules for the public to hear is a powerful message for reporters taking part. During preplanning, remember to practice the Q&A segment.

G) Closing statement: The closing statement is like the opening statement. This is a good time for the law enforcement leader to reiterate their message. Wish everyone a good evening or afternoon. Thank the media for being there and doing their jobs as an important conduit for the public.

Ending a press conference smoothly is a challenge. The PIO can wave when it's time to end, or the law enforcement presenter can decide. When it is time to end the PPC, say, "I am going to take one more question and then give my closing remarks."

Five Authentications to Convey to the Public

There are five authentications every PPC wants to convey. If the authentications are delivered in a manner where the viewing public *feels* them, the message will be more easily accepted and understood.

The five authentications are as follows:

1. Strike the perfect emotional tone.
2. Treat the media as a peer.
3. Be completely open.
4. Get in front of potential controversy.
5. Convey a sense of complete confidence (Phillips 2014).

An assessment of the five authentications at a PPC is available in Brad Phillips's article on the Throughline blog covering the PPC for the *COPS* Television Show OIS. His assessment highlights the five authentications; the only one where my view slightly diverges from his is that I prefer to view the media as a peer rather than an ally. As a learning tool, look up Brad Phillip's assessment of the 2013 COPS Television Show PPC. It can be found by googling "The Throughline Group Blog, A Perfect Example of a Great Press Conference, Brad Phillips 2014."

Conclusion

Chapter Six: Law Enforcement—Critical Media Strategy (B)—Mastering Policing Press Conferences has covered how to successfully conduct press conferences in the context of law enforcement. The PPC is a distinct skill from those involved in law enforcement, with its emphasis on influence, transparency, police–community relations, and specific insights relevant to law enforcement press conferences. The section on on-scene pressers was accompanied by a practice formula and real-world examples for added perspective.

The section on PPC pre planning provided insider tips and a comprehensive guide to ensure effective preparation for the PPC production. Suggested media rules and the pick-the-headline game were introduced to assist newcomers in conducting a successful PPC. Real-world pick-the-headline examples have been presented to illustrate these concepts to readers.

Lastly, the Actual PPC section described the acronym TTTRUS and provided a PPC formula as a guide. Five authentications to convey to the public were also covered. Law enforcement media insight was infused into this section as well.

Questions for Discussion and Review

1. What are the characteristics that separate a PPC from a regular press conference?
2. What is the purpose of a media staging area?
3. Provide three pieces of basic information available for an in-scene presser, regardless of the event?
4. Give two examples of critical events worthy of a PPC and why?
5. True or False: Any member of the public can attend a PPC. True or False: Transparency and time have a correlation or connection?
6. What is the value in releasing a still photo in conjunction with the entire video?
7. What is the value of a timeline of events segment during a PPC?

READER ASSIGNMENTS
On-Scene Presser
Write out your on-scene presser statement to the media for the following critical event.
On February 12, 2023, the New Orleans Police Department (NOPD) swiftly responded to a distressing 911 call originating from the vibrant French Quarter. The caller reported a recent shooting incident outside a bustling bar, with the grim revelation that three lives had been tragically taken. The officers promptly arrived at the scene to find three individuals fatally wounded and three others grievously injured. In an act of bravery, a responding NOPD officer confronted the shooter and, regrettably, had to use lethal force to stop the threat, resulting in the shooter's demise. Fortunately, none of the courageous officers were harmed during this harrowing encounter.

Pick the Headline
The pick-the-headline game is a good exercise for law enforcement commanders to galvanize their message. Choose a critical incident from Chapter Two: Omaha's National Crime Events—Unveiling the Impact and pick a headline you feel is

LAW ENFORCEMENT CRITICAL MEDIA STRATEGY (B)

prudent. Demonstrate for the class how you would emphasize the statement during the PPC so the media picks up on it.

Opening Statement

Refer to Chapter Two and select a critical event. Prepare a PPC opening statement based on the event. Write out the opening statement and verbalize it to the class.

Closing Statement

Refer to Chapter Two and select a critical event. Prepare a PPC closing statement based on the event. Write out the closing statement and verbalize it to the class.

"Synergy of Influence"

**The reader does not have to reach each chapter in order. Chapter 7 -12 can stand alone for the reader, or read in the order of the readers preference"

CHAPTER SEVEN

Brand Damage Control in Officer-Involved Shootings

Introduction

Officer-involved shootings (OISs) can be the greatest threat to a police agency's brand for obvious reasons; they represent real lives! A high degree of law enforcement deaths occur because of OISs. Across the country, major cities struggle with law enforcement and community relations. When the subject of race enters the mix, the stakes become even higher, and the cost to an agency's reputation can be steep.

In Chapter Eight: Race, Police, and Media—Unraveling the Puzzle, we will dive into the subject of race and how its presence in a situation heightens the need for a strong critical media strategy.

Since this is a book on law enforcement and the media, a premise that has been woven throughout has been that law enforcement leaders need to have insight and a strategy to enhance their agency's brand. When looking at OISs, two aspects come to mind:

First, it behooves a law enforcement agency to reduce the overall number of OISs in their society. A reduction in a society's macro-OIS numbers helps to preserve the agency's brand by supporting law enforcement. It is compassionate, just, and professional to reduce OISs for society.

Second is managing the media during the incident, the next day, and beyond when an OIS occurs. A law enforcement agency owes it to its professional officers and the community to give a complete, transparent, and competent accounting of an OIS critical event. Failure to have or to follow a critical media strategy after an OIS can have dire consequences. The community, the law enforcement agency, and the entire law enforcement profession can suffer, as was the case in the Michael Brown OIS in Ferguson, Missouri.

After reading this chapter you will be able to comprehend the significant impact of OISs as potent catalysts for detrimental effects on the reputation of law enforcement agencies. You will have gained a comprehensive understanding of the broader landscape of OIS incidents within the United States, encompassing both the intricate details and overarching trends, and acquired insight into the realm of fatalities arising from police encounters beyond OIS incidents. This will provide you with a nuanced understanding of the multifaceted challenges faced by law enforcement.

You will have a grasp of the intricate relationship that exists between the frequency of law enforcement gun seizures and the occurrence of OIS incidents, with an understanding of the underlying dynamics that shape these occurrences. You will also have developed a profound comprehension of the approaches that can be employed to effectively reduce the number of OISs in each society.

This chapter will help you cultivate an understanding of the OPD's reduction in OISs versus the macro-level national increases in the OIS landscape and gain a reference-worthy familiarity with the OIS Reduction Cocktail deployed by the OPD to curtail OIS incidents.

You will be able to discern the intricate media paradigm in the wake of a singular OIS event, gaining insights into the media's role in shaping public perception and narrative. You will also have acquired a comprehensive understanding of the law enforcement agency's responsibilities in the aftermath of a single OIS incident.

In Omaha, the OPD was able to reduce OISs over a ten-year period. In addition, a tremendous amount of planning has gone into how to be transparent and professional in giving a complete account of the event in the aftermath of a singular OIS. OPD's laser focus on reducing the aggregate number of OISs in the city has been successful and beneficial to police–community relations.

The additional components discussed in this chapter involve the media. Literature about OISs already exists. For example, the International Association of Chiefs of Police (IACP), a considerable resource for law enforcement agencies, has published a paper in conjunction with the Department of Justice about OISs because of their importance to community relations. The content of "Officer-involved Shootings, A Guide for Law Enforcement Leaders" (IACP 2018) covers OIS investigations and other intangibles associated with OISs. Yet, in this forty-six-page-long document, there are only a few paragraphs on the media portion in the aftermath of an OIS. In addition, there is no discussion, guide, or template in the document to reduce the overall number of OISs in a city.

There are currently no published guides to reducing OISs in a city or society and no preset formula for doing so. There are minimal collegial studies that indicate proper training correlates with a reduction in OISs. In addition, a law enforcement agency's use-of-force policy must be tight to reflect a decline in the total number of OISs. In short, through an examination of the available policing research, there are vast gaps in the knowledge of how to reduce OISs (PBS 2019).

BRAND DAMAGE CONTROL IN OFFICER-INVOLVED SHOOTINGS

We start with a look at the national statistics involving OISs to illustrate the current terrain in America. It will become clear that OISs are on the rise, and we will explore the potential reasons why. We will also look at national trends and data in comparison to Omaha's, plus OPD's template for reducing OISs. The chapter will end with a strategy on how to address the media in the aftermath of an OIS to augment the critical media strategy from Chapters Five: Law Enforcement—Critical Media Strategy (A) and Chapter Six: Law Enforcement—Critical Media Strategy (B)—Mastering Policing Press Conferences.

National data on the number of officer-involved deaths of civilians and police gun seizures is spotty. The FBI has taken measures to codify a national database; however, it is not yet fully dependable. Former FBI Director James Comey has acknowledged the shortcomings in data collection. In defense of the FBI, I am appreciative they are taking the lead, and it is up to the individual law enforcement agencies across the country to comply with the data collection for it to be dependable. *The Washington Post* has done an admirable job of filling the data collection void by gathering national data on police and citizen encounters that turn deadly (2022).

Disclaimer: This chapter provides a template for cities to reduce the total number of OISs. The template has been successful in Omaha, Nebraska, through OPD. Omaha police have sustained a ten-year reduction in OISs, giving credence to the template. However, the template has not been the subject of scholarly research. It is a suggested template with accompanying insight. It is up to the law enforcement agency to evaluate if the formula can be replicated in their city. As with any template, law enforcement agencies can adopt it in its entirety, in part, or even modify it.

National OIS and OPD OIS data is compared though the year 2022. The national data for 2023 was not available at the time of writing. In 2023, OPD had seven OISs.

National Officer-Involved Shootings

More people were killed in law enforcement encounters in America in 2022 than in any other year over the past decade. OISs represent 97 percent of police encounter deaths (Levin 2023).

I find this to be a shocking statistic. In 2015, in the aftermath of the OIS in Ferguson, Missouri, there was a large push for law enforcement reform, and many reforms were indeed enacted. In 2020, after the death of George Floyd, law enforcement agencies were scrambling to push through new or lingering reform protocols. The reforms centered around accountability and the use of force to reduce the number of police in-custody deaths, which are primarily OISs. Considering the double push for reforms, it is hard to swallow that OISs in America remain a prevalent statistic

US Fatal Police Shootings 2017-2022

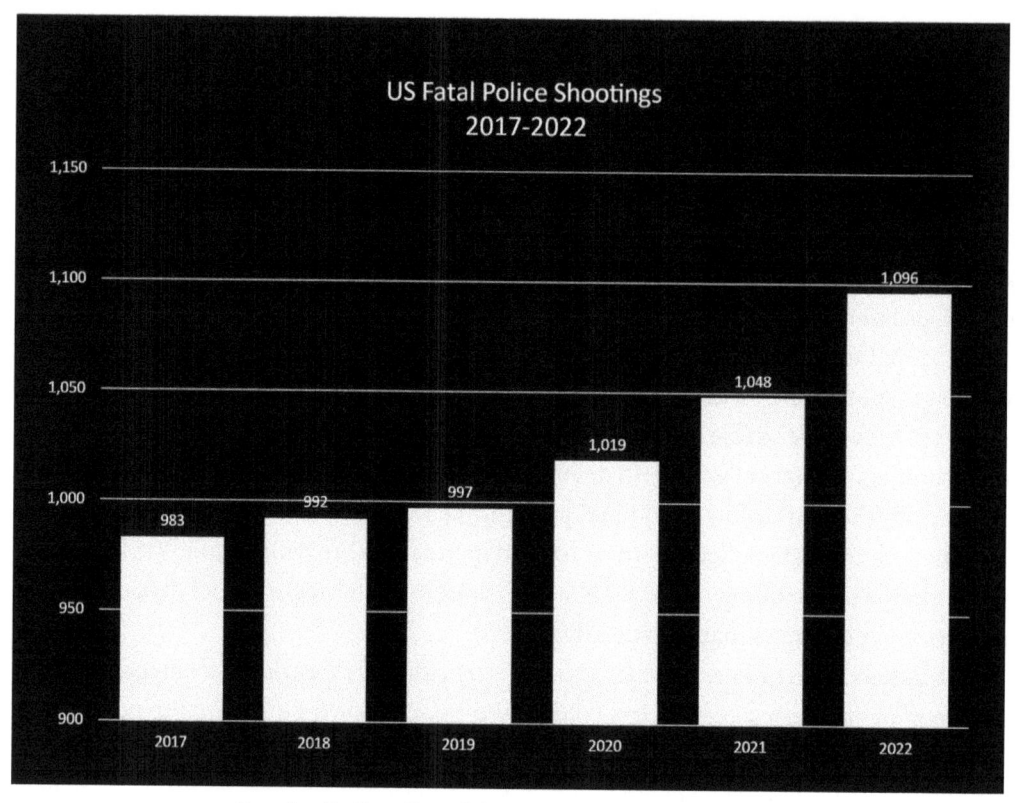

Year	Deaths
2017	983
2018	992
2019	997
2020	1,019
2021	1,048
2022	1,096

Omaha Police Graphic: National OIS Numbers
Source: *The Washington Post* 2022
Exhibit 1a

In 2017, there were 983 OIS deaths in America. Five years later, in contrast to the anticipation and hope of policing reforms, they had gone up to 1,096. OISs are on the rise. Because 97 percent of police encounter deaths are OISs, the focus of this chapter is on reducing them and their ability to damage the brand of policing. However, it is important to discuss the remaining 3 percent of law enforcement and citizen encounter deaths, as some have been extremely high profile and a catalyst to the reform movement (*The Washington Post* 2022).

The Other 3 Percent of Police Encounter Deaths

Citizens George Floyd, Tyre Nichols, and Zachary Bearheels (BWC Scorecard 2016) did not die from OISs (Berman and Nakamura 2023; KETV 2022). They died from the other category of law enforcement encounter deaths that makes up the remaining 3 percent of these fatalities. In the majority of these non-OIS citizen deaths, positional

BRAND DAMAGE CONTROL IN OFFICER-INVOLVED SHOOTINGS

asphyxia plays a role. Positional asphyxia occurs when someone's position prevents that person from breathing adequately (Lexipol 2017).

In Chapter Two: Omaha's National Crime Events—Unveiling the Impact, we presented the case of Zachary Bearheels. Zachary was lying face down on his stomach with officers on his back after being subdued. He died while he was in Omaha police custody. A factor in his death was the considerable number of officers trying to subdue him and hold him down. This shares an echo with the death of George Floyd, which we know involved an officer on his neck and back while he lay face down with handcuffs behind his back.

In police encounters, this is typical. A struggle ends, and the subject ends up face down with officers on the subject's back trying to subdue them. The arresting officers will apply handcuffs, and the suspect might continue to resist. The officers are on the person's back because it is the natural leverage point of control. It becomes exceedingly difficult to breathe with that body weight on top, and sometimes deaths occur because people become unable to breathe.

As an experiment, lie face down with your hands behind your back as if handcuffed. As you can feel, even with no weight on your back it is less natural to breathe in that position. Now imagine—do NOT simulate—if the situation included added body weight on your back; then, factor in a rush of adrenaline, panic, and a struggle. Can you see how the situation can turn deadly very quickly?

At OPD, our policy is that once the person is in handcuffs, get them in a different position! Sit them up or turn them to the side. Even if they are still fighting in handcuffs, control is maintained with a sitting position or to a side position if there are enough officers present (Omaha Police Policy and Procedure Manual 2020).

As chief, I have overseen over forty OISs and numerous other police-citizen-encounter deaths (PBS 2019). In Omaha, the term we use is *in-custody deaths*. The deaths could be anything from a heart attack where an arrestee dies on the way to jail, to suicide in front of the officer, or *suicide by cop*—which is more common than most realize. "Suicide by cop" is when the subject is suicidal and, instead of committing suicide themselves, they place themselves in a position where the police must respond with deadly force. They may, for example, raise a gun toward the officers. In 2023, two Omaha officers saw a female jump out of a ninth-story window to commit suicide in front of them.

READER ASSIGNMENT
***Suicide by cop* is a very real phenomenon. In the aftermath, officers can suffer from mental anguish and, in severe cases, post-traumatic stress. As a class discussion, brainstorm on ways to reduce suicide-by-cop incidents.**

I have also overseen the aftermath of positional asphyxia deaths and commanded scenes where it was prudent to get officers off the handcuffed subject's back. From the officer's point of view, they are trying to make an arrest and subdue a fighting suspect. An officer's priority is to affect the arrest and secure the suspect in handcuffs. The safety of the officer, the community, and the suspect is paramount until the suspect is fully secured. Priority two is getting the suspect off their stomach once the handcuffs are on.

Fifteen years ago, I was the commanding officer on the scene of a citizen's death. The suspect was naked and under the influence of an illegal drug, which made him impervious to pain and gave him superhuman strength. The person had committed crimes and was a danger to the public with his violent outbursts and demeanor. Omaha police officers encountered him, and a struggle ensued. The suspect fought the officers violently. Several officers were able to take him to the ground. The incident occurred before Tasers were in police use.

I arrived at the scene just as the handcuffs were applied on the man by the officers. He was sweating profusely from the fight and his actions leading up to the police intervention. His breathing was slow and labored, and sweat covered his entire body. I directed the officers to get off his back, as I could tell he was in a bad condition. The officers had not been on his back for long and were in the process of getting off anyway. After emergency medical aid, the man died.

The officers were valiant, acted in accordance with all our policies, and the suspect still died. Police work is exceedingly difficult, and it is a population certainty that law enforcement officers will encounter individuals who are suffering from mental illness or on an illegal substance. People will die in police custody; it is unavoidable. A person's medical condition can easily overcome them under such extreme duress. It is therefore imperative to have policies in place to mitigate the chances of police encounters turning into citizen deaths.

Why are OISs on the Rise in America?

The number of guns taken off the streets by law enforcement is said to have reached an all-time high in America. In my professional opinion, as the number of guns on the streets increases, the number of OISs will be commensurate. It makes sense that the greater the number of citizens with guns that law enforcement encounters, the more the number of OISs will rise.

Most people shot by law enforcement are armed with a gun. This was true of 633 of the 1,097 OIS incidents in 2022. The data surrounding law enforcement gun seizures is spotty, to say the least. Try looking up the number of gun seizures by police. What emerges is a very unreliable data set, yet there are more guns on the streets than ever.

BRAND DAMAGE CONTROL IN OFFICER-INVOLVED SHOOTINGS

Armed with Categories

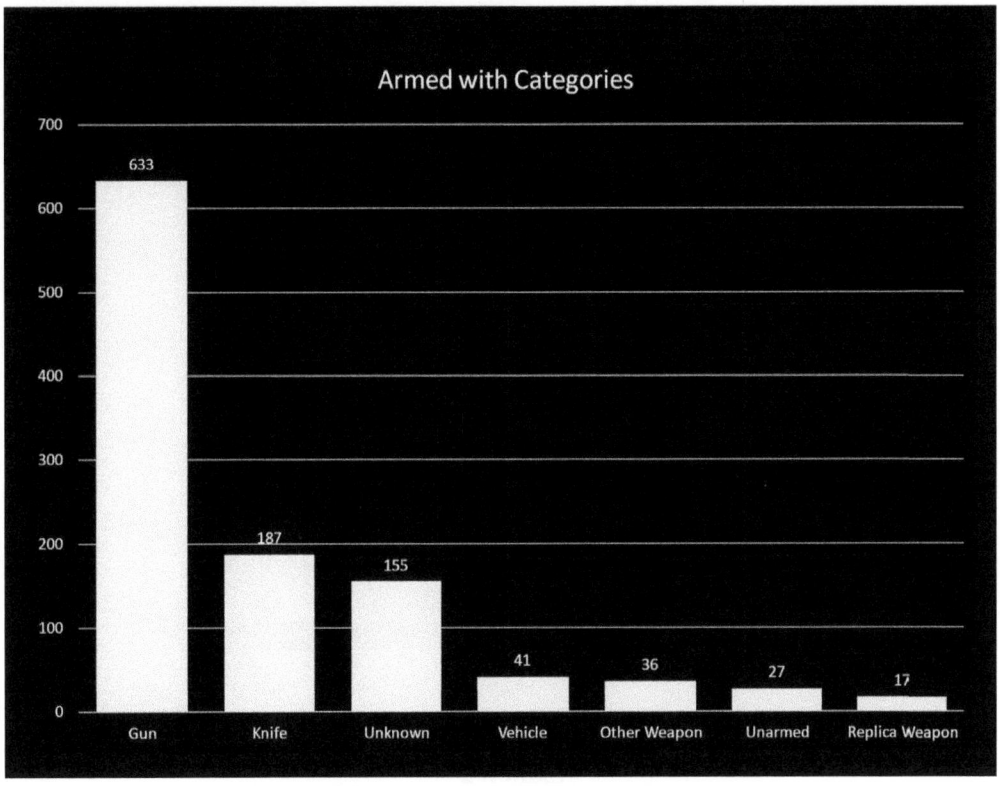

Category	Count
Gun	633
Knife	187
Unknown	155
Vehicle	41
Other Weapon	36
Unarmed	27
Replica Weapon	17

Omaha Police Graphic: National OIS Numbers
Source: *The Washington Post* 2022
Exhibit 1b

This is confirmed by some individual city's gun-seizure data, which shows the presence of guns in our society is on the rise (CNN 2022a; PBS 2019;).

Note: Gun-seizure data relates to any gun confiscated by law enforcement after an encounter, arrest, or search warrant. It does not include gun buyback or gun turn-in programs.

In 2022, CNN conducted a survey of the biggest police agencies in America to gauge the impact of guns on society. Law enforcement agencies in the largest cities in America seized a decade-high number of firearms in 2021 (CNN 2022a).

The increases are staggering.

- In NYC there was a 26 percent rise in gun seizures from 2019 to 2021.
- Of the eight major cities surveyed, all recorded more gun recoveries in 2021 than in 2020.
- In Philadelphia, police recovered 5,920 guns used or suspected in a crime; the highest in at least a decade for Philly.
- Chicago Police recovered 11,397 guns in 2020, increasing to 12,000 in 2021.

Look at the city of Los Angeles and their trend lines for guns recovered in Exhibit 2. With a population of 4,085,014 in 2023, Los Angeles is the number two most populated city in the United States (World Population Review, 2023a).

It makes sense that as the number of citizens with guns increases the number of police encounters with those citizens can lead to a rise in OISs in America.

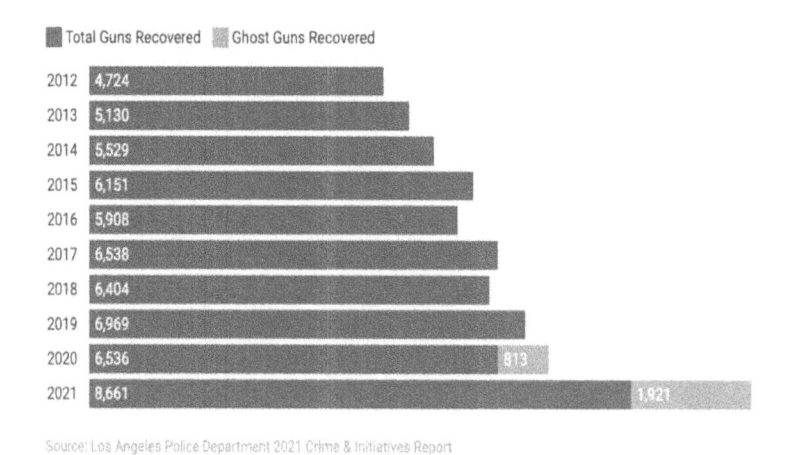

Year	Total Guns Recovered	Ghost Guns Recovered
2012	4,724	
2013	5,130	
2014	5,529	
2015	6,151	
2016	5,908	
2017	6,538	
2018	6,404	
2019	6,969	
2020	6,536	813
2021	8,661	1,921

Source: Los Angeles Police Department 2021 Crime and Initiatives Report
Exhibit 2

Omaha Police Gun Seizures

With just under half a million people living in Omaha, it is the thirty-eighth largest city, by population, in America. Its gun seizure increases are on par with the major cities and are remarkably like Los Angeles. In 2010, the police in Omaha seized 944 guns. By 2022, the number had gone up to 1,458, increasing by over a hundred from the previous year (see Exhibit 3). It is not hard to factor in the increase in the number of guns on the streets as a reason for why OISs are on the rise (World Population Review, 2023b).

READER ASSIGNMENT
The correlation between the rise in OISs and gun seizures by law enforcement is remarkable. What other factors may have contributed to the rise of OISs? The assignment could be a 1–2-page paper or a class discussion.

Omaha City Wide Gun Seizures

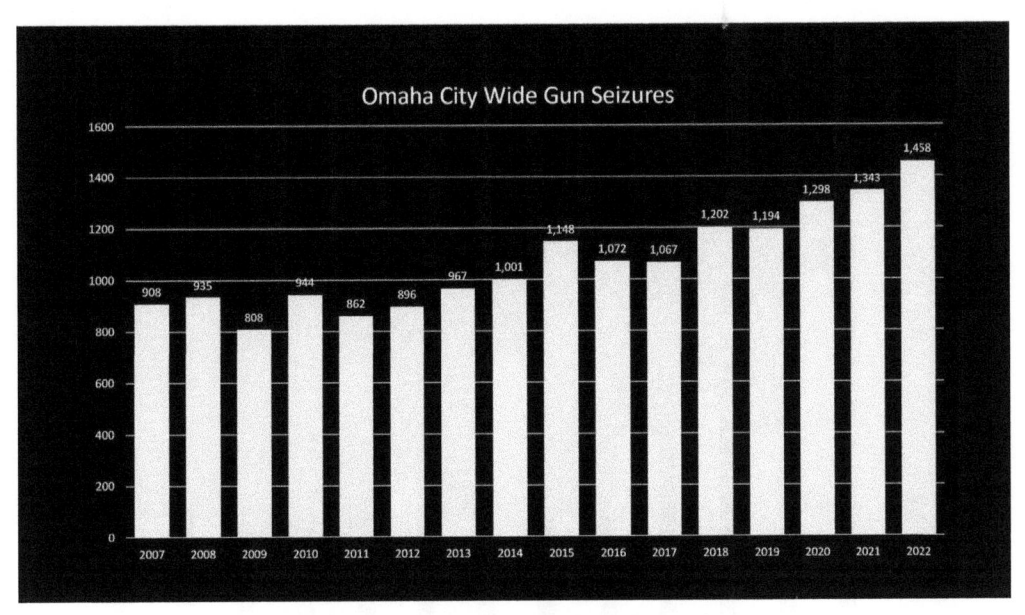

Year	Seizures
2007	908
2008	935
2009	808
2010	944
2011	862
2012	896
2013	967
2014	1,001
2015	1,148
2016	1,072
2017	1,067
2018	1,202
2019	1,194
2020	1,298
2021	1,343
2022	1,458

Omaha Gun Seizures 2008–2023 midyear
Source: Omaha Police
Exhibit 3

Officer-Involved Shootings Can Be Reduced

There are some numbers that seem to rise in parallel: the number of guns on the streets, the number of gun seizures, and the number of OISs. The question is, as gun seizures increase, can OISs be reduced? My professional opinion is yes, and the city of Omaha is an example of just that.

OPD's gun seizures are at an all-time high. However, in direct contrast to the nation, Omaha police OISs are near our baseline lows. In 2010, the OPD had eleven OISs and in 2011 there were ten. From 2019 to 2022, Omaha has averaged only 2.25 OISs a year. From 2017 to current times, Omaha has seen a sustained small number of OISs.

Exhibit 5 shows the stark contrast between Omaha's gun seizures and OISs. As the number of guns seized by OPD has increased, the number of OISs has gone down. In Exhibit 6, the national rise in OISs is compared with OPD's decline in OISs.

How is it that OPD numbers are in defiance of the national trend, where the number of OISs and the number of gun seizures have gone up in tandem? Why are Omaha's numbers divergent? As a precursor to providing Omaha's OIS Reduction Template, I wanted to provide readers with the contrasting data between the national rise and Omaha's decline in OISs as a selling point. The data also show an apples-to-apples comparison, as Omaha's gun seizures have risen in tandem with the nations.

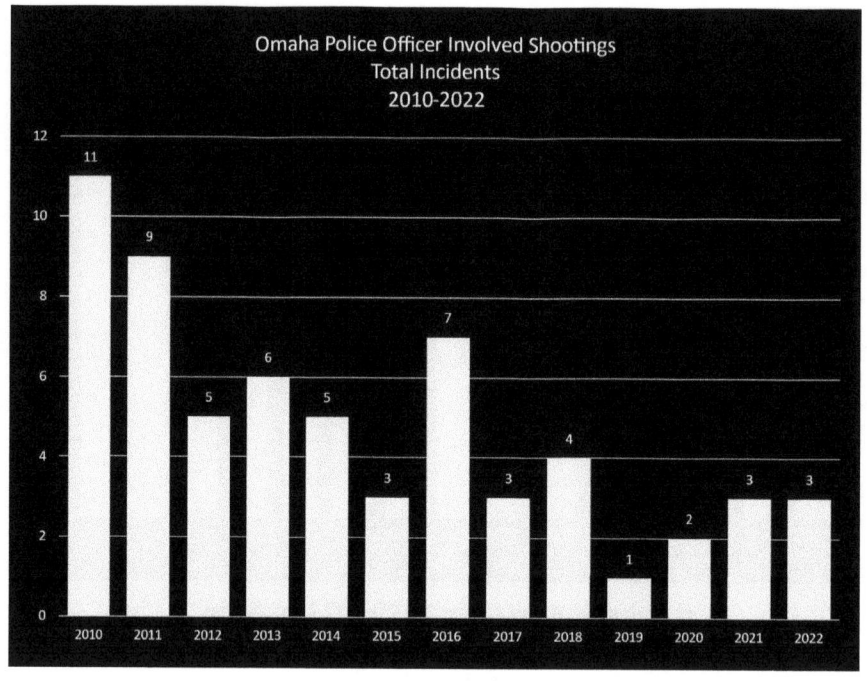

Omaha Police Officer-Involved Shootings 2010–2022
Source: Omaha Police
Exhibit 4

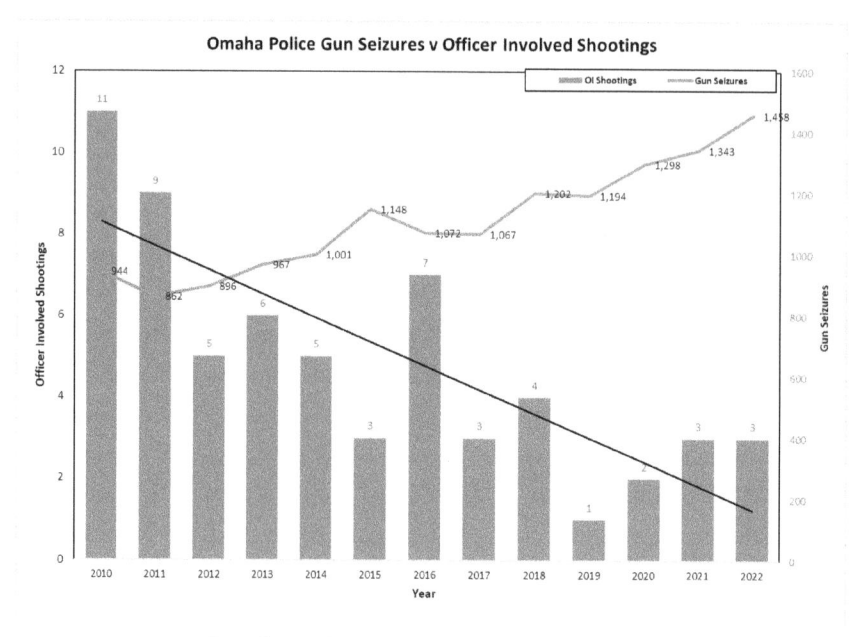

Omaha Police Gun Seizures versus OISs
Source: Omaha Police
Exhibit 5

BRAND DAMAGE CONTROL IN OFFICER-INVOLVED SHOOTINGS

OIS Reduction Template

In Omaha, we used a template to reduce OISs. Its implementation began in 2012, and by 2017, the OIS reduction program was fully in place. Since 2012, OPD has averaged under four OISs a year. Since full implementation in 2017, it has averaged under three (2.25) a year.

The data does not distinguish between OIS deaths and non-deaths. If an officer fired their service weapon and struck a subject, it was classified as an OIS.

In 2010, Omaha's population was approximately 460,000. An average of 2.2 OISs a year is a respectable average for a city that has a population of half a million in 2023. The OIS Reduction Template has had impressive success by numbers since 2010. Factor in one hundred more officers on the force since 2012, and a hefty population increase over the decade, and the numbers are even more impressive (United States Census Bureau 2019).

The OIS reduction programs implemented by OPD can have a positive impact on other cities as well. Academic literature is absent on the matter. To date, I have not been able to find any official studies on OIS reduction. As such, OPD fashioned its own. I want to extend Omaha's program to readers as an option for reducing OISs in other cities.

I completely understand that there are unavoidable OISs. Omaha had two recently: the Target store active shooter described in Chapter Two, and twelve hours prior, a burglary suspect shot two Omaha officers before they returned fire. All OISs are circumstance-based. The key is to change the circumstances and cut down on the number of OISs. In Omaha, it is one of our vital sign statistics for gauging our level of success in policing the community.

Most of all scholarly writings on reducing OISs will focus on training, training, and training. Studies have shown that proper training can reduce the overall use of force in a police agency. Training alone, however, does not count as an OIS reduction program or template (Bechtel et al. 2023; Engel et al. 2020; Klinger 2001).

The training spectrum of de-escalation, anti-bias, and dynamic skill development for officers is dutifully noted. As is the amount of training time needed to really instill the skills in officers. There is a minimum amount of time—a sweet spot—that an officer needs to train to gain proficiency and retention of the skills. I stipulate that training is imperative. Omaha's OIS reduction program is layered on top of proper training.

I believe in never inhibiting an officer's ability to protect themselves. I am also not in denial; officers face circumstances of life and death. It is hard to fathom, but there are theoretical discussions being held on officer use of force in complete denial of the danger that officers face. Theory butts up against reality.

It is important to assume that officers face danger in order to give them the best odds to come out alive, and to help prevent them from having to use deadly force. In addition to training and policies about the proper use of force, the OIS reduction program described next can provide a road map to reducing the aggregate number of OISs.

OIS Reduction Template—with Insight

1. Full Taser deployment
2. Crisis Intervention Team and Training
3. Full body worn camera (BWC) deployment
4. Retention gap mitigators
5. Evaluate and adapt
6. Championship team culture
7. Community relations

Full Taser deployment: Full Taser deployment means that every officer working the streets is assigned a Taser. This gives every officer a less lethal option before having to go to their duty firearm (at OPD that would be a 9mm, 40, or 45 caliber Glock handgun).

Officers face a plethora of dangers every day. They must have the tools to address the dangers without always having to resort to deadly force. The Taser can be effective in replacing a handgun, not all the time, but often enough. Taser usage should reduce the aggregate number of OISs over time in a society.

An analysis of the national OIS numbers highlights this point. How often are subjects shot when they are armed with a knife or other deadly object that is not a gun or a vehicle of some sort? Of the 1,097 people shot by the police in 2022, 187 were armed with a knife, 36 had a weapon other than a gun, 135 had an unknown weapon, and 36 were unarmed according to Exhibit 1b. There is potential for OIS numbers to go down with full Taser deployment (*The Washington Post* 2022).

San Francisco was one of the last major city police departments to issue Tasers in 2018. Some leaders in the city were in denial of the dangers officers faced and thought Tasers compounded the problem. San Francisco officers were shooting homeless persons who were suffering from mental illness and armed with edged weapons at a frequency high enough to cause concern. As such, the political will to avoid Tasers morphed into an agency willing to try them. This is a perfect example of theory butting up against reality (SPUR 2018; US Department of Justice 2016).

As the number of gun seizures rises in our country, it is important to cut down on the number of OISs involving weapons other than guns or vehicles. If a vehicle is running down citizens or is otherwise used as a weapon, the Taser is of no value. But with the luxury of a proper approach, crisis intervention training, and a lethal cover officer, the Taser can be highly successful in thwarting the need for deadly force in many

BRAND DAMAGE CONTROL IN OFFICER-INVOLVED SHOOTINGS

situations. A lethal cover officer is a backup officer who has their gun out in the event the Taser does not work and deadly force becomes imminent for the protection of life.

Crisis Intervention Team and Training: I have already stipulated that training is imperative in reducing OISs, so I will not go through each training subset. However, crisis intervention training (CIT) enhances knowledge for law enforcement on how to interact with those in a mental crisis. The mental health pool in our country is deep, and officers will oftentimes be the first to encounter those in a mental health crisis. This vital training can reduce OISs over the course of time.

CIT also helps with law enforcement culture as it builds a mindset that *talk and approach* can lead to better outcomes. CIT helps officers slow down the effects of the grind they face from going to 911 call after 911 call every shift. CIT prepares an officer's mind, even before contact with someone in a mental crisis, and gives the officer guidance as to how to successfully de-escalate the encounter.

Omaha police also added a *team* component, as the contact OPD was having with those in a mental crisis was vast. A crisis intervention team is composed of mental health specialists hired to respond with Omaha officers to 911 calls involving those in a mental health crisis. The premise is that the officer responds and, when it is safe, brings in the professional mental health team member. The civilian mental health specialist then takes it from there.

At first the officers resisted the notion of a civilian working alongside them, but now they frequently call for them. Officers have seen and felt the value of the team. The death of Zachary Bearheels gave a clear push toward the need for CIT and crisis intervention teams, as he suffered from mental illness (BWC Scorecard 2016).

Full body-worn camera (BWC) deployment: Omaha police were one of the first major cities to implement full BWC deployment in 2016.

All Omaha police officers who work the street have a BWC. All uniform patrol officers responding to 911 calls, all gang detectives, and all traffic officers wear a BWC. The camera must be on during all citizen contacts. The recordings provide an impartial account of an incident. The BWC increases officer professionalism and puts a suspect on notice that their actions are recorded, reducing the probability police intervention will turn into an OIS. There is some correlation between OPD's BWC program and a reduction in Omaha's OISs.

In addition, the BWC can help law enforcement commanders in the aftermath of an OIS because they will be able to see the footage to further the OIS investigation. The BWC also lends credibility to the community, as there is an unedited version of what took place. In addition, Omaha's BWC footage cannot be erased, as digital safeguards have been put in place to prevent any erasure and edits.

The BWC is a necessary tenet of the OIS Reduction Template. While the cost of BWC storage can make it prohibitive for many law enforcement agencies, even these days, a community that can raise the funds for full BWC deployment will realize the benefits in the long run.

Retention gap mitigators: Every time a case of alleged police misconduct occurs in our country, the first response from critics is that law enforcement needs more training and must be held accountable. I can tell readers that chiefs will hold officers accountable, and training is robust. The problem in policing is retention—it is hard to get rid of problem officers.

This is the nature of government work, unions, collective bargaining agreements, and arbitrations. The purpose of the book is not to denigrate unions or the arbitration process, as officers deserve to have an appeal process. The central principle is retention. There must be a way to safeguard the public from problem officers.

Non-governmental business and law enforcement employment are not comparable sectors when talking about retention. In the private sector, it behooves the business to shave off lower-performing employees and bring in higher-producing ones. The free market drives the push since companies strive to make as much money as possible. It is not uncommon to see the private sector let go of their bottom performers, and they are able to do so because they are at-will employees.

Law enforcement often must retain their low performers because of the dynamics of arbitrations, unions, and collective bargaining agreements. For example, if a non-governmental business has a thousand employees, management may cut 10 percent a year and replace them with higher-producing hires. If a police department has a thousand officers, there is no way to unilaterally remove the lowest 10 percent performing sworn law enforcement personnel.

There must be considerable cause to terminate an officer, and the termination is not necessarily final either, as it would be in the private sector. An officer can appeal to an arbitrator in most departments, under most collective bargaining agreements across the country. There is no way to unilaterally cut the lower-performing police officers, as they are not "at-will" employees.

My legal team used to joke with me that if we could pick ten officers who were underperforming and replace them each year, policing would incredibly improve. For illustration purposes, if a law enforcement agency must retain 1 percent of its lowest performing officers in a force of a thousand officers, that is ten officers a year the agency must keep. Ten officers may sound like a small number but consider the following: if each officer has twenty citizen contacts a day, which is two hundred police encounters the public is having with a law enforcement agency's lowest performer every day.

In Omaha, if an officer has lost our trust, management will find a job for them away from physical contact with the public. The officer might be assigned to the property room, or the report call center where citizen contact is minimal. A law enforcement

BRAND DAMAGE CONTROL IN OFFICER-INVOLVED SHOOTINGS

agency owes it to its professional officers to curtail the risk of less professional officers who may harm the reputation of the agency.

Certain officers are not cut out to make split-second decisions within a use-of-force continuum. It does not mean they are *dirty* officers or have corrupt mindsets. Some officers simply should not have made it through the hiring process and police academy training.

It is important to have an Early Warning Tracking System to identify officers in need of intervention by the law enforcement agency. It is imperative that the officers who struggle with the use-of-force continuum be assigned away from citizen contact. A department's Early Warning Tracking System should support officer reassignments when warranted.

During my time as chief, I have received over forty calls where a commander informed me of an OIS. I could tell just by the name of the officer involved whether it would turn out to be a justified shooting. Fortunately, for a great amount of the time, my comfort level was high, as OPD has top-notch officers. However, there were times I cringed when told who the officer involved was. Unfortunately, it turned out I was right. It is imperative a law enforcement agency segregates problem officers in a manner to keep the public safe. It is also high time that a real problem in policing—retention—comes to the forefront of reform discussion.

Evaluate and adapt: Law enforcement leaders should constantly evaluate deadly use of force in their agency. OISs from around the country need analysis as well. Why wait to make a correction when lessons can be learned from OIS preventative measures in another state? Learn from other cities to increase your agency's learning curve. OPD sits in on every national OIS Zoom or teleconference call to learn what went right and what wrong.

A 2012 evaluation of the OPD's OISs showed an elevated number of officers shooting at moving vehicles. As a result, OPD adopted new tactics and training. The training was crafted to minimize the number of times an officer found themselves in front of a moving vehicle and facing getting run over.

The training and new tactics cut down on the number of times officers fired at moving vehicles. Of the 1,097 subjects shot and killed by the police nationally in 2022, forty-one used a vehicle as a weapon (*The Washington Post* 2022).

In the aftermath of Michael Brown's death, the usage of BWCs expanded across the country. After George Floyd's death, the duty-to-intervene doctrine was implemented into law enforcement use-of-force policies across the county. The doctrine puts the onus on officers on the scene to stop excessive use of force they may witness.

READER NOTE
Axon Enterprise is the largest company in the BWC realm. In 2012, the stock price was under $20 per share. In 2024, it was over $616 per share (https://finance.yahoo.com/quote/AXON/history).

Breonna Taylor was a 26-year-old Black female, who, in March 2020, was shot in her apartment by the Louisville Metropolitan Police (BBC 2020). She was shot during a "no-knock" search warrant. No-knock search warrants allow for the law enforcement agency to enter an abode unannounced. Law enforcement rams the door and makes an "un-knocked or unalerted entry." No-knocks give the element of surprise, increasing officer safety and preventing the destruction of evidence, such as the flushing of a narcotic.

Law enforcement agencies across the country reevaluated their use of the no-knock search warrants in the aftermath of Breonna's death. Constant evaluation and adaptations need to take place to address trends in OISs.

Championship team culture: Championship team culture refers to the ideal culture for a law enforcement agency. In the early 1980s, law enforcement executives defended their officers to the extreme. BWCs and videos of any kind were nonexistent, leaving law enforcement executives with "he-said-she-said" scenarios and no independent video evidence. The executives would side with the law enforcement officer's version, as that was all they had to go on. The law enforcement dynamic in the 1980s was a culture of little accountability.

In the 2000s, law enforcement executives started to hold their officers accountable. The progression of professionalism took another stride forward. Strong law enforcement executives should also defend their officers, as the vast amount of time the officer's actions are justified. Since the OPD mandated full BWC deployment in 2016, I can say the camera footage exonerates the officer almost 95 percent of the time. OPD officers resisted the wearing of BWCs on initial implementation, but now officers will refuse to work without one.

The Championship team mindset is the next progression in professional law enforcement. Championship teams have players who are team leaders, and the players hold each other accountable. The coach does not necessarily have to intervene, as the players address problems among themselves in the pursuit of a championship.

A law enforcement agency can have a Championship team culture, empowering officers to hold each other accountable. Law enforcement commanders will hold problem officers accountable; when a Championship team culture forms, problems get solved at the ground level before they can reach the supervisor's desk. This type of culture is perfectly suited for professional law enforcement, and I believe it will reduce

BRAND DAMAGE CONTROL IN OFFICER-INVOLVED SHOOTINGS

OISs over time as the agency strives for professionalism. Law enforcement agencies should strive to reach the Championship team level in the progression toward professional law enforcement.

Community relations: Community relations play a role in the reduction of OISs. A city with strong law enforcement–community relations will have fewer per capita OISs over time than a city with struggles in this area. Community relations, therefore, are critical to reducing the aggregate number of OISs in a city. When a law enforcement agency views its citizens as partners and a community sees its officers as guardians, it is a powerful concoction.

In Omaha, for the last fifteen years, representatives from the community and OPD have met every Wednesday to go over crime trends and to resolve any relational matters. The sustained frequency of the meetings prevents problems from festering. All relationships will have rocky moments. Law enforcement and community relationships are no different. Omaha has half a million population and has over nine hundred officers, so it is a population certainty that there will be policing issues to address. Having a mechanism to address the issues head-on and right away is key to healthy police–community relationships.

Critical Media Strategy—Officer-Involved Shootings

How a law enforcement agency manages an OIS is integral to community relations and to the agency's professional officers. Dealing with the media after an OIS is often an afterthought, but it needs to be a forethought. Lack of preparation in managing the situation with the media can make an impressive law enforcement agency appear very ordinary. A professional law enforcement agency owes it to its community and employees to give a complete, timely, and transparent account of the OIS. It also owes it the nationwide profession of policing because an agency's OIS could become national news, and that reflects on other agencies across the country as well.

The Michael Brown OIS in Ferguson, Missouri, was national news and did not reflect well on the policing profession. OISs carry a social weight in our country, and law enforcement agencies should enact their critical media strategy as soon as one occurs (Hutchinson 2023).

The critical media strategy OPD uses for OISs has served the agency well within its own community and nationally. The formula for OPD's strategy is presented here as an instrument for learning, and it covers the period during, after, and beyond an OIS. It is a population certainty that OISs will happen; therefore, preparation in advance is indispensable.

SYNERGY *of* INFLUENCE

OIS Media Formula:
1. Assign duties
2. Instant social media
3. Alert community partners and trusted messengers
4. OIS investigation—immersive, transparent, and unbiased
5. An on-scene statement within an hour of the incident
6. Policing press conference (PPC)
7. Updated media releases
8. Community follow-up

Each of the eight formula points is covered as a learning exercise. Real-world examples are included in each formula point. It is up to each law enforcement agency to adopt, adapt, or add to the formula based on their unique circumstances with the media and community.

Assign duties: As soon as there is word of a confirmed OIS, assignments are given out. Through my experience, I have learned the following areas need a higher-level commander or a deputy chief (not all departments name each rank the same).

A) *OIS Investigation:* To oversee all aspects and coordination.
B) *Hospital:* In an OIS, there is at least one subject shot. There could be multiple suspects shot, and an officer could be injured or killed. The hospital is also a place where tensions are high. The suspect's family and friends, as well as law enforcement, will all be in the same place. Witnesses and other suspects may be present. The hospital is an extension of the OIS investigation, and a high-level commander should be assigned.

    In Omaha, there are two trauma centers, both of extreme medical prowess. The trauma centers alternate as the positioned trauma center for the day. If two rival gangs receive injured parties in a shooting, both sides will likely go to the same trauma emergency center.
C) *Family:* If an officer is shot, a commander or a co-worker officer should be assigned to the family. The family will have unique needs during this trying time, and the agency should be there to assist.
D) *Internal Affairs:* An OIS is an on-duty incident. The incident will need to be investigated criminally and internally by internal affairs.
E) *Media:* The press will be all over an OIS event, both at the scene and via social media. A commander needs to oversee these aspects as part of a critical media strategy. Policies, procedures, training, and practical "tabletop exercises" can instill preparedness.

BRAND DAMAGE CONTROL IN OFFICER-INVOLVED SHOOTINGS

F) *Community:* A commander should reach out to community partners, inform them of the OIS, and establish a point of contact as the situation unfolds. Community partners are salient to controlling rumors, as there is a direct link to the law enforcement agency; this can have a censorious function if there is controversy around the OIS.

As mentioned in Chapter One, in the societal monumental event related to Kerrie Orozco, community partner Pastor Greg Ashley was instrumental in dispelling a rumor. Gunfire-injured Officer Kerrie Orozco and the OIS suspect were both taken to the same hospital. An untrue rumor began to circulate that OPD had shut down the ER to all other patients. Pastor Ashley was able to dispel the rumor, as he had firsthand knowledge this was not the case.

Instant social media: The first communication to the public from the department will be through social media: Twitter (now called X) and Facebook. The PIO should instantly notify the community and press through social media and press release of the location of the OIS, with directions to stay clear of the area, as it is now a crime scene. Inform the community. The law enforcement agency will keep the press updated, and foremost, the only official source of information will come from the law enforcement agency PIO or executive.

Street rumors, speculation, and innuendo form in the aftermath of an OIS. A succinct social media message followed by a press release goes a long way toward curtailing the spread of the side talk.

Alert community partners and trusted messengers: Every community policing agency will have a network of community partners. It is prudent to notify community partners when an OIS occurs. Law enforcement agency community partners can assist in getting the agency's message out, dispelling rumors, and giving the public another avenue to ask questions. Notifying community partners is a layer of transparent communication befitting a partner.

OIS Investigation—immersive, transparent, and unbiased: The law enforcement executive should immerse themself in the investigation for knowledge, not as a micromanager. I would show my support to the investigators at the scene, get an initial briefing, and see the layout of where the OIS occurred. I would then receive briefings as the investigation unfolded, followed by a full-scale wrap-up presentation by the investigating detectives.

It is extremely important the agency executive has a mastery of the investigation for the press conference to follow. Complete knowledge of the investigation will also give the executive confidence when answering questions at the press conference. Complete knowledge is a function of being an executive, especially on critical events facing the agency.

An on-scene statement within an hour of the incident: An on-scene presser is prescribed with a critical media strategy. It is critical to get an early message to the public. Refer to Chapter Six: Law Enforcement Critical Media Strategy (B)—Mastering Policing Press Conferences for details.

Policing press conference (PPC): A PPC, as part of an agency's critical media strategy, will give a full account of the OIS. Refer to Chapter Six: Law Enforcement Critical Media Strategy (B)—Mastering Policing Press Conferences for details.

Updated media releases: Update the media regularly with press releases and social media supplements. Common supplements are the name of the officer, how long the officer has been on the force, and the name of the suspect. Another example is when and where the PPC will be held. If the information is verifiable and confirmed, an agency can release it after an evaluation of the benefit of doing so.

Community follow-up: Update the community; they were your partners prior to the OIS and will be again after. The law enforcement executive and commanders should be available to attend public sessions to answer questions and explain the OIS. All relationships have rocky moments. The police and community's relationship will be no different. It is compassionate and vital to have a mechanism to work through issues that affect the police and the community; this is usually done at the public session.

In Omaha, the chief and senior commanders will attend the weekly Empowerment Network 360 community group meeting, which gathers every Wednesday at 2:00 p.m. The meetings have evolved into a place where community members can get direct answers from the police command. Having a place for the community to go with their concerns has made an enormous impact on police–community relations.

Conclusion

It is imperative for law enforcement agencies to curtail the occurrence of OIS incidents for the preservation of human life, cultivation of positive community relations, and safeguarding of the agency's reputation. Despite significant waves of reform in 2015 and 2022, the escalation of OIS incidents remains a concerning national trend. Intriguingly, a simultaneous upsurge in the retrieval of firearms by law enforcement underscores a correlation between heightened OIS rates and increased gun seizures on a national scale.

Navigating the aftermath of an OIS mandates the activation of a well-prepared critical media strategy. Providing an influential, transparent, and timely account to the media regarding the OIS becomes a crucial therapeutic step for the affected community. The OIS Media Formula, which has been introduced in this chapter, serves as an invaluable guide for law enforcement agencies in times of OIS-related challenges.

BRAND DAMAGE CONTROL IN OFFICER-INVOLVED SHOOTINGS

Striving to diminish the cumulative count of OIS incidents within society is not only a noble pursuit but also a hallmark of professionalism within law enforcement. The adaptable nature of the OIS Reduction Template renders it an indispensable resource for agencies seeking to enact positive change. The success achieved by OPD in reducing OIS incidents over a decade underscores the potency of adhering to the principles outlined within the OIS Reduction Template.

Self-Assessment Questions

Attempt to answer the following questions before looking up the answers at the back of the book.

1. True or False: The rise in OISs across the country has a correlation with the rise in gun seizures by law enforcement.
2. True or False: There is a vast array of research and papers on the media portion of an OIS.
3. True or False: There has been a standard guide in existence for years on how to reduce OISs in a society.
4. True or False: More people were killed by American law enforcement in 2022 than in any other year in the past decade.
5. True or False: It is impossible to reduce the overall number of OISs, as each OIS is circumstance-based.
6. Why is it important to reduce the number of OISs on citizens not armed with a gun?
7. How does full Taser deployment reduce OISs over time?
8. True or False: The OIS Reduction Template cannot be changed.
9. True or False: The national databases on the number of OISs and gun seizures are spotty.
10. What is positional asphyxia?

CHAPTER EIGHT

Race, Police, and Media— Unraveling the Puzzle

In this chapter, we delve into the intricate dynamics of race within the realm of American law enforcement, shedding light on the factors that shape this complex landscape. By the end of this chapter, readers will have gained a comprehensive understanding of why race remains a crucial determinant in law enforcement practices, as well as the divergent perspectives held by Black and White communities.

Exploring Racial Disparities in Policing: We aim to comprehend the deep-rooted reasons behind the integration of race in American policing. Readers will not only grasp the historical underpinnings but also discern the ramifications that lead to a disproportionate number of encounters between Black citizens and law enforcement.

Challenging Misconceptions and Diverse Viewpoints: Delving further, we confront prevailing misconceptions about Black communities that have permeated our societal fabric through media coverage. Through a discerning lens, readers will decipher why divergent viewpoints exist between Black and White communities, drawing from historical and present-day disparities.

Analyzing the Influence of Race: As we navigate through various scenarios, readers will gain a profound insight into how race manifests as a consequential factor in law enforcement encounters. We will explore phenomena that arise in such encounters: 1) the "prove it to me" mentality 2) the "hands up" phenomenon, 3) critique by comparison, and 4) machination possibility.

Equipped for Critical Analysis: Upon completing this chapter, readers will possess the tools to critically assess law enforcement encounters regarding race. Readers will be adept at identifying the presence and impact of race as a determinant, sifting through evidence and nuances to draw informed conclusions.

This chapter is designed to equip readers with the insights needed to navigate the intricate interplay of race in American policing.

SYNERGY *of* INFLUENCE

"Race Is a Factor"

It was the summer of 1998, and I had been a police officer for two years, having come onto the OPD in 1996. In the embryo stage of my career, I was assigned to the highest crime area of the city on the evening shift (3:00 p.m. to 11:00 p.m.). My partner and I, both from the same academy class, worked in North Omaha in a Baker car. A Baker car is a two-officer patrol unit. Baker cars respond to disturbances and higher crime calls because there are two officers. The 911 calls would come in all night long, so we tried to "churn and burn" them; meaning, resolve the matter and go on to the next citizen in need.

It was an action-packed time in my career, and my partner and I both enjoyed collaborating with the community. North Omaha was good to us, and we were professional, respectful, and productive. Some nights we would mediate disputes from call to call. On other nights, we would try and talk to the community to make friends. Then on other nights, we would arrest felons in high-speed chases. We did it all, and every evening was different.

North Omaha, for those not familiar with the city of Omaha, Nebraska, is an African American community. North Omaha is rich in history and accomplishment, and many famous Black Americans such as Gale Sayers, Mildred Brown, Bob Gibson, Johnny Rodgers, Ernie Chambers, and, most recently, world champion boxer Terence Crawford, come from there. Malcolm X was born in Omaha. Lesser known nationally, but nonetheless very impressive leaders representing North Omaha are individuals such as Willie Barney, Robert Wagner, Ben Gray, Preston Love Jr., D'Shawn Cunningham, Teela Mickles, Chris Rodgers, Leo Louis, Chrome, Vicki Young, T. Michael Williams, Bryan Riley, Terrell McKinney, Justin Wayne, Tamika Mease, Willie Hamilton, Barbara Robinson, and the Interdenominational Ministerial Alliance, to name some.

During my tenure as chief, North Omaha has been my favorite sector of Omaha's diverse city. Insightful leaders, genuine people, and a passion for improving the quality of life in the area have made my time as chief enjoyable and sublime. The progress we have made together through reductions in shootings, homicides, and police complaints has made a substantial difference in the betterment of North Omaha.

Omaha's homicide clearance rate is a symbolic measure of how well the police and the community work together. OPD has averaged an 84 percent clearance over the course of a decade. A lot of major cities would love to hit 50 percent. In 2023, Omaha had a 100 percent clearance rate for homicides (twenty-eight homicides—twenty-six cleared in 2023, plus two homicides cleared from previous years—equaling 100 percent). A less formal measure of the cooperation among police and community is that community members call me all the time, and I will remain friends with them after I retire.

RACE, POLICE, AND MEDIA—UNRAVELING THE PUZZLE

I offer the following as a story indicative of this positive relationship: Two grassroots North Omaha community members, D'Shawn Cunningham, and Robert Wagner, protested my 2012 appointment to chief, interrupting the swearing-in ceremony. More than a decade later, I attended Robert Wagner's wedding, and I do meet with D'Shawn Cunningham on occasion. Each of us has proven ourselves, and through common goals and a healthy acknowledgment of each other's talents, they have become two people whom I hold in tremendous regard.

Back to the summer of 1998. One evening, my partner was off work for the shift, so I was assigned to work as a single-officer police car. This meant I would be taking some report calls, helping at bigger events, and responding to calls with other officers. My very first call, as I pulled out of the police station, was for an abandoned vehicle.

As I pulled into the neighborhood, I came across the abandoned vehicle and ran a check on it; the car had been stolen. I knocked on a few doors to see if anyone had seen where the car had come from, and I ordered a tow truck to get it. While waiting for the tow, I spoke with two elderly Black females on a porch, who had been good-naturedly teasing me.

As I was walking back to my police cruiser to wait for the tow truck, one of the elderly ladies yelled, "Look out!" I spun around, and there was a full-grown Doberman Pinscher dog jumping and biting at my neck. I pedaled back as fast as I could, and with the fortune of being twenty-five years old, I was able to avoid a bite taken out of my neck.

The Doberman was barking aggressively, salivating, biting, and jumping, trying to get at my neck. The animal was fixated on my neck and did not try to bite me anywhere else. With no other choice at my disposal, I pulled out my handgun and shot one time. The shot was six inches away from the Doberman. I shot the dog off my gun at chest level, as it was mid-jump and going for my neck. The dog whelped, stopped instantly, and ran back to the fenced yard it had come from.

I gathered myself from the sudden jolt of adrenaline and went to check on the animal. The dog was on the verge of dying. It was lying there, no longer aggressive and panting its last breaths. I wanted to put the dog out of its misery, but it was dying fast, and I did not want to scale the fence into someone's backyard and fire another round at the animal. I felt horrible about having to shoot the dog. It had been an unnecessary twist for towing a stolen car, but that is police work; one never knows what will come up.

Everyone in the all-Black neighborhood heard the gunshot and made their way outside, including the irate Doberman owner. From his perception, the dog was in its own backyard.

"How did my dog get shot?"

I explained the situation, and the owner was not having it, even though there was an obvious hole in the fence. The routine stolen-vehicle tow call was turning on me fast. Good people were irate, and I was the symbolic focus.

Many neighbors were outside, yelling at me for unjustifiably shooting the dog. None of them witnessed what transpired but were rapidly spreading rumors. The elderly females tried to explain to the crowd that the dog attacked the officer from behind in the street. The crowd did not want to hear it. I motioned my thanks to the elderly ladies and that it was OK to not get involved. I did not want them to be on the outs with their neighbors. I would eventually leave the call, but they lived there. The crowd grew hostile, and the anger toward me was boiling over. The slightest provocation was going to incite the crowd.

READER REFLECTION
Police departments routinely ask communities to help by stepping forward with information related to crimes, and I have even seen them chide a community for not doing so after a serious crime is committed. This is a completely myopic stance in my opinion. Consider this: If there is a shooting at a store, nowhere near your residence, with strangers, it is easy to step up and become a witness. When the shooting is down the street from where you live, and involves acquaintances seen in your daily travels, it is not so easy to get involved. Law enforcement agencies should realize this dynamic and tailor their requests for witnesses to come forward with information on how they can come forward in a safe or anonymous fashion. Failure to do so appears out of touch. Why would a witness come forward to help an agency that is not sensitive to this?

I radioed for more officers to come assist, and I pulled my police car to the end of the street. I wanted distance plus time to allow things to cool down, and there was no immediate crime I needed to tend to. Once the tow truck arrived, I followed it back in and stayed until the car was towed. Other officers arrived to assist, and we left just in time. The crowd was almost riotous over the dog that died at the hands of a White police officer.

The very next night, as if scripted for this book, a Black Omaha officer shot and killed a dog in West Omaha, where the population is predominantly White. The officer was lauded as a hero. I watched the news coverage, and all the White neighbors were thanking the Black officer. I will never forget the irony.

There was a complete acceptance that the Black officer had saved the day. Yet, in my circumstance, belief was hard to come by. My version of the dog escaping its backyard and attacking me was met with anger and disbelief. Even though it was clear the fence was broken and with two credible witnesses.

READER DISCUSSION
A White police officer kills a dog in a Black neighborhood. The outcome was a near riot. A Black officer does the same in a White neighborhood and is a hero. Was race a factor? Was mistrust of the police in play? Discuss.

This chapter will dissect the role of race in law enforcement and the media. An understanding of the differing perspectives between Black and White citizens is vital for tailoring a media message in law enforcement. When race is a factor, magnified insight is necessary when communicating with the media. Details of the magnified insight are explained in this chapter. There are also common misconceptions about race this chapter will anatomize. The chapter will end with a dissection of race as a factor or as evidence in some of the nation's highest-profile civilian deaths by law enforcement.

Race is emotional, polarizing, and a media darling.

Race is a scorching hot topic when combined with law enforcement. Victims of police misconduct are household names, and controversial police encounters rule the news cycles. Race and law enforcement in combination have given rise to the Black Lives Matter (BLM) movement (Lebron 2018). Civil rights activists and attorneys have become famous figures; Benjamin Crump and Al Sharpton are names nearly everyone in America is familiar with (Ben Crump Law, n.d.; CNN, 2021; The History Makers, n.d.; National Action Network, n.d.). The national media is eager to report on possible police misconduct or skewed judgment where race could be a factor because ratings soar on racial debates. The subject of race is wide-reaching, hitting every demographic for ratings, as every citizen in America can offer an opinion. When race and law enforcement are combined, a compelling story emerges, and polarizing viewpoints become fabulous fodder for talk shows.

Emotion and anger can never change the facts and become evidence, no matter how much dust is stirred up through media coverage. Our system of justice and jurisprudence would collapse under this fallacy. However, pressure works to a degree. The goal of some protests is to project anger and an inconsolable front so as to turn outrage into evidence. Anger is not evidence, but it draws attention to a subject. Race is not evidence on its surface, but it is a huge factor in American policing.

Race can certainly become evidence based on crime facts and the investigation, but anger cannot ever be allowed to speak as evidence. An understanding of the differing perspectives between Black and White citizens should galvanize a law enforcement agency's media message.

As a young officer, I assimilated race matters and committed myself to understanding the dynamics, as best as I could, as a White police officer. One dynamic I learned makes perfect sense and is understandable and reasonable based on historical and current experiences of a race.

Black communities want to know the branch of government (law enforcement) in place to protect them does not harm them because of race.

Historically, law enforcement in America has not been kind to Black people. With such history, dating back to law enforcement assisting with rounding up slaves, it makes perfect sense why Black citizens in our country have a "prove it to me" mentality on law enforcement encounters, especially when the situation involves the use of deadly force by the law enforcement agency. They want proof that their government (law enforcement) did not factor in race before making the decision to shoot, use force, or make an arrest. Fewer than one in five Black Americans feel confident that law enforcement in their area will treat them well. This could stem from a historical perspective of American law enforcement, their own negative experience, or familiarity with a person they know who had a negative experience (Drakulich et al. 2023; NAACP, n.d.; Pew Research Center 2022; Reichel 1988; Saad 2020).

White Americans, on the other hand, start out with acceptance that law enforcement was justified in making the arrest or shooting the suspect. In a poll conducted by Gallup Corporation (2020), 91 percent of White Americans say they are at least somewhat confident the police would treat them well. White Americans need convincing that law enforcement erred (Pew Research Center 2022). The White officer who shot the dog in a Black neighborhood could not get his version of events to be believed. The Black officer who shot a dog in a White neighborhood had instant acceptance and was lauded as a hero.

Why do White citizens accept law enforcement actions as valid at first sight? Why are Black citizens skeptical at first appearance? When factoring in the history of American policing, it is easy to understand Black Americans' "prove it to me" mentality. In the same vein, I surmise it is easy to understand why White Americans start with belief and acceptance of law enforcement actions in our country.

A look at the racial demographics of officer-involved shooting (OIS) national data should provide some insight. Does the data suggest that a "prove it to me" mentality is still warranted by Black citizens? I have elected to use OIS demographic data to illustrate my point, as OISs are often the greatest cause of breakdowns in police–community relations. This is true especially in urban areas, and especially when the subject is Black. OISs highlight the "prove it to me" thought process, and these situations can

RACE, POLICE, AND MEDIA—UNRAVELING THE PUZZLE

offer insight into the biggest perceptual differences between Black and White citizens, which makes the data salient to our learning.

Disclaimer:
- All White people and Black people do not think alike as a group. When factoring in socioeconomic conditions, where a person grows up, what school(s) they attend, and a host of other factors, people will have differing and individualized viewpoints. In addition, America is a melting pot, and a citizen could be of mixed race, so any wide-sweeping statements about groupthink are fallible.
- The chapter focuses on Black and White citizen perspectives and the disproportionality of their interactions with the police. Other races are not the focus of this chapter, as the treatment of Black citizens in the United States has brought substantial reform movements; nonetheless, all races are important and deserve impartial treatment from law enforcement. The 1960s, 1990s, and the era between 2015 and 2020 all saw major calls for police reforms because of the treatment of Black Americans.
- The chapter is designed to stimulate conversation through data, experiences, and layers of insight rarely or never talked about before. Through discussion of these matters, it is intended for readers to become more informed and to galvanize a higher level of discussion about race, law enforcement, and media.

Officer-Involved Shootings and Race

In Chapter Seven—Brand Damage Control in Officer-Involved Shootings, we explored how OISs are on the rise in America and how major cities are struggling with the increases. The data is shocking, as substantial policing reforms have taken place following the deaths of Black citizens Michael Brown in 2015 and George Floyd in 2020. The prediction and goal of the reform movements was to decrease disproportionality and the number of OISs as a micro subset. However, the prediction was faulty, as the disproportionality and total number of OISs remain intact.

Chapter Seven demonstrated the correlation between the rise in OISs and the rise in gun seizures. The two are going up in tandem nationally, and it is reasonable to assume a correlation. As the number of guns on the streets increases, the likelihood of OISs will also increase. In Omaha, gun seizures are at an all-time high, but there is no correlation between gun seizures and OISs. Omaha is on a divergent track from the rest of the country.

The OIS data in Chapter Seven did not dissect the potential role of race in these shootings. Historically, Black citizens have been shot by the police at a disproportionate rate in the United States. Are Black Americans, in current times, still being shot more often by the police? Or have OISs among the races become more proportional over the

SYNERGY *of* INFLUENCE

years? If it is still disproportional, what is the common justification to account for it? For this chapter, we are most concerned with whether there is still a disproportionality present today between Black and White Americans. A look at the OIS numbers will help answer the questions posed above.

United States Officer-Involved Shooting Racial Data

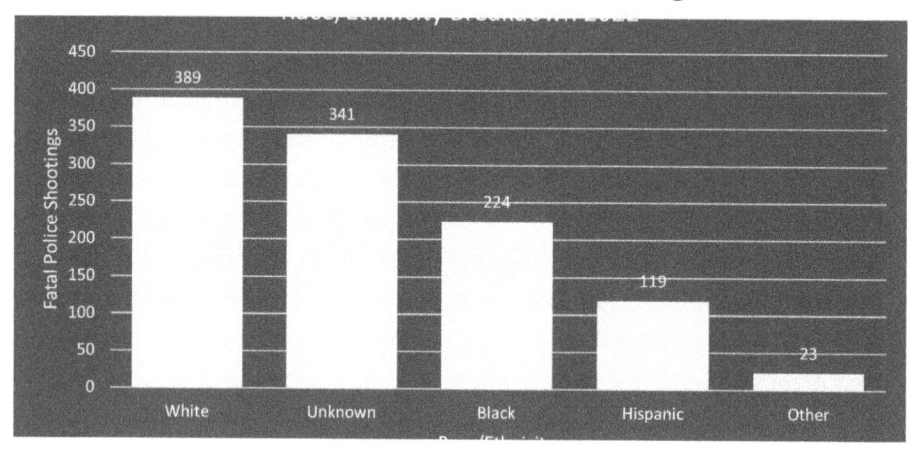

[Bar chart showing Fatal Police Shootings by Race/Ethnicity: White 389, Unknown 341, Black 224, Hispanic 119, Other 23]

Graphic: Omaha Police
United States Officer-Involved Shooting Racial Data
Source: *Washington Post*
Exhibit 1

The United States Fatal Police Shootings 2015–2023 YTD Racial Breakdown

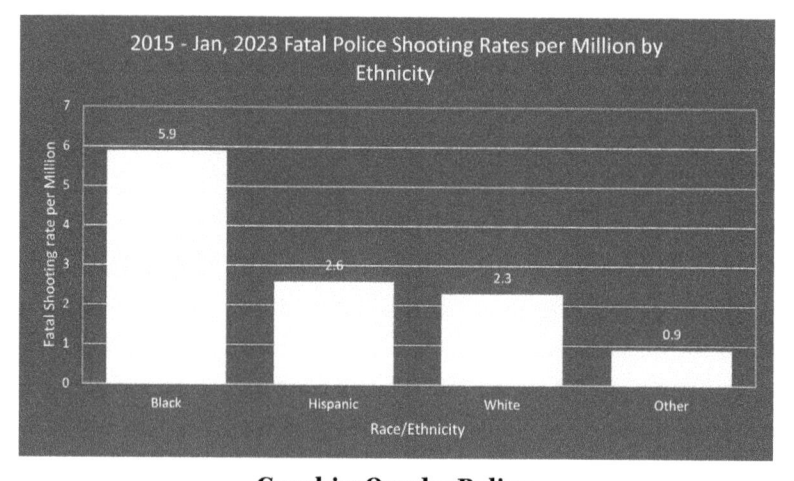

[Bar chart showing 2015 - Jan, 2023 Fatal Police Shooting Rates per Million by Ethnicity: Black 5.9, Hispanic 2.6, White 2.3, Other 0.9]

Graphic: Omaha Police
The United States Fatal Police Shootings 2015–2023 YTD Racial Breakdown
Source: *Washington Post*
Exhibit 2

To determine if there is still disproportionality in police behavior between the races, the data must be examined on multiple levels. I chose to look at fatal OISs, as these would theoretically cause the most harm to race relations and heighten the "prove it to me" mentality. There were 1,097 people shot and killed by the police in America in 2022. Of those killed that year, 224 were Black citizens. A look at Exhibit 2 shines a spotlight on disproportionality.

From 2014 to 2023, Black people were shot by law enforcement at a rate of 5.9 per one million and Whites at a rate of only 2.3 per one million. Even though 5.9 and 2.3 are incredibly small numbers and a person is just as likely to have a shark encounter, there is no overlooking the fact that the rate for Black Americans is more than double that of White Americans; Black Americans are 2.57 times more likely to be shot by the police. Black Americans continue to be shot by law enforcement at a staggeringly disproportionate rate.

Based on OIS death demographics, the "prove it to me" mindset of Black Americans is prudent and makes legitimate sense. In addition, many police chiefs today have the same mindset. To this day, the statistics surrounding police use of deadly force are disproportionately skewed against Black Americans. The "prove it to me" mentality essentially belies the fact Black citizens want to know that the training, policies, and culture of a law enforcement agency are strong, and that bias does not impact the way law enforcement is enacted. Many major city police chiefs share this sentiment, giving credence to the "prove it to me" stance.

Why Are Black Americans Shot and Killed More Often by Law Enforcement?

Why are Black Americans shot and killed more by law enforcement? The common answer is that Black people are more likely to live in areas of greater poverty, which is where most crime takes place, drawing in the most law enforcement officers. When there are more law enforcement officers working in Black communities, the number of encounters with the police will increase, increasing the chances of being shot.

This response is true on some fronts. Law enforcement officers will be assigned based on the number of crimes and victims in each area. In Omaha, North Omaha has historically had the highest concentration of officers assigned based on crime trends. But the "higher concentration of officers" excuse does not fully account for the more-than-double likelihood of Black people being shot by the police. Further examination will show that poverty (higher crime) areas cannot be the sole determinant for the disproportionate rate of law enforcement shootings involving Black citizens.

More Black Citizens are Shot while Unarmed than White Citizens

An alarming present-day statistic is that more Black citizens are shot while unarmed than White citizens (*The Washington Post* 2022). More than one thousand unarmed people were killed due to police action between the years of 2013 to 2019 (Police Violence Report, n.d.). One-third were Black (Mapping Police Violence, n.d.). Furthering the point, the fatal rate of police shootings of unarmed Black citizens in America was more than three times as high as it is among White citizens between 2015 and 2020 (Ethical Legal Data Science 2020; United States Census Bureau 2019).

According to the 2019 US Census, 60 percent of the population is White, while only 13 percent are Black. When you consider this demographic in the light of how many unarmed people were killed by police, we see a disproportionate effect on Black citizens: 45 percent of the unarmed subjects were White, while 25 percent were Black.

If the experiences of Black and White citizens were the same, we would expect only 13 percent of police-shooting victims to be Black and 60 percent to be White. However, we see a much lower number, proportionally, for White citizens and a much higher number for Black citizens. Therefore, a higher concentration of officers in areas affected by poverty cannot be the sole reason for Black OIS disproportionality.

Omaha Police OIS Data: From 2010 to 2022, there were sixty-two OISs at the OPD. The subject was White in twenty-five of those shootings, twenty-six were Black, seven were Hispanic, two were Native American, one Asian, and one was "other race." For a percentage breakdown, see the table below.

Omaha Police OIS Percentages by Race 2010–2023
- 40 percent White
- 42 percent Black
- 11 percent Hispanic
- 6 percent Native American, Asian, and Other Race combined

*Percentages were rounded; without the rounding, the total for all is 100 percent.

The Black population in Omaha is a little over 12 percent, the Hispanic population is a little over 14 percent, and the white population is about 66 percent (United States Census Bureau, 2023).

In Omaha, the racial disproportionality is obvious: Black people were the subject of 42 percent of OPD's OISs while comprising only 12 percent of the population. White people accounted for 40 percent of OPD's OISs while representing 66 percent of the population.

RACE, POLICE, AND MEDIA—UNRAVELING THE PUZZLE

READER NOTE
For purposes of the analysis, *unarmed* means that the subject shot by Omaha police did not have a gun and was not using a knife (or other hand weapon not a gun) or car as a weapon; this is same as the national OIS standard.

Omaha Police Officer-Involved Shootings
2010–2023 Racial Breakdown

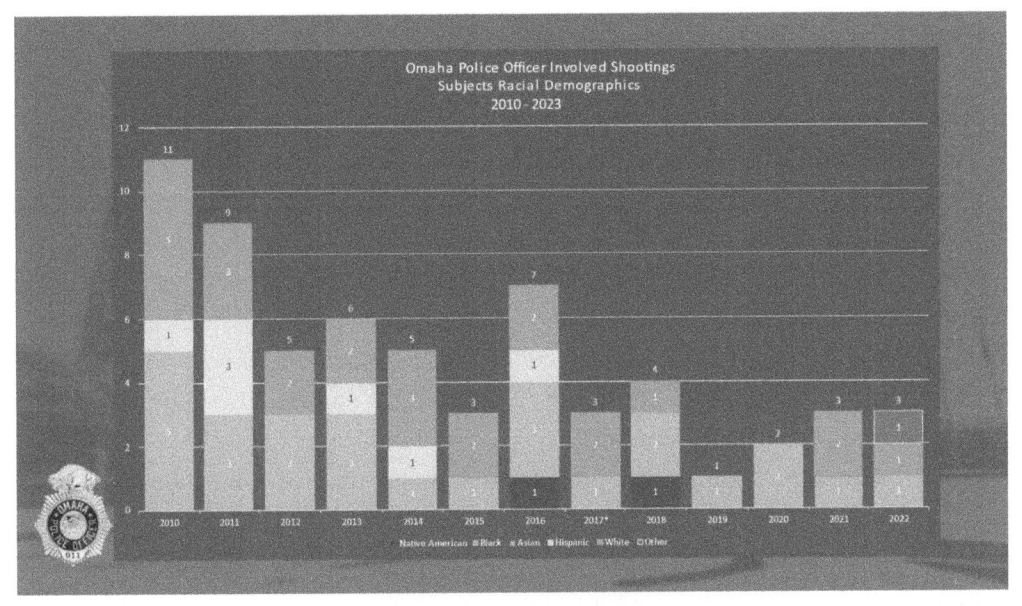

Graphic: Omaha Police

From 2014–2024, Omaha Police have shot three unarmed men. In 2015, a White, unarmed male named Danny Elrod was shot. In 2018, a White, unarmed male named Dillon Trejo was shot, although he acted as if he had a gun with his movements. In 2024, a Hispanic male named Jonathan Hernandez-Rosales was shot as an unarmed front seat passenger when the driver leaned over Hernandez-Rosales and fired a gun out the passenger window at a crowd. OPD has not shot an unarmed Black person since George Bibens was shot in 2000. Omaha has been in defiance of the national trend, where, of those shot while unarmed, 14.8 percent were Black Americans and 9.4 percent were White.

Disclaimer

On August 28th, 2024, two days before the scheduled release of this book, Omaha police shot and killed a Black male named Cameron Ford. The OPD SWAT team was serving a *"no-knock" search warrant at Ford's residence when he was shot one time and killed by OPD. Ford was unarmed. In one incident, Omaha police ended the impressive run of not killing an unarmed Black citizen. The investigation into the incident is ongoing at the time of publication for this book. I encourage the reader to look up the results on the internet.*

Black Communities Will Accept and Recognize Policing Improvements

In response to the OPD's reduction in OISs, Omaha's Black community has accepted and recognized the improvements in policing in the city. OPD has gained strides with our Black community, and in return community relations have improved. The "prove it to me" mentality accepts the facts and effort. The "prove it to me" mentality is functionally fair, as Black communities will acknowledge and recognize concrete proof of policing improvements.

Black communities want to know that the branch of government put in place to protect them will not harm them because of race, and they want this fact supported by data. When the data shows an improvement in policing, Omaha's Black community has acknowledged it. This leads me to the statement, "Black communities have an understandable feel for policing in America."

Black communities want police presence, but they want professional and unbiased policing. This is a stance that reflects the position of many major city chiefs who have spent their educational and professional lives studying policing. According to polls, 81 percent of Black communities want the police to spend the same or more time in their area (Saad 2020; Withrow 2023). Black communities recognize the need for law enforcement—but they will also maintain their "prove it to me" mentality. However, when it is proven by data that law enforcement will be conducted without bias, Black communities accept the proof. This is fair enough from my perspective, and many major city chiefs of police agree.

Why Is There Disproportionality in Unarmed OISs?

Why is there a heavy disproportion of unarmed Black citizens shot by the police? This question raises a host of further qualifying questions about this topic. Let us address them:

- Do some Black citizens distrust the police so much that it causes them to act more aggressively with the police, as any person would do under perceived duress?

- Are some law enforcement officers more fearful of Black people, leading to more unarmed shootings?
- Is there subconscious or overt bias on the part of law enforcement?
- Can an argument still be made that a larger amount of police in high-crime areas is the reason?
- Or is it a combination of all the above?

Let us add one more variable discussed in a leadership class at which I was presenting.

In August 2023, I was a featured presenter for the DC Police Leadership Academy. The academy draws in law enforcement commanders from around the world to prepare future law enforcement leaders. The class was cross-sectional and large, with seventy-five commanders in the class. The class commanders theorized that law enforcement officers are not used to policing in Black communities and that policing in Black communities is a specialty in policing. In short, urban poverty areas require highly professional and experienced law enforcement officers—officers who have gained a cultural understanding of the community.

According to the class discussion, Black citizens are generally more energized in their manner of communication. Black people are more dynamic than White people in their communication styles, and someone not used to this kind of interaction could perceive a *threat* to the officer, when there is no threat. Talking loudly and using strong body movements are less typically a hallmark of White communities, as a Black community often expresses themselves in a livelier fashion. One basic question was thrown out by the class, which is hard to ignore: "How could a white rookie police officer possibly understand an urban Black community and know how to police it?"

Golden Opportunity

The class's opinion at the police leadership academy lends strong credence to the value of diversity in law enforcement. A diverse law enforcement agency will not only have a better understanding of different viewpoints, but employing a diversity of officers provides opportunities for setting an example of how to communicate and understand different communities. It is ideal for a law enforcement agency to be reflective of the community it serves.

Law enforcement agencies across the country are hemorrhaging employees amid a national staffing crisis. Since 2020, law enforcement agencies have struggled with a decreasing applicant pool and an increase in veteran officers leaving the profession. Historically, law enforcement enjoyed high application numbers and retention of veteran officers. The new dynamic of low applicant numbers in combination with lower

SYNERGY of INFLUENCE

retention of veterans has had a debilitating effect on the profession and the communities law enforcement serves.

An excellent opportunity exists right now for major law enforcement agencies to expedite an increase in diversity within their departments. Increasing diversity in a major law enforcement agency has traditionally been a *crawl*. It happens slowly and only when there is an intentional push. Law enforcement agencies operating at full strength find it difficult to increase diversity, as the number of new hires amounts to a "drop in the bucket."

For example, OPD increased its number of Black officers in the agency, but it took ten years to go from 7 percent to 10 percent. The annual academy classes only accounted for a small percentage, so the needle of diversity was hard to move. If an agency has a thousand officers and puts on a class of forty recruits every year to replace retirements and other vacancies, it will take decades to meaningfully increase the agency's diversity. Conversely, if an agency has an authorized strength of a thousand officers and puts on two recruit academy classes of sixty (120 total) because the agency is down 12–15 percent of its workforce, there is an opportunity to change the demographics of the agency very quickly. What would have normally been three years of hires can now be done in one year.

READER NOTE:
There are no guarantees law enforcement applications will increase; however, I believe they will. The OPD used to have nearly two thousand applicants per year, but in 2021 it was down to 375. However, there are signs the profession is making a comeback:
1. **Pay is rising in the profession across the country. Officer shortages have stimulated the free market of America, and pay is being increased to attract new recruits.**
2. **Student enrollment in the University of Nebraska at Omaha's (UNO) Criminal Justice program is near its all-time high. The UNO Criminal Justice program is a strong "feeder" to law enforcement agencies in the Omaha metro area.**
3. **The "defunding" movement has nearly ceased, and cities are trying to restore money to law enforcement.**
4. **The entertainment business has rebounded with police and detective shows. During the civil unrest in 2020, law enforcement television series and movies went into the abyss. They were pulled from television, and new movies were not made. Television and movies with law enforcement plots have**

returned to mainstream channels and theaters. This is an anecdotal example, but nonetheless, it indicates a renewed interest in the profession.

In terms of staffing, in 2023, the average major law enforcement agency in America was down anywhere from 8–12 percent. Some agencies were down much more. If a large recruit academy class is saturated with diversity, the agency can very quickly increase its overall diversity percentages. The national staffing crisis that law enforcement agencies are facing right now has been a leadership challenge. However, the silver lining is that, right now, a *golden opportunity* exists to increase diversity and improve the culture of law enforcement in large strides. I encourage law enforcement leaders to take advantage of this unique opportunity.

READER ASSIGNMENT
Discuss as a class the variables leading to OIS disproportionality that we have mentioned up to this point. What is the class's position on why there remains a heavy Black disproportionality with OISs, especially for the unarmed category?

Racial Bias Does Exist

Racial bias does exist in individuals. It can also exist in institutions. It is present in every facet of life where people are involved. The professions that encompass healthcare, finance, housing, policing, and journalism all have some bias (Withrow 2023). Policing has historically been labeled as an institution with racial bias. Some Black communities and chiefs of police know this and realize that the only way to guard against it is through proper hiring, training, policies, and culture. It does not mean all Black communities want the police to go away. It means that Black communities want fair and professional policing.

This chapter started with the story about the dog to illustrate a position. White America is more likely to give law enforcement a pass, especially in scenarios where the police shoot an unarmed subject. The national data for OISs suggests that it makes sense for White Americans to feel this way. For Black communities, it needs to be proven to be a justified shooting, and the data suggests this is a reasonable stance. The differing viewpoints and the "prove it to me" prism are justified given the history of policing Black Americans.

Race Matters When Communicating through the Media
&
Race is a Factor in All Police Encounters

Law enforcement needs to recognize the differing perspectives held by some Black and White citizens and account for these differences in their communications with the press. It is critical to understand why different communities have different viewpoints. The historical treatment of Black citizens by law enforcement and the current disproportionality (for example, the OIS data) make race a factor in all police encounters involving Black citizens. Law enforcement's critical media strategy must consider race as a factor when explaining a high-profile event involving the Black community.

The subject of race and law enforcement in our country is often misunderstood. Effective reporting on race and law enforcement by the media is subject to debate. A dissection of the evidence is rarely used to tell the story. Rather, emotion and sensationalism are the hooks used to reel in viewers or draw clicks. The dissection of the role of race is fodder for talk shows and water cooler chat.

Law enforcement needs to rise above the chatter and enact a critical media strategy that lays out the evidence in a manner that takes into account the historical and current contexts of policing. A critical media strategy that is infused with racial insight can go a long way toward community relations and proper media coverage. In addition to the critical media strategy taught in Chapters Five and Six, the law enforcement agency must give extra care to the details when race is involved, especially in the death of a Black person by White officers. The evidence must show if the law enforcement officer was justified. The evidence must be laid out in a way to disprove the negative assumptions.

OISs and controversial law enforcement encounters, regardless of race, should prompt a transparent and copious account of critical events with the press. Critical media communications should be done in a way that everyone can be assured of what happened. The public should be shown the law enforcement officer's justification without gaps, or the public should be shown that the situation was not in accordance with policy; it depends on the facts and evidence of the event or OIS.

Magnified Insight
&
Nuances Are Present When Race Is a Factor

Consider the nuances discussed below that are present in the aftermath of an OIS. A law enforcement agency's PPC or critical media press release should account for all citizens. The nuances of machination possibility, demands for release of the video, critique by comparison, and the "hands up" phenomenon are considerations found in some Black communities.

The nuances discussed next are seldom—if ever—talked about. However, it behooves a law enforcement agency to be cognizant of their existence when considering the "prove it to me" starting point of view. An understanding of the nuances is fair to Black communities who want to be assured that the arm of government in place to protect them will do so without bias.

Machination Possibility

A law enforcement agency needs to be thorough in its critical media strategy to account for machination possibilities. According to the Merriam-Webster dictionary (Merriam-Webster.com), machination is a plot or a scheme. The act of machinating is scheming, or crafty or artful design intended to accomplish some usually evil end. In short, the question that needs to be accounted for is, "Has a plot taken place to cover up a mistake or act of bias brought on by the color of some one's skin?"

Some in the Black community are understandably more desiring of an explanation of the facts where the suspicion of a plot or scheme can be dispelled. A law enforcement agency needs to account for this nuance when addressing the media. The institution of policing is faced with historical and present-day skepticism from some Black communities. The officer's race does not matter. What matters is a law enforcement officer is present, representing the government, regardless of the race of the officer.

Some in the Black community may call into question a police encounter involving race, and street rumors can also spread:

- Rumors about the gun being planted by the police.
- Questions about why the person was shot so many times by the police, and was this a by-product of the person's race?
- If there were several officers on the scene, was an officer shot by friendly fire and not the Black subject?
- The police are asking for help solving a crime, but is Crime Stoppers really anonymous?

All the above are "machination possibility" thoughts that can play out in the aftermath of an OIS where race was involved. And let us face it, somewhere and somehow through the course of law enforcement history, a plot or scheme has taken place by law enforcement against the Black community. The following are some examples:

During the late 1990s and early 2000s, the Rampart scandal took place in law enforcement. This was about police corruption that unfolded in Los Angeles, California.

The scandal concerned widespread criminal activity within the Community Resources Against Street Hoodlums (CRASH) anti-gang unit of the LAPD's Rampart Division. More than seventy police officers were initially implicated in various forms of misconduct, including unprovoked shootings and beatings, planting of false evidence, stealing and dealing narcotics, bank robbery, lying under oath, and cover-ups thereof (PBS 2015).

In 2015, a citizen's video was provided to the *New York Times* showing a police officer in North Charleston, South Carolina, shooting an apparently unarmed man after a scuffle following a traffic stop. The white police officer was charged with murder when the video surfaced showing the officer shooting in the back and killing an apparently unarmed Black man while the man ran away. The officer, Michael T. Slager, thirty-three, said he had feared for his life because the man had taken his stun gun in a scuffle after a traffic stop. A video, however, shows the officer firing eight times as the man, Walter L. Scott, fifty, fled, dispelling Slager's account (*New York Times* 2015).

In Omaha in 2013, a police corruption scandal also took place, involving two Black Omahans and White Omaha police officers. See Chapter Two for full details. Based on the three examples of Rampart, South Carolina, and Omaha, it is prudent and reasonable to want to eliminate the possibility of a cover-up.

Some might say that the chances of a plot or scheme are extremely rare and should never enter a society's mindset. My response to that is threefold:

1) Tell that to the citizens of Rampart or North Charleston.
2) If it has happened once, it will be considered a possibility no matter how rare it is. There is not a person alive who has swum in the ocean and has not had a fleeting thought of a shark biting them. Shark attacks do happen, and because they happen it is prudent to try to minimize the occurrences, as they are rare but devastating. Police misconduct or an after-the-fact "machination" is rare but extremely devastating, and it has happened before—not to mention how many times it may have occurred and went uncovered.
3) Professional law enforcement officers and agencies know the "machination possibility" is unfair to them, but they understand why it can be an issue.

Let us now consider the possible scenarios.

Was the gun planted? If a Black suspect is shot by law enforcement and the person has a gun, some in the community will question if the gun was planted. I have heard it many times over the years. A few ways to combat the rumor is to show a crime scene photo of where the gun was at the scene. Or show a BWC still photo where the gun is clearly in the hands of the suspect. If the suspect fired the gun, they would have gunshot residue (GSR) on their hands. Making note of the GSR positive test result can allay the

RACE, POLICE, AND MEDIA—UNRAVELING THE PUZZLE

community's concerns. A gun trace can also be valuable, especially if it can be traced to the suspect. This kind of extra diligence can go a long way toward dispelling rumors and benefiting community relations.

Disclaimer: If there is evidence of a plot or a scheme, come right out and say it along with a criminal arrest and termination of the officers.

Was the officer actually shot by the suspect? If an officer is shot and a Black person is arrested, street rumors can form around whether the officer shot was by the suspect or by another officer. Did the officers inadvertently or recklessly shoot each other and are now pinning it on the Black suspect in a cover-up? In the case of Officer Kerrie Orozco, Kerrie was shot by a Black suspect, and then a White police sergeant shot and killed the Black suspect.

OPD took extra care in the investigation and worked with the media to lay out the evidence and disprove the negative by eliminating the possibility that another officer had shot Kerrie. The suspect's gun was given to him by his girlfriend through a *straw purchase*. A straw purchase is when a legal gun owner buys the gun to give it to someone who is unable to buy one, such as a felon.

OPD took great effort to show the gun trace linked to the suspect. In addition, the suspect's gun was of a different caliber from the ones carried by the officers on the scene. It was clearly denoted in the PPC that the caliber of gun and round recovered that struck Kerrie was from the suspect's and not an officer's gun. Lastly, a still photo of the gun lying on the ground at the crime scene was shown to the public.

Conversely, in the case of the *COPS* television show's OIS, friendly fire did strike and kill soundman Bryce Dion (see Chapter Two). The investigation showed the Black suspect to be armed with a pellet gun. It was imperative and clear from the evidence that friendly fire from a police officer had struck Bryce. In the critical media strategy PPC, it was clearly laid out for the media and public.

Why was the suspect shot so many times? The Black suspect in the *COPS* television show incident was shot at over thirty times by the officers. There were many who questioned why the Black suspect was shot so many times (struck 9 times). Officers shot at the suspect thirty-two times and continued to fire at the suspect until he was no longer a threat in accordance with OPD policies and training. The *COPS* video showed that the suspect was impervious to being hit by gunfire and was a continued threat until the officer's rounds finally put him down.

The video was clear: the suspect would not go down and, once in the parking lot, continued to point his pellet gun at the officers. The *COPS* TV show camera person was able to continue filming when the shots were fired inside the Wendy's. The video of the shooting as well as the OPD press conference the next day can be found on the internet.

CLASS ASSIGNMENT
Watch the *COPS* video and the OPD press conference that followed. Discuss among the class what was done well and what could have been done better.

Are Crime Stoppers really anonymous? Crime Stoppers is an anonymous way to send a tip to law enforcement. Crime Stopper programs do not work for the police. A reward is given to the tipster. When advertised correctly, Crime Stoppers can be a great community tool to catch offenders. I have heard many times that people do not believe Crime Stoppers are anonymous, even though there has never been one example of a tipster being "outed" in Omaha. It is a good idea to periodically explain how Crime Stoppers work to eliminate concerns law enforcement is behind the tip line.

A tipster calls the Crime Stoppers number and reaches a call center in another state. The tipster is not asked for their name. The tipster never talks to law enforcement and is given a code number to retrieve their reward if the tip pans out and leads to an arrest. The tipster is then given a bank where they can go pick up their reward anonymously by giving the code. The tipster can even authorize another person to pick it up if they wish. The law enforcement agency never knows the bank being used.

"Release the Video" Demands

Some Black communities are more likely to demand the release of BWC footage. They want to see for themselves what occurred after an OIS. The intensity of chants during protests for the release of BWC footage is more intense when the subject of the law enforcement encounter is Black.

During my time as chief, only a few have manifested protest demands to release the BWC footage. In every one of those times, the subject was Black. The same is demonstrated on a national scale. How many times is the community protesting to see the BWC where the subject of the law enforcement encounter is White? Few, as demands to see BWC footage are a product of community's mistrust of law enforcement.

Strong consideration should be given to showing the BWC footage to the family and community in the aftermath of a critical event or OIS. However, making the BWC footage available must be balanced with the laws of each state, the integrity of the court process, and an understanding it may foster a *court of public opinion*. A court of public opinion is a metaphorical concept, describing the collective judgment of a society regarding a particular issue, often formed through media coverage, social discourse, and public discussions rather than legal proceedings.

Differing State Laws

Each state has differing laws for the release of evidence. In some states, law enforcement can release BWC footage immediately, while in some it can only be done after a defined period, and other states are in flux. Nebraska has a prescribed way that evidence and BWC footage should be released. The law prescribes the footage to be released after grand jury (GJ) proceedings. In Nebraska, if there is a death while in police custody, a grand jury is automatically convened to determine if a "true bill" or no "true bill" is the finding. A true bill means the GJ determined a crime was committed by the officer(s). No true bill means the officer(s) were justified in their actions (City of Omaha Legal Department, n.d.).

Nebraska's evidence release laws are confusing. The prescribed manner is that the evidence should be released after the GJ. Yet there is no language in the law saying that a law enforcement agency cannot release the BWC footage before the GJ. Does the chief of police wait until after the GJ or release the footage before the GJ? Releasing BWC footage before the GJ is quintessential to holding a "court of public opinion" before the legal GJ proceedings—a perilous move toward affecting a fair and impartial GJ process.

At OPD, we have taken the position of releasing still photos from the BWC immediately after a critical event. The BWC footage is released after the GJ to parse transparency with the GJ process. However, on rare occasions, given the historical and present-day context of policing in our country, it may be prudent to release the BWC footage shortly after an incident. If the incident is of such interest and may cause potential damage to community relations, releasing the video may have to occur before the GJ.

My preference would be for Nebraska's BWC evidence law to become clear. It is currently *cloudy*, so a case-by-case determination is in order. My command staff and I showed the family BWC footage one time because of the ramifications it had for community relations. In the incident, a Black male was running from OPD and stopped and shot himself in the head. The officer was close enough to capture it on his BWC. This was hard to fathom by the family, and the rumor on the street became that OPD shot him unjustifiably and was covering it up. After all, who would just stop and shoot themselves?

On this occasion, I found it vital for community relations to show the family the BWC. One of my deputy chiefs and I met with the family to go over the incident. The family was distraught but appreciative of the meeting. It gave the family closure and conveyed to the community that it was indeed a suicide. It was also a professional and respectful way to treat a family suffering from the loss of a loved one. The determination to release the bodycam video must be weighed against state laws and the potential for interfering with a fair trial versus the need to know right now what happened and officer morale.

READER ASSIGNMENT

Is it right to release body cam footage within days of an incident? Is holding the court of public opinion the right thing to do when releasing the video? Do community relations require immediate release? These are consideration points for a law enforcement agency executive. Draft a paper two to five pages long on your thoughts and perspectives.

The media will always push for the body camera video to be released. It is obviously good for their industry and ratings. Any stance contrary to the media on this front will be drowned out by the press themselves. I attempted to explain Nebraska law as it relates to the release of evidence in the aftermath of the Kenneth Jones OIS. A specific reporter directly ignored my explanation on two separate occasions.

A Black man named Kenneth Jones was shot by two White police officers in November of 2020 (Hayes 2020). The Kenneth Jones case is covered in Chapter Two. The case highlights the media ecosystem surrounding Black citizens who are shot by the police. Protests occurred in front of police headquarters for several nights. The theme of the protests was a request to release the BWC footage of the OIS. The calls to release the BWC footage were intense, and the media coverage reflected that. Anywhere from twenty to sixty protestors gathered in front of OPD headquarters for several nights to pressure for the release of the BWC footage.

I elected to not publicly release the BWC. My reasons were threefold:

1) A detailed PPC was held the day after the incident, where the public was given still photos and a complete review of the incident. The two officers involved were both wearing BWCs, so the timeline of the incident could be weaved together with no gaps.
2) The officers' actions were legally justified and followed the OPD use-of-force policy. They deserved an untainted GJ process.
3) The pressure demands by the crowd were designed to intimidate, and they threatened violence if the BWC was not released. A law enforcement leader can never be extorted into a decision. My officers deserved a fair review from the GJ and not a "court of public opinion" by those willing to intimidate and threaten. If I caved, would this have opened the door for more intimidation tactics? Would the officers of the OPD, who are sworn to protect the city, have been thrown under the bus by the BWC release? There are many variables for chiefs to consider before releasing BWC footage. Another variable to consider is respectful protests by the public, which are lawful and not designed to intimidate or threaten violence. This variable is hard to ignore.

RACE, POLICE, AND MEDIA—UNRAVELING THE PUZZLE

Critique by Comparison

Critique by comparison is the perception that an investigation would have been conducted differently for a White person or that the action taken by law enforcement would not have occurred if it was a White suspect.

A few national examples expose the prudence of considering critique by comparison. Would Minneapolis Officer Chauvin have knelt with his knee on the neck of a White person for as long as he did? Would a White person have been left to lay in the street for hours like Michael Brown did? These are examples of critiques by comparison, which are often made in the aftermath of a controversial law enforcement encounter with a member of the Black community.

A poignant Omaha example of critique by comparison is the task force convened to catch serial killer Dr. Anthony Garcia (see Chapter Two). The murders went back five years, and several persons of interest were spread around the country and in Canada. The FBI was needed, as the investigation was clearly going to cross state lines and go out of the country. The task force was needed to enlist the FBI as a full-time member of the work group. OPD does not have jurisdiction outside of the state of Nebraska, and the FBI does.

To ensure there were enough detective personnel to pour through Creighton Medical Center's files, follow up on new tips, and review the original double-murder investigation, a task force was set up. This model allowed assisting agencies to supply detectives to the task force on a full-time basis, creating a force multiplier. Full-time assistance was needed, and the task force allowed for multi-agency collaboration and coordination.

The task force included OPD detectives, Nebraska State Patrol detectives, and the FBI. The day of the PPC that announced the task force, and periodically over the years, there have been critiques by comparison regarding its formation. People asked, "Why isn't a task force set up for Black victims?" The answer is that the serial killer aspect, in combination with the workload and the five-year hiatus between murders, mandated the task force model.

This has always bothered me because OPD has pulled out all the stops in every murder investigation. If the investigation is going to cross state lines or go out of the country, the FBI is needed. The FBI's full-time seat on the task force was instrumental to its success. As big as the task force investigation was, the Peyton Benson murder investigation (see Chapter Two) was equally as grand. The investigative hunt for serial killer Nikko Jenkins (see Chapter Two) was massive. The difference was that the Benson investigation and Jenkins's arrest required local work. There was nothing about the investigations taking OPD to other states or out of the country. In addition, OPD worked with federal law enforcement agencies on both cases.

The OPD has a limited jurisdiction, which consists of the Omaha city limits and the state of Nebraska under certain circumstances. The resources used were equal; the investigations simply did not have the task force label. However, at the end of the day, as I look back, the critique by comparison was reasonable, and I wish I had explained it better at the PPC announcing the task force. If I had explained why the creation of the task force was needed at one of the press conferences, it would have gone a long way for some. Instead, I lacked insight at that point in my career.

"Hands Up" Phenomenon

In at least three of the OISs involving Black males in Omaha, a witness would say the suspect had his hands up when he was shot. On a few occasions, the witness said he was on his knees with his hands up—but then all the other witnesses (many of them Black), disputed the notion, and all video evidence and forensics also dispelled it. So why would a Black witness to an OIS say the Black suspect had his hands up when it did not occur?

It all goes back to the perception starting point. Black witnesses will see a situation differently, and the power of persuasion or the notion of what someone assumes could happen affects perception. In the Ferguson, Missouri, police shooting of Michael Brown, the very same phenomenon occurred. A Black witness said that Michael Brown had his hands up, and the Department of Justice determined it was not true. Hands up, don't shoot" became a common chorus in the case.

A law enforcement agency's critical media strategy must be aware of this phenomenon. The assertion that a suspect's hands were up when they were shot, if not dispelled by other witnesses, video footage, or other evidence, will cause massive damage to community relations.

Oftentimes, the rumor on the street becomes that the suspect had his hands up when shot. Unfortunately, I have seen this play out on several occasions. It is imperative that the street rumors are dispelled when they are this polarizing. In short, the "hands up" phenomenon is real, and it will manifest itself with witnesses and rumors. The damage of this phenomenon is devastating to a community when it is not factual. Law enforcement agencies need the insight to guard against it and get out in front of it when not supported by evidence.

Disclaimer: If it is true, and the Black suspect was shot while their hands were up, then the community should also be informed of the next steps of arresting and charging the officer.

Miscellaneous Nuances

Diversity at the PPC: Some Black communities want to see someone who looks like them at a law enforcement press conference. If a PPC is held after an OIS of a Black person, it behooves the agency to have diversity at the PPC. A PPC with only White law enforcement officials will cause mistrust. Law enforcement agencies should be diverse and have high-ranking commanders of color. The community is much more amenable to investigation if a commander of color has a role. It is important to have a diverse staff visible to the public.

My suggestion is to have command officers stand behind the executive at the PPC, where the public can see the diverse command. If the chief and everyone behind them is White, the optics say the agency does not understand, appreciate, or value diversity. I made the mistake of holding a press conference where a Black man was killed by OPD, and I had all White commanders stand behind me. My critics pointed this out, and I thank them for doing so, as it has shaped my future approach.

Transparency: Transparency is more than being thorough with a PPC or press release in the aftermath of a critical event. Timing is transparent as well. Transparency requires communicating with the public through the media at the scene of a critical event, with an on-scene presser. A PPC done the next day will solidify the transparency timing. Otherwise, the law enforcement agency will run the risk of street rumors and conjecture creeping in.

> **READER NOTE**
> **It is fine to wait two days or a little more after a critical event for a PPC, but the media must be kept apprised as to the reason for the delay.**

History of the Officer: What is the law enforcement officer's history in the department? Are they a veteran or a rookie? Has the officer received discipline in the past? If the officer is a veteran with a clean work history, the public is much more likely to accept what the critical event investigation shows. If the officer has a history of disciplinary action, no matter how justified the present incident is, there will be community skepticism. Veteran officers will get more deference from the community as well.

Rumor Antagonist: There is a small percentage of people or groups interested in sowing discord in the community, commonly through spreading false rumors. Unfortunately, I have heard false rumors several times in the aftermath of an OIS where a person of color was shot. In addition, I have seen some sophisticated attempts to sow discord in the community.

SYNERGY *of* INFLUENCE

Disclaimer—I struggled with where to place this section in the book, as during my time as chief, it has not been the product of Omaha's Black communities; rather, most traces after a rumor antagonist led us to a White person. I placed it in this chapter because it was mostly used as a means to sow racial discord.

During the 2020 Omaha civil unrest (see Chapter Two), a White bar owner shot and killed a Black protestor. A rumor was intentionally spread that I was personal friends with the bar owner. The rumor was false. In fact, I had met the bar owner only one time previously, as he was part of a downtown Omaha business contingent complaining about policing in the Old Market area of Omaha. The meeting took place in the mayor's office. This was the only time I ever met the man, and quite frankly, we had been at odds with each other in the meeting. The rumor was designed to make it appear that the OPD had taken sides against the Black protestor. The OPD took no side, and our role was to conduct a thorough investigation, which we did.

Another sophisticated but crude attempt was made to sow discord during the 2020 Omaha civil unrest period. Someone in the community took a video of Omaha police officers talking to a crowd and then kneeling with them. The video was cropped and cut down all the way to the point where it looked like an OPD officer was on his knees giving the "Heil Hitler" sign: a stiff arm pointed straight out and slightly up. The OPD press information office had a video of the incident and played it to the public. The video showed the officer merely waving over a protestor from the kneeling position. However, stopping the video at the right time and intimating it was a picture of a Nazi pose was a clear attempt to sow discord. OPD never found out who was responsible.

Omaha Police photo: Cropped video still photo where it appears an Omaha police officer is holding up the Heil Hitler sign. In reality, the video was stopped when the officer was in mid-wave, making it appear to be the Nazi salute.

Show Me the Body: Some in the community want to see their deceased loved ones for proof and closure when they die. The death could be a homicide investigation or a law enforcement shooting. A law enforcement agency should try to carve out an opportunity for the family to see the body. The criminal investigation can determine when and how the body is viewed to ensure the integrity of the investigation. The point is that if they are not able to see the body, the family can lose trust in the investigation.

Prevalent Misconceptions

There are some prevalent misconceptions about Black Americans in our country, no doubt fostered by poor media coverage and cable talk shows looking to portray a certain image. The biggest misconception is that Black communities care more about police shootings of Black people than Black-on-Black crime.

Do Black communities care more about police killings than Black-on-Black crime? No, they do not, and the protocol to address each problem is quite different. I hear it all the time on cable talk shows, and it makes me cringe. Black citizens care deeply about Black-on-Black crime. I know this firsthand.

The efforts to reduce Black-on-Black crime are grassroots and driven by addressing the root causes, like poverty or education gaps. If there is a murder, the Black community wants it solved. Solving homicides and reducing gang and gun violence is a top priority of the Omaha community. It is a top priority across the country as well, in my professional opinion.

On the other hand, when law enforcement shoots a Black person, grassroots efforts to reduce poverty are not the prescribed remedy. An agent of the government has just taken the life of a community member. As such, the response is designed to address the government's perceived failure. Government failures are addressed by protests, demands, court actions, and sometimes civil unrest. These are all methods a citizen can exercise to challenge the government.

The two different rallying cries make sense when comparing solutions for Black-on-Black crime versus law enforcement misconduct toward the Black community. When Black Lives Matter (BLM) was formed, many white Americans were offended. "All Lives Matter" was the retort, as BLM only came out when there was police involvement. "All Lives Matter" is missing the mark. BLM was not formed to address gang and gun violence or Black-on-Black crime; rather, BLM was formed to keep law enforcement in check. Black men were dying disproportionally at the hands of law enforcement, and BLM assumed the cause.

When BLM does not come out for the high number of Black-on-Black murders in Chicago, it is because their mission was to stand up for people of color who may have been wrongfully killed by law enforcement. The Black community is already addressing

Black-on-Black crime via legislative and grassroots efforts. When White America compares the two, perpetuated by some segments of the press, it is truly an apples-to-oranges comparison. This example does not imply across-the-board approval of the BLM's actions.

Class Discussion

What does the class think of the author's position that race matters if the government is involved, and Black-on-Black crime is addressed every day from a grassroots standpoint?

Omaha Example: Race as a Factor

The story of Omaha's 2020 civil unrest was first recounted in Chapter Two: Omaha's National Crime Events—Unveiling the Impact. The critical event between Black Omaha citizen James Scurlock and White Omaha citizen Jake Gardner exemplifies the role of race as a factor. Following this case study, readers will then be taken through four of the biggest policing events in America as an analysis of race as a factor.

The case of James Scurlock and Jake Gardner beckons the sometimes-differing viewpoints of Black and White America. Their deadly encounter considers whether race was a factor. Both Black and White citizens of Omaha saw a video showing the incident described below.

On May 30, 2020, around 11:00 p.m., James Scurlock and a group of protestors were in the Old Market area of Omaha, Nebraska, during the George Floyd protests. During the protest, Scurlock was filmed vandalizing inside a building, including exterior windows and interior office spaces, on the corner of 13th and Harney Street. Scurlock then headed east toward the business belonging to Jacob Gardner, a white bar owner. Gardner and his father stood guard inside his business, The Hive. After a window was broken by protestors, the two men exited The Hive and walked east down the Harney Street sidewalk. Gardner's father pushed two people, telling them to leave. Gardner's father was then knocked to the ground by one man.

A verbal altercation between Gardner and a group of people he believed pushed his father ensued. Gardner positioned himself amid the protestors. He lifted his shirt, making it known he was carrying a concealed handgun in his waistband. He then withdrew the handgun from his waistband and held it at his side. As he turned his back, he was tackled to the ground by two people.

Gardner fired two shots in the air (which he would later describe to the police as warning shots), and his two attackers fled. It was then that Scurlock jumped on Gardner's back as he was getting up. After both had struggled for around twenty seconds, Gardner fired a third shot over his own shoulder, striking Scurlock in his clavicle.

Scurlock was taken to Nebraska Medicine, where he died from his injuries.

Omaha's Black community viewed the video as Scurlock protecting others by jumping on Gardner's back, possibly even intervening in an active shooter scenario, or preventing Gardner from firing his weapon again, not knowing the direction of the next shot. Omaha's white community saw it as a case of self-defense.

How can two different sets of people view the same video in such vastly diverse ways? It all goes back to differing Black and White histories in our country, leading to differing prisms through which Black America and white America look at these events (*New York Times* 2023).

Analysis

Was race a factor? Yes. Even though the police were not involved in Scurlock's death, it was during a time of civil unrest stemming from the murder of George Floyds by White police officers. Thus, the Black community was outraged that Gardner did not initially get charged with murder. The County Attorney is a law enforcement official, and as such the prism of history will be in effect. Recall that, given the history of law enforcement in America and the current disproportionality in OIS data, we know that if law enforcement is involved, even if not directly, race is a factor.

Is race evidence in the case? No, not on its surface. However, I do not know how Gardner would have testified or if there was evidence in other ways that would bring race into the courtroom legally. Race as a factor will certainly be in the courtroom.

Four National Law Enforcement Critical Events That Have Shaped Our Country:

The following section offers a look at four infamous deaths involving Black men and law enforcement that have shaped our country. An analysis is provided as to why race was or was not a factor. You may be wondering why the question of whether race is evidence is also being analyzed. There is great dissension between White and Black Americans on the subject, and its understanding is important for law enforcement, all government officials, and our country.

George Floyd: On May 25, 2020, George Floyd, a forty-six-year-old Black man, was murdered in Minneapolis, Minnesota by Derek Chauvin, a forty-four-year-old white police officer. Floyd had been arrested after a store clerk alleged that Floyd made a purchase using a counterfeit $20 bill. Chauvin knelt on Floyd's neck for over eight minutes while Floyd was handcuffed and lying face down in the street. Two other police officers, J. Alexander Keung and Thomas Lane, assisted Chauvin in restraining Floyd.

Lane had also pointed a gun at Floyd's head prior to Floyd being put in handcuffs. A fourth police officer, Tou Thao, prevented bystanders from intervening.

Prior to being placed on the ground, Floyd had exhibited signs of anxiety, complaining about having claustrophobia and being unable to breathe. After being restrained, he became more distressed, still complaining of breathing difficulties, of the knee on his neck, and of fear of imminent death. After several minutes, Floyd stopped speaking. For the last few minutes, he lay motionless, and Officer Kueng found no pulse when urged to check. Despite this, Chauvin ignored pleas from bystanders to lift his knee from Floyd's neck. Floyd died after nine minutes of being restrained (*New York Times* 2020).

Analysis

Was race a factor? Yes. Derek Chauvin was a white police officer, and George Floyd was Black.

Is race evidence in the case? No, but read below.

Former Minneapolis Officer Derek Chauvin did not testify at his murder trial, so we will never know what was truly in his heart. However, we can make reasonable inferences. For starters, holding your knee on someone's neck for over eight minutes is very personal, and we saw that Chauvin did not seem to care. Chauvin knew Floyd was Black. Chauvin also disregarded Black bystanders who pleaded with him to get off Floyd's neck. Chauvin knew the bystanders were Black because he looked at them.

The bystanders had no effect on his actions. A reasonable inference is that race had to have crossed Chauvin's mind. A reasonable question is, would a White suspect and white bystanders have led Chauvin to a different outcome? It is also possible that Chauvin drowned out points of view different from his own after spending over twenty years working the streets; this is something for law enforcement executives to watch out for. The grind of being a law enforcement officer can sometimes desensitize. The officer can grow angry over years of street policing. We do not totally know if race would have been evidence in the trial because Chauvin did not testify.

*Disclaimer: There is a documentary titled *The Fall of Minneapolis* that asserts the Maximum Restraint Technique (MRT)—the position Chauvin was in with his knee on George Floyd—was a technique taught by the Minneapolis Police Department. Even if the MRT was a taught position (I am not saying it was, and court testimony claimed it wasn't), and the paramedics took longer than normal to arrive, it does not eliminate the fact Officer Chauvin seemed to ignore the crowd and showed little emotion for Mr. Floyd's well-being. Mr. Chauvin was found guilty in a court of law.

Michael Brown: On August 9, 2014, eighteen-year-old Michael Brown was shot and killed by police officer Darren Wilson in Ferguson, Missouri, a suburb of Saint Louis (Department of Justice 2015).

Brown was accompanied by his twenty-two-year-old male friend Dorian Johnson, who later stated that Brown had robbed a convenience store before the shooting occurred.

Wilson, a white, male Ferguson police officer, said that an altercation ensued when Brown attacked him in his police vehicle for control of Wilson's service pistol. The struggle continued until the pistol fired.

Johnson said that Wilson initiated a confrontation by grabbing Brown by the neck through Wilson's patrol car window, threatening him, and then shooting at him.

At this point, both Wilson and Johnson state that Brown and Johnson fled, with Wilson pursuing Brown shortly thereafter. Wilson stated that Brown stopped and charged him after a short pursuit.

Johnson contradicted this account, stating that Brown turned around with his hands raised after Wilson shot at his back. According to Johnson, Wilson then shot Brown multiple times until Brown fell to the ground.

In the entire altercation, Wilson fired a total of twelve bullets, including twice during the struggle in the car. Brown was struck six times, all in the front of his body (History.com 2020; Suggs, n.d.). This event ignited unrest in Ferguson. Witnesses to the shooting claimed Brown had his hands up in surrender or said, "Don't shoot," so protestors later used the slogan "Hands up. Don't shoot." A subsequent FBI investigation said that there was no evidence that Brown had done so. Protests, both peaceful and violent, continued for more than a week in Ferguson (Henderson 2023).

Analysis

Was race a factor? Yes. Michael Brown died at the hands of a white officer, so the historical prism on race is in effect.

Is race evidence in the case? No. Race cannot be attributed to any evidential string in this case (legally).

Miscellaneous comments: The "hands up" phenomenon was in full play. In addition, the aftermath was managed poorly by the Ferguson Police Department. Brown's body lay in the street for four hours, which came across as disrespectful, and the perception was that this would not happen to a White citizen. The agency took five days to release any information, and then when something was released, it was the video of Brown acting aggressively in a convenience store. This was poor decorum, which made it look like race was a factor in the shooting.

I am hoping this book helps future law executives in their analysis of events and media preparation with insight. There is not any piece of tangible evidence that shows Brown may have been shot because he was Black. However, how the case was overseen in the aftermath sure left the door open for that assumption.

Trayvon Martin: On the evening of February 26, 2012, in Sanford, Florida, George Zimmerman fatally shot Trayvon Martin, a seventeen-year-old African American teenager.

Zimmerman, a twenty-eight-year-old man of mixed race who identifies as Hispanic, was a neighborhood watch coordinator for the gated community where Martin was visiting relatives at the time of the shooting. Zimmerman became suspicious of Martin and called the police. Zimmerman was injured during a physical altercation between the two and shot Martin in self-defense with a pistol he was licensed to carry.

In a widely reported trial, Zimmerman was charged with murder of the second degree for Martin's death but acquitted on all counts by the jury after claiming self-defense. The incident was reviewed by the Department of Justice for potential civil rights violations, but no additional charges were filed, citing insufficient evidence.

The shooting: On the evening of February 26, 2012, Zimmerman observed Martin as he returned to the Twin Lakes housing community after having walked to a nearby convenience store. At the time, Zimmerman was driving through the neighborhood on a personal errand.

At approximately 7:09 p.m., Zimmerman called the Sanford police non-emergency number to report a suspicious person in the Twin Lakes community. Zimmerman said, "We've had some break-ins in my neighborhood, and there's a real suspicious . . ." He described an unknown male "just walking around, looking about" in the rain and said, "This guy looks like he is up to no good or he is on drugs or something."

Zimmerman reported that the person had his hand in his waistband and was walking around looking at homes. He also mentioned that Martin was wearing a "dark hoodie, like a gray hoodie." On the recording, Zimmerman is heard saying, "These assholes; they always get away."

About two minutes into the call, Zimmerman said, "He's running."

The dispatcher asked, "He's running? Which way is he running?"

Noises on the tape at this point have been interpreted by some media outlets as the sound of a car door chime, possibly indicating that Zimmerman opened his car door. Zimmerman followed Martin, eventually losing sight of him. The dispatcher asked Zimmerman if he was following him. When Zimmerman answered, "Yeah," the dispatcher said, "We don't need you to do that." Zimmerman responded, "Okay." Zimmerman asked that the police call him upon their arrival so he could provide his location. Zimmerman ended the call at 7:15 p.m.

After Zimmerman ended his call with the police, a violent encounter took place between him and Martin. It ended with Zimmerman fatally shooting Martin 70 yards (64 m) from the rear door of the townhouse where Martin was staying (CNN 2013; History.com 2012).

Analysis:

Was race a factor? Yes, and no. No, because Zimmerman was not a police officer. Yes, because Zimmerman was not Black and exerted authority over Trayvon Martin as a security guard. Also, Zimmerman's analysis as to why Trayvon was running was skewed and could be based on bias.

Is race evidence in the case? No, not officially. However, it could have slipped into the minds of the acquitting jury.

Miscellaneous comments: Law enforcement grimaces when Trayvon's death is used as a rallying cry for law enforcement reform and accountability. George Zimmerman was far from a police officer and indeed was not one. If an off-duty officer had been working in replacement of Zimmerman that day, I believe this incident would have been avoided. Officers I know can process what Zimmerman saw and would not have been so aggressive when contacting Trayvon Martin. In the event an officer had confronted Trayvon Martin, in my hypothetical scenario, it is likely that Trayvon would have complied because it was a police officer rather than a security guard. Most people show more skepticism when faced with a security guard rather than a law enforcement officer.

Tyre Nichols: Tyre Nichols, a twenty-nine-year-old Black man, was beaten by Memphis police officers for roughly three minutes on the evening of January 7, 2023, after he was stopped for what the police initially said was reckless driving. The stop escalated into a violent confrontation that ended with Mr. Nichols hospitalized in critical condition. Three days later, he died.

Five police officers, all of whom are also Black, have been fired and were charged on January 26, 2023, with various felonies, including second-degree murder. A sixth officer was fired on February 3, and another has been suspended. Also, two sheriff's deputies have been taken off duty, and three fire department employees have been fired.

Was race a factor? Yes. Even though all the officers were Black, they were still police officers for the Memphis PD. As such, the history of how Black Americans are treated by the police comes into play, making race a factor. After all, history is full of Black lawmen who did the White man's bidding in early policing (Alfonseca et al. 2023, Franklin and Bowman 2023).

Is race evidence in the case? No. With all the officers being Black, it would be a huge stretch to think race is going to be part of the evidence at trial.

Miscellaneous comments: What we witnessed on primetime television of the arrest, beating and murder was pure criminal, in my opinion. There is no space to argue self-defense, officer safety, or police tactics. What was needed here was arrests and indictments—which the country received—and then reform. I noticed four areas of concern and potential reform when I watched the video:

1. The plainclothes police officers did not have BWCs.
2. There was no supervisor on the scene until the end.
3. The duty to intervene was ignored.
4. The Scorpion Unit appears to have developed its own criminal subculture.

The suspect officers are considered innocent until proven guilty in a court of law. It is possible that new evidence will become known during the trial. However, the videos released by Memphis Police are persuasive in forming an opinion on what occurred.

Final Analysis: Black Communities and Major City Chiefs of Police Align

A theme has been woven throughout this chapter, which leads to a final analysis based on data, experience, and piecing together shared positions. In general, city chiefs of police of major cities and Black communities align and have similar trains of thought on policing. The alignment of these two thought processes is interesting and compelling. The chiefs, through careers of education and professional experience, and Black communities, through life experience, share the same perspectives.

Chiefs of police and Black communities share the same macro perspectives on the following:

1) The branch of government (law enforcement) in place to protect should not harm anyone because of race.
2) The "prove it to me" attitude of Black communities is reasonable and understandable.
3) Law enforcement hiring, training, and culture need to be strong to prevent negative encounters because of race.
4) Black communities will accept and embrace positive and professional policing, for which is something chiefs of police strive for.
5) Positive police–community relationships are valued and imperative (81 percent of those surveyed want the police in their area).

7) Negative police encounters involving race need to be diminished, and this is a shared goal. Reducing the disproportionality of OISs in America is a prime example.

The macro alignment of perspectives and goals between Black communities and chiefs of police are astounding. This convergence is a reason to hold hope for the future of community relations. How then is there seemingly a perpetual struggle across America with many Black communities and law enforcement? Let us examine this by looking at some of the bigger divergences between law enforcement and Black communities.

Divergence Between Black Communities and Law Enforcement

1) Micro Encounters: There are bound to be singular law enforcement and individual citizen encounters in which the subject of the encounter is left with a negative impression. When the subject is Black, the negative impression carries greater significance for all the reasons we have talked about in this chapter. In addition, citizens struggle with an understanding of police procedures, such as when a law enforcement officer can search a car, affect an arrest, tow a vehicle, or use force.

    Law enforcement must recognize that singular citizen encounters, when race is a factor, can exacerbate a problem and cause it to spread. Many Black communities will pay attention to how law enforcement treats their community and, as such, many more Black citizens will be aware of negative police encounters with Black subjects than those that occur with a White subject. How many times have you turned on the news to see a single police encounter played on the news repeatedly? Even if the negative encounter did not occur in your city, it can still have devastating community relations effects if race was a factor. Singular negative encounters spread fast among Black communities and not so much in White communities.

2) 30/30/30 Blend: The 30/30/30 blend refers to the ideal formula for policing: 30 percent enforcement, 30 percent intervention, and 30 percent prevention. The remaining 10 percent can be applied wherever the need arises. Divergence from agreement with law enforcement in Black communities can form when they perceive that the enforcement role is getting too much emphasis and the community feels overpoliced. The problem lies in the 30/30/30 formula because it takes time to implement successfully. It may take a decade for a city to get to the ideal mix.

SYNERGY *of* INFLUENCE

In Omaha in 2012 OPD, was probably 80 percent enforcement and 20 percent intervention and prevention. It took us until 2018 to reach 30/30/30. Omaha was experiencing an epidemic of shootings in our city in 2012, so the enforcement component needed to be heavier to arrest the violent offenders and bring them to justice. The community was afraid of the violent offenders, and OPD needed to get them off the streets for the community to feel safe. Increased intervention and prevention would not have been successful in getting the violent offenders off the streets. It took precision enforcement. *Precision* is a keyword, as the enforcement was not geared to the community in general but rather to individual violent offenders

The "defund the police" movement missed its mark because it failed to account for the role of enforcement and failed to understand that all cities were not at the point where increasing intervention and prevention would be successful. Cities with aggressive high street crimes (shootings) need to have a heavier percentage of enforcement to "stop the bleeding" before intervention and prevention can really take hold. As such, the 30/30/30 blend can cause divergence in communities. Finding the right blend is an art, and major city police chiefs have a strong understanding and feel for the "mix" needed in their cities. The key is to know when to dial the enforcement piece back and segue more into intervention and prevention.

3) Media Coverage: No profession benefits more from a negative police encounter caught on video, when race is involved, than the media. Ratings become remarkably high, and the "discussion" in the aftermath can carry an entire cable show or radio broadcast. Unfortunately, the discussion is rarely all-encompassing and has caused disagreement among many Black communities with the police.

4) Staying Power: Major city police chiefs seldom last more than three years before there is turnover. I have seen many community leaders come and go in the Black community across the country. This instability is bad for community relations and stalls progress.

Omaha has had community leaders in place for over a decade, and the list of names I mentioned earlier in this chapter are examples of them. A prominent city council member for Omaha's Black community was in place for over a decade. I have been chief for twelve years. This level of staying power is rare and has allowed Omaha to reach historic lows for shootings in the city. A chief or community member that takes their fifteen minutes of fame and then runs is a problem for many major cities and breeds divergence.

5) Culture: While the goals of many major city chiefs and Black communities align, that does not imply that the alignment has reached all the way down to the rank-and-file officers. Hiring, retention, training, and diversity must be in place in the agency to ensure the culture is taking place at the top and the bottom. Far too often, it takes years to establish the correct culture and, until then, a divergence with Black communities can embed.

6) Politics: Many political officials reach into the law enforcement perspective and upset the 30/30/30 progression. This is an unpleasant fact in law enforcement. In Omaha, the mayor has been in place for three terms, and she is known as a staunch public safety mayor; however, she has allowed me to do my job. The chiefs of police I talk to do not always have this luxury with their mayors. Political interventions can cause a divergence with Black communities if the political pressure amounts to a poor understanding of the 30/30/30 blend. The mayors who "defunded" their police departments seem to regret it.

Reader Discussion

Major city chiefs of police and Black communities share common goals. I have listed six areas where the commonalities are in jeopardy. Discuss among the class some other "divergences" present within some Black communities and law enforcement, which may harm community relations.

Conclusion

This chapter provides an appreciation for the divergent starting perceptions of Black and White Americans during police encounters. The divergent starting points call for more *insightful* law enforcement communications with the media and during a PPC. Black Americans are shot by the police at a disproportionate rate even today, compounding the effects of the poor history of policing Black Americans in this country. Even more egregious is the percentage of *unarmed* Black people who are shot versus their white counterparts.

There are some common misconceptions from the public about race. In addition, there are unique nuances at play when a Black American is shot by the police. Law enforcement agencies need to adapt to the nuances. Race is an interesting subject in the sense that it can be a barrier between the police and the community. Law enforcement agencies need to break down the barrier on a macro and an individual scale. The goal is to someday have no disproportionality between the races in policing.

Reader Discussion

Chapter 8 focused on Black communities and the police. What about the other races? For example, what is the status of police–community relations with Asian, Hispanic, and Native American communities? Will the border crisis America is facing change the dynamics of police–community relations in our country? Will the lessening or strengthening of gun laws in America affect the prevalence of officer-involved shootings as a whole? What other factors does our country face that could affect the disproportionality and prevalence of officer-involved shootings in America?

Questions for Discussion and Review

Attempt to answer the following questions before looking up the answers at the back of the book.

1. True or False: Emotion and anger can be considered evidence.
2. Do you agree the "prove it to me" stance of Black Americans is reasonable?
3. The disproportionate rate at which Black Americans are shot by law enforcement is a) less than white Americans, b) about the same as white Americans, c) more than double that of white Americans, d) five times as often as white Americans.
4. True or False: Unarmed Black Americans are shot by the police at a higher percentage rate than unarmed white Americans.
5. Do you agree with the premise that race is a factor in all law enforcement encounters with Black Americans?
6. Does releasing BWC footage after an OIS start the "court of public opinion" trial?
7. Why is an officer's discipline history relevant in cases where race is a factor?
8. Under the section Prevalent Misconceptions, the notion that Black Americans care more about police killings than Black-on-Black crime is dispelled. Do you agree with the author's conclusion?

CHAPTER NINE

Media Self-Rule and Its Effects on Law Enforcement

In this chapter, we will explore key challenges and ethical issues for law enforcement when dealing with the media industry, which is currently struggling to adapt and survive to the changes brought about by the internet. We will start by understanding the concept of media oversight hypocrisy and the roles of important organizations such as the Federal Communication Commission (FCC) and the Society for Professional Journalists (SPJ). These discussions will help us appreciate the complexity of issues like the Great Conundrum and the importance of protecting confidential sources, along with the rare exceptions that might force a reporter to reveal them. We will also examine media bias, introducing terms such as *affinity reporting*, the "look at me" reporters, *headline distraction*, *layout lean*, and *photo lean*, to understand how media shapes public perception. Additionally, we will cover guidelines for addressing issues with journalists and media agencies, including the steps that lead to a reporter being banned from access to a law enforcement agency. This chapter aims to provide a straightforward overview of these important topics, helping readers navigate the media landscape more effectively.

Throughout this book, reporters and journalists have been referred to as peers, and, indeed, most reporters are true professionals. As with any profession, however, the media is far from perfect. The news industry is an incredibly competitive business in generating traffic to its sites, and this naturally forces sensationalism. Some news agencies in Omaha have gone from fact-reporting to clickbait headlines. In a fight-to-survive industry, papers must be sold, viewers must tune in, and the online news must be read. We cannot just assume that local news sources will be impartial and independent when it comes to reporting police incidents.

As with any industry, including law enforcement, some officers are better than others. Some reporters and news agencies are also better than others. Some news agencies will take shortcuts to get ahead, and some have Pulitzer-standard reporters. Henry Cordes with the *Omaha World Herald* is one of the best journalists in the region. His in-depth stories are layered in research and deep coverage. Among his signature features was the *Sunday World Herald* exclusive "What Went Wrong at 72nd and Dodge?" June 21, 2020. The piece dissected the civil unrest that occurred in Omaha and what may have touched it off (Cordes et al. 2020). Cordes also wrote an investigative series of articles on Nebraska's prison system, which was stellar and illuminating (Cordes 2022).

There are reporters I have lost regard for, and they will not be mentioned by name in this book. However, no book on media insight for law enforcement agencies is worth its salt if poor reporting is not discussed. I draw upon my years as chief to provide readers with insight into media misconduct. The chapter will begin with media oversight hypocrisy, The Great Conundrum, the sanctity of confidential sources, media self-rule, and guidelines for addressing problem journalists and news agencies.

Note: The terms used in this chapter are my own. These terms were fashioned so law enforcement personnel could relate and benefit from the insight. The media self-rule examples were designed and based on my experience as chief. There may be some unintended similarities to media bias terms and definitions from other sources. The guidelines for addressing problem journalists and news agencies is my own formula. As such, traditional citing of references is not present.

Media Oversight Hypocrisy

The discussion about media oversight hypocrisy is related to the lack of accountability of the press. Hypothetically, let's say you have an issue with a story that has aired or a newspaper article you assess as unfair. Where can an individual , chief, or company's legal team take their complaint? Is there a neutral third party who can investigate the journalism and provide remedies if necessary?

The answer is yes, if you live in Canada (Media Council n.d.) or the United Kingdom (IPSO, n.d.; SPJ, n.d.). The answer is a resounding *no* if you live in the United States. There is no oversight board of the media in the United States where a person or company can file a complaint for investigation and rectification.

All news agencies will advocate for police oversight and transparency, and yet, the press has none. Thus, the term *media oversight hypocrisy*. In the 1980s, civilian oversight of the police was virtually nonexistent. We see the same situation with the media today.

The media covers civilian police oversight heavily, yet they do not freely disclose that there is zero independent oversight for their profession. The subject of independent civilian police oversight is, of course, an important topic in policing and for society, so it makes sense that the press covers the issue. It is typical to see the outcome of an investigation by a civilian police oversight board as front-page news and the opening story for the nightly news. But where do the media report on their own investigations about their behavior?

MEDIA SELF-RULE AND ITS EFFECTS ON LAW ENFORCEMENT

The Society of Professional Journalists (SPJ) has a code of ethics, and it ends with the line, "Abide *by the same high standards they expect of others.*" Oversight boards are there to foster higher standards. However, it is hard to conclude that a profession that does not have adequate checks and balances is striving for higher standards. This lack of accountability poses a challenge for law enforcement executives and others when seeking remedy for a media story assessed as biased, underreported, or overreported.

Let me provide an example with an "in the room" perspective to demonstrate the challenge facing police executives trying to find redress. There was a time when there was media bias playing out in a series of segments on the same subject, involving the OPD. The OPD PIO was unable to get any resolution with the reporter on the matter, so I called the news director and asked for the reporter's work to be investigated.

The news director instantly started defending the reporter, leaving the distinct impression that my complaint was not going to be investigated. My response to the news director was as follows: Imagine if I, as chief of police, instantly defended the actions of my officers when receiving a complaint. What if a chief of police blindly supported an officer and didn't even bother to investigate the situation? It would not be the type of response a person would want from a chief. It was not the response I wanted from a news executive. It reminded me of the way policing had been in the 1980s, when countless citizens lodged complaints against the police and scarce oversight took place to manage the complaints.

In the 1980s, many police chiefs defended officers in the same vein as some news executives do in 2024. Thirty to forty years ago, cell phones and video evidence were hard to come by, and BWCs did not exist (Bhattar 2021). The lack of evidence, coupled with the staunch defense and backing by police agency leaders, stymied the progression of the policing profession. The public became frustrated by the lack of police responsiveness, and the culture of law enforcement agencies drifted into unaccountability. Is the lack of a media oversight board, where an independent investigation, determination, or review could take place, also causing a stall in the advancement of journalistic professionalism?

Months later, I tried to get a resolution for the same media bias complaint from the news. I lodged a complaint laying out dates, times, and circumstances, as evidence of the bias. I crafted a second complaint, months later, with further evidence; indisputable facts were laid out. The news director acknowledged that the reporter may have developed an affinity for one side of the story over the other. It was a difficult progression to receive the acknowledgment, and this is a good example of a culture that can develop when there is no independent oversight. The news executive is a top-notch media executive and someone for whom I have high regard. Can you imagine how the problem would be compounded if the news executive were not in the upper echelon of their position? Like police chiefs in the 1980s who may have overlooked problem officers, the lack of independent oversight of the media today can cause news executives to inadvertently overlook or miss biased reporting.

Would this be the level of oversight we would want for policing? Or the level of oversight we would want for attorneys or doctors? Every major law enforcement agency has some form of civilian police oversight. OPD, for example, has a civilian complaint review board. If you want to lodge a complaint against a lawyer, there is the American Bar Association, which then investigates, and discipline is meted out, sometimes in the form of a disbarment. There are also medical review boards for doctors where the loss of a medical license is possible. However, there is nothing for the press, and therein lies the *independent oversight hypocrisy* and the danger it can bring to society.

Disclaimer:

There are libel and slander laws in place and there is legal recourse in that regard; however, they are designed for individuals or businesses to seek redress. The redress is framed toward the person or entity that created the slander or libel; not for the news media that reported it occurred. Law enforcement agencies are public entities and are much more impervious to being a legal victim of slander or libel.

This book is designed to give media "insight" and should not be construed as a legal template or as providing legal advice.

The Federal Communication Commission (FCC)

The FCC is a regulatory body in the United States responsible for overseeing all interstate and international communications by radio, television, wire, satellite, and cable (FCCa, n.d.; FCCb, n.d.; FCCc, n.d.; SPJ, n.d.). It also grants licenses for news agencies to operate on television. When there are issues with broadcast journalism, a complaint can be made to the FCC, as it provides accountability. For example, the FCC clearly states that broadcasters may not intentionally distort the news: "rigging or slanting the news is a most heinous act against the public interest."

However, if you have a complaint about a television news story, the FCC will refer you to the news network. The FCC can only interfere as a last resort, and only under the strictest of measures; for example, only if there is "documented evidence from persons with direct knowledge of an intentional falsification of the news."

For a regular citizen, elected official, or even a law enforcement executive to receive any sort of intervention from the FCC, would take an extreme case. The reporter would have to be caught on a wiretap admitting to slanting a story or giving an inordinate amount of time to one side over the other. The FCC does not cover online, print, or social media, and in fact, there is no independent recourse for redress with this latter type of media. So, why wouldn't news agency executives defend their reporters and move on just as police chiefs did in the 1980s? Who or what holds reporters accountable?

Society of Professional Journalists

The Society of Professional Journalists (SPJ) was formed to promote and defend the First Amendment guarantees of freedom of speech and freedom of the press. There are almost three hundred chapters across the United States, and it has a prominent legal defense fund to wage court battles to protect First Amendment Rights (SPJ, n.d.).

The SPJ also has a code of ethics, which aims to "inspire" journalists to have lofty standards of reporting (the full text of the code of ethics is available in Addendum 4).

Can the SPJ help to hold journalists accountable? If there is a complaint or concern about a story, journalist, or news agency, one could contact the SPJ, and the organization may put some peer pressure on the reporter or news agency. However, there is no official remedy. The SPJ will not function as an oversight entity and investigate the complaint, nor issue any findings, corrections, or censures (SPJ, n.d.).

Accountable Journalism Organization

Accountable Journalism is an organization designed to be the world's largest collection of ethical codes of conduct for press agencies. If you go to the website (https://accountablejournalism.org), under the dropdown menu of Press Councils, there is a host of countries with a press council. The press council is, in effect, responsible for investigating potential breaches of the ethical codes adopted by the media. The United States is not one of those countries.

In short, the only thing keeping journalists ethical in the United States is the honor system. Fortunately, professional news organizations will create a culture of *just* journalism. It is only hope that the righteous nature of reporting stays intact against a backdrop of heavy industry competition. As chief, I have been fortunate that the Omaha area news industry generally strives for fair and ethical journalism.

Great Conundrum

The SPJ's Code of Ethics is a framework for ethical journalism, but it is voluntary and not enforced. Why isn't there an independent review board for journalism like there is for law enforcement? Wouldn't an oversight board advance the professionalism of journalism as it did for police officers, doctors, and lawyers? The answer is a great conundrum.

The reason there is no oversight board is because of the First Amendment right of freedom of speech and freedom of the press. The immense value that the freedom of the press brings to a society is sacred. Freedom of the press is the hallmark of any free democracy. A press corps, free from government control, functions as a watchdog that can investigate and report on corruption or other government wrongdoing. Freedom of the press is sometimes the only entity keeping politicians and corporate executives honest. The other entity is law enforcement in America (ACLU, n.d.).

For decades now, the SPJ has pondered and debated the question of an oversight board. The majority sentiment has always been that establishing such a media oversight board, as in other professions, could be the first step toward restricting the free press. Preserving the freedom of the press is just as important as ethical journalism, and any negative effect on constitutional rights just is not worth the risk. (SPJ , n.d.).

There is thoughtful debate taking place about an independent media oversight board. Canada and the UK have such boards; can the United States live with their blend of oversight and freedom of the press? There will come a time when the strive for journalistic professionalism hits a tipping point, and the creation of an oversight board is worth the risk. When professionals debate an issue, it is encouraging. Fortunately, the oversight board discussion happens regularly among journalism professionals. Until then, mayors, governors, law enforcement executives, celebrities, and star athletes are at the mercy of the media with no independent journalism oversight.

READER ASSIGNMENT
What do you think of the author's comparison between policing in the 1980s and modern-day journalism? Is it time for journalistic oversight in America? Draft a two-to-four-page paper covering the two questions.

READER NOTE
The final segment of this chapter gives a guide for addressing problematic media. This is a guide developed by the author in the absence of an independent oversight board to register journalism complaints.

Sanctity Of Confidential Sources

All good reporters seek out sources, because those sources are the driving force behind a reporter's insight. Since policing in major cities drives the media market, reporters seek sources from within law enforcement agencies. Reporters have successfully sought sources from within OPD and every major law enforcement agency in the country.

MEDIA SELF-RULE AND ITS EFFECTS ON LAW ENFORCEMENT

There are press sources within the White House, the Federal Bureau of Investigation (FBI), and even the Central Intelligence Agency (CIA). If it is of public interest, reporters will seek and commandeer sources (Centre for Ethics in Journalism, n.d.).

Every major law enforcement agency, city hall, or government division will have leaks—employees who divulge insider information to reporters (Bennett 2023, Bertrand et al. 2023; Fisher 2023). OPD is no different. In 2012, the agency was akin to Swiss cheese, with all the leaks coming out of the police department. By the time 2016 rolled around, OPD's leaks were shored up. It remained that way until around five years later, when it came to my attention that a high-level source was gathered by a reporter under dubious circumstances.

READER NOTE
Chapter Ten will cover media leaks within a law enforcement agency and how to uncover and address those leaks.

The freedom of the press and the protection of press sources find their roots in the First Amendment of the United States Constitution. Adopted in 1791 as part of the Bill of Rights, the First Amendment safeguards freedom of speech and freedom of the press by preventing the legislative branch from enacting laws that infringe upon these fundamental liberties. Specifically, the Free Press Clause enshrines the right to publish information and opinions without government interference, applying to all forms of media, whether print, broadcast, or digital (Cornell Law School, n.d.).

Journalists operate under the principle of a "reporter's privilege," which theoretically and legally allows them to protect the confidentiality of their sources and never be compelled to reveal them in court. However, reporters also rely on standard, on-the-record sources that are openly identified and referenced in their articles. As a chief, I have been quoted and credited as a source in numerous articles over the years. Nonetheless, it is the confidential sources—those insiders who choose to remain anonymous—who often provide reporters with the most valuable and exclusive information that would otherwise remain hidden from public view.

A confidential source may divulge various scenarios to a reporter, including when an arrest is about to be made, the details of a large investigation, when a police officer is getting terminated, the release of a new pharmaceutical drug, or a government kickback scheme. An hour before the PPC for the officer-involved death of Zachary Bearheels, the *Omaha World Herald* reported that four officers were going to be fired. The reporter clearly had a confidential source, and the reporter was able to break the news story (See Addendum 3: Omaha's National Crime Events for details on the Bearheels case) (KETV 2022).

The reporter never disclosed the source, but those of us familiar with the circumstances have a fairly good idea who it was. The suspicions fell on another member of the criminal justice system and not an OPD employee.

It falls upon the reporter to carefully vet the credibility and truthfulness of their sources. Crucially, the reporter must determine whether the source truly has insider knowledge and access to the subject matter at hand. As a chief of police, I have witnessed instances where reporters have overestimated a source's level of insider access or expertise—resulting in claims that do not align with the source's actual position or involvement.

Confidential sources may harbor ulterior motives that call into question the integrity of the information they provide. A source is seeking to undermine a rival's chances for a coveted promotion. Oftentimes, confidential sources are disgruntled former or current employees, so reporters must approach their claims with prudent skepticism. A thorough examination of the source's role, potential biases, and motivations is imperative.

Journalists rely on confidential sources whose identities are carefully guarded and never revealed, as this protection is a cornerstone of the media's role as neutral observers. Professional reporters can rightfully refuse to testify in court about how they obtained information or from whom, as the public interest in protecting confidential sources outweighs the need for disclosure in specific cases.

The First Amendment ensures the source can never be compelled in a court of law, with a few exceptions. Some states have taken an extra layer of press protection by implementing shield laws. Shield laws prevent the disclosure of confidential sources, without exceptions (Marburger, n.d.; Omachonu 2023).

Exceptions to Revealing Confidential Sources

There are a few exceptions where a reporter can be compelled to reveal a confidential source. First, the government must show there is probable cause to believe a reporter possesses relevant information. Second, it must be shown there is no alternative way to retrieve the information. This is a high bar, because if the reporter got information from a confidential source, why can't the government also get the same information from the same source? Third, there must be a compelling and overriding interest by the state for the information in question. Another high bar to get over, as knowledge of a confidential source's use is oftentimes a "so what" moment.

For example, when a reporter broke the story that officers were going to be fired before the Zachary Bearheels PPC, it was a "so what" moment because Omaha residents were going to find out the same information at the press conference just an hour later anyway. The court would not compel a reporter to divulge a source under this kind of "so what" condition.

Only pertinent and propriety information, gained by a confidential source, is grounds for compelled disclosure of the source by the journalist. Even when journalists are ordered to disclose their sources, some will not do so. In 1972, a reporter was sent to jail for forty-six days for refusing to identify his confidential source for an article on the Charles Manson murder trial. A *New York Times* reporter was ordered to jail for refusing to reveal her source in connection with a government investigation into the leaked name of a CIA operative (Eggen 2007). Prosecutors alleged that the George W. Bush administration leaked the name of the CIA operative in an act of retribution after the operative's husband authored an article criticizing President Bush (The Reporters Committee for Freedom of the Press, n.d.).

Confidential Sources Exposed

While some journalists will go to jail to protect their sources, do not expect this to be the rule for every reporter. Talking to reporters may not always be as protected as you think. As unlikely as it may sound, I have had reporters reveal their confidential sources to me. This included a few young reporters who left the profession and an executive-level media employee. Newcomer reporters are young, likely in their twenties, and looking to make a name for themselves in their first real career. Many leave the business after a few years because the pay is better elsewhere, which leads me to reinforce my opening statement: not all reporters will protect their sources. Young reporters have left the business and called me to report their sources. Who knows why reporters do this? But it happens.

On one occasion, a young reporter had left the news profession disheartened because of their low salary. They reached out to me and outed their confidential source, saying it was an OPD officer. My response was to ask who it was because I knew the officer rank would not have access to information on higher-level investigations or internal affairs matters. The officer would have to be directly involved, or they would have to be the responding officer to the original 911 call.

The reporter, clearly disgusted with the confidential source, told me a name but did so "off the record." The reporter said they would not repeat the name to internal affairs, nor would they testify in any disciplinary investigation the officer may have. As such, there was not much I could do with the information other than to be aware of it. The officer's name came as a shock, and I am still unaware of their motivation. The officer who acted as a confidential source seemed only to want to help OPD, but nonetheless, all media communications from the department must originate from the chief or PIO.

On another occasion, when a reporter revealed a source, it was because they had been in a romantic relationship with the source. I gather that when it ended, they took revenge by outing their behavior to me. It did give me an officer to investigate. During my time as chief, an employee has been terminated who was deliberately leaking confidential case information to a reporter.

Even veteran journalists will not always protect their sources. On one occasion, under an agreement that I would take no action with the information, an executive-level news official told me who the leak was within OPD. The news agency had been burned by the source, and the news executive refused to use the confidential source any longer. The source was a disgruntled OPD employee with an agenda.

I kept my end of the deal and took no official action, but I kept it as "back-pocket information." Of course, I had to give something to the news executive in return. So be aware of who you may be dealing with. Reporters—both newcomers and veterans—have, for a variety of reasons, revealed their sources to me throughout my time as chief.

Assumed Standards

The assumed standards of many professions cannot be taken for granted. For example, attorney–client privilege. I have had many defense attorneys break this confidentiality. Some have done so while running scenarios by me and seeking my opinion on their cases and clients; fortunately, for the client, I was a trusted sounding board and not interested in ever repeating the conversations.

Consider the following scenario: Lawyers work for law firms. The lawyers run their cases by the other attorneys in the firm. It may make good sense to provide the client with an expert opinion, but now other attorneys know your attorney–client privileged information. It is easier for the second or third attorney to divulge it to their spouse, boyfriend, another attorney, neighbor, or whomever. The same is true for doctors' offices; lots of employees know about your medical condition, not just the doctor.

The same goes for the clergy. What is said in the sanctity of a confession to a priest does not always stay sacred. Indeed, priests have come forward to OPD about crimes learned in confession. The assumed sanctity does not always exist. Defense attorneys and priests are human and as with any sector of human beings there is a bell curve of responses. Most are great, a smaller percentage is exceptional, and an even smaller percentage will break the confidentiality and sanctity codes of the vocation.

READER ASSIGNMENT
Brainstorm either in person or online some other examples of professions where the sanctity of assumed standards could be broken.

MEDIA SELF-RULE AND ITS EFFECTS ON LAW ENFORCEMENT

Media Self-Rule

Media self-rule, for our purposes, is defined as selective revelations, selective emphasis, suppression of information, self-investigation of complaints, or unjust favoritism by journalists or news producers, which leads to misinforming readers or viewers. In succinct language, media self-rule means the media will use their own tilts, leans, and favoritism in reporting the news (LeBlanc et al. 2017). As discussed earlier in the chapter, the media also investigates and determines their own outcomes for complaints, without any independent review. The most prevalent examples of media self-rule that law enforcement agencies will face are the following: affinity reporting, "look at me" reporters, headline tilt, selective coverage, photo lean, and lack of responsiveness.

Disclaimer:
The terms affinity reporting, "look at me" reporters, headline tilt, selective coverage, photo lean, and lack of responsiveness were named by myself to tailor them to law enforcement. Media and journalism books refer to the same concept with different terminology.

Affinity Reporting

The biased reporter has an affinity for one side of the story over another. Reliable news stories recapture what has occurred and paint a picture of the terrain of a situation. The affinity reporter distorts the terrain and wants the audience to view a situation from their preferred point of view. Affinity reporting shines through when there are two sides to the story being pitted against each other. The affinity reporter has a preferred side and reports or writes the story in a way that reflects their bias. The story will have omissions of pertinent facts for one side and a heightened emphasis on details germane to the other side.

Let me use a national example to demonstrate what I mean. CNN and FOX News both have an affinity for political sides. Both cable news stations have biases that fall on opposite sides of the political aisle. Their reporting and the coverage of world events bear this out plainly. In some media books, this is referred to as ideological bias (University of Wisconsin–Green Bay 2023). For our purposes, it is referred to as affinity reporting. The cable stations mentioned have a clear affinity for one side of the political spectrum over the other.

Law enforcement agencies work with the local media, and local reporters can develop affinities for one side over another. Major law enforcement agencies have reporters assigned to them. I can easily remember all the *Omaha World Herald*, KETV, and WOWT reporters assigned to OPD over the years. Each one of them was looking for a story and asked the PIO to forward stories their way. There is daily news to fill up, and it is a puzzle to put together a daily paper or news broadcast.

The stories that OPD would push out were, of course, positive stories, but OPD will fully participate in negative stories as well. An agency needs to embrace flaws and positives alike. The reporter's affinity is shown through the stories they elected to take on. If the story goes against their narrative, it will not be aired.

During Omaha's 2020 civil unrest period, it was impossible to push out a positive story about OPD. The self-rule media chose to take on stories where the protester side was dominant. A reasonable explanation of OPD's actions was not fully covered, as it would have easily been understood. After the initial week of civil unrest, OPD still had protests contained to either the OPD headquarters or the city's Old Market area. These protests began nightly, before tailing off to weekly, then monthly, and finally, the wintry weather months ended the protests altogether. The coverage of the protest by the television media was misleading and affinity laden.

The media covered the story in a way designed to portray excess intensity to the situation and widespread support for the protestors (after the initial week). The media exaggerated crowd sizes by conducting interviews with the same activists over and over, without challenging what they were saying. The media omitted the obvious, which was that the protests were the same twenty to forty people every time, which is hardly widespread. Lastly, the protestors were chanting for a police union's officers' death during this time, and it went unreported. The Omaha Police Officers Association (union) president was in critical condition due to complications from the COVID virus. The protestors took the approach of calling for his death, but their chants went unreported by the media.

READER NOTE
Does the reader feel the press should have reported on the protest chants calling for a police union officials' death? Would the reader or viewer of the news feel they received the "real terrain" of the protests when considering the omission?

Media self-rule will follow the topics that sell. If negative news stories about a mayor sells, then good luck getting a positive story published. The belief that negative news sells better is common. In the early part of my career as chief, positive OPD coverage was the norm. Stories showing progress on OPD's three vital sign markers of shootings, homicide clearance rates, and OISs were robust. There was a string of good stories and editorials about the city's police force. The media affinity for OPD was high.

Now, the stories mostly lean negative as the affinity has changed. It is a post-2020 phenomenon. In the span of sixteen hours during one week in February 2023, there were two incidents. The first was that two Omaha officers were shot as they valiantly confronted a man with a gun inside a storage unit. The second happened the very next day, when OPD responded with precision to calls of an active shooter inside a Target store, took the necessary action, and killed the gunman. During my early years as chief, an editorial would have been published, thanking the officers and the police department for protecting the public. There was nothing in 2023; not even a hint of an editorial thanking OPD.

The city of Omaha is lauded nationally for reducing shootings and for its community engagement. CNN, ABC News, and *The Washington Post* have all given attention to the success. There has been national applause for OPD's collaborative work with the community and especially for The Empowerment Network, an umbrella organization that brings everyone together to focus on crime, poverty, and education by addressing root causes. Presentations are put on in major cities across the county, trying to replicate Omaha's success. Yet locally, there was minimal coverage of the positive trend lines, until the national stories started to air, and bandwagon coverage was given locally. When the terrain of a matter is abdicated, that is bias or media self-rule (AllSides, n.d.).

Omaha received national coverage for reducing shootings and homicides. Some samples of the national coverage are below:

- "How one city cut gun violence in half and may become a model around the country: Omaha, Nebraska, has seen a marked decrease in shootings," Ella McCarthy (ABC News, February 22, 2023)
- "Omaha 360 cuts shootings by 50 percent , other cities to follow," Ezekiel J. Walker (The Black Wall Street Times, February 22, 2023)
- "Omaha police chief on city's decline in gun violence," Washington Post Live (April 27, 2023)

A "Look at Me" Reporter

For the purposes of our instruction, a "look at me" reporter is a journalist who weaves together optics and coincidences to make them appear as fact. The reporter overly portrays a subject and uses a tabloid manner to try and pull in readers. This sensationalist reporter is easy to spot because every story they write is the biggest piece in the world. This type of reporting encourages bias and emotionally charged impressions of events rather than neutrality, which can cause manipulation of the truth (Frye 2005; Vanacore 2021).

If a single journalist has a consistent stream of sensational and monster news stories, the reader or viewer needs to be aware that the reporter might have a "look at me" persona. The Omaha area has had a few "look at me" reporters over the years. Everyone

Omaha Police photo: CNN interview on how Omaha succeeded in drastically reducing gun violence. CNN host with Willie Barney of the Empowerment Network and Omaha Police Chief Todd Schmaderer.

in law enforcement knew who the reporters were. Their stories repeatedly had flamboyant and misleading headlines, and their style led to manipulation of the truth. The "look at me" reporting continues because the stories were enjoyable to read or view, and they would draw in an audience. I will withhold my specific examples of a "look at me" journalist, as they would unnecessarily identify the reporter(s), and that is not the purpose of this book.

In summary, a "look at me" reporter will try to *make* the news rather than *report* the news. The best analogy I can give is the referee who makes the game about him. Good referees and reporters should be in the shadows; the sensationalist referee and reporter are on full display, as if to say, "Look at me." As such, lots of dramatic calls, technical fouls, flamboyant headlines, and cute quotes will weave throughout the game and story.

Headline Tilt

When headlines are misleading or designed to convey excitement on a dull story, this is an example of headline bias or tilt. Clickbaiting is a hallmark of headline tilt.

Clickbait headlines are written in a way that sensationalizes or misleads to attract clicks on the story (Coschedule, n.d.; University of Washington Library, n.d.). I have been the subject of clickbait on many occasions, in my opinion. Having been around for a while now, I have been through several management contracts and pay increases. They have all been commensurate with industry standards or what other chiefs in

MEDIA SELF-RULE AND ITS EFFECTS ON LAW ENFORCEMENT

comparable cities make for salary and benefits. Nonetheless, each time, a headline tilt was used to draw in readers.

Not once has there been a comparison between my salary and what other chiefs earn in comparably sized cities. There was a comparison once to the surrounding cities' police chiefs' salaries. Omaha's was naturally the highest. Omaha is by far the biggest city and has the biggest police force in the state of Nebraska. It was an apples-to-oranges comparison. There was never a true comparison to large comparable cities like Oklahoma City, or Minneapolis for chief salaries.

Here is an example from 2023: "Former (well-known Nebraskan name withheld), sues city of Omaha, Police Chief Todd Schmaderer." The headline was clickbait and designed to get the viewer or reader to click on the story. The implication was that I had some personal contact with the well-known person, and it was negative. If you are a reader or viewer, would the fact that there might be a personal connection with the chief interest you more?

Does the headline "Former (well-known Nebraskan name withheld) sues city of Omaha, Police Chief Todd Schmaderer" entice an audience more than "former (well-known Nebraskan name withheld) sues the city of Omaha"? I would argue the personal nature of the headline, ----- versus Schmaderer, entices more clicks. What makes the headline clickbait is that I had no role in the investigation that led to the person's arrest. Note that the well-known person was found "not guilty" at trial, and the verdict must be respected. Chiefs are named in a lot of lawsuits involving their agency, as the agency's head. These lawsuits happen all the time in major law enforcement agencies. The clickbait headline made it unnecessarily personal, which it was not, to entice an audience to click on the article or news clip.

Reader Note:

The court would eventually dismiss me on the above lawsuit, in 2024, as I had no tangible role in the matter. The media failed to report on the dismissal, even though the original lawsuit was "breaking" news. Attorneys know this, and sometimes will use a lawsuit to smear someone knowing when it gets dismissed, the dismissal will not receive the same "splash." The Omaha media market has been sub-par on their follow-up stories in this regard. Disclaimer: I am not alleging this occurred on this example.

Selective Coverage

Selective coverage refers to where a story is placed in the news coverage; this indicates its value to the news agency. A story can be *buried* by placing it in a less-read section. It can also be buried at the end of the nightly news broadcast, or it can be ignored altogether (Aliprandini and Flynn 2016).

In Chapter Two: Omaha's National Crime Events—Unveiling the Impact, there is a story of a public corruption scandal. The media adopted the name "33rd and Seward" for the story, as it was the location in the city where the scandal took place (KETV 2023). In the 33rd and Seward scandal, the news agency that broke the story ran it at the beginning of their nightly newscasts for days. The other stations, likely because they did not break the story, ran it deeper in the nightly news broadcast. We all know the first story is the biggest on the nightly news. As the story grew, and the Omaha community began to take notice, only then did all news agencies report on it as the main story.

For print media, this effect is much easier to spot. Stories the paper wants to highlight will be front and center in the hard copy or the online version. Stories that need to be reported on, but the paper wants to minimize will be deeper in the print paper and harder to find online (Steppat et al 2022).

Photo Lean

Photographs can serve as a powerful medium for selling a story (Barrett and Barrington 2005; Reza 2022). There are many professional photos of public figures online. In contrast, enter any major law enforcement executive into Google and see what comes up.

For law enforcement personnel, inevitably, photos are taken during normal times when the executive is not looking or during interviews and PPCs. Many of the photos will be in mid-speech or action, thereby distorting the image. Law enforcement agencies do provide the media with professional photos of law enforcement executives for usage in their broadcasts or print. It is fascinating to see which news agencies use the professional photo versus those that use candid, distorted photos.

Political candidate photos are often shown next to each other during election cycles on the news. The photo of the candidate the media agency prefers will be a studio photo. The photo of the other candidate will be unflattering. Never underestimate the intelligence of the population, though, as people see right through the subliminal photo messaging.

Articles critical of the police will use unflattering photos of the chief or ones where they look angry, in my opinion. Other media outlets will ensure the chief looks stately and professional. It is easy to detect the new agency's subliminal support or opposition by the photos they use; or the photo is used to bring in viewers or was captured during a press conference on the story at hand.

In another example of photo lean, there was a story that played out for over a year in the media. The city and I were being sued by a command officer who worked for OPD. The city and I eventually lost a lawsuit in court. The photo of me used by some news organization was of a stern or mean look. This photo was always put side by side with the plaintiff's photo, which was a professionally taken department photo.

MEDIA SELF-RULE AND ITS EFFECTS ON LAW ENFORCEMENT

Photo courtesy of the *Omaha World Herald*.

OPD professional photo available to all local media agencies for media use.

I always laughed because my commensurate official photo could have been used but was not.

In the starkest example of photo lean, a contradictory photo was used to pull in readers, though the actual story delivered a different message. During a front page story shortly after the major 2020 protests and civil unrest in Omaha, regarding the number of times Omaha police officers used force to make an arrest, the story laid out how rare and minuscule the number of occurrences are. However, the photo accompanying the story was of an Omaha officer using his baton on a protester (Connely 2020). A whole host of potential issues come to mind when the photo lean is contrary to what the story says (Nikolaev 2009). Such as the subliminal perception the OPD uses a lot of force; a reader could see the photo and be left with the wrong impression unless they read the story.

"Use of force rare among Omaha police; decrease in shootings 'impressive,' expert says" *Omaha World Herald,* July 27, 2020

Photo courtesy of the *Omaha World Herald.*

Readers should know that I consider the *Omaha World Herald* to be a highly professional news entity. The photo lean is one example of a divergent photo and storyline. The paper has written hundreds of stories about OPD or myself during my career, and I seldom take issue with the reporting, because it is thorough journalism. In addition, I chose not to complain about this story's photo lean at the time. If I had complained, I trust that a professional review of the matter would have taken place, followed by professional reasoning and a response.

MEDIA SELF-RULE AND ITS EFFECTS ON LAW ENFORCEMENT

READER ASSIGNMENT
How much emphasis do you put on photos? A photo can be used to denote a favorable or unfavorable view of a person. For example, look up former President Donald Trump's photos. Can you tell by the photo the impression the news outlet wants you to have of the former president? In a one- or two-page paper, show a positive image of Trump and one where the photo shows him in a negative light. Explain the photos in your paper.

Lack of Responsiveness

On occasion, there will be a distinct lack of responsiveness by the media. Law enforcement agencies work around the clock, 365 days a year. The major media nationally and locally are supposed to work 365 days around the clock as well. However, the time and day of a major event matters.

The following is an example that demonstrates what I am talking about. The incident was a call about a domestic assault, and OPD responded on a Saturday morning in 2023. The 911 call led officers to another location, where a man was found shot and murdered in his house. It was determined that the suspect was the same man who had just committed the domestic assault. Further information led officers to another house, where the suspect was trying to track down females with whom he had been in a prior relationship. At this location, the suspect rammed the house with his car and fired a gun at a neighbor when his ex was not there.

The suspect was on the run, had committed a domestic assault and murder, and had fired a gun at three different crime scenes, all during a Saturday morning hour. It was clear the suspect was a grave danger to society. OPD put out a press release to all media and asked the media to run a scroll at the bottom of the television. The scroll never occurred, and OPD struggled to get any media present at our on-scene pressers, even though it was a grave and imminent public safety concern.

Later in the day, the suspect was located, and a high-speed police pursuit went into two states. The suspect was finally stopped after police rammed his car, and he was subsequently shot and killed. In the suspect's possession was a hit list of people he wanted to kill for revenge. The Omaha area had a "spree killer" that day, and if it had not been for the professional intervention of law enforcement, they would have killed more. Yet OPD could not get the media to respond. The reasonable inference is that the early morning hours of a Saturday were shallow in staffing for the media, and this had been a case of lack of resources.

However, a lack of responsiveness can occur for nefarious reasons as well. The media is self-ruled and run by human beings. Human beings are not always professional. In fact, they come with weaknesses and biases. Without industry checks and balances, those weaknesses can turn into unresponsiveness.

Guidelines for Addressing Problem Journalists and News Agencies

How to contest an already written or aired news story

There are going to be incomplete, poorly aired, and/or poorly written news stories. There will also be daily stories involving major law enforcement agencies and their personnel, crime, societal matters, or interesting court cases. The point is, there will be so many stories that some will be wrong. If the mistakes are minor, and not germane to the story, just let them go. If they are minor but material to an important matter, direct the PIO to point it out.

But what about major mistakes by the media? For major mistakes, consider this progression formula:

Step 1. Use the department's PIO

First, see if the PIO can fix the problem. The PIO should reach out to the reporter first for a correction. If that fails, the PIO should call the reporter's supervisor. If that also fails, go to Step 2.

Step 2. Reach out to the editor or news director

If the PIO is unable to correct the falsehood, only then should the law enforcement executive reach out to an editor or news director. A chief of police should not ever squabble with an entry-level reporter. A chief, sheriff, or superintendent should reach out to their peer in the news agency, an editor, or a news director. If Step 2 fails, there are three ways to proceed. They are outlined below as Steps 3a, 3b, and 3c.

Step 3a. Use the law enforcement agency's social media

As a last resort, if the news director or editor will not correct the falsehood, the police department can use their own social media to correct the situation. The following anecdote provides an actual example of such a scenario.

On this occasion, a news entity reported an attempted child abduction at a school, which caused concern. But there had been no attempted child abduction; it had been something far less, and by no means did the public need this level of alarm. The news director was contacted, and they did not want to deal with it so, OPD put out what

MEDIA SELF-RULE AND ITS EFFECTS ON LAW ENFORCEMENT

really happened through the official Omaha police social media accounts. The reasoning for OPD taking this action was spelled out in the social media post. The post was effective. The situation was cleared up for the public, and OPD's social media followers ate the media organization alive with negative comments.

Step 3b. Going to the news agency president or publisher

As a last resort, there is the option of going to the news agency president or publisher. You could also consider going to the parent company's president or board of directors. Most local news agencies work under a parent company. The fact that you are going to the top means you have exhausted all other means and denotes a profoundly serious matter. Some parent companies that have many local news agencies under their ownership are Lee Enterprises and Hearst Television. I have previously come close to contacting their corporate headquarters. However, the news director addressed my concern before it got to that point.

Lee Enterprises is the parent company of the *Omaha World Herald* and Hearst is the parent company of KETV. Please do not read into their parent company being noted. Both news entities are highly professional and managed well. On a national level, six news companies control 90 percent of the media in the United States: AT&T, CBS, Comcast, Disney, News Corp, and Viacom (Nalbandian 2022).

Step 3c. Banning a reporter

Banning a reporter is the nuclear option and should only be used in the most extreme of circumstances. I would only ban a reporter from OPD or from access to myself or my staff as the very last resort. I have only ever banned one reporter in over eleven years as chief.

Law enforcement leaders should try to work through the situation before banning reporters. Oftentimes, the reporter's supervisor will intervene or at least mitigate enough for the situation to pass. However, when the reporter's behavior or reporting is outlandishly atrocious, or the issue being reported on is of a severe and serious nature then, a reporter may need to be banned. In my real-world example, the reporter was trying to make a name for themselves and went too far. Unfortunately, the reporter's supervisors then fell into the trap of blindly supporting their reporter.

Banning a reporter example

A heinous set of murders took place in Omaha. A killer stabbed his mother and murdered her during an argument and then was suspected of throwing his four-year-old half-sibling over a bridge into the Elkhorn River. It was unknown if the child was thrown over the bridge or not, but the river was an area we decided to search for good reason. The child could have been missing somewhere else too.

OPD, Omaha Fire Dive team, and other search-and-rescue water workers spent days looking for the child, particularly searching the Elkhorn River. While we were looking at the Elkhorn River, there was no definitive proof the child had been thrown into it. We did not know where he was. A missing child was out in Omaha, and until the child was found, it was imperative the search continued.

It was during this crisis that a local reporter was banned from the OPD. This journalist was about to break a story that OPD had located the child. I received word of the reporter's intentions through my PIO, who was enraged. At the time, we had no idea where the child was. The child could be in the river but had certainly not been located. For the sake of everyone, especially the child and his family, a reporter cannot report a child was located when they have not been.

I eventually contacted the reporter's news director. The news director said their reporter had reliable information that the child had been located. I retorted in a stern manner, "You have the ultimate authority on the phone, and I am telling you we have not found the child." To my disbelief, I was totally ignored, and the story moved forward.

Given the serious nature of the situation, it was life and death—a death penalty case where a plea is the only reason a life sentence is happening—the nuclear measure of banning the reporter from access to the OPD commenced. I do not mean physical access; the reporter could have come to the police department, but we were not going to work with them again. The news entity would have to send someone else if they wanted cooperation from us.

The reporter's boss was not happy about the ban. I feel they had blindly and erroneously supported their reporter on this occasion, and the gravity of the story had pushed a desire to have breaking news. It is hard to tell. It is the only time in over twelve years in which I have banned a reporter, so, let that be an illustration that this is an exceedingly rare circumstance.

Chapter Conclusion

The chapter, Media Self-Rule and Its Effects on Law Enforcement, covers the lack of accountability for the media and the consequences this can have on law enforcement. The media operates in a highly competitive *for-profit* industry. The media is a professional entity that wrestles with whether to have an oversight board to strive for further professionalism. The Great Conundrum is the premise of the First Amendment as "freedom of the press" butts up against the creation of a national media oversight board.

MEDIA SELF-RULE AND ITS EFFECTS ON LAW ENFORCEMENT

The sanctity of confidential sources is discussed, while real-world examples of affinity reporting, "look at me" reporters, headline tilt, selective coverage, photo lean, and lack of responsiveness demonstrate the media's self-rule. The chapter ends with a progression guide for addressing problem journalists and news media agencies.

The following chapter covers law enforcement agency *leaks* and types of leakers. It looks at how to narrow down the leak through real-world examples and provides insight on how to minimize such situations. It discusses the Freedom of Information Act (FOIA) and covers the public's right to government information and law enforcement exceptions.

Questions for discussion and review

Attempt to answer the following questions before looking up the answers at the back of the book.

1. True or False: The media is in a not-for-profit industry, so journalistic standards are regulated.
2. True or False: In Canada, there is a media oversight board regulating media standards.
3. The author compares the media today to policing in the 1980s. Why?
4. True or False: Confidential sources never have to be disclosed.
5. True or False: Shield Laws are in place via individual states to bolster the protection of confidential sources.
6. What is the author referring to when the term "assumed standards" is used?
7. Are the guidelines for addressing problem journalists or news agencies a progression formula?
8. True or False: Banning a reporter is an early step in the progression when dealing with a problem reporter or news agency.
9. True or False: Contacting a news agency's parent company is an option when addressing a problem news agency.

CHAPTER TEN

Freedom of Information Act and Leaks—Navigating the Maze of Information Access

Introduction

After reading this chapter, you will gain a comprehensive understanding of law enforcement leaks, the dynamics between reporters and leakers, and the legal and ethical considerations surrounding the disclosure of confidential information. You will learn what constitutes a law enforcement leak, the process by which reporters actively seek out and engage with leakers, and the importance of verifying the accuracy, legitimacy, and truthfulness of the information obtained.

The chapter will delve into the circumstances under which leaking information can be considered a criminal offense, as well as the nuanced process of acquiring and possessing confidential information. You will become familiar with the four distinct character types of leakers and the key role that motivation plays in preventing and detecting leaks. Specifically, the chapter will explore the four primary motivations that drive individuals to leak information.

Furthermore, you will gain insights into the methods and techniques for uncovering leaks, as well as the differences between the phrases "sources close to the investigations" and "law enforcement source," which are commonly used in reporting. The chapter will also clarify the distinctions between the terms "off the record" and "on background," which are essential for understanding the boundaries of information sharing.

Finally, you will learn about the Freedom of Information Act (FOIA) and the specific exceptions that apply to law enforcement agencies, providing a comprehensive understanding of the legal framework governing the disclosure of sensitive information in the context of law enforcement.

Leaks

Every major law enforcement agency will eventually encounter leaks (Freedom Forum, n.d.; The Free Dictionary, n.d.). While there are existing books and writings on this subject, *Synergy of Influence* stands out as the first comprehensive exploration of leaks as they pertain to law enforcement agencies. With law enforcement agencies comprising hundreds, thousands, and even tens of thousands of employees, leaks are an unavoidable reality. Even an agency with just two deputies can be susceptible to leaks.

Information from a law enforcement agency does not only get released through leaks. There is also the FOIA, and it holds paramount significance for a law enforcement agency. A strong understanding of FOIA is imperative, as failure to grasp its intricacies can subject the agency to high-level embarrassment through information releases. The FOIA grants the media and private citizens access to government documents, such as emails, police computer-aided dispatch comments, text messages, and phone logs. However, it is crucial for agencies to be aware of certain exceptions to FOIA.

What is Considered a Leak?

Let us define a leak for the purposes of this book in the context of law enforcement. A leak occurs when an employee of a police agency or another individual within the criminal justice system discloses information not authorized for release to a member of the press (Clark 2017). Leakers may include contractors with database knowledge, detectives with sensitive case information, members of the prosecution team, defense lawyers (yes, this happens), or courtroom employees before a trial.

In approximately 95 percent of leak instances, the leaker prefers to remain anonymous when sharing information with reporters. However, there are some examples of retired or fired officers who leak information. In these rare instances, the generally disgruntled former employee seeks to attach their name to the leak. It is up to the local press to discern the former employee's motives behind the leak and decide whether to report on it.

Many years ago, around late 2012 or early 2013, a significant story emerged about an OPD police supervisor who was arrested for driving under the influence. Despite the arrest, the supervisor retained their command position within the department's homicide unit. A leaker, who had contacted the media, portrayed the supervisor's twenty-day suspension and continued role in the homicide unit as a miscarriage of justice. The leaker's position to the reporter was that the supervisor should not have been allowed to stay in such a coveted position and trusted unit after the arrest.

However, the truth behind the leak revealed a different story. The leaker was likely an Internal Terrorist (one of the four-character types of leakers discussed later in the chapter) acting out of vengeance due to another matter that did not go their way. Upon learning of the leaked information, I promptly contacted the news director to clarify the situation. I explained that the homicide supervisor was retained in their position due to their extensive knowledge and involvement in critical ongoing cases. Moreover, during that period, the homicide unit was not considered a coveted position, as the OPD faced challenges in solving homicides, and there was a lack of interest in working in the unit. To support my assertion, I decided to present the news director with the list of supervisors who had expressed interest in working in the homicide unit when the next opening became available, and to my surprise, there were no names on the list.

The news director acknowledged the validity of the bid sheet and took immediate action to make redactions to the story. Though the identity of the leaker remained undisclosed to me, I was informed that the news agency would not use this person as a source again, as they felt manipulated and taken advantage of. While I have personal certainty about the leaker's identity, I lacked concrete evidence to take formal action or initiate an internal investigation. As an executive, sometimes the most one can obtain is informal information, which can be used for personal judgment in future decision-making.

Leaks Are a Violation of Policy and Sometimes the Law

Releasing confidential information, as exemplified in this case, violates the department's policies and procedures and can even be illegal in certain instances. For instance, leaking knowledge of a wiretap is a crime, and disclosing national defense information with the intent to harm the United States or another nation is also a criminal offense (though typically more relevant to FBI/CIA cases than municipal police departments). Moreover, releasing something of value to the United States, such as sensitive records and documents, straddles a fine line in terms of criminal implications.

A reputable law enforcement agency must have a comprehensive policy against information leaks. The public has the right to know that the agency investigating their crime, or the natural or accidental death of a loved one will not release sensitive information to the media. A prominent example of the consequences of such leaks is the case of Los Angeles Sheriff's deputies who released photos of Kobe Bryant's deceased body after his helicopter crashed, leading to a lawsuit settlement by Kobe's wife for $28.85 million (Schrotenboer 2023).

Whistleblowers

Not all sharing of information goes against department policy. Some individuals who leak information are considered whistleblowers, as the information they disclose is protected by the Whistleblower Protection Act. This act ensures that whistleblowers cannot be fired or discriminated against for exposing abuses of authority, law violations, or wasteful spending of money (US Department of Labor, n.d.).

Leaks Are a Challenge for Law Enforcement Executives

The challenge of leaks can drive law enforcement executives crazy. As I mentioned in the last chapter, back in 2012, the OPD was plagued by leaks. Leaks have a detrimental impact on public trust in the agency, individual case investigations, the culture set by the law enforcement executive, and the integrity of the internal affairs process with employees. Furthermore, leaks project the image of an unprofessional agency incapable of competently fulfilling its duties.

Agency executives who oversee sensitive information must establish clear policies on handling leaks and improper transfer of materials or information. Valuable advice that I received as a new chief still holds true today. A former Omaha police chief once told me that the "walls have ears." This referred to the morning briefings in the chief's office, during which deputy chiefs and the PIO briefed the chief of police on matters related to their bureaus. Though these discussions are highly sensitive and confidential, one must be mindful that the walls have ears, meaning that the subject matter may circulate beyond the room.

Learned Process

Agency executives must recognize that maintaining sensitive information is a learned process. Topics such as internal affairs (IA) investigations, homicide details, budget matters, and personnel issues are all discussed during the chief's briefings. It has been my experience that newer deputy chiefs may unintentionally slip up, driven by their newfound access to highly sensitive information. The temptation to share enticing information can be strong, particularly among those recently assigned to sensitive units like the child victim unit.

In my approach, I exercise caution with new high-level commanders concerning the information they can access and when. On the other hand, seasoned deputy chiefs have learned to preserve confidentiality and hold on to sensitive information. I adopt a layered approach to handling sensitive data, with certain highly sensitive information remaining solely with me. There have been rare occasions when the FBI involved me in extremely sensitive matters, and I found it best not to even discuss them with my deputy chiefs.

Sensitive case investigation materials should only be known to the criminal investigation's deputy chief, the executive deputy chief, and the chief of police. Similarly, IA sensitive information should be restricted to the IA deputy chief, executive deputy chief, and chief of police. This ensures that the *walls* will not inadvertently reveal sensitive information.

In general, a chief or executive overseeing an agency housing sensitive information should establish comprehensive policies and procedures regarding the unauthorized release of such information. Training should emphasize the importance of confidentiality, and staff should receive frequent reminders about overseeing confidential matters with utmost care. Swift action must be taken against leakers, especially in significant investigations like the 33rd and Seward police corruption scandal or the Nikko Jenkins serial killer case (see Chapter Two for descriptions of both these investigations). Detectives should be made aware of the severe consequences of leaks, and stern warnings about leaks should be part of their expectations.

Media Recruitment of "Leakers"

Dealing with the media is no walk in the park for a law enforcement leader. Journalists and reporters relentlessly seek out confidential informants as part of their professional duties. At the conclusion of every news story—whether on the online version of a television broadcast or an online newspaper—the reporter's contact information, including email and phone number, is typically available at the bottom. Sometimes, these reporters even solicit news stories directly from the law enforcement agency. As another example of how commonplace this activity is, the Society of Professional Journalists (SPJ) has a dedicated section on their website called "Leak Seeker," where they encourage sharing information with reputable news media (SPJ, n.d.).

A fundamental principle of successful journalists and reporters is their ability to secure confidential sources. Naturally, these sources must come from areas of public interest, which is what drives the media market. A source within the White House would be monumental, while one within the University of Alabama football team would be considered an asset. Similarly, having a source within a major police department is seen as a remarkable achievement.

In my experience, I have come across emails where reporters directly approached several OPD employees, explicitly requesting them to be future sources. At that moment, there might not have been a specific story in mind, but the reporters were strategically trying to establish sources for potential future stories. Additionally, I have personally been asked to serve as a source, and my commanders have informed me that they, too, have been solicited as sources. This emphasizes the importance of preparing and reminding staff members of their responsibilities, as reporters will actively pursue them for information. As the saying goes, "Hate the player (reporter), not the game."

An excellent example of the relentless pursuit of leakers can be found in WikiLeaks, which epitomizes the search for confidential sources. This website operates under a unique business model, exposing corporations, governments, foreign countries, and anything else that can capture an audience's attention. The founder of WikiLeaks, Julian Assange, remains a household name, with opinions about him ranging from hero to traitor. Such is the nature of exposing leaks, with some lauding its cause and others expressing collective disapproval (WikiLeaks, n.d.).

News agencies highly value reporters with a network of confidential sources, recognizing the valuable insights they provide. However, from the perspective of a law enforcement agency executive, having such sources may not be as favorable, considering the delicate nature of managing sensitive information. Nevertheless, I fully comprehend that reporters are merely doing their jobs. On a related note, when faced with a heinous crime, I often consult with the deputy chief of detectives to determine whether our confidential sources possess any relevant information, or if they can aid in uncovering what occurred. Such reliance on confidential sources is an indispensable aspect of journalism and police work. At a higher level, it plays a vital role in national security efforts aimed at keeping our country safe.

The Four Character Types of "Leakers"

Over time, I have developed character types to describe the four kinds of leakers that exist in law enforcement agencies. An understanding of the leaker's motivation is key to the prevention and detection of the leaker. Let us go through all four of the characters.

1) Status Seeker

The status seeker is an employee who constantly seeks recognition and a prominent reputation. In the realm of law enforcement, many police officers exhibit type A personalities, embodying the courage to take charge and be present on the scene. The entry-level position of a police officer comes with considerable authority, unlike some other professions where the bottom rung holds minimal power. A newcomer police officer possesses the legal authority to make life-altering decisions under extreme circumstances, such as taking someone's life, depriving them of their liberty (arresting them), and seizing their property (such as towing a car). However, within the agency's internal dynamics, a police officer does not hold a decision-making role, as the chain of command prevails.

Imagine having the responsibility of managing every 911 call and making critical decisions that impact people's lives, yet, upon arriving at work and being in an assembly, having limited decision-making authority. For such decisions, veteran officers, sergeants, lieutenants, captains, and deputy chiefs hold the reins. Thus, for some officers, being a confidential source for a reporter provides them with a sense of status and decision-making power.

Officers are typically the first responders to crime scenes, as illustrated by the Kobe Bryant example, and they possess firsthand knowledge of the initial incident. Consequently, officers make compelling sources for reporters, given their immediate and direct access to crucial information. Higher-ranking officers can also fall into the category of status seekers. The desire to be self-identified as important becomes a driving force for many individuals. Savvy reporters recognize this aspect and, much like skilled salespeople, subtly leverage it to gain access to a source.

2) Mr. or Ms. Personal Gain

Who does not want to advance in the world? Some individuals are willing to compromise policies and take career risks to get ahead, driven by a misguided perception of how to achieve success. In my experience, I have come across employees who engage with the media as sources for personal gain. This personal gain could take various forms, ranging from seeking a romantic chance with a reporter, entering a desired social circle, or, in extreme cases, hoping for material benefits like money or tickets to events. I must clarify that I do not have examples of officers agreeing to be sources for financial or material gain, but I have encountered instances where they sought a romantic or social connection.

Some years ago, my deputy chiefs and I noticed a series of leaks in the department. Although these were low-level leaks with limited information, we suspected they were coming from one of our officers. While these leaks did not cause substantial harm, they did create the perception of sloppiness within the OPD. As it turned out, the leaks originated from an employee who was in a relationship with a reporter. During their social interactions, certain information came up and got leaked.

I am aware of a few instances where young officers expressed a desire to date certain reporters, and I can only assume that this worked to the reporters' advantage. Additionally, there have been circumstances where reporters actively pursued some of the officers, seeking opportunities to secure sources within our department. The NYPD, with its vast workforce of nearly 50,000 employees, presents even more possibilities for such dynamics than the OPD with 1,200 employees.

It is essential to understand that the examples I have provided pertain to the dynamic of reporters seeking sources, but I want to make it clear that most officers do not break the rules or compromise their oath of service. Officers are remarkable individuals who demonstrate important levels of integrity and professionalism, yet they sometimes face unfair criticism due to the actions of a few individuals.

3) The Vendetta Seeker

This type of employee poses a danger but is situationally motivated. They are not chronic sources or leakers, but when an opportunity arises to carry out a vendetta, they will not hesitate. As discussed in a previous chapter, allegations of police misconduct are of significant interest to the media, both nationally and in local markets.

For instance, if an officer is being investigated for a serious allegation by internal affairs, whether the media knows about it depends on how the investigation was initiated. If a command officer turned in the officer to internal affairs, the chances of the public knowing about it are slim. However, the officer's fellow crew members may be aware of the situation or the rumors surrounding it. Inquiries from the media about the case often lead prudent chiefs to conclude that someone within the department leaked the information and that the Vendetta Seeker is a likely culprit. They may have personal grudges or unresolved issues with their co-worker and might even have been the ones who reported the officer.

The scenarios described above are relatively low-level examples of a Vendetta Seeker, but the situation can become much worse. Imagine being passed over for a promotion, and the person who got the promotion made a mistake. The Vendetta Seeker may exploit this opportunity to anonymously share information with the media. The point I am emphasizing is that the Vendetta Seeker awaits the right circumstances, and if the chance presents itself, they will act on their vendetta.

Vendetta Seekers can inflict real harm on a police agency, making it imperative for internal affairs to be tightly managed. Your senior command staff should also be well versed in maintaining confidentiality. Any leaker, regardless of their motivation, can cause damage, especially when they hold sensitive positions such as internal affairs investigators or homicide detectives. It is crucial to select the right personnel for such sensitive roles. I can confidently say that within the OPD, true insiders who leak information are rare. While there have been occasions when sensitive information was withheld from a deputy chief or other commander to prevent any leaks, actual insiders involved in the cases are uncommon. Cops are professionals, and after more than a decade as chief, I say that with pride.

4) The Internal Terrorist

The internal terrorist is different from the Vendetta Seeker. This employee is a constant threat and not motivated by specific situations. They seize every chance to undermine the department or spread negativity, and their chosen outlet is the media. The internal terrorist understands that public perception is crucial for police departments. They strike at the agency's public image through the media as a confidential source.

FREEDOM OF INFORMATION ACT AND LEAKS

Internal terrorists sometimes emerge because their thirst for power and ego is not satisfied by their current position in the police agency. OPD is a member of the Major Cities Police Chiefs Association (MCCA), and the subject of Internal Terrorists is talked about on breaks among the chiefs. Most chiefs I have spoken to have encountered Internal Terrorists among their ranks, often right below their own rank, such as individuals who aspired to become the chief of police. These internal terrorists brood daily over why they were not chosen for the top position.

An esteemed and successful college basketball coach was once asked what he looked for in his assistant coaches. He replied that he sought individuals who could be successors but were not seeking to overthrow him. He lamented that he had encountered Internal Terrorists who craved his job title so much that they would covertly attempt to undermine him. Such Internal Terrorists can be found in all professions.

The government's structure in policing creates a unique dynamic compared to the private sector. In policing, the executive (the chief) does not have the freedom to fully select their leadership team. The upper commanders are already in place upon the chief's appointment, and, in most cases, the chief cannot remove or replace personnel. While there is some flexibility to reassign personnel to different bureaus, the commander would retain their rank.

Vacancies are filled through a testing process, and while there may be some flexibility to skip the rank order, bypassing a commander in favor of someone the chief deems more suitable can lead to bitter feelings and potential lawsuits. These hurdles can be challenging for chiefs to navigate.

The second dynamic in policing that hampers chiefs is the competition among deputies for the chief's position. When a chief is appointed, it is highly likely that the other candidates for the job are the deputy chiefs within the agency. Ultimately, one deputy chief is appointed as the chief of police, while the others become their deputies.

When I became chief in 2012, the competition was fierce, with fifty-three existing chiefs from around the country and sixteen internal Omaha Police candidates vying for the position. The interim chief at that time was also in the running for the permanent position. Can you imagine the awkwardness of taking over from the current interim chief and flipping the rank structure? One day, as a deputy chief, I was answering to the interim chief, and the next day, he was answering to me as chief.

The same dynamics can apply to other candidates who were not selected. While most commanders align themselves and act in a professional manner, others may turn into Internal Terrorists. This situation occurs less frequently in the private sector, where employment is often at will, and individual contracts may include an exit clause.

In law enforcement leadership, no such dynamic exists, and Internal Terrorists may try to destroy the agency and undermine the agency executive without being detected. I know of several major city chiefs who lament this dynamic. The Internal Terrorist will seek out a reporter and attempt to become a confidential source, giving the impression that they have an *army* of insiders supporting them. Oftentimes, disgruntled or terminated officers may be prone to recruitment by Internal Terrorists, becoming part of their army.

Is there a way to reverse the Internal Terrorist and make them an ally? In my opinion, the chances of that happening are slim. The other three types of leakers can be won over, but an Internal Terrorist is deeply entrenched in their own mindset and motivations, making it difficult to change their behavior. Reporters should be vigilant and thoroughly vet their confidential sources to guard against using an Internal Terrorist as a reliable source, as they are too compromised to be trusted.

To deal with an Internal Terrorist, they must be marginalized and managed like any other subordinate. Clear directions and expectations must be given to minimize their opportunities to go off script and harm the agency. Sensitive information must be withheld from the Internal Terrorist, and the chief may need to find ways to separate them from highly confidential investigative information. However, this can be challenging if the Internal Terrorist is one of the top commanders and a direct report who participates in briefings with the chief.

Internal Terrorists are obsessed with trying to build a network. If the Internal Terrorist can become a media source, and then add a politician who carries the Internal Terrorist mantra, it can cause real problems in a law enforcement agency. Sometimes a representative group of police officers can be compromised by the Internal Terrorist, as the Internal Terrorist will hide their true motivations. If the internal Terrorist is a high-ranking commander, they will ensure that every beneficial move done for a law enforcement officer comes with a "You owe me!" battle cry to build their army. In conversation with me, other major cities' chiefs have mentioned this dynamic playing out in their departments.

Uncovering the Leaker

How can the leaker be uncovered? The following section offers some tips on how to proceed with uncovering the leaker in your department.

1. Pay attention to the information released in the news story. The chief should have a good understanding of who would have access to certain levels of knowledge, which can help eliminate or include certain ranks as potential leakers. For example, let's say there is an internal affairs investigation into a highly publicized police misconduct case. The internal affairs unit and the chief will know the most details. If the *leak* does not entail the *juicy* information and instead is more focused on the circumstances below the

FREEDOM OF INFORMATION ACT AND LEAKS

juiciest information, then it can be assumed the leak did not come from internal affairs. Why leak lesser information when the juicy information is at your disposal?

2. Engage with reporters and compare notes through the Public Information Officer (PIO). While reporters will not divulge their sources, engaging in conversation can help pinpoint where the leak might have come from. Asking questions about the reporter's relationship with the source or when they first learned about the information can provide valuable insights. While they will not directly divulge their source, reporters also will not want to be rude, so they will respond around the subject. The reporter desires to have a *peer* relationship as much as the law enforcement agency does; therefore, the reporter will not totally shut down when questioned about the identity of the source. What the reporter says instead will help pin down the *leaker*. For example, asking the reporter if they knew the leaker before the story can be telling. The reporter will likely answer the question because it does not directly expose their source, but the answer is valuable. If the reporter covers the evening shift for the media, the reporter's connections will likely come from the evening shift of the law enforcement agency. That one question helps pin down the leaker and provides a segue for a follow-up question with the reporter.

3. Analyze how the source is referenced in the story. The way the reporter categorizes the source can narrow down the search. For instance, specific terminology used in the story might indicate whether the source is an insider or an external party. If the story says a "source close to the investigation," that is quite telling. The fact that the story did not say it was a law enforcement source or a source "within the agency" tells me the leaker is not from the law enforcement agency. The source could now be someone from the county or district attorney's office, or someone else outside of the law enforcement agency. If the story says a "law enforcement source" but does not say "close to the investigation," that tells me it is a general source. A general source is someone in the agency who the reporter goes to for information, but this individual is not an "insider," so the best they can do is repeat *water cooler* talk. This is why it is important to pay attention to how the source is described in the story.

It is also important to understand the distinction between "off the record" and "on background" information (Flegenheimer 2008). Knowing the reporter's usage of these terms can help narrow down the source. "Off the record" means that information the source shares with the reporter cannot be used in any way. When information is given "on background," it means that a reporter can use the information but cannot attribute it to the source.

Therefore, watch for words the reporter uses in the story. If it is verbiage unique to an officer, commander, or case information, the source can be uncovered. For example, if the verbiage used in the story refers to a case nickname, like "purple crew," then one can narrow the source to someone in the agency working the "purple crew" case. Reporters want their source to be "on background" rather than "off the record."

Off the record is a place to start for the reporter, as they must verify the information elsewhere to use it. Asking the reporter if the source originated from an off-the-record conversation is a good question to ask. If the reporter says yes, it tells me that an insider could be the source and does not want to be tracked. "On background" is an effective way to correct errors the reporter may have in their story construction. Always get an agreement in writing for off-the-record or on background information. I know of an example where a source texted a reporter, wrote "off the record," and gave investigative information. The reporter outed the source in the article because the one-sided text did not symbolize an agreement to be off the record.

4. Check city emails and phones for cross-referencing with the reporter's personal contact information. Leakers will often call a reporter's personal number, not knowing it is identifiable, to avoid detection on government property.

5. Consider using false information to flush out the leaker, particularly if a deep inner circle is suspected. By presenting false information at a high-level briefing and monitoring its dissemination, the source can be exposed. The reporter will then contact the chief or PIO for comment on the leak, and it can be debunked at this time. A leaker can easily be ferreted out this way, but it only works on insider personnel. Most of the time, the law enforcement executive will learn the leak is not in their inner circle.

6. Initiate an internal affairs investigation if enough evidence points to a suspect officer. Follow the collective bargaining rules for internal affairs investigations, specific to each law enforcement agency, but also note that some allow for taking the officer's personal phone if it is carried on duty, and then it can be checked for contact with the reporter.

7. Establish counter sources within the newsroom to receive information on upcoming stories. While these sources may not reveal the leaker's identity directly, they can provide valuable leads. I do know of chiefs who have counter sources in the media. The reverse source tells the chief of large stories on the horizon, and in return, the counter source may receive more access to the law enforcement agency.

8. Familiarize yourself with the Associated Press (AP) rules for using anonymous sources. This can help determine the credibility and level of the leaker. The following are the AP source rules:

i. The information is not an opinion or speculative and is vital to the story.

ii. The information is not available except under the condition of anonymity by the source.

iii. The source is reliable, and in a position to have direct knowledge.

Based on the AP's rules, one can ascertain more about the identity of the leaker.

FREEDOM OF INFORMATION ACT AND LEAKS

During a conversation I had with a reporter, I was told one source is all that is needed if the source is of high rank, such as a chief, deputy chief, or the head of an investigative unit such as the homicide unit. If a lower-ranked source is used, or someone not related to the case investigation, more than one source is needed. If the story makes reference to the sources in the plural, e.g., "sources have told," this would indicate that there are a few lower-level sources and not a single high-ranking source. A high-ranking source would come across as singular in the story, such as "a reliable police source."

Remember that having one high-ranking reliable police source is sufficient for the reporter. Peripheral sources may require multiple individuals to corroborate information, while a reliable police source typically indicates one singular member of the police department with direct involvement in the case.

The Freedom of Information Act

The Freedom of Information Act (FOIA) is a federal law that mandates the partial or full release of government documents at the federal level (US Department of the Treasury, n.d.). It defines the types of agency records subject to disclosure, such as emails, cell phone logs, texts, and files. Although primarily utilized by reporters, any regular citizen can request and receive federal government information through FOIA.

The purpose of the act is to promote transparency and accountability within the United States government, much like open public proceedings in courtrooms. However, it is essential to note that FOIA only applies to the federal government. Each state has its own set of freedom of information laws, governing the release of information for county, city, and state governments, including law enforcement agencies.

Having a clear understanding of freedom of information laws is crucial for police agencies, as reporters and citizens may use them to engage in "fishing expeditions" for information. Proper policies and procedures governing freedom of information should be in place, ensuring that officers are aware that work emails, phones, and computer communications are property of the city and thus subject to requests covered by freedom of information laws.

Numerous examples exist of officers' communications being exposed by reporters through FOIA, leading to job losses and severe embarrassment for departments. Leaked emails containing offensive content or inappropriate discussions about citizens can seriously damage the public's respect for the agency.

An illustrative example comes from a scandal involving a newly hired public schools superintendent about a decade ago. The superintendent appointment was derailed when a reporter, searching for unrelated information, stumbled upon emails exchanged between the superintendent and her lover on school email accounts.

As a chief, I can personally attest to my emails being subject to regular FOIA requests. Senior commanders and all city government employees should be well informed about what can and cannot be communicated via email. It is essential to understand the exceptions to freedom of information laws, especially those applicable to law enforcement:

a) Records developed or received from law enforcement during ongoing investigations, including supplemental detective reports, citizen complaints, informant identifications, information used in police tactics training, and intelligence data.
b) Communications protected by attorney–client privilege, particularly when high-ranking police officials interact with the city's legal team.
c) Personnel information, except for salaries and routine directory data, can be excluded, including police officers' personnel files.

To ensure compliance with the law and prevent any mishaps, all police agencies must establish clear policies and provide regular reminders about freedom of information records. Proper vetting for law enforcement exceptions should be conducted by both the legal department and a designated member of the agency before releasing any requested documents (US Department of Justice, n.d.).

Chapter Conclusion

This chapter began with a definition of a law enforcement leak and moved into why law enforcement executives are challenged and troubled by leaks. Reporters will always seek out sources and confidential sources, but they should thoroughly vet confidential sources to determine their motivation, accuracy, reliability, and truthfulness.

There are four-character types of leakers in law enforcement agencies, with The Internal Terrorist being the most damaging to an agency. Chapter Ten also covered how to prevent and uncover a leaker. The Associated Press rules for confidential sources are covered, which gives insight for law enforcement executives to understand the terrain from the reporter's operating instructions. The chapter also discussed law enforcement exceptions to the FOIA, instances where the information does not have to be released.

Up next is Chapter Eleven—Chief's Perspicacity. *Perspicacity* means the quality of having a ready insight into things. In the next chapter, the chief gives insight into policing matters and philosophy. This provides a "what works and what doesn't work" perspective for policing in a large city. The chapter provides quick-hitting executive viewpoints and a way for law enforcement agencies to avoid image damagers.

FREEDOM OF INFORMATION ACT AND LEAKS

Questions for discussion and review

Attempt to answer the following questions before looking up the answers at the back of the book.

1. What is considered a law enforcement leak?
2. If a contractor working with a police department leaks material, is it considered a law enforcement leak?
3. True or False: Most of the time, a leaker requests to be anonymous.
4. True or False: A reporter should take a confidential source at face value.
5. Give an example of when leaking law enforcement information is a crime.
6. Why do leaks pose a challenge for law enforcement executives?
7. True or False: All law enforcement employees are well suited to maintaining confidentiality on important matters.
8. Describe the four-character types of leakers.
9. What is the difference between the Vendetta Seeker and the Internal Terrorist?

CHAPTER ELEVEN

Media Case Study—The Enigma of Serial Killer Dr. Anthony Garcia

In the previous chapters, we discussed the theoretical foundations for creating a critical media strategy, the rationale behind why it is necessary, and what constitutes a societal monumental event. This chapter serves as a culmination of the theory already discussed in this textbook, applying those concepts to a real-world case study.

The investigation into the serial killer Dr. Anthony Garcia is an example in which the success of our critical media strategy was a literal matter of life and death. In this chapter, I will go through that strategy stage by stage.

The OPD critical media strategy was on full display during Dr. Anthony Garcia's five-year reign of terror. Garcia killed in 2008 and struck again in 2013, leaving four innocent victims murdered in the city of Omaha. Garcia was a former doctor and resident at the Creighton University School of Medicine. His motive stemmed from a bitter grudge against the medical school after he was fired in 2001 amid allegations of erratic behavior. Over a decade later, between 2008 and 2013, Garcia meticulously planned and carried out four revenge killings.

This chapter proceeds in the following order, beginning with the four victims.

1) The Victims
2) Who is Dr. Anthony Garcia?
3) Five-Part Case Study
    1. The Murders
    2. Task force Investigation
    3. Garcia's Arrest
    4. The Trial, Verdict, and Sentencing
    5. Where Are They Now?

The Victims

The victims of Dr. Anthony Garcia are listed in order of their deaths. Thomas Hunter and Shirley Sherman were killed at the same crime scene in 2008. Dr. Roger Brumback and his wife, Mary Brumback, were killed at the same crime scene in 2013. The Omaha community has forever been impacted by their deaths, as each one of them was a special contributor to their family and friends. They were tremendous people.

Solving their murders and preventing future killings was a top priority of the OPD and mine personally. The victims' names will be used in the chapter case study, and it is imperative to me that readers know who they are *first* before delving into who Dr. Anthony Garcia really is.

Thomas Hunter

Thomas Hunter was a vibrant eleven-year-old boy from Omaha, Nebraska. He was murdered on March 13, 2008. Thomas was the youngest son of four boys born to Drs. William Hunter (pathologist) and Claire Hunter (cardiologist). Both worked at Creighton University Medical Center. Thomas was quite a bit younger than his brothers; the second youngest brother, for example, was in college at the time of his death. Thomas's surviving brothers are Timothy, Robert, and Jeffrey.

Thomas was a sixth grader at an Omaha school where math and science were the specializations. He was a passionate gamer who loved rushing home from school to play on his Xbox. In an interview with KETV News, Claire Hunter described her son as "a wonderful, lively boy who didn't deserve what happened to him." The entire Omaha community felt the same way.

The magnitude of the murder of an innocent eleven-year-old boy was not lost on the community of Omaha, Nebraska. The death of a priceless child ramped up the intensity and emotion surrounding the case for the entire community and the OPD. There is no doubt that one of the reasons the media went into overdrive in 2013 was because of the innocence lost and extra agony associated with the unexplained murder of an eleven-year-old.

Shirley Kay Waite Sherman

Shirley Sherman, fifty-seven, was a rock for her family. She was the matriarch all families love and are lucky to have. She worked a few days a month as a housekeeper for the Hunter family to supplement her income as a single mother. Her death was a case of her being in the wrong place at the wrong time.

Shirley was a lifelong resident of Omaha and had two children. She also had five grandchildren, whom she adored. Shirley loved gardening and crafts. I had the pleasure of meeting Shirley's brother Brad and other members of her family for lunch and a stock car racing event. It was apparent she was adored and loved. Her infectious laugh is a strong memory of her personality.

Media coverage referred to Shirley as "the housekeeper." Her family hated that portrayal, and so did I. Shirley was working to make ends meet, and to the media, she was just "the housekeeper." After meeting with her family, however, I learned very quickly who she was and how she should be defined: as the heartbeat of an amazing family.

Dr. Roger Brumback and Mary Brumback

The Brumbacks were murdered in May 2013 at their home in Omaha, Nebraska.

Dr. Roger Brumback was born in 1948 in Washington, DC. He was highly accomplished academically and professionally. He finished his undergraduate degree in less than two years and was the youngest in his class at Pennsylvania University College of Medicine in Hershey, Pennsylvania. In 2001, he was appointed as professor and chair of the Pathology Department at Creighton University School of Medicine in Omaha, Nebraska.

Roger loved reading books and edited or co-authored at least nineteen books himself, including a series about cognitive disorders and Alzheimer's disease as a guide for families and caregivers. He received numerous prestigious awards for his medical acumen, including being elected to the Alpha Omega Honor Medical Society and the Creighton University Chapter of the Gold Humanism Honor Society.

The impact he had on society through his medicine was impressive. Roger loved traveling the world with his wife, Mary. Some of his other interests were square dancing and genealogy research.

Mary Brumback was born and raised in Richland, Washington, in 1947. She attended Pennsylvania University after a robust and successful high school period. It was at Pennsylvania University where she met her husband, to whom she was a devoted wife and mother to their kids. Mary was a pharmacist and highly accomplished professionally herself. She co-authored a book with her husband titled *The Dietary Fiber Weight Control Handbook*. Mary enjoyed cooking, gardening, and genealogy research. She was an avid art enthusiast and visited many museums during her world travels with her husband.

Roger and Mary were greatly loved. Roger's sister, Carol Brumback, said in a KETV media interview, "Whenever they say the death penalty is going to happen, I'm going to be there. Even if it is ten years down the road, I'm going to be there, because the man deserves to die."

The news media noticed the connection between the four murders very quickly when the Brumbacks were found murdered. Dr. Thomas Hunter's son had been killed five years previously, and now Dr. Roger Brumback and his wife were killed. The media is savvy and instantly grasped the connection of both doctors to the Creighton University Pathology Department.

The Brumbacks' murders obviously heightened the tension and fear of the entire Omaha community. The deaths were the talk of the town, and the media dug in hard. The four murder victims are now forever linked in Omaha history, and the common portrait used in the media shows all their faces in a row.

Who is Dr. Anthony Garcia?

It behooves readers to know the man behind the killings to set the stage for the media chess match in which the OPD partook.

Dr. Anthony Joseph Garcia (date of birth June 7,1973) is a former medical doctor and an American serial killer. You can find him on Wikipedia's "List of Serial Killers" under his surname (Wikipedia, n.d.(b)). Garcia was born in Los Angeles, California, to Fred and Estella Garcia. His father, Fred, was a postal worker, and his mother, Estella, was a nurse. He has two younger siblings and has no children that law enforcement is aware of.

Garcia was arrested in July 2013 and went to trial in October 2016, where he was found guilty on all counts. He was convicted of two separate double murders committed in 2008 and 2013 in the city of Omaha, Nebraska, and is currently on death row in a state prison facility in Nebraska.

The media coverage of Garcia's five-year reign of terror in Omaha was the most robust I have seen in my time as chief. For five years, the Omaha community lived under a dark cloud of fear. It was a fear that engulfed the University of Creighton Medical Center and the neighborhoods where his murders took place. The local media coverage was on top of it as a feature case.

The enigma of Garcia was also the subject of national news coverage following the murders and his arrest. In addition, the national show *48 Hours* reported on the case with an episode titled "Resident Evil." *Dateline NBC* did a two-hour episode called "Haunting," and a fictionalized version of the case was made into a true crime series, James Patterson's *Murder is Forever* on the Discovery Channel. The famous television show *Law and Order* did a spinoff of the case, and the book *Pathological* was written by two *Omaha World Herald* journalists, Henry J. Cordes and Todd Cooper, about the case.

All the news coverage, national and local, has been in-depth and exhaustive. There is not a person in Omaha who was an adult during his five-year reign, who does not know who Anthony Garcia is. However, the critical media strategy and deeper insight into Garcia and the investigation that took him down has never been discussed until now. The media aspect and my own professional assessments will be new for readers, even if they are already well versed in the case.

Early Life and Family

A high proportion of serial killers are survivors of childhood trauma. The common traumas are sexual abuse, physical abuse, family dysfunction, and emotionally distant or absent parents. In the biographies of most serial killers, because of their childhood trauma, they suppress their emotional responses, and their emotional growth is stymied. Consequently, serial killers never develop healthy or normal emotions, so they find it difficult to empathize with others.

Serial killers tend to be loners who fear intimacy and seek to control the outcome of relationships to eliminate the possibility of a humiliating rejection. Criminologists who endeavor to study serial killers believe that they are partly motivated by the attention and fame that mass media can provide.

How to Spot a Serial Killer: History of Serial Killers—Research Guide

In the manifestation of serial killer Anthony Garcia, his childhood upbringing was *not* the cause of his lack of emotion. By all accounts, Fred and Estella were good parents and people who wanted the best for their kids. The common theme of childhood trauma does not apply to the case of Garcia. He is an enigma on this front and in many other aspects of his demented mind.

When Anthony Garcia was arrested in 2013 for the four murders, his parents went through their own personal hell being by his side. Fred and Estella leveraged all the finances they could produce to provide their son with a law firm to give him the best defense possible. Garcia's parents were also emotionally supportive and by his side in every way. In return, Garcia refused to—or feigned not being able to—talk to his parents. I can only imagine the personal toll all of Garcia's actions have had on his parents and family, who are good people.

In my opinion, Fred and Estella, like most parents, originally thought their son had been wrongfully arrested. Clearly, it would be hard to believe your son was responsible for four murders. However, over the course of Garcia's trial, Fred and Estella accepted the evidence as a reality. Their son had killed four people. Fred would later go on to tell the media that he and Estella wanted to apologize: "We are sorry [for] what took place. We hurt. We feel their hurt. We are not an evil family. We hope they find peace." I believe Fred and Estella are still in disbelief that the son they raised could commit such acts, and they are victims of Anthony Garcia as well.

Medical School

Garcia received his medical degree from the University of Utah in 1999. After that, he began a residency at Saint Elizabeth's Medical Center, where he remained for approximately six months before being forced to resign for "unprofessional and inappropriate conduct."

In July 2000, Garcia moved to Omaha, Nebraska, where he began another residency in the pathology department at the Creighton University Medical Center. Garcia struggled in the program. One of the doctors responsible for Garcia's performance appraisals was Dr. Chhandra Bewtra. Dr. Bewtra clearly—prophetically—spotted an issue with Garcia from the onset.

In one of her performance appraisals, Dr. Bewtra had the foresight to note, "He had an attitude problem. He just did not want to learn. I thought he was arrogant; he was mean. He liked to hurt people and derive pleasure from there. And so, he was not a nice person."

The two doctors who dismissed him from medical school were William Hunter and Roger Brumback, operating in part from Dr. Bewtra's performance appraisals. In complete contrast with Garcia, these three doctors (Bewtra, Hunter, and Brumback) are professionals who have contributed to the advancement of medicine in their field of pathology. They also clearly understood medical talent and the social intelligence required to be a medical doctor. Garcia did not have it.

In an infamous story, Garcia, during one of his petulant acts as a pathology resident, overturned a body on an autopsy table face down, so the blood would pool to the facial region, disfiguring the appearance. Garcia only lasted nine months at Creighton University Medical Center and was removed in 2001.

Garcia then enrolled in a psychiatry residency program at LSU Health Sciences Center Shreveport in Shreveport, Louisiana. He remained there until February 27, 2008, when the State Board of Medical Examiners informed him that he might not qualify for a medical license, due in part to the fact he had not reported his failure to finish the pathology program at Creighton University Medical Center.

Garcia went on to just squeak by and get a medical license in another state. He then worked as a doctor at a prison and other lower-level doctor jobs. I cannot imagine he was respected, but even though he was on the bottom rung of the medical profession, he was a doctor.

MEDIA CASE STUDY

Pre-arrest Dr. Garcia Persona

Garcia liked his strippers and beer. He relished his popularity at the local strip clubs where he lived in Indiana. When he walked in, the DJ booth master of ceremonies would announce, "The *doctor* is in the house!" It was all a façade. The strippers had no real respect for the odd doctor. Garcia ate it up though, as it fed his powerful impulse to be an important and respected figure. This impulse was an indicator that the odd doctor could not face rejection. Rejection ate away at him and triggered a rare, demented mode.

We know how the strippers felt because of court testimony. One of the strippers testified that Garcia bragged about killing an old woman and a young boy to be a "bad boy." Garcia tried to use the image to bolster his romantic chances with the dance club entertainer. She politely rejected his advances and told him she was not interested in a romantic relationship. He had mistaken her role as an entertainer for more. The rejection prompted the spontaneous, incriminating response from Garcia that he had killed before.

I found the entertainer to be of high credibility in court. She stepped up to do the right thing, in the face of a blistering cross-examination from Garcia's lead defense attorney. Who makes such a statement within the confines of a strip club? The demented personality of Anthony Garcia does. The club entertainer, unbeknownst to her at the time, unearthed the real Garcia when she rejected his romantic advances.

Garcia's house, at the time of his arrest, was in Terre Haute, Indiana. The way he lived was befitting of a fraud. His abode hardly had any furniture, and his refrigerator was empty, except for his beer. His residence was pathetic on the inside, yet he had a nice sports car to present a false front to the world, to look like he was a successful doctor. He flaunted this false front at his favorite strip clubs because there, he felt like an elevated customer—a doctor that was in the house.

Post-arrest Dr. Garcia Persona

Anthony Garcia went mute shortly following his arrest. He would not speak. During the trial, he pretended to be sleeping. He barely communicated with his attorneys and sat comatose during the trial as if he were suffering from a mental breakdown. He would not even speak to his family, who had traveled from Los Angeles to be by his side during the trial.

Regarding Garcia's mental condition, I do not believe it for a minute! It was feigned. Anthony Garcia is a phony. He is a coward who cannot face his parents or the world and account for what he has done.

His act of pretending to sleep in the trial was akin to a spoiled toddler throwing a tantrum. Garcia talked when he wanted to. He would wake up to ask the deputies to take him back to his cell so as not to miss his jail dinner. He would miraculously become lucid and speak up if he needed a personal amenity. It was all an act, in my professional opinion, to not face humiliation for what he had done. Even Nikko Jenkins, a fellow serial killer who had a cell near Garcia, thought he was odd and gave up on trying to talk to him, as the story goes.

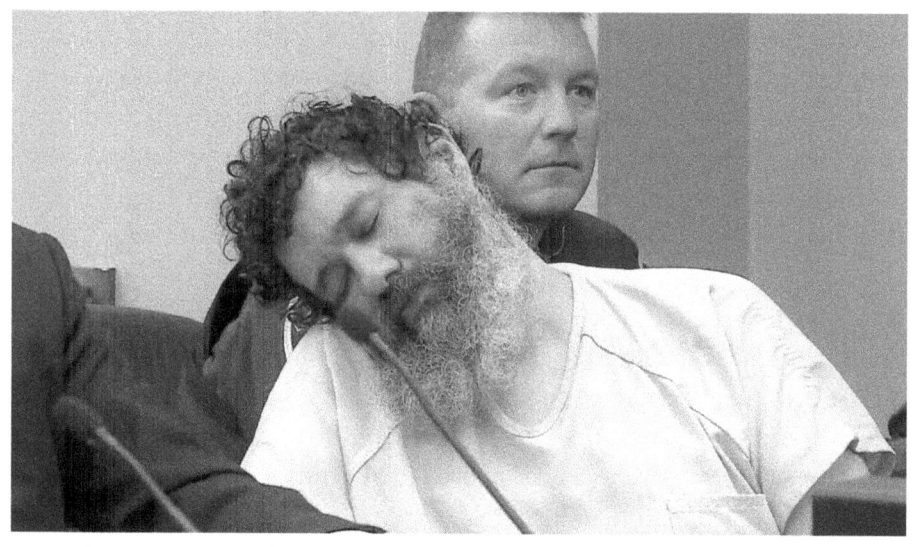

Photo courtesy of WOWT: Garcia appears to sleep during his trial. The Douglas County Sheriff's Deputy in the background is Forrest Christiansen, a friend of mine from high school. For every bad person, there is an honorable person who protects others from evil.

Motive

REVENGE.

Garcia is a cold-blooded killer who stewed for years over his performance evaluations and dismissal from the Creighton University Pathology Department. His dismissal from Creighton University Medical School after only nine months haunted him repeatedly as he applied for doctor jobs. Each time he would lose a job or be eliminated from a program, heavy humiliation would set in.

In Garcia's mind, if Creighton had not fired him as a resident, he would have gone on to "bigger and better" doctor jobs. He could have then walked into his strip clubs and been an even bigger draw. Maybe then the dancers would not have romantically rejected him. He had been humiliated repeatedly and wanted revenge for it all.

MEDIA CASE STUDY

Modus Operandi and Killing Signature

The modus operandi—or method of operation—and killing signature are the personal marks of a serial killer. They come from the psyche of the offender and reflect a deep fantasy that the killing represents. Sometimes, the fantasies develop slowly and increase over time. Some serial killers begin with the torture of animals during childhood. Not Garcia, though; his fantasy began slowly after each professional rejection he attributed back to his dismissal from Creighton University. Each murder was a fantasy to quench his thirst for revenge and momentarily get a release from all his humiliation, in my informed opinion.

Serial Killers: Modus Operandi, Signature— Staging and Posing, 2015

Garcia's modus operandi was to arrive in Omaha, drink alcohol, and get the courage to go right up to the front door of his victims. He carried a gun, presumably to control his victims if needed, and killed them with knives from their own residence.

The killing itself was a series of puncture stabs with a knife behind the ear. As a doctor, he knew this would cause the most damage. It is a unique killing signature because it is based on science and an understanding of the human body. Many other serial killers will try to recreate what they have seen on television or use trial and error to see what kills the best. Garcia's final hallmark was to leave the knife in the neck of the victims.

Garcia also understood the critical nature of DNA at crime scenes and was adept at not leaving any behind. Let me rephrase that: either he was adept because of his medical background, or he was sloppily lucky—I cannot fully decide. Law enforcement did not find any DNA at the two crime scenes where he was killed inside the homes.

Five-Part Case Study

Now that we have some background information, let's examine the substance of the case study through five segments, ending with an exploration of where those involved in the case are now. Each segment brings the reader into the stages of law enforcement's contact with Garcia as a known suspect and during the time he was an unknown serial killer. The critical media strategy to apprehend the unknown serial killer was intense and required scrupulous strategy and execution. Once Garcia's second set of murders took place, our critical media strategy took on new twists and turns. This chapter will take readers through the media and law enforcement *chess match* of the Anthony Garcia serial killer case.

1) The Murders
2) The "Task Force" Investigation
3) Garcia's Arrest
4) The Trial, Verdict, and Sentencing
5) Where are They Now?

1) The Murders

The 2008 Double Murder

On March 13, 2008, about two weeks after Dr. Anthony Garcia was told to leave LSU and seven years after being kicked out of his pathology residency at Creighton, Omaha's five-year interlude of terror commenced. Dr. William Hunter returned home from work to find his son and housekeeper deceased. His son, Thomas, was in the formal dining room, and Shirley Sherman was found dead in a hallway near a bathroom. Both victims bore Garcia's killing signature from knives missing from the kitchen.

The Hunter residence is in the historic Dundee neighborhood, known for its pride, class, and famous neighbor Warren Buffet. Dr. Hunter would have known instantly upon finding the victims of the medical certainty of their deaths.

There would be no emergency medical measures that could bring them back to life. Dr. Hunter would also have known they had been murdered. Garcia's "killing signature" left no doubt. I have so many images burned in my brain from being a chief for over twelve years and a twenty-eight-year police veteran. I pray Dr. Hunter does not. The image of his murdered son, ingrained in recurring visions, would be torturous. His son, Thomas, was eleven years old. We all know that eleven-year-old boys deeply look up to their dads, and Dr. Hunter was a man to look up to.

There was a child murderer in Omaha, who was willing to strike in the middle of the day in a historically low-crime neighborhood. Omaha has just been put on notice by the brazen killings. There was a killer in Omaha, and it seemed that his targets could be anyone, because the murder of an eleven-year-old and Shirley Sherman appeared indiscriminate at the time. As one would expect, the media coverage was ferocious. The national news reported on it, but the local media professionals really dug in as the public yearned for every piece of reporting on the killings.

Shirley's murder was a case of being at the wrong place at the wrong time. Garcia did not have her on his radar when driving to Omaha to kill. His primary victim was likely to have been Dr. William Hunter, the man who had fired him from Creighton. Since Dr. Hunter himself was not home, his son would have to do.

Thomas was killed first, and then Garcia went after Shirley. She had come into the dining area and would have seen Garcia after he had killed Thomas. Detectives believe

MEDIA CASE STUDY

Shirley was trying to run out the back door when Garcia caught up to her. Shirley was unknown to Garcia, but she was a witness and had at least some connection to the Hunter residence, so she was killed too.

Omaha was shocked and befuddled as the collective sense of security in Dundee and Omaha was broken. The murders were the buzz of the town and became ingrained as a subconscious layer of thought in Omaha.

Speculation on the murders was rampant in the city and within the newsrooms of the Omaha media market. Because of where Thomas had died, rumors began to circulate about Dr. Hunter's potential involvement. Shirley Sherman's family had to endure the rumor mill as well, and let's just say rumors have no regard for feelings. People love to take optics, weave them with speculation, and play detective. That is not a negative statement, it is a fact. For what it is worth, OPD never bought into the rumors.

Omaha Police Department (OPD) Players

I was a mid-level commander in 2008, running OPD's training academy. I was not involved in the case and, given the nature of my position, had no direct knowledge of the case investigation. It was not until I became chief in 2012 that I became knowledgeable about it.

Imagine being elected president of the United States—what would be the first thing you would ask about? Who shot President Kennedy? Is Area 51 really the site of a downed alien aircraft? The first things I wanted to know when I became chief were about the Sherman and Hunter homicides and one other child murder case from the 1990s in North Omaha.

Omaha Police had some big-time detectives on the case. Detectives Derek Mois and Scott Warner were the responding homicide detectives to the Hunter residence in 2008 and the Brumback residence in 2013. They are strong veteran detectives with a wealth of experience and steely demeanors.

Cold Case Detective Ken Kanger was working on the 2008 murders when I took over as chief. Ken would go on to be one of my deputy chiefs many years later and oversee the entire criminal investigations bureau for OPD. If I had a loved one killed, I would choose these three to be the detectives on the case.

This case certainly had many layers, motives, and angles. It was not until the second set of murders five years later, in 2013, that the triangulation took place. A target could then be developed.

The media gamesmanship also started in 2013. What I will now discuss is the critical media strategy needed to catch a killer, buy time to prevent other murders, and calm a community in fear.

Personal photos: Detectives Scott Warner and Derek Mois and Omaha police deputy chief Ken Kanger (retired) with Chief Schmaderer.

The 2013 Double Murder

The second set of murders in Omaha came in 2013, five years after the first set and twelve years since Garcia had received his walking papers from Creighton. This was his grudge playing out again. Garcia's expulsion from Creighton had haunted him as he had attempted to advance his medical career and secure other doctoral positions. Every time he would apply somewhere, his background check would bring his Creighton past back.

On May 12, 2013, Omaha homicide detectives Mois and Warner responded to the Mary and Roger Brumback residence. As they passed by the uniformed officers already on the scene and lifted underneath the yellow crime scene tape, they were seconds away from being stunned. The 2008 murderer had struck again.

The dead bodies of Roger and Mary Brumback bore an unforgettable "killing signature." The veteran detectives knew it instantly when they saw the knives in the necks of the bodies. There was no mistaking what the veteran detectives had seen; there was now a serial killer targeting Omaha.

The media coverage went into overdrive once the connection was made between Dr. William Hunter and Dr. Roger Brumback, the two men in charge of Creighton's Pathology Department and linked with the two sets of murders. Coincidences like this do not occur every day.

On Mother's Day in 2013, Roger Brumback responded to a knock at his door in the middle of the day. The Brumbacks lived near 114th and Pacific Street in a serene, quiet neighborhood. Upon opening his front door, Roger would have come face to face with his former pathology student, who immediately pulled a gun on him.

READER NOTE
I can only imagine what went through Roger Brumback's mind when he opened the door and saw his former pathology student with a gun. Roger had lived five years with the agonizing mystery of who killed his colleague's eleven-year-old son. At that moment, when Roger saw Garcia, the mystery would be over for him. The killer had been his former pathology student, Anthony Garcia. Roger also would have known that Garcia was not at his house on Mother's Day, five years later, to talk. Roger could only react as he knew instantly he was in a fight for his life.

In addition, can you imagine the hunger Garcia must have had to risk knocking on a door on Mother's Day to kill his target? Garcia could have very easily walked into a situation where ten people were at the house. Taking such a risk was a strong indicator that Garcia was in an extremely heightened mode to kill. It was a factor the Behavioral Analysis Unit (BAU) and the task force considered in making the assessment that the killer was in a *killing* state of mind and would do it again if not caught ASAP. The pressure was high to *pause* Garcia so the task force could identify him before he struck again.

Roger fought mightily right after realizing who was at the door. Roger knew that if he were to be controlled by the gun-toting Garcia, his death would have been tortuous, and his wife Mary would be done for. Roger fought like a warrior before succumbing to a gunshot that was clearly fatal. Even then, detectives believe he continued to fight until his body gave out. Garcia then moved into the living room area as Mary had heard the commotion.

Mary fought ferociously but was overpowered by a knife—Garcia's gun had been damaged in the fight with Roger. The Brumbacks were professional, civilized people who had to turn into warriors at the end of their lives. This made for a sobering reality.

For what it is worth, as detectives assessed the crime scene and tried to profile the killer, the fortitude and the fight put up by the Brumbacks caught their eye. Roger had been fighting for his life and his wife's life and was willing to do so courageously. Mary fought harder than anyone could imagine as evidenced by her injuries. There would be no hostage situation where the Brumbacks could be controlled by Garcia. The detectives were impressed with the couple's character, courage, and warrior mindset.

The press were carnivores, piecing together the connection between doctors, poking and waiting for the next move from the OPD. Any tidbit we could give them was eaten up and devoured. OPD waited five days to hold the first press conference. There was a reason. We needed to get our ducks in a row because the stakes were immeasurably high. The press conference had ramifications far beyond informing the public of what occurred. It was also a chess match with the killer.

Dr. Bewtra's House

The media did not know this other fact at the time of the Brumback murders: Garcia had gone to Dr. Chhandra Bewtra's house first, but no one had been at home. Dr. Bewtra reached out to us after the Brumback murders, informing us of an alarm that had gone off at her house. Drs. Bewtra, Hunter, and Brumback all worked for the Creighton University Pathology Department. The triangulation was made everywhere, by the detectives, media, and the public. Creighton was the glue.

The investigation eventually led to the realization it was Garcia who had set off the alarm. Garcia had traveled from Indiana to Omaha on Mother's Day in 2013. He had used his cell phone to look up the Brumback residence after he had gone to the Bewtra residence, and no one had been at home. We eventually found DNA from Garcia on the back doorknob of the Bewtra residence but had no one to compare it to until the killer was found. No other DNA was recovered in the investigation.

A Task Force is Formed

The media was on our time frame. From the moment the Brumbacks had been found, we knew we would not be giving a press conference until we were ready. A hasty press conference could have had dire consequences. At that moment, the media would only get a statement saying that OPD was looking into the connection between the two sets of murders.

MEDIA CASE STUDY

Within the OPD, however, we knew there was a serial killer. We were also preparing for a press conference of monumental importance. We needed five days to get our strategy in order. The media chess match had arrived, and the stakes were life and death.

I made the determination that a task force was needed to catch the killer or killers. Given the amount of time between the two sets of murders, the force multiplier of extra agencies was going to be of immense value. Here we had two sets of murders, linked by the connection to the two doctors, which had taken place five years apart. The murders were brutal and gory, and there was every indication that the search for the killer would take us out of the country.

The workload was going to be immense. We needed to revisit the 2008 case, pore over the Creighton connection, follow up on current leads, and get another murder case and person of interest "on or off the plate." All the while realizing that the killer might strike again at any time.

READER NOTE
The task force knew the investigation would take us out of the country because a person of interest still lingered from the 2008 double murders. The person of interest was a former colleague of Drs. Hunter and Brumback. The person also contacted detectives after the Brumback murders, which we found suspicious. We traveled to Canada and determined that this person of interest was not our killer.

The task force was set up with the best each agency had to offer for detectives and resources. It was comprised of the OPD, FBI, and the Nebraska State Patrol. Omaha was the lead agency, and the task force worked out of a meeting room just down the hall from my top (sixth) floor chief's office. The room was modified to encompass many computers, functional working props, locks, and window blocks to ensure confidentiality.

I received a briefing every day on the progress of the investigation as well as providing overall direction on day one of the task force convening. The work that was done in the war room was of the highest detail and impressive beyond belief. The investigation was all-consuming, yet the daily business of being chief still went on. For the months that the task force was in operation, my top commanders and I worked nonstop.

Leaks were a concern, and the detectives selected were the absolute best. The order was given that any leaks would lead to termination, but to be frank, I only gave the order because of the magnitude of damage any leaks would cause in the investigation. These detectives would never leak information, as they were consummate professionals.

Serial killer investigations historically have leaks, as the press probes and tries harder than ever to generate sources and leaks. The task force that was conducting the largest and most sensitive investigation in the history of Nebraska at the time had *zero* leaks. This is an unheard-of accomplishment and a testament to the professionals in the task force. The press was going to be our tool, our weapon, in this investigation—not the other way around.

I should say that at the time, this was arguably the largest investigation in the history of Nebraska. One would have to look at the Charles Starkweather investigation or the child serial killer John Joubert investigation to have something comparable in Nebraska. Starkweather killed eleven people in a murderous spree over a little more than two months in 1957. John Joubert was convicted of killing three boys, ages twelve and thirteen, one in Maine and two in Nebraska. Both killers received the death penalty and were executed.

The FBI Behavioral Analysis Unit

The task force was now fully in place. The next step was a meeting, via conference call, with the FBI's Behavioral Analysis Unit (BAU)—yes, the famed unit from the famous television series *Criminal Minds*. We asked for the BAU to look at the case files for both sets of murders. Their insight was impressive and helped form the strategy for the first press conference. The media was kept in the dark.

We did not want the community or the killer to know we were interfacing with the BAU prior to the press conference. Why? The BAU is used to establish a profile of the killer as a place to start the investigation. The BAU's role is known to the world because of the television show. We did not want to signal to the killer that we had no idea who the perpetrator was, as evidenced by needing a profile to get started. This was an important theme of ours for the first press conference.

The BAU and the task force all felt the killer was in a heightened state to kill again. Something had triggered the killer, and we all felt he was posed to strike again soon. The serial killer was in *killing* mode. We did not know at the time how accurate we were. Garcia's grudge was not over, and he had been looking to kill again when he was finally arrested. The press conference was vital for making Garcia *pause* and for buying us time to land on a suspect. Our strategy for the press conference was formed.

> **READ NOTE**
> **The BAU had our case files and had been looking through them. They did not come to Omaha. Instead, we consulted via a conference call. On one of the calls, they made an intriguing observation. The BAU noted that a witness had seen a man walking up to the Hunter residence in 2008 with a limp or a stagger. The BAU said this was going to be an important detail.**

MEDIA CASE STUDY

Now that we know Garcia's penchant for drinking beer, I surmise that he was drunk. He drank for liquid courage to get up the gumption to brutally kill. He drank before both killings to deaden his inhibitions and heighten his satisfaction, I believe. His alcohol intake was the cause of his unsteady walk.

The First Press Conference Strategy

- The press conference needed to convey to the public that we had a handle on the situation; to persuade them of calm and rationality. The killings were five years apart. Omaha had never gotten over the Dundee killings in 2008, and people were keenly aware that the Brumback murders were connected. The Creighton medical community was severely unnerved, for obvious cause, as individual doctors wondered if they might be next.
- The press conference needed to convey a message to the killer. The message was, "There is a powerful entity coming after you," but it had to convey this in a way that did not incite the killer to move up his time frame for the next killing(s). The task force represented the powerful entity, and this was one of the strategic reasons it had been formed. At the press conference, I described the prowess of the team of detectives and the agencies involved. This was all part of the strategy to show both the public and the killer that we had the best of the best on this investigation, and we were joining forces together as a task force. The message was that this is an immensely powerful entity, so think twice before killing again!

The task force members knew I would be questioned by the media about the viability of the task force and that I needed to "pick the headline" to instill our critical media strategy. So, a response was prepared in advance of the question. The public and anyone watching the press conference assumed I was merely answering a reporter's question. That was not the case. We had a carefully scripted response to the question we all knew was coming.

The question was, "Will the task force catch the killer, and are you confident in the task force?"

The scripted answer was, "I would not want this task force coming after me." Later, we would be told this was the headline quote the media was looking for. Thank you to the media for playing along with our strategy. The answer was intended to get media attention and instill both our primary strategy points. The public could be assured we had a powerful team in place to protect society, and the killer needed to *pause* and think twice before killing again. Our goal was to convince the killer to pause and think, rather than incite anger in the killer.

As the chess match continued with the killer, we knew the media would ask if we had made any progress on the case. I wanted my next scripted answer to be accurate, yet strategic because we had nothing at this point. The two crime scenes did not lend themselves to solving the case instantly. The DNA on the Bewtra residence did not come back until later, and it needed to be compared to Garcia anyway. But in no way were we going to let the killer know we had nothing.

My answer was, "Yes, there is early progress already on the case," and I gave no further explanation as to what that meant. No one could know from watching the press conference that the progress I was referring to was merely the formation of the task force. It *was* progress to bring together three law enforcement agencies at the federal, state, and local level so quickly under one task force.

The audiences of that press conference were the community and the killer. Neither of them needed to know that we had *no* leads at that point. If I had admitted we had no leads early on, panic would have increased exponentially in the community, and the killer would have been empowered. An empowered killer, in a heightened *killing* state of mind, would have led to more murders before we could catch him.

The initial press conference was the first *tightrope* critical media strategy used in this case. Pushed too far, and the bravado could incite Garcia to strike again, and much sooner than we would have wanted. It was crucial to give the task force time to develop a suspect. It was pivotal that Garcia thought the task force was making progress to give him pause.

If Garcia spent time thinking back to the Brumback murders, wondering if he'd made any mistakes, we had just gained precious time—time where Garcia wasn't focused on his next murder(s) and taking active steps toward that.

At the time of the first press conference, we had no idea if our strategy worked.

Had we made him pause?

In retrospect, we had nailed it.

The initial press conference was on May 20, 2013, and Garcia did not head off to kill others until July 14 (more on this in the segment about his arrest). The press conference had bought the task force almost two months.

Those two months were invaluable in identifying him as a suspect. If he had killed again right away, the triangulation of the Creighton doctor connection would have been thrown into an abyss of other avenues. When Garcia was eventually arrested, he was pulled over driving toward New Orleans, which is where the task force felt he would kill again. Garcia had a grudge in Louisiana as well—someone who worked for LSU Medical Center.

MEDIA CASE STUDY

READER ASSIGNMENT
Consider the following scenario: In the midst of the hunt for the serial killer, another murder takes place, outside of Nebraska and unconnected to Creighton. Can you consider how many possible other trajectories and channels would have opened for the task force's investigation?

I suspect it would have been like drinking out of a firehose for the task force. The Creighton connection was a significant help in triangulating the murders. If that connection had been muddied, there could have been delays in identifying Garcia as a suspect.

As a class, discuss the other possible trajectories and channels another murder would have posed.

2) The "Task Force" Investigation

The task force received a break in the case about one month into the investigation. We had very little at that point, as some of our better leads had fallen through. Detective Mois was going through Creighton University Medical Center personnel files and came across a termination letter signed by none other than Drs. Hunter and Brumback. The termination was of Anthony Garcia's residency in Creighton pathology. Further digging uncovered that Garcia's professor was Dr. Chhandra Bewtra, and things started to get interesting.

Detective Mois continued to probe into Garcia's background. So many times, in police investigations and media investigations, the theory falls apart after three or four cuts into the story. Garcia's did not. Mois then checked what kind of car Garcia had owned in 2008, as witnesses had seen a silver Honda CRV parked nearby on the day of the Sherman and Thomas Hunter murders. Garcia owned a silver CRV at the time and, to further pique our interest, the license plate of the CRV described by the witness was an out-of-state plate with the same colors as Garcia's out-of-state plate at the time.

I recall running into Mois in the elevator at OPD headquarters and asking him how the investigation was going. His response was mild but curious to me.

"I have a person who intrigues me. I am going to continue digging," Mois said. I continued the questioning, and he said it was a former resident terminated by the doctors, and he had been driving a Honda CRV at the time. His appearance also came close to the composite drawing based on the witness from the 2008 homicides.

The task force now had enough to start zeroing in on Garcia and get his cell phone records. I will never forget the call I got when the first batch of cell phone records was received.

"Chief, guess who was in Atlantic, Iowa, sixty minutes after the 2013 murders?"

"Garcia," I said.

"Bingo," was the reply.

Atlantic, Iowa, is about an hour east of Omaha. This was an "aha!" moment for sure. It was the first real piece of the puzzle, which means you can start to see the picture come together. It was the turning point between someone being a person of intrigue to becoming a full-blown suspect.

The task force went on to develop much more evidence. The gun Garcia used in 2013 was recovered after his fight with Roger Brumback, with the missing parts that matched those we found at the scene. The purchase of the gun could be tied to Garcia as well. Further phone records showed his internet search history, where he looked up the Brumback house, around the same time the Brumbacks had just got off a Skype call with their kids. This gave us a tight timeline.

Garcia was in Omaha at the time, based on his cell phone location and searches. Plus, he was caught on camera buying beer the morning of the 2013 murders in Council Bluffs, Iowa, at a convenience store; only the Missouri river separates Council Bluffs from Omaha. There was much more evidence, and we knew we had our man. Garcia lived in Terre Haute, Indiana at the time of the 2013 double murders. A GPS tracking device was placed on his car in Terre Haute, and the task force began tracking him.

3) Garcia's Arrest

On July 15, 2013, the FBI had been following Garcia on the interstate in the direction of New Orleans. After dramatically losing him for a while, Illinois State Troopers were able to locate him and pulled him over. Garcia's driving was erratic. If he had not been intoxicated and posed a danger to other drivers, the plan would have been to continue following him. Instead, he was arrested.

Garcia's blood alcohol level was twice the legal limit, and a search of his car found a sledgehammer, crowbar, .45 handgun, fifty bullets, an LSU lab coat and LSU bag, a stethoscope, and, of course, his beer. A search of his residence located a self-written note with ominous writings. Parts of the note included the words *gun, invade, torture, kill*.

When I was told of the note and the belongings in his car when he had been stopped, I knew Garcia had started into his "killing" mode again. The purpose of the initial press conference had been to pause the killer. In my heart and in my mind, I believed right then that the press conference had paused him long enough for the task force to identify Anthony Garcia. Otherwise, he would have attempted to kill sooner before we could get on to him. The task force and I uncovered that he was on his way to the French Quarter in New Orleans for another grudge killing.

MEDIA CASE STUDY

The arrest of Anthony Garcia posed the need for a continued critical media strategy.

During the second live press conference announcing his arrest, coffee shops in Dundee were filled and work stopped, while regular broadcasting was halted to cover the press conference live.

Second Press Conference

The second press conference had three goals, in the following order of priority.

1) We needed to convey that we had arrested the right guy so the city could feel a sense of peace. I wanted the city to give a "sigh of relief" that it was finally over. The task force had been working diligently and wisely to track down our killer and had been successful.
2) We needed to convey that Garcia would have killed again and had been on his way to kill when the police had stopped him. The community needed to know the layers associated with the killer and his arrest.
3) The community needed to know that Garcia was a serial killer.

My team and I wanted a headline that depicted the arrest and the fear that he would have killed again. We tried to convey that headline by playing the pick-the-headline game.

I did not want to come right out and say he was a serial killer at the press conference because the serial killer aspect was not the first priority of the stories we wanted to relay at the arrest press conference. That was the third storyline.

The question arose: How does one convey to the public that Garcia is a serial killer without it becoming the headline? I did not want the sexy appeal of a serial killer overshadowing the top two points.

The best way to accomplish this would be to have the media ask me, "Do you feel Garcia is a serial killer?" If it came during the question-and-answer session at the end, and not from my prepared remarks, the serial killer notion would not be front and center. I needed the media to do their job and ask.

In an interview with *Omaha World Herald* reporter Maggie O'Brien on a different story the day before the second Garcia press conference was announced, I hinted at the notion our arrest was a serial killer. Maggie, who is an outstanding writer and reporter, took the not-so-subtle bait and asked me at the second press conference if Dr. Garcia was a serial killer.

My response was, "I see elements of a serial killer in Dr. Garcia."

Mission accomplished. The serial killer aspect fell third in line out of the conveyed messages. See the headline photo from the *Omaha World Herald* (three pages from

275

here), which covered the Creighton killings with precision and skill: "Police Pounced Fearing More Killings." Note the right side underneath the headline, where it says, "Omaha chief sees 'elements of a serial killer' in Dr. Anthony J. Garcia III."

Our strategy worked nicely. This chapter is a case study of the media chess match from law enforcement's perspective. The Creighton murders could also be a case study in journalism from the media's viewpoint. I know I would be interested in hearing about it from a counter-strategy point of view.

The Defense Team

After the arrest and the second live press conference, we were under the impression that the media chess game was over. We were wrong! Garcia's defense team had different thoughts. They were not going to go along with the task force narrative, and they were not going to play nice. Right out of the chute, Garcia's legal team was incensed at my reply that I saw "elements of a serial killer" in Dr. Anthony Garcia. That was all I had said. There was no elaboration at the press conference or follow-up questions on the subject.

Garcia's legal team consisted of a Chicago husband and wife. Augmenting their team nicely was the father of the husband, an attorney who had once been a member of famed serial killer John Wayne Gacy's defense team.

John Wayne Gacy (March 17, 1942–May 10, 1994) was an American serial killer and sex offender who raped, tortured, and murdered at least thirty-three young men and boys in Norwood Park Township, Illinois, a suburb of Chicago. He became known as the Killer Clown due to his public performances as Pogo the Clown. Gacy was executed in May 1994, with large crowds in a celebratory atmosphere outside of the penal institution (Crime Museum, n.d.).

The Gacy trial was called "the case of the century" by the media and remains the highest-profile case in the history of Illinois jurisprudence. Without question, Garcia's legal team posed a significant challenge to the media strategy aspect of this case. They would go on to force our media hand and continue the media chess game (A&E True Crime Blog 2022).

Motta & Motta LLC

Garcia's legal team was found and commandeered by Garcia's brother. Motta & Motta LLC accepted the challenge and answered the call. All defendants deserve a robust defense. It is crucial in our legal system in America. The Motta's gave a robust defense and a fight to be remembered.

MEDIA CASE STUDY

The defense team was highly bombastic with the media and willing to publicly fight for their client, which I respect. They were outspoken and tried to convey the strength of their case with definitive speech. According to their law firm's website, they have a "take-no-prisoners" approach to defending their clients.

"When your enemy is weak expose their weakness," their website states. "When your enemy is strong delay the battle, and when your enemy is angry make them angrier because mistakes are sure to follow." (Motta & Motta LLC, n.d.)

If you happen to be their client, I imagine you would love their passion.

The Motta defense team was not afraid to talk to the media, show passion, and take a hard line. According to them, Omaha had the wrong guy under arrest. Garcia was not the killer, and they were going to portray that stance to the media and all of Omaha.

There have been many other murder investigations in Omaha, and the defense teams carried themselves differently from the Motta's. The local defense teams were not as bold and brash with their comments to the media. The Motta stance puts pressure on the work of the task force through the media.

Here we had a serial killer that had killed four people in Omaha over a period separated by five years. The citizens of Omaha had to endure the dark cloud over the city since the 2008 murders. The murders that followed in 2013 took the community's fear to a new level. I cannot tell you the number of times Creighton doctors called me explaining their fears and uncertainties. I saw the trepidation in their eyes when I went to speak to the Creighton medical teams after the Brumback murders.

There was no way I was going to allow Omaha to feel this way any longer. Omaha needed to know that their police department had arrested the right suspect. As such, I felt compelled to release a piece of photo evidence for the mental well-being of Omaha.

The Omaha community was worn down, and back-and-forth debates on whether OPD had arrested the right killer would have been a continual drain; not to mention, the fear would linger until the trial verdict. Knowing this, and for the benefit of Omaha, we released a photo to the press of Garcia buying beer at a convenience store in Council Bluffs (a few minutes from Omaha) on the day of the murders.

As soon as the photo was released, it was on every news channel and the front page of the *Omaha World Herald*. It was difficult to explain why Garcia would be there on the day of the murders buying beer, when he lived in Terre Haute, Indiana. I felt my hand had been forced on this one by the defense team. Omahans could now rest and not have to live on edge until the trial started.

SYNERGY *of* INFLUENCE

Omaha Police photos: Dr. Garcia bought beer the morning of the 2013 murders at a convenience store in Council Bluffs, Iowa (minutes from Omaha and part of the Omaha Metropolitan area.)

In addition, the *Omaha World Herald* (OWH) gave me an assist when Team Motta took exception to my comment during the arrest press conference that I saw "elements of a serial killer" in Dr. Anthony Garcia.

Team Motta called it "patently absurd" that Garcia was a serial killer. Three days later, the OWH ran a front-page story where experts agreed with me that Garcia was a serial killer. Thank you, OWH. The headline read, "Creighton deaths the work of a serial killer? Experts say yes."

The four front pages of the OWH, after the second press conference, show an intense media playground. In a perfect world, chiefs of police would not have to use a critical media strategy; all cases would play out only in the court of law. The paradigm has changed, and law enforcement agencies are now forced to have a baseline media strategy and a more intense one for critical events. The Mottas forced a media chess game, and quite frankly they were doing their job. It is clear they would never back away from a challenge.

MEDIA CASE STUDY

Omaha World-Herald

TUESDAY, JULY 16, 2013 — SUNRISE EDITION — LOCALLY OWNED SINCE 1885

CREIGHTON SLAYINGS

THOMAS HUNTER | SHIRLEE SHERMAN | DR. ROGER BRUMBACK | MARY BRUMBACK

POLICE POUNCED, FEARING MORE KILLINGS

Omaha chief sees "elements of a serial killer" in Dr. Anthony J. Garcia III

By HENRY J. CORDES
TODD COOPER AND MAGGIE O'BRIEN
WORLD-HERALD STAFF WRITERS

When Dr. Anthony J. Garcia III exhibited what was viewed as erratic, rude and insubordinate behavior, Creighton University officials booted him out of his pathology residency in 2001.

Omaha police believe that a festering grudge born in that years-ago firing ultimately led to four killings tied to the two people most responsible for the termination.

And had Garcia not been arrested by a state trooper in rural Illinois on Monday, Omaha Police Chief Todd Schmaderer thinks still more could have died.

"We did not feel this individual would stop unless an arrest was made," Schmaderer said in a late afternoon press conference in Omaha. Schmaderer said he saw in the murder suspect "the elements of a serial killer."

The arrest of 40-year-old Garcia Monday morning provided a dramatic turn in a pair of double homicides that had rocked Omaha and baffled police: the March 2008 deaths of 11-year-old Thomas Hunter and Shirlee Sherman, the son and house cleaner of Creighton pathologist William Hunter; and the deaths this May of Creighton pathologist Roger Brumback and his wife, Mary.

So short was Garcia's stint in the pathology department, and so much time had passed since his exit from it, that he apparently didn't emerge as a suspect after the 2008 killings. Police did not interview him at that time.

"The first time we (confronted) Dr. Garcia physically and in person was today," a source close to the investigation told The World-Herald.

But the two-month work of a task force Schmaderer formed in the wake of the Brumback deaths, with officers going through "file after file," ultimately led to Garcia as a

See Garcia: Page 2

Dr. Anthony J. Garcia III, 40, who was kicked out of his pathology residency at Creighton in 2001, was arrested Monday in Illinois on a warrant charging him in a pair of double slayings in Omaha.

MORE COVERAGE INSIDE
» **A LOOK AT THE FOUR VICTIMS** More on Thomas Hunter, Shirlee Sherman, Dr. Roger Brumback and his wife, Mary Brumback. **Page 2A**
» **HOW THE CASES UNFOLDED** A timeline of major events in the two double homicides. **Page 3A**

ON OMAHA.COM
» **MISSED THE PRESS CONFERENCE?** Watch a video replay of and read the full transcript from the Omaha Police Department's press conference.
» **REACTION TO THE ARRESTS** Quotes from family members of the slaying victims and from Creighton University.

A police sketch from 2008 of the suspect in the slayings of Thomas Hunter and Shirlee Sherman.

Suspect appeared to blame firing from Creighton for his struggles

By ROSEANN MORING
WORLD-HERALD STAFF WRITER

Anthony J. Garcia III tried to be a good neighbor, but the mild-mannered doctor who is now accused of four grisly revenge slayings in Omaha was dubbed "weird" by his neighbors who said he had some odd habits.

He also came and went at "strange hours" of the day and night, and never appeared to entertain visitors at his three-bedroom home in a middle-class neighborhood in Terre Haute, Ind.

"The whole time that he lived in this area, he never, ever put any trash out — never," said a neighbor, who lived in the same cul-de-sac as Garcia and awoke Monday to a flood of police vehicles swarming the neighborhood.

Omaha police announced Monday that they had arrested Garcia in the May deaths of Dr. Roger Brumback of the Creighton University

See Garcia: Page 2

INSIDE

The humble T-shirt turns 100
Whether advertising our team or just keeping us comfy, the classic T has never gone out of style. **Living**

More details on Gretna slaying
Gretna farmer William H. Braesche's three granddaughters were in his house when he was fatally shot Saturday. **Midlands**

Beginning of a beautiful friendship?
The U.S. Senior Open went so well that the USGA is eager to bring more national events to Omaha. **Sports**

Omaha weather
Today's forecast
High: 88
Low: 69
Full report: Page 6B

Index
Classifieds....40
Comics....4E
Movies....36
Obituaries....36
Opinion....4&5B
30 PAGES   75 CENTS

SYNERGY *of* INFLUENCE

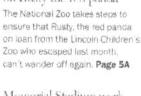

MEDIA CASE STUDY

SYNERGY *of* INFLUENCE

Courtesy of the Omaha World Herald: All four front page photos

MEDIA CASE STUDY

Serial Killer Criteria

What is a serial killer? According to the FBI, the definition of a serial killer is as follows: The unlawful killing of two or more victims by the same offender(s), in separate events.

Serial killings account for no more than 1 percent of all murders committed in the United States. Based on recent FBI crime statistics, there are approximately 15,000 murders annually, so that means there are no more than 150 victims of serial murder in the United States in any given year. The FBI estimates that there are between twenty-five and fifty serial killers operating throughout the United States. at any given time (World Atlas, n.d.).

Dr. Anthony Garcia killed four people in two separate incidents. He clearly fits the technical definition of being a serial killer. There are a few more characteristics behind his murders that further characterize Garcia as a serial killer. In 2005, the FBI brought together 135 investigators, mental health professionals, and academic scholars to provide law enforcement background information to help catch serial killers.

The FBI group noted that a "cooling-off" period is a crucial factor in identifying serial killers. The cooling-off period can be days, months, or even years—it was five years, in the case of Anthony Garcia. Shirley Sherman and Thomas Hunter were killed in 2008, and the Brumbacks were murdered in 2013. How long would his cooling-off period have been after the Brumback murders? It was a question that haunted the task force at the time. We all felt the killer was in a heightened state. It is why we spent so much time preparing for the initial press conference. We wanted to extend his cooling-off period, and we did for two months.

Garcia is a case study for a long cooling-off period. One of the most prominent examples of such a long cooling-off period was the BTK Killer from Wichita, Kansas. BTK stands for bind, torture, and kill. Dennis Lynn Rader (born March 9, 1945) was the BTK Killer between the years of 1974 and 1991. During that time, he killed ten people in Wichita and Park City, Kansas, and sent taunting letters to police and media outlets describing the details of his crimes.

During his cooling-off periods between murders, Rader would take pictures of himself wearing women's clothes and a female mask while bound. He later admitted that he was pretending to be his victims as part of a sexual fantasy. After a decade-long hiatus, Rader resumed sending letters in 2004, leading to his 2005 arrest and subsequent guilty plea. He is currently serving ten consecutive life sentences at the El Dorado Correctional Facility. (Wikipedia, n.d.(a)).

The gruesome nature of Garcia's killing signature is also a hallmark of serial killers. Eric Hickey, Dean of the California School of Forensic Studies at Alliant International University, was quoted as saying, "This guy was angry and enraged, not too many killers who choose knives target the neck. That makes him unique." (*Omaha World Herald* 2013).

The most disturbing aspect of the Garcia murders in my mind is the killing of eleven-year-old Thomas Hunter. I believe Garcia did not travel eleven hours by car to kill the boy. Thomas was home and his dad was not, plain, and simple. In Garcia's mind, killing Dr. Hunter's son would cause great pain and harm to the person against whom he held a grudge, Dr. William Hunter. In my professional opinion, I believe his thought process was, "If I can't kill Dr. Hunter, I will kill his son, and take away someone important to him."

What was most important to Garcia? From what we were told at the trial, its potentially beer, or strip clubs, or his doctor status. Look at it this way: the minute Garcia was arrested; he was deprived of three things he held most important. Maybe this is why Garcia stopped talking?

The next section touches on the trial, verdict, and death sentence of Garcia. When imposed, the death penalty may take twenty years to carry out, or it may never take place at all. However, closure can be found by knowing that he lost all his most important reasons for living when he was arrested. I say this for the families of the victims, who know he is alive and on death row.

4) The Trial, Verdict, and Sentencing

The Trial

Anthony Garcia's trial was Omaha's version of the O. J. Simpson trial, as far as media coverage. There was daily coverage of the court wrangling, and the trial was as intense as they come. The Mottas would not back down to anyone and fought tooth and nail the whole way through.

Anthony Garcia play-acted like he was sleeping the whole time. The Mottas met head-on with the Douglas County Attorney Don Kleine and Deputy Attorney Brenda Beatle. I did not attend the trial. It was not my place to do so, but I did attend the day of the verdict.

The Verdict

The verdict was important for Omaha, my detectives, and the victim's families. I attended court the day of the verdict to show support. As I walked through the courthouse rotunda, there was a large crowd waiting to get into the courtroom, and the media was brimming. This was clearly a big day, and the verdict was going to be relayed live as soon as it came in.

As I walked into the courtroom, the Mottas took note that I was in attendance and spoke among themselves upon their realization. The Mottas and I never met, but if we did, I would shake their hands. Defense attorneys play a vital role in our society, and the Mottas were doing their jobs.

The verdict came back as guilty on all four murders. I felt that two important messages had come from the guilty verdict. The first was that the task force had gotten the right guy. Thomas Hunter's mom, Dr. Claire Hunter, took care of sending that message to the media for me, giving a quote indicating just that. She picked the headline:

"'They got the right guy,' Thomas Hunter's mother says; Anthony Garcia is found guilty on all counts" (Cooper et al. 2019).

The second media message was that Omaha did not have to worry about Anthony Garcia any longer, and that the community's focus should forever be on the victims now that Garcia was convicted. I gave a statement outside of the courtroom and let the media play it on the nightly news. It was my way of using the media to put a period on this dark chapter in Omaha's history.

The *Omaha World Herald* used that statement to close out an editorial on the murders and task force arrests. The last paragraph of the OWH's editorial was as follows:

Garcia evaded justice for years until a storm of evidence developed through dogged, professional police work and prosecutors did him in. "As we move forward, we are left to remember the victims, and there is no need to mention or worry about Anthony Garcia any longer" [Chief] Schmaderer said after the trial. That is the gift police and prosecutors gave the city. Justice. (*Omaha World Herald* 2016)

The Sentencing

Dr. Anthony Garcia was sentenced to death. I did not weigh in with the media when asked about the sentence. My opinion on the death penalty is not germane, as I will support whatever feelings the victims' families have on the death sentence. It was the task force's job to catch the killer, and we did.

5) Where Are They Now?

The murders were an emotional and terrifying time for Omaha. Serial killers are extremely rare, and Garcia was unique among them. His motive of revenge and modus operandi brought a lot of attention. To this day, the OPD's Press Information Office still receives inquiries from documentaries and shows looking to highlight this case.

The media "chess match" related to this investigation has never been talked about in detail or exposed until this book. My intention in sharing it here is for it to be a learning tool. I know in my early days as chief it would have been helpful to have had such a resource to rely on. I would like to close this chapter by giving a synopsis of where those involved in the case are now.

The Families: The victim's families still live in Omaha, and I am happy they stayed. They have my utmost respect.

Team Motta: They are still practicing law together in Chicago. They dropped out of representing Garcia after the trial, and Garcia's appeals are being delegated by other attorneys. Bob Motta Jr. has an informative and entertaining podcast called, Defense Diaries Podcast; check it out.

Derek Mois: Derek is still a detective in OPD's Cold Case Homicide Unit. This should be a comforting thought to crime victims' families.

Scott Warner: Scott is still working at the OPD. He is now a supervisor in the Robbery Unit nearing retirement.

Ken Kanger: Ken retired from OPD as a deputy chief. He is now the Omaha Airport Authority chief of police.

Douglas County Attorney Don Kleine and Deputy Attorney Brenda Beatle: Both are still in the same roles, protecting Douglas County and ensuring justice for victims.

Omaha Police Chief Todd Schmaderer: I am still the chief of police for Omaha. About a month after the task force arrested Dr. Anthony Garcia, we had to regroup and track down Omaha's next serial killer. Nikko Jenkins had just begun his reign of terror, killing four people in Omaha.

It was a rare and unique time in Omaha, having two serial killers back-to-back. In Omaha's and Nebraska's crime history, it must rank up there near the topmost intense crime era. I want to thank the top commander of the task force, Deputy Chief Mary Newman. Mary has since retired and is teaching a homicide class at the University of Nebraska at Omaha. Her work on this case was behind the scenes, and worthy of Hall of Fame status.

Dr. Anthony Garcia: Garcia is a death-row inmate being housed at the Tecumseh State Correctional Institution.

The last person to be executed in Nebraska was Carey Dean Moore on August 14, 2018. Moore was given a lethal injection for killing two cab drivers. Moore committed his murders in 1979 and was one of the longest-serving death row inmates in the United States.

The death penalty is a slow process. There is no telling when the next death-row inmate in Nebraska will be slated for execution. There is no way of knowing when Garcia's number will be up, or if it will ever happen. For all practical purposes, the families of the victims received their closure at the time of arrest. The task force's strong motivation was to prevent other murders and give some measure of closure to the victims' families.

Anthony Garcia is inmate #88303 / Death Row / Nebraska Department of Correctional Services, Tecumseh Prison.

CHAPTER TWELVE

Chief's Perspicacity

This chapter breaks away from the traditional chapter objectives and gives quick-hitting executive viewpoints on law enforcement and leadership. *Perspicacity* means the quality of having a shrewdness or a ready insight into things. In this chapter, I look back at over a decade as chief of police to give insight into my law enforcement philosophy. This provides a "what works and what doesn't work" perspective on law enforcement, including commonly misunderstood situations, from my personal perspective and opinion. All these thoughts are about bridges I have crossed in my career.

Final Thoughts and Words of Wisdom

I would rather have one thousand more jobs than one thousand more officers to reduce crime.

One thousand strategically placed good jobs would go a long way toward changing the environment of crime and its root causes.

Managing expectations is the hardest challenge of being a law enforcement executive.

The internal and external expectations on a chief of police are arduous and oftentimes emotional and unreasonable. A law enforcement executive is best served by instilling the barometers for success with buy-in from both the internal and external environments. The internal environment is the rank-and-file officers and their representative union. The external environment is made up of the community, media, and politicians.

As a leader, strive to be respected over being liked. This is the message I told the new Omaha police supervisors. When a leader strives to be liked, corners will be cut, and accountability is lost. The leader may be liked by his/her subordinates but not necessarily respected as accountability can be lost. For example, a new supervisor may overlook an officer being late for roll call, to be liked. Though, what message does this send to the specific late officer and what general message is being sent to the rest of his/her subordinates? When a leader strives to be respected, he/she will be liked for their just stance. In the officer that was late example, addressing tardiness appropriately will be respected and an understandable "tone" has now been set, leading to respect, and being liked by the subordinates.

Hiring a major city chief or superintendent because of their views on social justice, or their gender, or ethnicity alone is a recipe for disaster. Look for a candidate with executive skills and who is a strong communicator. If the executive-skilled candidate has a solid understanding of law enforcement and their social justice views align with yours, you have your hire.

The appointed position of a major city chief of police or elected sheriff will require executive skills first and foremost. OPD has 1,200 employees and a $200-million-dollar budget to police a city of half a million population. First and foremost, it takes a polished executive to formulate and implement strategic planning to move a large agency forward. If the candidate is not an executive-level leader, any other of the candidate's strong social justice suits will not be able to shine through.

Never underestimate your audience (the community) because if you are seeing it, they are too.

Listen to—and value—your critics because they will make you better.

Never lambaste or degrade your entire agency for mistakes. When the controversy is over, you will need your employees to move forward.

CHIEF'S PERSPICACITY

Faith leaders are important message-holders in a community.

As policing advances, other societal advances tend to follow.

A small percentage of the population commits violent crimes.
   In crime-ridden cities, there is a misbelief that there are a lot of violent criminals, but there are not. A small percentage of the population commits violent crimes. The violent offender will continue until stopped (Falk et al. 2014).

Never lay blame on the community or place unrealistic expectations on them to come forward as witnesses to all violent crimes.
   You would not come forward either if the perpetrator lives next to you or down the street. A proper policing plan will have workarounds such as Crime Stoppers, witness relocation, confidential informants, technology, community partnerships, and major investigations to catch the most violent offenders where law enforcement is the witness.

Ensure that your top commanders are overseeing the most mission-critical units, such as Homicide, Gang, PIO, Child Victims and Sexual Assault, Narcotics, and so on.
   Otherwise, the media will embarrass you with mistakes.

The problem in policing is not backgrounds for hiring, training, or oversight—it is retention.
   It is hard to replace problem officers in government work. The private sector gets rid of their lowest 10 percent every year. In policing, this does not happen.

Specialized units reduce crime.
Uniformed officers are your first responders for 911 calls, and they cannot be in the complete know as to who the violent offenders are. The units that reduce crime are your Gang Units, Violent Crime Task Forces, Homicide (to eliminate repeat offenders), Narcotics, and Felony Assault Units. These units can dissect crime and know who the problem offenders are.

Strive to not be "defensive" as a leader. It is important for an agency to embrace flaws and positives alike.

Try to focus on the violent offenders and chronic property crime felons and leave everyone else alone.

The police are expected to solve the greatest affronts to society—homicides. If your agency cannot solve them, why should you be trusted on the lesser crimes?

Fixing a crime problem is a progression.
    At first, it should be 80 percent enforcement with 20 percent intervention and prevention (10 percent each). Eventually, as the bleeding stops, your agency should gravitate toward the optimal 30 percent enforcement, 30 percent intervention, and 30 percent prevention. The remaining 10 percent can be applied extra to enforcement, intervention, and prevention, however the commanders deem appropriate.
    Stop the bleeding first, so addressing the root causes have a chance to work. (Examples of root causes of crime would be poverty, educational gaps, and the breakdown of the family.)

CHIEF'S PERSPICACITY

Avoid yo-yo decisions. One year, the school system cannot get enough school resource officers (SROs). The next year, the schools want them gone. Consistency is leadership; the yo-yo effect is not.

Prior to 2020, school mass shootings were a societal problem, and their prevention a high priority. The community wanted more SROs for protection. In 2020, there was a push to eliminate SROs for social justice reasons, and many jurisdictions did so. In 2021, mass shooting phenomena started to manifest again as a top public safety priority. Eliminating SROs in blindness from one year to the next year shows poor leadership and vision.

Civilian oversight of police departments is paramount.

However, do not go so far with it that the chief's capacity to set the culture for the department is undermined.

There are many forms of civilian oversight; there are review boards, auditors, and federal monitors. If there is only a single auditor . . . then who monitors the auditor?

Best practices in policing are ever changing. Have a good relationship with your local university to stay ahead of the game.

Zero-tolerance operations cause more harm than good.

Zero tolerance is when a law enforcement agency saturates an area after a spike in crime and writes citations and makes arrests for every little violation they can find. The problem is that criminals have moved on, and now you are punishing the mostly law-abiding citizens that live there.

SYNERGY *of* INFLUENCE

Officer-involved shootings (OISs) can be reduced. OISs are circumstance-based; it is up to the law enforcement agency to change the circumstances as best as possible.

Holding officers accountable initiates a culture progression.

First, the chief will be viewed negatively by the agency issuing accountability discipline. Over time, and with consistent accountability discipline, officers will accept that their fellow officers made a mistake.

Do not weigh in on other cities' poor performance unless it is necessary.

Being pitted against other law enforcement agencies is not how to control your message.

Be good at addressing the five vital signs of any major city's law enforcement agency: 1) homicides, 2) shootings, 3) officer-involved shootings, 4) complaints about officers, and 5) homicide clearance rates.

The public responds well to transparency and acknowledgment of a poorly handled situation.

If a persistent problem is identified, come at it from at least three different angles.

Said another way: attack it from all angles. A singular attack on a problem prolongs the problem.

CHIEF'S PERSPICACITY

With the advent of all the camera footage now available, it was predictable that American society would lash out over law enforcement's use of force, since the use of force is never pretty.

In addition, all the camera footage was bound to catch some police wrongdoing.

A primary function of a leader is to control the messaging for their organization, whether it is a law enforcement agency or a Fortune 500 company.

Stern policies governing off-duty social media activity are necessary. Otherwise, the agency will inevitably be faced with an image damager. Off-duty officers cannot identify themselves as agency police officers and weigh in on matters on social media. A thousand or more employees will not all be on the same page as the agency leader.

Utilize your federal partners (FBI, DEA, ATF, Homeland Security, etc.) to address your priorities as a force multiplier.

Every major city will have spikes in crime. Be known for how well you can address them.

Chiefs need to delegate minor discipline to their command staff. It empowers them and keeps the chief away from daily gripe sessions.

There are five major blocks for law enforcement executives: the media, unions, politicians, special interest groups, and the public.

SYNERGY *of* INFLUENCE

Strive for higher pay and benefits for your officers, as it goes toward a positive culture.

Show me a city with a low homicide clearance rate, and I will show you a city with poor police–community relations.

Consider having a designated second-in-command (executive deputy chief or chief deputy sheriff) because you cannot be everywhere, and the rank and file and the public will identify with this secondary leader.

The law enforcement executive should participate in high-profile charity events once a year if possible (Trek the Tower, Guns and Hoses, or Dancing with the Stars) to show the more relatable, human side of their personality, or they will only be known as the serious executive. I have participated in all three.

Your law enforcement agency is not an army, and the citizens are not enemy combatants.

Have advisors outside of law enforcement who you can trust.

Be on the alert for subcultures that can form within a law enforcement agency.

In the case of the "scorpion unit," of the Memphis police department in custody death of Tyree Nichols. The street level "scorpion unit" clearly developed a dangerous sub culture. In large agencies, sub cultures can form under poor supervision and accountability.

CHIEF'S PERSPICACITY

Pay attention to patterns.

Your belief that something will not happen, or someone would never take an action is not evidence. Human beings are good at masking themselves.

Optics and coincidences mean something, as people will form conclusions.

Law enforcement ensures your freedom. How free are you if a bully can shove you out of your place in line? How free are you if an intruder is trying to break into your home and there is no one to call?

There is no Super Bowl for law enforcement agencies.

There is no way for the public to know what cities have good law enforcement agencies. The law enforcement executive should define his/her agency's barometers for success and ensure that the media knows what they are.

Law enforcement agencies are in various stages of progression. It is wrong to paint all agencies in the same colors.

Police work is like an airline—if you are not hearing about it, things are good. If the plane crashes, everyone will be talking about it.

SYNERGY *of* INFLUENCE

—«««•»»»—

Positive publicity can come from a movie. If a movie producer wants to highlight your department, at least consider it for a morale boost.

Personal photo: Chief Schmaderer and cast on the set of *Going for Two* filmed at Omaha Police Headquarters

—«««•»»»—

A police officer's mindset should be of a guardian and not a warrior.
    Avoid photos of a warrior depiction.

CHIEF'S PERSPICACITY

Personal photo: A picture of my crew when I was a young sergeant in 2001 (yellow stripes). They were super officers who loved the community and treated people right. The picture comes across as a *crew of warriors*, and it is misleading because we were *guardians*.

Be neutral. For example, I am a registered independent. Also, avoid weighing in on non-law-enforcement, personal-choice matters, such as abortion or political elections. Why lose the trust or cooperation of 50 percent of the population you are trying to work with and protect? A law enforcement agency is supposed to be there for everyone, equally.

The few times I have weighed in on politics as chief of police, I regretted it. I was proud of the candidate, but in retrospect I feel that entering politics as an endorser distracted from the *neutral* standpoint all law enforcement executives should have.

Always support red! The fire department is your partner and, quite frankly, saves lives.

**Photo courtesy of the Omaha World Herald:
Trek the Tower with Omaha Fire**

Vent behind the scenes, never in the public eye.

As a law enforcement executive, be mindful of your office décor, as visitors will form an opinion.

You want visitors to read your décor as neutral, and any photos you display should be viewed as positive for all. If you have a picture with a Republican president, only hang it if you have another picture with a Democrat president for balance. If the photo can be viewed negatively, some visitors will do so.

**READER ASSIGNMENT:
Have a class discussion of the following: Would a photo of a president that resigned be a good look for an executive law enforcement office?**

Two vital leadership variables are seldom talked about in law enforcement: one, the officers must want to be led by the executive, and two, the leader must be allowed to lead.

The rank and file must respect the law enforcement executive (chief, sheriff, superintendent, or agent in charge)—and the mayor, governor, or president must allow them to lead.

CHIEF'S PERSPICACITY

**Omaha Police photo: President Richard Nixon
with Omaha police officers**

The 1960s race riots were needed for fundamental changes in how Black Americans were treated. The 2020 national civil unrest forced lower-performing law enforcement agencies to evolve, and society advanced. However, caution is needed; be careful not to go too far. The Defunding Movement, the elimination of qualified police immunity in some states, and the vitriolic talk about the law enforcement profession have caused a national hiring crisis where citizens of color have been hurt the worst.

A Golden Opportunity: America is going through a national staffing crisis for law enforcement agencies with unprecedentedly high vacancies of sworn personnel. As damaging as this is to the communities these law enforcement agencies serve, a golden opportunity lies underneath. If law enforcement agencies filled the vast vacancies with enhanced diversity, the sheer number of openings would change the demographics of law enforcement across the county. It would make law enforcement agencies representative of the communities they serve in one large sea change.

SYNERGY *of* INFLUENCE

READER NOTE
The pictures in the textbook are provided for proof of concept only. All major city chiefs will have impactful scenarios in their careers. From my vantage point, the country is in good hands with the major city chiefs I have met.

ADDENDUM ONE

"Kerrie's Writings"

8/22/13

Kerrie Oks

It could have been me. I have children, I'm young, I'm beautiful inside and out. I sometimes drive home alone late at night after work. I have hobbies, dreams, and goals for myself and my family. All of the story hasn't been released yet, but I could fit right into the victim's shoes. Except someone thoughtlessly took the victim's life.

They haven't caught the suspect(s), YET. I don't know who they are, I don't know anything about them. I don't know how old the person responsible is. I don't know what race, sex, nationality, or gender this person is. I don't know their ideology. I don't think any of that matters. I don't know the background of this person, yet I don't think that any sort of messed up childhood, adulthood, addiction, abuse or anything should excuse this kind of behavior.

Even if I couldn't compare myself to the victim, any victim of a horrific crime such as this doesn't deserve to be killed in a senseless matter. No parent, child, friend or family member should have to deal with the pain and questions of why after such a horrible ordeal.

The world is headed into a dangerous and scary direction. The price of life is worth far much less than it ever has been. Loved ones are being killed for money, drugs, possessions, greed, respect, publicity, for the name of the 'hood', and even out of boredom. We no longer have a common sense of belonging or responsibility to each other. Sometimes I think our 'freedoms' are used as an excuse to do whatever we want and demonize whoever dare question us. We've put personal choice above common sense. We support those who don't feel the need or satisfaction to work for themselves and build something.

It could have been me. It could have been you. It could have been anyone, in that spot at the same time under the same circumstances. But instead of pointing the finger at the person(s) responsible, we will divide ourselves and fight over silly things should never play a role in the case. People will lay blame on the victim for working late, the gun for shooting her, the parents that didn't raise the person(s) responsible the "right" way. The mental health system will bear blame, the criminal justice system will feel the burn if the person was let out early. All the while, the pain will be felt by the victim's family, friends, husband and children.

When will we learn?
Again, they haven't caught the suspect(s), YET. When that day comes, let's put all of the conversation about who's fault it is stay on the suspect. There is no excuse for this action. Let's join together and let them know, we know it's their fault and they will pay for their crime.

SYNERGY *of* INFLUENCE

      I've recieved many gifts in my lifetime. Wether the material presents I got as a toddler still exist, I
couldn't tell you. On the other hand, the gifts my friends and family gave to me that weren't physical

goods have stayed with me through today.

      My patience was given to me the moment my sister was born. It accumulated in size each time

my parents brought my brothers home from the hospital too. I had been an only child for three years

and now I had to wait to play with my favorite toy, watch my favorite cartoon. I even had to wait to be

fed. The diaper clad sibling always came first.

      Work ethnic was handed down to me from my dad. Many storms came and went and still he

trudged through the mud, snow, and rain just to get the chores done. I remember one night Dad stayed

at the hog confinement all night and slept in an empty pen so he'd be sure to keep the electricity running

and the hogs in check.

      My grandpa gave me my sense of humor. He'll laugh at anything, no matter how overused the

joke. We kid him about the time he wasn't wearing his seatbelt and instinctively pulled it across his chest

when he saw the blinking lights.....of the postman's car. He gets a kick out of that one everytime.

      My mom gave me my love of sports. It wasn't that she was a star in school, but she made sure I

made it to every Little League practice those first few years. It was her pushing that kept me out for the

sport of the season since I regularly hated the sport we were in. Every year I would pull the stunt that I

hated losing, that i couldn't hit the ball or catch it, and she'd make me stay out.

      I'm certain these gifts and the ones I was unable to mention will surely stay with me the rest of

my life. Sometimes it's not about what the people you love give youin presents, but it's the friendship

and traits they give you that really count. Count your blessings.

"KERRIE'S WRITINGS"

My Philosophy of Life   Kerrie Holtz
                            Oct 9, 2002

To breathe in nature and partake as much of it as one can, that should be my goal. Too often I get caught up in the fast lane of life, never stopping to take in some of the important stuff. Nature provides little (and big) opportunities to relax you and let you get in touch with your inner self. Nature lets me be silly and no one will see or judge me on it. Nature allows you a short break from reality, a time-out to sit out and look at your life.

Nature teaches me to be optimistic. A fire may destroy a forest for that moment in time, but what about the next spring? Those plants grow right back and the forest floor seems greener than ever, as if mocking the fire saying "Nah, nah you can't get me".

I believe that one is in control of one's own life. If you don't like what you're doing, you have the power of changing it to fit what you want. Don't like your job? Get a new one. Keep in mind that this may seem easier said than done, but don't let the fire put you out. You can bounce right back too. Fulfill your life with everything you need or want, luxuries included, not with what the "standard" is. Do your own thing, and be your own person.

True happiness doesn't come only in enjoying the small things. You also have to enjoy everything else too. By this, I mean your chores, your job, and your schoolwork. There are some things you *have* to do. Change your perspective and you'll be much happier, guaranteed. Look at washing the dishes as you *get* to wash them, not *have* to. You don't *have* to watch your little brother; you *get* to. Make little games out of life, you'll have more fun. After all, life is one big game; you just have to win.

Don't take life for granted, it will be gone and past before you know it. I've already been here seventeen years and what have I done that I want to accomplish? I could name a few things worthwhile that I spent my time wisely on, but that's not all I want to do. I have plenty of work cut out for me, if I want to fulfill my life before it's over.

True happiness is one of my goals. It should be one for everyone. The definition of "true" happiness may be varied, but that's because we all are different. Maybe it has something to do with our social position, or lack thereof. If you were born into a modest household, with the basic necessities, but few luxuries, of course you would wish to be higher up on the social ladder, where more luxuries might occur. Material possessions are taken more for granted if you are up higher class-wise. I think people who have everything just begin to take the little things for granted. They might be nice to have, but you can't beat the homemade toys, or the hand-me-down outfits. Those retain many fond memories.

Success in life is self-determined, although there is a model for it. The model states the successful to be living in a close to perfect home, a good family, no police record, one being a model citizen. What about that middle-aged man living across the street for the model of success? He has seen his share of bad days, but he has a home in which he owns, a good sum of retirement money, and a few young grandchildren who like to hear stories about the "good old days." He is a success in his family's eyes. I define success for me as having a job I love to go to everyday, a stable home, some money saved up, and a loving family. The next person might say "A good-paying job." This is where I stress the difference in goals.

One piece of advice I want to offer to fellow passerby is to have fun in life, while you can. I don't mean go out for 90 mile an hour joy ride cruising through town, but enjoy the little things. That will be my everlasting memory. A friend told me this a while back and I have realized that he is absolutely right. Picture your life dragging on forever. Are you going to want to reminisce that when your telling your good buddies up in heaven? Of course you don't. You would want to tell them of the time you made a bet with the guys that you would win a volleyball match and they had to shave their legs the next day.

The true purpose in life can be whatever you believe. I believe I am here now because someday I'm going to make a difference in someone's life. Maybe it would be broadcast on every channel on the T.V. when I make my famous speech, or maybe it'll be on the last page of the small local newspaper. Whatever that may be, but I do believe that is the reason I am here. When I see the bright light, I'm going to look back at my life and hoped I fulfilled my need. Otherwise, I'm going to tell God, "Wait, I forgot to do something," and get back to what I need to do.

The last piece of advice I would like to give is to stop worrying. We live worried lifestyles, and need to quit. Often I hear my friends complaining they have a test next period, and quickly hurry and try to squeeze and retain every ounce of information that they can, sort of like sponges. I'm not saying studying is bad, but why stress your self out so much? I prefer to look at my notes, take a deep breath and do my best. After the test I might check the hard problem that I know I probably missed, but after that I hope for the best and leave the subject alone. As for the grades at the end of quarters, I admit to falling into that same pattern, worrying about the hard class I opted to take but worry about lower grade. I always try my hardest but there is a sense of failure when I get a grade that isn't up to my standard, when I know I could have done better.

All in all, the meaning and purpose of life is just what it says. Live it.

SYNERGY *of* INFLUENCE

51315 Pinoak Road
Walnut, IA 51577
January 23, 2002

Patti Peppermint
1234 Candy Cane Lane
Yummy, China 12345

Dear Patti:

Hello. My name is Kerrie. I have two brothers and a sister. I just turned 16 on September 19. We live on a farm and have cows and pigs. The horse we have just had a colt this past spring. I have two dogs and a lot of cats. I go to Walnut High School, and I am in the tenth grade. Walnut, Iowa is in the middle of the United States. I like riding my horse and playing basketball. Basketball is my favorite sport. I love to read too. Everyone makes fun of my car because it is so old. Don't worry, I'm going to get a new one soon. When I get out of school I'm going to go to college but I don't know what I am going to be when I grow up.

We were told to tell you about our two holidays Christmas and Thanksgiving. Thanksgiving is on the third Thursday in November. We celebrate the pilgrims and the Native Americans having a feast together after the pilgrims first arrived here. My family goes to my grandma's house and we have a big dinner. We get out of school for a couple days too. Christmas is on December 25. We celebrate Jesus Christ's birth. We get two weeks off of school, and my family and I go to both my aunt and grandma's houses. Everyone exchanges presents. This year I got four shirts and a telephone line that I have to share with my sister.

On weekdays, I have school and after that I go to basketball practice. Wednesday nights I have a piano lesson and church classes. Friday and Saturday nights that I don't have basketball games I work at a restaurant. Sundays I have church and I tutor two junior high girls in math. I play softball, basketball, volleyball, and I am in jazz band and show choir. When I find free time I go to the movies and out to eat with my boyfriend. I love driving, and I just bought a new car so I won't have to drive my junkie one.

So, how is your life going? Do you play any sports? Tell me about what you do every day. Hope to hear from you soon!

Your friend,

Kerrie Holtz

Kerrie Holtz

ADDENDUM TWO

Verbatim transcripts and video from two press conferences following Officer Kerrie Orozco's murder.

Excerpts from Police
Chief Todd Schmaderer's remarks at press conference
- May 21, 2015, Omaha World Herald

With Creighton University Medical Center staff members and other officials at his side, Police Chief Todd Schmaderer speaks Wednesday after Officer Kerrie Orozco's death.

CHRIS MACHIAN/THE WORLD-HERALD
From staff reports

"This is a somber day for the city of Omaha. My Omaha police officers especially and the entire law enforcement community. It is with deep sorrow and pain that I have to announce that 7-year veteran officer — Officer Kerrie Orozco — has died after being shot in the line of duty. Kerrie Orozco, 29 years old, has been in the department for 7 years and 5 months. She worked in the gang unit and she has since March 2012.

Her husband is Hector Orozco. She has ... a stepdaughter, 8-year-old Natalia, and a stepson, Santiago, who is 6 years old. Kerrie had a newborn baby that was born February 17th and is in ... UNMC in an intensive care unit right now. Her name is Olivia Ruth. She is set to be released from the hospital tomorrow. ...

A little bit about Kerrie: She was a tremendous officer, an even better person. She coached baseball since 2009 in a north Omaha Boys & Girls Club. She volunteered with the Special Olympics, she was president of the Police Officers' Ball to benefit the Special Olympics, she took in rescue dogs, she was a Girl Scout mentor, she spoke at Girls Inc. frequently.

She was a friend, a popular officer, a top-notch person, and I just can't imagine that this has even happened. But Officer Orozco is a top-notch individual, and the city of Omaha owes her a debt of gratitude, and her family, like no other.

I'm going to get a little bit into the incident that had occurred, but before I do, I want to make note that the suspect in the case, Mr. (Marcus) D. Wheeler also died of gunshot wounds after being transported to Creighton University. Our condolences to the family of Mr. Wheeler, as well. ...

―⋘⋙―

The Omaha Police Department is a very professional entity and what you're seeing is the men and women of the Omaha Police Department doing their jobs right now. And I'm standing here doing my job even though inside I'm churning. My message to them is they are special individuals in this community, something the community desperately needs is that law enforcement presence and those willing to step up and apprehend violent offenders and those willing to put themselves in harm's way. ... My message to them is to keep your head held high, we'll do our job professionally and we're going to grieve. We'll grieve like everybody else. This is a very tough day for the Omaha Police Department, for the city of Omaha, law enforcement in general.

―⋘⋙―

I think Omaha is a tremendous community. I've said all along that north Omaha (is a) tremendous community. And we're going to work through this issue with the community side by side. It's why we're here right now: to give as much information as we possibly can.

―⋘⋙―

But the community should be very confident in knowing that we're doing our jobs professionally, we're overseeing this investigation and even though we're grieving ... like no other right now, we'll maintain that professionalism and do what we need to do.

―⋘⋙―

"KERRIE'S WRITINGS"

We are the community. That's why I don't feel that this will cause any negative police-community relations. I think you'll see the city of Omaha band together, look for the outcome of this investigation, and support the Omaha Police Department and certainly support Officer Orozco for her sacrifice and what has taken place.

Transcript of Police Chief Todd Schmaderer's remarks at OPD Headquarters on Kerrie Orozco murder press conference the day after she died.— *Omaha World Herald*

On behalf of the Omaha Police Department, I want to thank the citizens of Omaha and the law enforcement community — locally and nationally — for their overwhelming support they have shown us. It is humbling and it makes all of us proud to serve our great city. Mayor Stothert and I continue our constant communication on the incident that occurred yesterday. Mayor Stothert is going to make early arrangements to come home — she's at her son's wedding in Florida. She's going to come home early to attend the funeral. Today's press conference will be a clinical briefing on the events that occurred yesterday. It is designed for transparency, just like we would do in the aftermath of any large-scale occurrence that occurs in the city of Omaha. So please bear with me, there are quite a few details to go through. We have prepared a media packet, and at the end of my briefing I will take some questions.

On Monday, May 20th, at 12:58 p.m., Omaha police officers assigned to the Metro Area Task Force were conducting surveillance in the area of Martin Avenue and Read Street. Sgt. Jeff Kopietz, a 24-year police veteran, and Officer Robert Laney, a 25-year police veteran, were attempting to locate and arrest 26-year-old Marcus D. Wheeler. Wheeler was wanted on a felony warrant on first-degree assault as a result of a shooting that occurred on September 5th, 2014; you should have copies of this in your media packet.

Sgt. Kopietz and Officer Laney were watching the residents at 3057 Martin Ave., additional officers assigned to the multiagency task force began responding to their location to assist with locating Wheeler. Among the responding officers were officers Jeff Shada, 21-year police veteran, and officer Kerrie Orozco, a seven-year police veteran. Officer Laney observed a suspect, which matched the description of Wheeler on foot near the intersection of Vane Street and Martin Avenue. Officer Laney drove to the intersection of Vane Street and Martin Avenue, where he observed Wheeler walking in a grassy area on the north side of Vane Street across from the address of 3159 Vane Street. Officer Laney radioed to Sgt. Kopietz that he had the suspect. Officer Laney parked his unmarked vehicle equipped with emergency police lights in front of 3159 Vane Street. The red-and-blue emergency police lights were flashing at this time. Officer

Laney got out of his vehicle and called Wheeler by his name and told him to stop. Wheeler responded by pulling a handgun and firing at least three gunshots at Officer Laney. One bullet struck the lower portion of the driver-side door of Laney's vehicle — it's depicted in the photo. Officer Laney did not have a chance to discharge his handgun in response. A second bullet struck the back window of a parked vehicle in the driveway of 3159 Vane Street. A female witness was standing near this vehicle and witnessed and corroborated the confrontation between Wheeler and Officer Laney. Wheeler then fled north toward the rear of 3057 Martin Ave.

At this point, Officer Laney radioed to Sgt. Kopietz that shots were fired and that Wheeler had fled to 3057 Martin Ave.

Sgt. Kopietz quickly drove his unmarked vehicle into the driveway at 3057 Martin Ave. and turned on his red-and-blue emergency lights.

Sergeant got out of his vehicle and observed Erica Coppage-

Williams and a small child come out of the front door of the residence. Sgt. Kopietz yelled out to Coppage-Williams to come out away from the residence to him. So he's motioning her, "Come to us."

Sgt. Kopietz described Coppage-Williams' appearance as agitated and stressed as she yelled back at him. Sgt. Kopietz then observed Wheeler appear from the back of 3057 Martin Ave. walking across the driveway from the west to the east. There was a green four-door sedan parked in the driveway that was between Wheeler and Sgt. Kopietz.

Sgt. Kopietz gave Wheeler loud verbal commands to stop and get on the ground. Wheeler instantly responded to the verbal commands by quickly turning toward Sgt. Kopietz, taking a crouched, shooting position, pointing a handgun and firing multiple gunshots at Sgt.

Kopietz. Sgt. Kopietz at this time returned gunfire toward Wheeler.

At this moment, Officer Orozco and Officer Shada ran up to the driveway and formed a tactical approach behind Sgt. Kopietz's position. Wheeler continued east over a fence and into the backyard of 3055 Martin Ave. The sergeant, followed by Officer Orozco and Officer

Shada approached the backyard along the west side of 3055 Martin Ave. Sgt. Kopietz observed Wheeler in the backyard. Wheeler was again crouched down in a shooting stance and fired a second volley of multiple gunshots at Sgt. Kopietz. Sgt. Kopietz also fired multiple gunshots at Wheeler in return. Immediately after this exchange of gunfire, Officer Orozco yelled out that she had been hit. Sgt.

Kopietz turns toward her, observed her bleeding and yelled for her to get on the ground. Sgt. Kopietz then lost sight of Wheeler as he fled toward the east. During the exchange of gunfire, Wheeler fired at least six gunshots from a 9 mm caliber handgun equipped with a high drum capacity type magazine — it should be depicted in one of the photos. This exchange of gunfire was witnessed by a citizen. Officer Shada and Orozco did not discharge their duty weapons. Their duty weapons were .45-caliber. Officer Orozco suffered a lethal gunshot wound to her upper chest area, just above the front panel of the ballistic vest line. Officer Shada pulled Officer Orozco to the front yard of 3055 Martin, where Officer Shada began to administer first aid. Two uniform patrol officers arrived on scene and began CPR on Officer Orozco until the Omaha Fire Department arrived and took over the emergency medical procedures. Wheeler was struck by two gunshots. One was a lethal gunshot wound to his chest. However, he was able to continue eastbound through the backyards along Martin Avenue to the rear of 3043 Read Street. A witness observed Wheeler collapse in the yard in the southeast corner of the residence at this address. The witness also observed a handgun fall to the ground with Wheeler. Witnesses alerted officers to Wheeler's location. Sgt. Kopietz,

Officer Laney and other officers that had arrived to the scene located

Wheeler lying on the ground in the rear of 3043 Read Street. Lying next to Wheeler was the 9 mm Glock handgun. The uniform patrol officers began CPR on Wheeler until the Fire Department could take over. Officer Orozco and Wheeler were transported to CHI hospital in extremely critical condition with CPR in progress for both. Officer Orozco was treated by a trauma team at the hospital. Officer Orozco succumbed to her injuries and was pronounced dead at the hospital. Preliminary autopsy results show that Officer Orozco died from a gunshot wound to the upper chest just above the ballistic vest line. Further evidence showed that the bullet that struck Officer Orozco passed through her chest and exited her back. A bullet was recovered from inside of the rear of her ballistic vest panel. This bullet was examined by the Omaha Police Department forensic firearms examiners. The bullet was fired from a 9 mm handgun. The only person at this scene that had a 9 mm handgun was our suspect, Wheeler.

Wheeler was also treated by a trauma team at the hospital. He also succumbed to his injuries and was pronounced dead at the hospital. Preliminary autopsy results have not been completed and are not available at this time. To summarize, the firearms involved in this incident, including the 9 mm handgun, fired 9 times by Wheeler, at least 3 gunshots fired at Officer Laney on Vane Street and at least 6 gunshots fired at the officers in the driveway at 3057 Martin Ave. Wheeler was armed with a Glock, 9 millimeter handgun with a high capacity drum-type magazine with a 50 round capacity. Wheeler's handgun was loaded with 45 rounds of 9 mm ammunition when it was recovered. An additional Glock, 9 mm magazine, with a magazine capacity of 15 rounds was located on the ground in the backyard of

3055 Martin Ave. This magazine contained 8 rounds of ammunition.

Sgt. Kopietz was the only police officer that discharged his duty weapon. Sgt. Kopietz fired between 3 to 4 shots at Wheeler. All four officers in this incident were armed with Glock 45 handguns. Law enforcement officers assigned to the Metro Area Task

Force wear a modified, tactical police uniform due to the nature of their work. The uniform typically consists of tan pants, a dark shirt and a black tactical vest clearly marked with police on front and back. At this point in the investigation, 13 sworn law enforcement personnel and 11 civilian witnesses have been interviewed by the Omaha Police Department's officer-involved investigations team. This investigation continues at this time. Autopsy and toxicology results are pending, and forensic firearms and ballistic examinations will be conducted. Wheeler is a convicted felon, he's also a known gang member. He was convicted for federal narcotics distribution charge. He was sentenced to 5 years, 6 months in federal prison. According to court documents, he ended his term of federal supervised release on Nov. 5, 2013. Douglas County Attorney Don Kleine has been contacted and briefed on this incident. The sergeant who discharged his weapon, 51-year-old Jeffrey Kopietz, again he's a 24-year veteran assigned to the Omaha fugitives squad. He's been a supervisor in that squad for many, many years. Per Omaha Police Department policy, any officer who discharges his or her firearm that results in injury or death is placed on paid administrative leave pending the officer-involved investigations team and internal affairs investigations. Sgt. Kopietz has been placed on paid administrative leave. A grand jury will be convened to investigate, per state law.

The actions of my officers were justified, as they were attempting to apprehend a dangerous suspect who engaged them in gunfire on at least two occasions.

"This is a somber day for Omaha: City mourns a mother, a mentor, an officer killed in the line of duty.

By Alia Conley, Maggie O'Brien and Alissa Skelton / World-Herald staff writers

A month ago, Omaha Police Officer Kerrie Orozco was proud of the weight her premature daughter had gained.

"She's pretty close to 6 lbs!" Orozco wrote on Facebook, underneath photos of her two stepchildren holding baby Olivia Ruth.

Orozco had been looking forward to today — the day when she could take Olivia home after three months in the neonatal intensive care unit.

But she didn't make it.

Orozco, 29, was killed Wednesday, her last day of police duty before taking the rest of her maternity leave to spend with her first-born child.

Gunfire erupted when Orozco and other officers attempted to arrest **Marcus D. Wheeler**, on a felony warrant for first-degree assault about 1 p.m.

Orozco, who was part of the gang unit, is the first female police officer in the department to die in the line of duty. She is the 25th Omaha officer killed on duty overall and the first since 2003.

"KERRIE'S WRITINGS"

Wheeler, 26, also died of injuries from the shooting near 30th Street and Martin Avenue. Wheeler was a convicted felon and a known gang member, police said.

Police are planning a 4:30 p.m. Wednesday press conference to provide more information on the shootings.

In a press conference late Wednesday afternoon, Police Chief Todd Schmaderer said Orozco, who was a seven-year-veteran, dedicated her life to service.

"This is a somber day for the city of Omaha," Schmaderer said.

"**Officer Orozco was a top-notch individual**, and the city of Omaha owes her a debt of gratitude, and her family, like no other." Schmaderer laid out a basic time line of events:

At 12:58 p.m., Orozco and other members of the Metro Area Fugitive Task Force were near Martin Avenue and Read Street, looking for Wheeler, when they spotted him about a block away, near 31st Avenue and Vane Street.

Wheeler shot at officers, then ran north through a wooded area toward the backyard of a house at 3057 Martin Ave.

Orozco, another officer and a sergeant confronted Wheeler, and shots were exchanged. Orozco collapsed.

While officers rendered first aid to Orozco, Wheeler ran east and collapsed in the backyard at 3042 Read Street. A semiautomatic handgun with a drum magazine was found near him.

A man living at the Read Street house said he saw Wheeler lean against a downspout and fall to the ground. He said Wheeler was pointing at his chest, where he had been shot.

Officers performed CPR on Orozco and Wheeler, Schmaderer said.

"It was really sad," Valentine said, "really heart-wrenching, watching the officer."

Both Orozco and Wheeler were taken by ambulance to Creighton University Medical Center in extremely critical condition. They were pronounced dead at the hospital.

Angela Valentine, who lives just east of 3057 Martin Ave., was taking a nap Wednesday afternoon when her son walked in and said, "I think I heard shooting." Valentine then heard what she thought were police outside the house say, "Get down! Get down on the ground!" The officers were yelling toward the back of the neighbor's house.

Valentine then heard two shots, then many shots.

She looked outside and saw a female police officer on the ground near the corner of her house. "There was blood on her pants and the upper part of her body," Valentine said. Other officers were trying to keep the officer calm, she said, and were "going into CPR mode."

Following the news of Orozco's death, condolences began pouring into social media from across the nation. Hundreds of people, including law enforcement officers and police departments, posted comments, many containing the hashtag #SupportBlue.

Crime scene tape remained around 3057 Martin Ave. on Thursday morning. The Omaha Police Department's mobile command center was parked directly in front of the house, and the crime lab van also was parked in front of the command center. Eastbound Martin Avenue was blocked from Vane Street to Read Street.

After looking at a photo of Wheeler on Thursday, a neighbor said, "I've absolutely seen him hanging around, kicking it in the driveway. I've seen him coming and going, but not causing any trouble. Of course, if you're laying low, you wouldn't want to cause any trouble."

He said he recently started seeing people coming and going, mostly at night.

Orozco was the second female law enforcement officer in the state to be killed in the line of duty, according to the Nebraska Law Enforcement Memorial. Amanda Baker, a Scotts Bluff County corrections officer, was strangled in February 2014 by a 15-year-old inmate at the Scotts Bluff County Detention Center.

Schmaderer said he had spoken with Orozco's family. At the press conference he also offered condolences to Wheeler's family.

Mayor Jean Stothert, who was out of town for her son's wedding, said in a statement:

"Officer Orozco will be honored by the entire community for her service and bravery through our prayer and our continued community support for all police officers."

Stothert ordered flags in the city to be lowered to half-staff in Orozco's honor until dusk on Monday. In addition, the lights on the Heartland of America Fountain and the Bob Kerrey Pedestrian Bridge will be blue through Memorial Day.

After the shooting, more than 20 bystanders gathered at the crime scene, which spanned 30th to 33rd Streets and from Read to Whitmore Streets.

Outside 3057 Martin Ave., where gunfire had been exchanged, police were talking to Erica Coppage-Williams. She had recently moved into the house, said her father, Anthony Williams.

Coppage-Williams, 24, appeared distraught as she sat in her front yard. She let out tearful screams and called out to her father while talking to police.

Wheeler and Coppage-Williams had a child in 2009, court records show.

Coppage-Williams was booked by Omaha police Wednesday night on suspicion of obstructing a peace officer, aiding consummation of a felony and disorderly conduct.

Authorities had been searching for Wheeler in connection with the

Sept. 5 shooting of Antonio Martin near 60th Street and Curtis Avenue. Wheeler was released from federal prison in February 2014 after being convicted of possession of cocaine with intent to distribute.

Schmaderer called Wheeler "a very dangerous individual" and said the community needs brave individuals to apprehend such serious criminals. Orozco and the Metro Area Fugitive Task Force officers go after "the worst of the worst," he said.

"KERRIE'S WRITINGS"

Orozco returned to work shortly after giving birth to Olivia on Feb. 17.

With Olivia facing an extended stay in the NICU at the Nebraska Medical Center, Orozco wanted to save her maternity leave for when Olivia left the hospital.

Before she had her own child, Orozco served as a mother and a mentor to other children, coaching baseball and volunteering with numerous community organizations.

She was a stepmother to Natalia, 8, and Santiago, 6, children of her husband, Hector Orozco Lopez. They were married in a civil ceremony in 2011, then had a church wedding in 2012.

The Police Department was collecting food donations for Orozco's family. By 10 p.m., so much food had been dropped off at precinct stations that the department was suggesting that any additional donations be taken to homeless shelters in memory of the officer.

The Omaha Police Foundation announced Wednesday night that it would give all of its Omaha Gives donations to the Orozco family.

The donation total has topped $75,000, from more than 1,800 donors, the most of any nonprofit in the campaign.

Asked at the press conference whether the shooting would damage police-community relations, Schmaderer rejected the idea. Officers are also a part of the community, he pointed out.

"I think you'll see the city of Omaha band together ... and certainly support Officer Orozco for her sacrifice," he said.

"I think Omaha is a tremendous community. I've said all along that north Omaha (is a) tremendous community," he said. "And we're going to work through this issue with the community side by side."

Many details about the shooting haven't been released. A press conference may be held later today, officials said.

"My greatest concern is with my officers and their families and the integrity of this investigation," Schmaderer said.

By Wednesday night, flowers, candles and other tokens were being left as makeshift memorials at the crime scene and outside Omaha Police Headquarters.

The chief had a message for his officers, who were struggling with the loss of their well-liked colleague.

"Keep your head held high, we'll do our job professionally, and we're going to grieve," Schmaderer said. "We'll grieve like anybody else."

World-Herald staff writers Kevin Cole, Christopher Burbach, Bob Glissmann and Emerson Clarridge contributed to this report.

Contact the writer: 402-444-1068, alia.conley@owh.com

+23

ADDENDUM THREE

Society for Professional Journalism
"Code of Ethics"
https://www.spj.org/images/blurbs/t-ethicscodedl.jpg

Society of Professional Journalists

CODE of ETHICS

PREAMBLE
Members of the Society of Professional Journalists believe that public enlightenment is the forerunner of justice and the foundation of democracy. Ethical journalism strives to ensure the free exchange of information that is accurate, fair and thorough. An ethical journalist acts with integrity. The Society declares these four principles as the foundation of ethical journalism and encourages their use in its practice by all people in all media.

SEEK TRUTH AND REPORT IT
Ethical journalism should be accurate and fair. Journalists should be honest and courageous in gathering, reporting and interpreting information.

Journalists should:

- Take responsibility for the accuracy of their work. Verify information before releasing it. Use original sources whenever possible.
- Remember that neither speed nor format excuses inaccuracy.
- Provide context. Take special care not to misrepresent or oversimplify in promoting, previewing or summarizing a story.
- Gather, update and correct information throughout the life of a news story.
- Be cautious when making promises, but keep the promises they make.
- Identify sources clearly. The public is entitled to as much information as possible to judge the reliability and motivations of sources.
- Consider sources' motives before promising anonymity. Reserve anonymity for sources who may face danger, retribution or other harm, and have information that cannot be obtained elsewhere. Explain why anonymity was granted.
- Diligently seek subjects of news coverage to allow them to respond to criticism or allegations of wrongdoing.
- Avoid undercover or other surreptitious methods of gathering information unless traditional, open methods will not yield information vital to the public.
- Be vigilant and courageous about holding those with power accountable. Give voice to the voiceless.
- Support the open and civil exchange of views, even views they find repugnant.
- Recognize a special obligation to serve as watchdogs over public affairs and government. Seek to ensure that the public's business is conducted in the open, and that public records are open to all.
- Provide access to source material when it is relevant and appropriate.
- Boldly tell the story of the diversity and magnitude of the human experience. Seek sources whose voices we seldom hear.
- Avoid stereotyping. Journalists should examine the ways their values and experiences may shape their reporting.
- Label advocacy and commentary.
- Never deliberately distort facts or context, including visual information. Clearly label illustrations and re-enactments.
- Never plagiarize. Always attribute.

MINIMIZE HARM
Ethical journalism treats sources, subjects, colleagues and members of the public as human beings deserving of respect.

Journalists should:

- Balance the public's need for information against potential harm or discomfort. Pursuit of the news is not a license for arrogance or undue intrusiveness.
- Show compassion for those who may be affected by news coverage. Use heightened sensitivity when dealing with juveniles, victims of sex crimes, and sources or subjects who are inexperienced or unable to give consent. Consider cultural differences in approach and treatment.
- Recognize that legal access to information differs from an ethical justification to publish or broadcast.
- Realize that private people have a greater right to control information about themselves than public figures and others who seek power, influence or attention. Weigh the consequences of publishing or broadcasting personal information.
- Avoid pandering to lurid curiosity, even if others do.
- Balance a suspect's right to a fair trial with the public's right to know. Consider the implications of identifying criminal suspects before they face legal charges.
- Consider the long-term implications of the extended reach and permanence of publication. Provide updated and more complete information as appropriate.

ACT INDEPENDENTLY
The highest and primary obligation of ethical journalism is to serve the public.

Journalists should:

- Avoid conflicts of interest, real or perceived. Disclose unavoidable conflicts.
- Refuse gifts, favors, fees, free travel and special treatment, and avoid political and other outside activities that may compromise integrity or impartiality, or may damage credibility.
- Be wary of sources offering information for favors or money; do not pay for access to news. Identify content provided by outside sources, whether paid or not.
- Deny favored treatment to advertisers, donors or any other special interests, and resist internal and external pressure to influence coverage.
- Distinguish news from advertising and shun hybrids that blur the lines between the two. Prominently label sponsored content.

BE ACCOUNTABLE AND TRANSPARENT
Ethical journalism means taking responsibility for one's work and explaining one's decisions to the public.

Journalists should:

- Explain ethical choices and processes to audiences. Encourage a civil dialogue with the public about journalistic practices, coverage and news content.
- Respond quickly to questions about accuracy, clarity and fairness.
- Acknowledge mistakes and correct them promptly and prominently. Explain corrections and clarifications carefully and clearly.
- Expose unethical conduct in journalism, including within their organizations.
- Abide by the same high standards they expect of others.

The SPJ Code of Ethics is a statement of abiding principles supported by additional explanations and position papers (at spj.org) that address changing journalistic practices. It is not a set of rules, rather a guide that encourages all who engage in journalism to take responsibility for the information they provide, regardless of medium. The code should be read as a whole; individual principles should not be taken out of context. It is not, nor can it be under the First Amendment, legally enforceable.

ADDENDUM FOUR

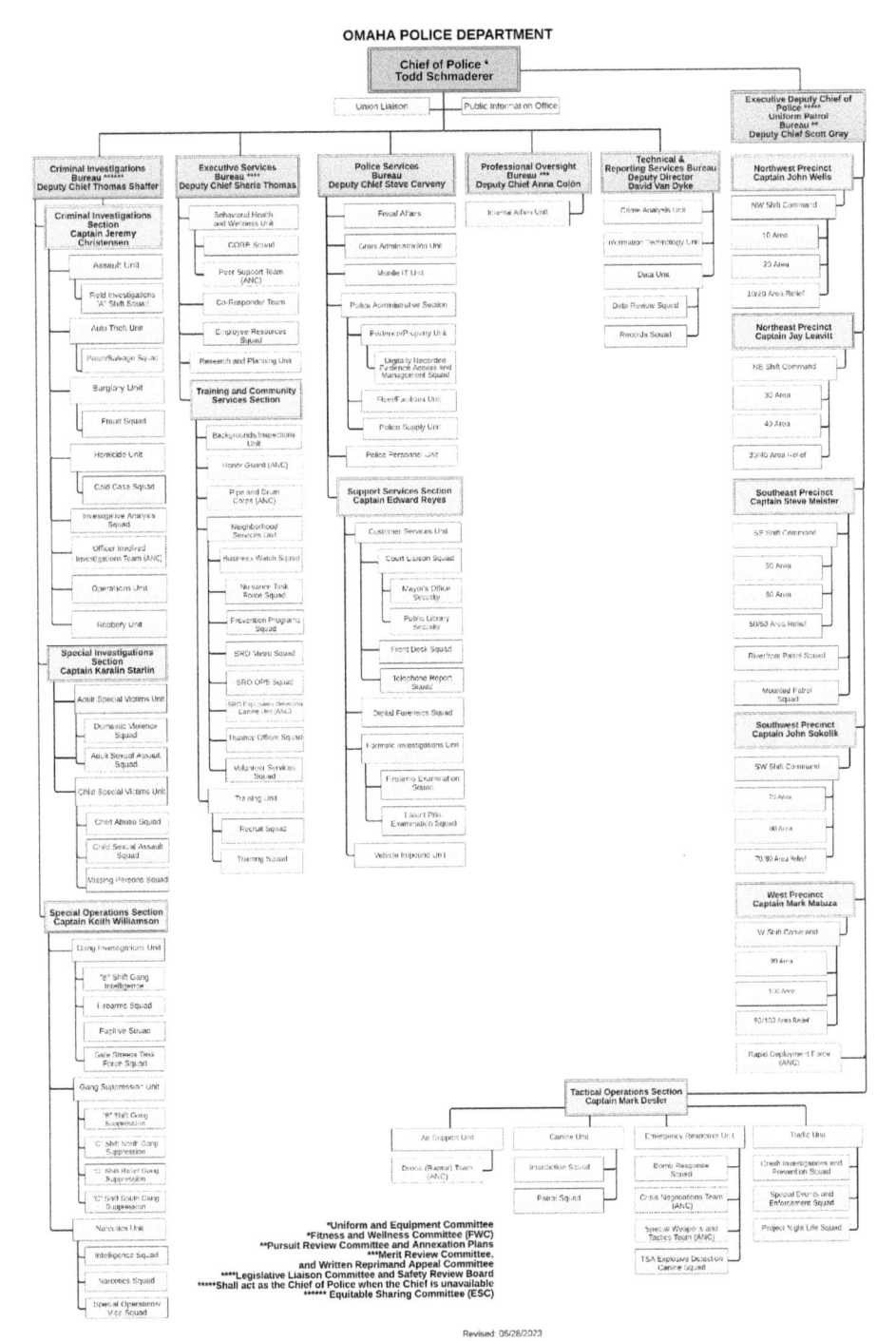

OMAHA POLICE DEPARTMENT

Chief of Police *
Todd Schmaderer

- Union Liaison
- Public Information Office

Executive Deputy Chief of Police *****
Uniform Patrol Bureau **
Deputy Chief Scott Gray

Criminal Investigations Bureau ******
Deputy Chief Thomas Shaffer

Criminal Investigations Section
Captain Jeremy Christensen
- Assault Unit
- Field Investigations "A" Shift Squad
- Auto Theft Unit
- Pawn/Salvage Squad
- Burglary Unit
- Fraud Squad
- Homicide Unit
- Cold Case Squad
- Investigative Analysis Squad
- Officer Involved Investigations Team (ANC)
- Operations Unit
- Robbery Unit

Special Investigations Section
Captain Karalin Starlin
- Adult Special Victims Unit
- Domestic Violence Squad
- Adult Sexual Assault Squad
- Child Special Victims Unit
- Child Abuse Squad
- Child Sexual Assault Squad
- Missing Persons Squad

Special Operations Section
Captain Keith Williamson
- Gang Investigations Unit
- "B" Shift Gang Intelligence
- Firearms Squad
- Fugitive Squad
- Safe Streets Task Force Squad
- Gang Suppression Unit
- "B" Shift Gang Suppression
- "C" Shift North Gang Suppression
- "C" Shift East Gang Suppression
- "C" Shift South Gang Suppression
- Narcotics Unit
- Intelligence Squad
- Narcotics Squad
- Special Operations/ Vice Squad

Executive Services Bureau ****
Deputy Chief Sherie Thomas

- Behavioral Health and Wellness Unit
- CORE Squad
- Peer Support Team (ANC)
- Co-Responder Team
- Employee Resources Squad
- Research and Planning Unit

Training and Community Services Section
- Backgrounds/Inspections Unit
- Honor Guard (ANC)
- Pipe and Drum Corps (ANC)
- Neighborhood Services Unit
- Business Watch Squad
- Nuisance Task Force Squad
- Prevention Programs Squad
- SRO Metro Squad
- SRO OPS Squad
- SRO Explosives Detection Canine Unit (ANC)
- Truancy Officer Squad
- Volunteer Services Squad
- Training Unit
- Recruit Squad
- Training Squad

Police Services Bureau
Deputy Chief Steve Cerveny

- Fiscal Affairs
- Grant Administration Unit
- Mobile IT Unit
- Police Administrative Section
- Evidence/Property Unit
- Digitally Recorded Evidence Access and Management Squad
- Fleet/Facilities Unit
- Police Supply Unit
- Police Personnel Unit

Support Services Section
Captain Edward Reyes
- Customer Services Unit
- Court Liaison Squad
- Mayor's Office Security
- Public Library Security
- Front Desk Squad
- Telephone Report Squad
- Digital Forensics Squad
- Forensic Investigations Unit
- Firearms Examination Squad
- Latent Print Examination Squad
- Vehicle Impound Unit

Professional Oversight Bureau ***
Deputy Chief Anna Colón

- Internal Affairs Unit

Technical & Reporting Services Bureau
Deputy Director David Van Dyke

- Crime Analysis Unit
- Information Technology Unit
- Data Unit
- Data Review Squad
- Records Squad

Northwest Precinct
Captain John Wells
- NW Shift Command
- 10 Area
- 20 Area
- 10/20 Area Relief

Northeast Precinct
Captain Jay Leavitt
- NE Shift Command
- 30 Area
- 40 Area
- 30/40 Area Relief

Southeast Precinct
Captain Steve Meister
- SE Shift Command
- 50 Area
- 60 Area
- 50/60 Area Relief
- Riverfront Patrol Squad
- Mounted Patrol Squad

Southwest Precinct
Captain John Sokolik
- SW Shift Command
- 70 Area
- 80 Area
- 70/80 Area Relief

West Precinct
Captain Mark Matuza
- W Shift Command
- 90 Area
- 100 Area
- 90/100 Area Relief
- Rapid Deployment Force (ANC)

Tactical Operations Section
Captain Mark Desler

- Air Support Unit
  - Drone (Radial) Team (ANC)
- Canine Unit
  - Interdiction Squad
  - Patrol Squad
- Emergency Response Unit
  - Bomb Response Squad
  - Crisis Negotiations Team (ANC)
  - Special Weapons and Tactics Team (ANC)
  - TSA Explosive Detection Canine Squad
- Traffic Unit
  - Crash Investigations and Prevention Squad
  - Special Events and Enforcement Squad
  - Project Night Life Squad

---

*Uniform and Equipment Committee
*Fitness and Wellness Committee (FWC)
**Pursuit Review Committee and Annexation Plans
***Merit Review Committee, and Written Reprimand Appeal Committee
****Legislative Liaison Committee and Safety Review Board
*****Shall act as the Chief of Police when the Chief is unavailable
******Equitable Sharing Committee (ESC)

Revised: 05/26/2023

Answers to the Questions

Chapter One

1) What is media ecology? Media ecology is the study of the media and how it affects the human environment through perception, understanding, and feelings.

2) What is the function of a presidential watch for the press? A presidential watch is when major news correspondents travel wherever the president goes, presumably so the press never misses a national moment involving the president.

3) How was the media a vital aspect of Officer Kerrie Orozco's death?
It was vital for OPD to communicate about Kerrie's death and what it meant to our society. In addition, it was important to provide a clinical account of what took place for transparency with the community.

4) Describe what is a societal monumental event. A societal monumental event can be described as an occurrence so impactful it changes the course of history and/or the collective thoughts or consciousness of a population. A societal monumental event is a defining moment for a country, state, or city and has historical significance. Collective consciousness is the shared morals, beliefs, and ideas that operate as a unifying force within society.

5) What is considered a society for the purposes of Chapter One? Society could be a nation, state, or city.

6) What are the three tenets of a societal monumental event? There are three tenets to a societal monumental event. One, the occurrence will be embedded in the collective consciousness of a society (which could be a nation, state, or city). Two, the impact of the occurrence was so colossal that the populace can recall where they were and what they were doing when the event happened. Three, the event is covered extensively by the media when it occurs, every step of the way after, and on anniversary memorials for years after, possibly forever.

7) What is an individual monumental event? An individual monumental event captures the consciousness of an individual and/or the individual's inner circle. An individual monumental event does not capture the collective consciousness of an entire society. In fact, there may be no media coverage of the event at all because it is individualized. An example of an individual monumental event is the birth of a child, a marriage, or a death in a family.

8) What is a signature occurrence? A signature occurrence is one step below a societal monumental event. Signature occurrences are different than societal monumental events. A signature occurrence is an event where everyone in society knows what occurred. It has received in-depth media coverage, but the collective consciousness of society has not been altered by the signature occurrence.

9) Give two examples of a societal monumental event, an individual monumental event, and a signature occurrence in society.

Two examples of societal monumental events: 9/11 for the nation and Kerrie Orozco's death for Omaha.

Two examples of individual monumental events: a divorce and the birth of a child.

Two examples of signature occurrences: teens killed in a drunk driver car crash and an OIS resulting in death.

Chapter Three

1. Define what a media ecosystem is and its significance today.

A media ecosystem refers to the complex interplay between humans, technology, media, and the environment. It encompasses various forms of media, including print, broadcast, digital, and social media, working together to create an information environment of interest to society. In recent years, crime, law enforcement scandals, and racial issues have garnered significant interest in American society, shaping the media landscape.

2. Explore and discuss the role of the media in shaping public opinions and attitudes about various subjects.

The media plays a crucial role in shaping public awareness and opinions by providing information through various channels such as television, radio, and the internet. Social media has further amplified the media's influence in our daily lives.

3. Examine the concept of the media acting as a watchdog in a democratic free press society.

In a democratic free press society, the media acts as a watchdog by holding politicians and public officials accountable. Major city newspapers have been particularly adept at exposing wrongdoing or corruption of public officials.

4. Describe the unique characteristics and dynamics of a Law Enforcement Media Ecosystem.

The law enforcement media ecosystem is highly intense and ranks second only to the White House Press Corps in its significance. It demands continuous attention during large events and day-to-day policing activities. Understanding and managing the police media ecosystem is essential for any major police department.

5. Discuss the importance of media training for law enforcement agencies and its impact on public perception.

ANSWERS TO THE QUESTIONS

Law enforcement agencies must train their officers in various aspects of policing, but often they neglect the critical component of media handling and interaction.

6. Analyze why instances of police misconduct in one city can have implications for law enforcement agencies in other cities.

The public tends to view all police officers and agencies as one entity, emotionally connecting the actions of one officer to the entire profession, regardless of the agency's performance.

7. Explore how CALEA accreditation can set a law enforcement agency apart and enhance its standing in the community.

The Commission on the Accreditation of Law Enforcement Agencies (CALEA) serves as a prestigious recognition for law enforcement agencies, setting them apart with its professional accreditation.

8. Assess the impact of George Floyd's murder on policing practices and reform efforts in the United States.

The murder of George Floyd prompted widespread protests and civil unrest, forcing law enforcement to reassess and implement best practices across the profession to address public concerns and improve community relations.

9. Identify the ranking of Atlanta, Georgia, in the list of top ten media markets in America.

Seventh

10. Compare and contrast the historical effects of the 1960s race riots and the nationwide civil unrest in 2020.

Social advances in America were influenced by the 1960s race riots. Moving forward to modern times, the civil unrest witnessed in 2020 resulted from the disproportionate treatment of Black citizens compared to White citizens by law enforcement. This upheaval sparked discussions and actions aimed at promoting social change. Major corporations pledged to achieve greater diversity in their hiring, leadership, and board of director positions. Policing also underwent advancements, with many departments striving to keep up with the changing social landscape.

11. Investigate the reasons behind the extensive media attention given to cases of police misconduct.

When law enforcement officials make mistakes, violate policies, commit crimes, or are involved in controversial events, they become subjects of intense media scrutiny. As public employees, paid by taxpayers and entrusted with significant authority and responsibility, it is natural for the press to closely monitor such cases. Police officers wield considerable power, being authorized to curtail a person's freedom, confiscate property, or, in extreme circumstances, take a person's life. As a result, these incidents naturally attract media attention.

12. Explain the concept of a media market and how it influences news coverage and consumer access to information.

A media market is a group of consumers who have access to the same marketing material. Typically, media markets involve radio, television, and print mediums like newspapers and magazines. The internet also serves as a media market, and unlike other mediums, it can reach a global audience. In simpler terms, a media market defines the coverage area for a station or newspaper, and in the case of the internet, it extends worldwide. It encompasses the area where the local populace can access local news coverage.

Chapter Four

1. The difference between "new media" and traditional media lies in their platforms and modes of communication. Traditional media encompasses conventional channels such as television, radio, newspapers, and magazines. New media refers to digital platforms like social media, websites, podcasts, and online streaming services.

2. Traditional media is important to law enforcement agencies because it remains a primary source of information for the public. It allows agencies to disseminate important announcements, safety information, and updates to a wide audience, including those who might not be active on new media platforms.

3. The three ways a law enforcement agency can be in a relationship with the media are as an enemy, peer, or ally. These relationships dictate the agency's attitude toward the media and the level of collaboration or opposition in which they choose to engage.

4. The "peer" relationship with the media is the most coveted because it fosters mutual respect and collaboration. Viewing the media as peers allows law enforcement agencies to establish open lines of communication, share information transparently, and work together to achieve common goals while maintaining a balanced portrayal of events.

5. Private businesses and nonprofits can have any of the three relationships (enemy, peer, or ally) with the media, depending on their communication strategies, goals, and the nature of their interactions. Just like law enforcement agencies, their relationships are influenced by how they perceive and engage with the media.

6. The five components of a law enforcement baseline media strategy are:
- Day-to-day media interactions
- Highlighting agency accomplishments and addressing needs
- Defining the agency's image
- Defining measures of success
- Troubleshooting media-related challenges

7. Using barometers for success with the media and the public is essential for a law enforcement agency to gage the effectiveness of its communication efforts. It helps

them assess how well their messages are resonating, whether their objectives are being met, and if adjustments are needed to maintain public trust and positive relations.

8. Some characteristics of a good Public Information Officer include a calming demeanor, humility, trustworthiness, and believability. These traits enable the PIO to effectively communicate with the public and media, fostering a sense of credibility and transparency.

9. False. Law enforcement executives should not deny all requests for national shows and movie productions. Positive portrayals in such media can contribute to officer morale and community positivity, enhancing the agency's public image when handled thoughtfully.

10. An example of when a law enforcement agency should consider using a media scroll is during a developing crisis or emergency. A media scroll, which provides real-time updates on a screen, can disseminate important information rapidly to the public, keeping them informed and safe as events unfold.

Chapter Five

1. True or False: Law enforcement controversy and significant occurrences have only recently become national news.

False. Law enforcement controversies and significant occurrences have been part of national news for a long time. However, advancements in communication technology and the rise of social media have made it easier for such news to spread quickly and reach a larger audience. Controversies related to law enforcement have been reported for decades, but the speed and breadth of coverage have increased in the digital age.

2. True or False: The audience will govern your tone, demeanor, and message in critical communications. How important is it to consider the audience when crafting a message?

True. The audience plays a pivotal role in shaping the tone, demeanor, and message of critical communications. It's highly important to consider the audience because different groups have varying perspectives, concerns, and sensitivities. Tailoring your message to the audience helps ensure that it is relatable, empathetic, and effectively addresses their specific needs, which is crucial for maintaining trust and understanding.

3. Describe the two phases of the critical media strategy—the evaluation phase and the transition phase. Why is it crucial to have a well-defined strategy in place to address critical events?

Evaluation Phase: In this phase, the situation is assessed, potential impacts are identified, and a response plan is developed. Gathering accurate information and understanding the context are key.

Transition Phase: This involves the actual communication process, including crafting messages, selecting appropriate spokespeople, and engaging with the media and public. The goal is to convey accurate information, manage perception, and uphold transparency. Having a well-defined strategy is crucial because critical events can escalate quickly, and the public's perception can have lasting effects. A strategy ensures consistent messaging, minimizes confusion and helps maintain public trust during times of crisis.

4. True or False: Law enforcement agencies should not admit fault for legal reasons. Discuss the implications of admitting fault and the importance of transparency in critical communications.

False. While legal considerations are important, admitting fault when appropriate demonstrates transparency and accountability. Failure to admit fault, when necessary, can erode public trust and exacerbate controversies. Transparency builds credibility and allows for constructive dialogue, potentially leading to better resolutions and improved community relations.

5. Describe a time when a press conference can be used to make a social or community statement. How can law enforcement executives effectively utilize press conferences to convey important messages to the public?

A press conference can be used to make a social or community statement after a contentious incident, like a use-of-force case involving someone in a mental health crisis. Law enforcement executives can use a press conference to express empathy, acknowledge community concerns, announce steps for investigation, and lay out plans for improved practices. Effective communication during a press conference involves clear messaging, active listening, and a commitment to addressing community grievances.

6. Describe what is meant by "distancing your agency from controversy." Why is it important for law enforcement agencies to proactively address and mitigate controversies that may arise?

"Distancing your agency from controversy" means taking proactive steps to mitigate situations that could bring negative attention or harm the agency's reputation.

7. True or False: Law enforcement agencies should regularly comment with the local media on other city policing events. Discuss the potential risks and benefits of commenting on other agencies' actions.

False. Law enforcement agencies should exercise caution when commenting on other cities' policing events. The risks include misunderstanding the full context, commenting without complete information, or inadvertently taking sides. It also opens the door for other agencies to comment back and is not the preferred way to lead.

8. Explain what a news embargo is and how it can be beneficial for both law enforcement agencies and the media.

A news embargo is an agreement between a news source (like a law enforcement agency) and a media outlet to release information at a specific time in the future. It benefits both parties by allowing the agency time to prepare accurate information and the media time to develop a well-informed story. It also helps manage the timing of sensitive announcements and avoids premature or inaccurate reporting.

9. Explain what a news exclusive is and how can it be strategically used by law enforcement agencies.

A news exclusive is when a media outlet is given exclusive access to a story or information before it's released to other outlets. Law enforcement agencies can strategically use this approach to control the narrative, ensure accurate reporting, and build a positive relationship with a specific media organization. However, agencies need to ensure that granting an exclusive does not compromise transparency or fairness.

10. Describe what "off the record" means and discuss the importance of establishing clear agreements with reporters when providing information.

"Off the record" means that the information provided is not to be attributed to the source and is not for publication. Establishing clear agreements is crucial to prevent misunderstandings, protect sensitive information, and maintain trust between law enforcement agencies and reporters. Without a clear understanding, information could be used inappropriately or harm the agency's reputation.

11. Describe what "on background" means and discuss situations where law enforcement executives may choose to provide information on background.

"On background" means that the information provided can be used in the story but without attributing it to a specific individual. Law enforcement executives might provide information on background when discussing sensitive topics, revealing behind-the-scenes details, or sharing context that could be important for accurate reporting without compromising the individual's position.

12. True or False: The reporter must agree that the communication is "off the record." Why is mutual understanding and agreement crucial when engaging in off-the-record communications?

True. Mutual understanding and agreement are crucial in "off the record" communications. Both parties need to explicitly agree that the information shared will be treated as confidential and not used in public reporting. Without this clear understanding, misinterpretations or breaches of trust can occur, leading to unintended consequences and potential damage to relationships between law enforcement and the media.

Chapter Six

1. What are the characteristics that separate a PPC from a regular press conference?

A PPC is specifically tailored for law enforcement and focuses on critical incidents related to policing.

It incorporates strategic insights and offers a detailed account of the incident, aiming to establish public trust and transparency.

The law enforcement executive takes live questions from reporters, fostering direct communication with the community.

1. What is the purpose of a media staging area?

The purpose of the media staging area is to provide a designated location for reporters to gather and receive information from the law enforcement agency. It serves as a central point of communication during a press conference, ensuring that reporters have easy access to the necessary information.

1. Provide three pieces of basic information available for an on-scene presser, regardless of the event:
   - The current condition of the suspect or any injured civilians and officers.
   - The original 911 call time and officer arrival time.
   - The investigating agency responsible for handling the critical event.

1. Give two examples of critical events worthy of a PPC and why.:
   - OIS resulting in loss of life: This event requires transparency and thoroughness to address potential public concerns and to maintain trust in the law enforcement agency.
   - Announcement of a major public safety concern or formation of a task force to address a serial killer: This event demands clear communication to reassure the public and provide information on the steps being taken to address the situation.

1. True or False: Any member of the public can attend a PPC

Only credentialed media are allowed into the PPC to maintain control over the conference. Allowing only professional, credentialed reporters ensures that the press conference proceeds smoothly and limits the potential for disruptions or chaos caused by non-credentialed individuals.

1. True or False: Transparency and timely communication have a correlation or connection.

True: Timely communication with the public during a critical incident is crucial for maintaining transparency and public trust. Delaying or withholding information can lead to community mistrust and rumors.

1. What is the value in releasing a still photo in conjunction with the entire video?

The value of releasing a still photo in conjunction with releasing a video during a PPC is to provide a slowed-down, detailed view of critical moments in the incident. Still photos allow the public to better understand what occurred and can support the narrative presented in the video.

8. What is the value of a time line of events segment during a PPC? The time line is presented to offer a chronological and clinical account of the critical incident. It

ANSWERS TO THE QUESTIONS

demonstrates transparency, thoroughness, and mastery of the incident, fostering public confidence in the law enforcement agency's handling of the situation.

Chapter Seven

1. True or False: Does the rise in the number of OISs across the country have a correlation with the rise in gun seizures by law enforcement? This statement is true. There is a correlation between the increase in OISs and the rise in gun seizures by law enforcement.

2. True or False: There is a vast array of research and papers on the media portion of an OIS. False. The subject has not received a great amount of attention in law enforcement research and papers.

3. True or False: There has been a standard guide in existence for years on how to reduce OISs in a society. False. There isn't a single standardized guide that has been universally adopted. Different law enforcement agencies may adopt their own approaches based on their specific circumstances and needs.

4. True or False: More people were killed by American law enforcement in 2022 than in any other year in the past decade. True.

5. True or False: It is impossible to reduce the overall number of OISs, as each OIS is circumstance-based. False. While each OIS incident is indeed unique and circumstance-based, it is possible to reduce the overall number of OISs through strategic measures.

6. Why is it important to reduce the number of OISs on citizens not armed with a gun? It is important to reduce the number of OIS incidents involving citizens not armed with a gun, as approach, training, and less lethal options have a greater chance of preventing an OIS when the subject is not armed with a gun. Thus, by reducing non-gun OIS incidents, the overall number of OISs should go down.

7. How does full Taser deployment reduce OISs over time? Full Taser deployment can reduce OIS incidents over time by providing officers with a non-lethal alternative for subduing individuals who may pose a threat. *Training and a lethal cover officer are strongly recommended for officer safety.

8. True or False: The OIS Reduction Template cannot be changed. False. The OIS Reduction Template, like any strategy, can be adapted and refined based on evolving circumstances, new insights, and the unique needs of each law enforcement agency. Flexibility in modifying the template allows agencies to tailor their approach to effectively address specific challenges.

9. True or False: The national databases on the number of OISs and gun seizures are spotty. True. National databases on the number of OISs and gun seizures

can sometimes be inconsistent or incomplete due to variations in reporting practices among different jurisdictions. This can make it challenging to obtain a comprehensive and accurate overview of these statistics on a national level.

10. What is positional asphyxia? Positional asphyxia refers to a potentially fatal condition that occurs when an individual's body position restricts their ability to breathe. It can happen during physical restraint, particularly when an individual is lying face down or in a position that compresses the chest and airways. This restriction can lead to a decrease in oxygen levels, respiratory distress, and in extreme cases, death. Positional asphyxia highlights the risks associated with certain restraint techniques and the importance of monitoring individuals in custody.

Chapter Eight

1) True or False: Emotion and anger can be considered evidence.

False: Emotion and anger are not considered concrete evidence in a legal or factual context. They are subjective feelings and reactions rather than tangible pieces of evidence.

2) Do you agree that the "prove it to me" stance of Black Americans is reasonable?

This is a subjective question and depends on individual perspectives. Some may find the "prove it to me" stance reasonable considering historical experiences of racial discrimination and lack of trust in institutions. Others might view it differently.

3) The disproportionate rate of Black Americans shot by law enforcement is: c) More than double white Americans: Statistics consistently show that Black Americans are shot by law enforcement officers at a higher rate than white Americans, more than doubling the rate.

4) True or False: Unarmed Black Americans are shot by the police at a higher percentage rate than white Americans.

True: Multiple studies have indicated that unarmed Black Americans are shot by the police at a higher percentage rate compared to unarmed white Americans.

5. Does the reader agree with the premise that race is a factor in all law enforcement encounters with Black Americans?

The answer will depend on the reader's personal perspective and understanding of the issue. The ability to discuss is what is germane.

6. True or False: Releasing BWC footage after an OIS starts the "court of public opinion" trial.

True: Releasing BWC footage after an OIS can indeed lead to public scrutiny and discussions in the "court of public opinion."

7. Why is an officer's discipline history relevant in cases where race is a factor?

ANSWERS TO THE QUESTIONS

An officer's discipline history can be relevant because it might indicate a pattern of behavior, use of force incidents, or bias that could contribute to racial disparities or discriminatory practices. It provides context for understanding the officer's conduct and potential biases.

8. Under the section Prevalent Misconceptions, the notion of Black Americans caring more about police killings than Black-on-Black crime is dispelled. Do you concur with the author's conclusion?

This is subjective and depends on personal views. Some may agree with the author's conclusion that this notion is a misconception, while others might have different perspectives on the matter. The ability to discuss is the germane factor.

Chapter Nine

1. True or False: The media is in a "not-for-profit" industry, so journalistic standards are regulated.

False: The media is often in a for-profit industry, and while journalistic standards are upheld by professional ethics, they might not always be strictly regulated.

2. True or False: In Canada, there is a media oversight board regulating media standards.

True: Canada does have regulatory bodies, such as the Canadian Radio-television and Telecommunications Commission (CRTC), that oversee broadcasting standards, including aspects of media content.

3. The author compares the media today to policing in the 1980s. Why?

Independent oversight of the policing profession was lacking in the 1980s as it is today for the media profession.

4. True or False: Confidential sources never have to be disclosed.

False: While confidential sources are protected in many cases, there might be situations where they could be compelled to be disclosed, particularly in legal proceedings.

5. True or False: Shield laws are in place via the states to bolster the protection of confidential sources.

True: Shield laws vary by jurisdiction and aim to provide legal protection to journalists, preventing them from being compelled to reveal confidential sources in certain circumstances.

6. What is the author referring to when the term "assumed standards" is used?

"Assumed standards" refers to widely accepted practices or elements that are integral to a particular field or context, in this case, the media industry.

7. Are the guidelines for addressing a problem journalist or news agency a progression formula?

Yes, the guidelines for addressing a problem journalist or news agency outline a step-by-step approach or formula to navigate and address issues arising from problematic journalists or news agencies.

8. True or False: Banning a reporter is an early step in the progression when dealing with a problem reporter or news agency.

False: Banning a reporter is typically considered a more serious measure and might come after other attempts to address issues have been exhausted.

9. True or False: Contacting a news agency's parent company is an option when addressing a problem news agency.

True: Contacting a news agency's parent company can be an option to escalate concerns and address issues with a problem news agency.

Chapter Ten

1. What is considered a law enforcement leak?

A law enforcement leak is the unauthorized disclosure of confidential or sensitive information related to law enforcement activities or operations to the media.

2. If a contractor with a police department leaks material, is it considered a law enforcement leak?

Yes, if a contractor with a police department leaks material that pertains to law enforcement activities or operations, it would be considered a law enforcement leak.

3. True or False: Most of the time a leaker requests to be anonymous.

True: Leakers prefer to remain anonymous to protect their identity and avoid potential repercussions.

4. True or False: A reporter should take a confidential source at face value.

False: Reporters should exercise due diligence and verify the information provided by a confidential source to ensure accuracy and credibility.

5. Give an example of when leaking law enforcement information is a crime.

An example of a leak that is a crime would be leaking information of a federal wiretap to those under investigation.

6. Why do leaks pose a challenge for law enforcement executives?

Leaks pose a challenge for law enforcement executives because they can undermine ongoing investigations, compromise operational strategies, erode public trust, and potentially expose sensitive information that could harm individuals or the agency's effectiveness.

7. True or False: All law enforcement employees are well suited to maintain confidentiality on important matters.

ANSWERS TO THE QUESTIONS

False: While many law enforcement employees are trained to maintain confidentiality, not all may possess the necessary skills or commitment to do so effectively. It can be considered a learned trait to maintain confidential information.

8. Describe the four character types of leakers.

The four character types of leakers are:

1. Status Seeker: Motivated by enhancing their reputation or position.

2. Mr. and Ms. Personal Gain: This personal gain could take various forms, ranging from seeking a romantic chance with a reporter, entering a desired social circle, or, in extreme cases, hoping for material benefits like money or tickets to events.

3. Vendetta Seeker: Seeking revenge or settling personal scores.

4. Internal Terrorist: Intending to undermine or disrupt the agency's operations.

9. What is the difference between The Vendetta Seeker and the Internal Terrorist?

The Vendetta Seeker's motivations are situational, while The Internal Terrorist will seek to disrupt or cause chaos within the agency any chance they get.

References

Accountable Journalism. n.d. "Homepage." Accessed March 1, 2024. https://accountablejournalism.org/.

Alfonseca, Kiara, Nakylah Carter, and Ivan Pereira. 2023. "Tyre Nichols: A timeline of the investigation into his death." *ABC News*, September 12. https://abcnews.go.com/US/tyre-nichols-timeline-investigation-death/story?id=96695791.

Aliprandini, Michael, and Simone Isadora Flynn. 2016. "Media Bias: An Overview." Columbus State Library, March 1. https://library.cscc.edu/mediabias/typesofmediabias.

AllSides. (n.d.). Media Bias. Retrieved 1 March 2024, from https://www.allsides.com/media-bias.

American Civil Liberties Union (ACLU). n.d. "Freedom of the Press." Accessed March 1, 2024. https://www.aclu.org/issues/free-speech/freedom-press.

American Press Institute. 2023. "What is journalism?" Accessed April 6, 2024. https://www.americanpressinstitute.org/journalism-essentials/what-is-journalism/.

Associated Press. 2019. "Timeline of events in shooting of Michael Brown in Ferguson." APnews.com, August 8. https://apnews.com/article/shootings-police-us-news-st-louis-michael-brown-9aa32033692547699a3b61da8fd1fc62

Authorization for Use of Military Force, Public Law 107–40, 107th Congress (September 18, 2001), https://www.congress.gov/107/plaws/publ40/PLAW-107publ40.pdf.

Barr, Luke, and Kyla Guilfoil. 2022. "Minneapolis Police Department to Hire New Police Chief 2 Years After George Floyd Killed." *ABC News*, June 21. https://abcnews.go.com/US/minneapolis-police-department-hire-police-chief-years-george/story?id=85536430.

Barrett, Andrew W., and Lowell W. Barrington. 2005. "Bias in Newspaper Photograph Selection." *Political Research Quarterly* 58 (4): 609–618. https://doi.org/10.1177/106591290505800408

BBC. 2020. "Breonna Taylor: What happened on the night of her death?" *BBC News*, October 8. https://www.bbc.co.uk/news/world-us-canada-54210448.

Bechtel, Trevor, Mara C. Ostfeld, and H. Luke Schaefer. 2023. "Evidence on Measures to Reduce Use of Force by the Police." University of Michigan Center for Racial Justice. Accessed April 6, 2024. https://sites.fordschool.umich.edu/poverty2021/files/2023/01/final-Policing-pb.pdf.

Bell, K. (Ed.) 2013. "Collective consciousness." *Open Education Sociology Dictionary*. Accessed December 22, 2023. https://sociologydictionary.org/collective-consciousness/.

Ben Crump Law. n.d. "Homepage." Accessed April 6, 2024. https://bencrump.com/.

Bennett, Geoff. 2023. "Guardsman Accused of Leaking Classified Information Charged under Espionage Act." *PBS*, April 14. https://www.pbs.org/newshour/show/guardsman-accused-of-leaking-classified-information-charged-under-espionage-act.

Berman, Mark, and David Nakamura. 2023. "Memphis Tyre Nichols Case Prompts Police Reform Discussion." *The Washington Post*, February 2. https://www.washingtonpost.com/national-security/2023/02/02/memphis-tyre-nichols-police-reform/.

Bertrand, Natasha, Sean Lyngaas, Zachary Cohen, and Haley Britzky. 2023. "Accused Pentagon Leaker's Violent Rhetoric Raises Fresh Questions about Top Secret Vetting Process." *CNN*, April 28. https://www.cnn.com/2023/04/28/politics/pentagon-leaker-red-flags-fresh-questions-top-secret-vetting/index.html.

Bhattar, Kala. 2021. "The History of Policing in the US and its Impact on Americans Today." *UAB Institute for Human Rights Blog*, December 8. https://sites.uab.edu/humanrights/2021/12/08/the-history-of-policing-in-the-us-and-its-impact-on-americans-today/

Black Lives Matter. n.d. "Homepage." Accessed April 6, 2024. https://blacklivesmatter.com.

Boren, Cindy. 2020. "Colin Kaepernick: Kneeling History." *The Washington Post*, June 1. https://www.washingtonpost.com/sports/2020/06/01/colin-kaepernick-kneeling-history/.

Burbach, C., et al. 2023. "Omaha City Councilman, Former Police Officers Face Federal Felony Charges." *Omaha World-Herald*, April 22. https://omaha.com/news/local/crime-courts/omaha-city-councilman-former-police-officers-face-federal-felony-charges/article_1f97090e-e08a-11ed-8b95-576d44fdfb02.html.

CALEA. n.d. "CALEA Client Database." The Commission on Accreditation for Law Enforcement Agencies. Accessed March 4, 2024. https://www.calea.org/calea-client-database.

Camaj, Lindita. 2013. "The Media's Role in Fighting Corruption: Media Effects on Governmental Accountability." *The International Journal of Press/Politics* 18 (1): 21–42. https://doi.org/10.1177/1940161212462741

CBS News. 2023. "Minneapolis: Derek Chauvin Settlement Lawsuits." Accessed March 1, 2024. https://www.cbsnews.com/news/minneapolis-derek-chauvin-settlement-lawsuits/.

Centre for Ethics in Journalism. n.d. Accessed March 1, 2024.

Cheung, H. 2020. "George Floyd Death: Why US Protests Are So Powerful This Time." *New York Times*, June 8. https://www.nytimes.com/2020/05/31/us/george-floyd-investigation.html

Christian, D., S. Jacobsen, and D. Minthorn. 2011. *The Associated Press Stylebook and Briefing on Media Law 2011*. Basic Books.

Clark, Charles S. 2017. "When Does a Leak to the Media Violate the Law?" *Government Executive*, February 27. https://www.govexec.com/management/2017/02/when-does-leak-media-violate-law/135737/.

Clementson, Julia. n.d. "What is an Editorial? Its Purpose and Types." *Azura*. Accessed September 6, 2024. https://azuramagazine.com/articles/what-is-an-editorial-its-purpose-and-types.

CNN. 2013. "Trayvon Martin Shooting Fast Facts." *CNN.com*, June 5. https://www.cnn.com/2013/06/05/us/trayvon-martin-shooting-fast-facts/index.html.

CNN. 2021. "Benjamin Crump: The attorney behind the civil rights cases." *CNN.com*, May 22. https://www.cnn.com/2021/05/22/us/benjamin-crump-attorney-profile-blake/index.html.

CNN. 2022a. "High Number of Firearm Recoveries Underscores America's Worsening Gun Violence Epidemic." *CNN.com*, January 30. https://www.cnn.com/2022/01/30/us/firearm-recoveries-gun-violence/index.html.

REFERENCES

CNN. 2022b. "No-knock Raid That Left Breonna Taylor Dead Changes Policing." *CNN.com*, August 4. https://www.cnn.com/2022/08/04/us/no-knock-raid-breonna-taylor-timeline/index.html

Cohen, Zachary, and Sean Lyngaas. 2023. "Washington Post: Person Behind Leaked Pentagon Documents Worked on Military Base." *CNN.com*, April 13. https://edition.cnn.com/2023/04/13/politics/pentagon-leaked-documents-military-base/index.html.

Collins Dictionary. n.d. "Definition of 'Editorial'." Accessed March 4, 2024. https://www.collinsdictionary.com/us/dictionary/english/editorial.

Community Tool Box. n.d. "Section 8. Arranging a Press Conference." Accessed March 4, 2024. https://ctb.ku.edu/en/table-of-contents/participation/promoting-interest/press-conference/main.

Conley, Alia. 2020. "Use of Force Rare among Omaha Police; Decrease in Shootings 'Impressive,' Expert Says." *Omaha World Herald*, July 27. f https://omaha.com/news/local/crime-and-courts/use-of-force-rare-among-omaha-police-decrease-in-shootings-impressive-expert-says/article_31f8b976-5dba-558e-89b1-61998e619e24.html.

Constitution Annotated. n.d. "Amdt 1.9.1 Overview of Freedom of the Press." Accessed March 1, 2024. https://constitution.congress.gov/browse/essay/amdt1-9-1/ALDE_00000395/.

Cooper, T., A. Conley, and C. Burbach. 2019. "OPD Chief Schmaderer: There Really Isn't Any Reason to Mention or Worry about Anthony Garcia any Further." *KETV.com*. Accessed March 18, 2024. https://www.ketv.com/article/opd-chief-schmaderer-there-really-isnt-any-reason-to-mention-or-worry-about-anthony-garcia-any-further/7865245.

Cordes, H., et al. 2020. "What Went Wrong at 72nd and Dodge: The Anatomy of Omaha's May 29 Street Conflict." *Omaha World-Herald*. Accessed March 3, 2024. https://omaha.com/news/local/what-went-wrong-at-72nd-and-dodge-the-anatomy-of-omahas-may-29-street-conflict/article_d943cc78-52a3-5f67-8f43-ac642922e5bc.html.

Cordes, H. 2022. "Paying the Price: An investigative series looking at Nebraska's prisons." *Omaha World Herald*. Accessed March 18, 2024. https://omaha.com/paying-the-price-an-investigative-series-looking-at-nebraskas-prisons/collection_93d24054-9e64-11ec-80f3-378ae5c01389.html.

Cornell Law School. n.d. "Legal Information Institute." Accessed August 21, 2024. https://www.law.cornell.edu/.

CoSchedule. n.d. "What is Click Bait?" Accessed March 1, 2024. https://coschedule.com/marketing-terms-definitions/what-is-clickbait.

Crime Museum. n.d. "John Wayne Gacy." Accessed March 2, 2024. https://www.crimemuseum.org/crime-library/serial-killers/john-wayne-gacy/.

Gorman, Ryan. 2014. "Tragedy as Girl, 5, Shot Dead by Stray Bullet while She Ate Breakfast." *Daily Mail*, January 15. https://www.dailymail.co.uk/news/article-2540371/Girl-5-shot-dead-stray-bullet-ate-breakfast.html.

Davenport, Debra. n.d. "The 3 most effective crisis communication strategies." Purdue University.

Delorme, Aurnaud, Cassandra Vieten, and Dean Radin. n.d. "Collective Consciousness." Accessed December 22, 2023. https://noetic.org/research/collective-consciousness/.

Democracy & Me. n.d. "The Role of the Media." Accessed March 1, 2024. https://www.democracyandme.org/the-role-of-media/.

Department of Justice. 2015. "Department of Justice report regarding the criminal investigation into the shooting death of Michael Brown by Ferguson, Missouri police officer Darren Wilson." Accessed April 6, 2024. https://www.justice.gov/sites/default/files/opa/press-releases/attachments/2015/03/04/doj_report_on_shooting_of_michael_brown_1.pdf.

Dershowitz, Alan. 2019. *Guilt by Accusation: The Challenge of Proving Innocence in the Age of #metoo*. Hot Books.

Dizikes, Peter. 2018. "Study: On Twitter, False News Travels Faster than True Stories." *MIT News*, March 8. https://news.mit.edu/2018/study-twitter-false-news-travels-faster-true-stories-0308.

Drakulich, Kevin, Eric Rodriguez-Whitney, and Jesenia Robles. 2023. "Why White Americans More Frequently Fail to View the Police Critically: A Subtle but Vital Shift in Focus." *Du Bois Review: Social Science Research on Race* 20 (1): 57–88. doi:10.1017/S1742058X22000133

Eggen, D. 2007. "Key Players in the CIA Leak Investigation." *Washington Post*, July 3. https://www.washingtonpost.com/wp-srv/politics/special/plame/Plame_KeyPlayers.html.

Ellison, Keith. 2021. "The Death of George Floyd, the Trial of Derek Chauvin, and Deadly-Force Encounters with Police: Have We Finally Reached an Inflection Point? Or Will the Cycle of Inaction Continue?" *Annual Review of Criminal Procedure* 50: i–xiv.

Encyclopedia.com. n.d. "Race riots of the 1960s." Accessed April 6, 2024. https://www.encyclopedia.com/history/encyclopedias-almanacs-transcripts-and-maps/race-riots-1960s.

Engel, R. S., H. D. McManus, and G. T. Isaza. 2020. "Moving Beyond 'Best Practice': Experiences in Police Reform and a Call For Evidence to Reduce Officer-Involved Shootings." *The Annals of the American Academy of Political and Social Science* 687 (1): 146–165.

Ethical Legal Data Science. 2020. "Police Shootings: A Closer Look at Unarmed Fatalities." *Data Science W231*, June 24. https://blogs.ischool.berkeley.edu/w231/2020/06/24/police-shootings-a-closer-look-at-unarmed-fatalities/.

Falk, Orjan, Märta Wallinius, Sebastian Lundström, Thomas Frisell, Henrik Anckarsäter, and Nóra Kerekes. 2014. "The 1% of the Population Accountable for 63% of All Violent Crime Convictions." *Social Psychiatry and Psychiatric Epidemiology* 49 (4): 559–571.

FBI. 1993. "World Trade Center Bombing." Accessed March 1, 2024. https://www.fbi.gov/history/famous-cases/world-trade-center-bombing-1993.

FCCa. n.d. "What we Do." Federal Communications Commission. Accessed March 1, 2024. https://www.fcc.gov/about-fcc/what-we-do

FCCb. n.d. "Complaints about Broadcast Journalism." Federal Communications Commission. Accessed March 1, 2024. https://www.fcc.gov/sites/default/files/complaints_about_broadcast_journalism.pdf.

FCCc. n.d. "Broadcast News Distortion." Federal Communications Commission. Accessed March 1, 2024. https://www.fcc.gov/broadcast-news-distortion.

Fisher, M. 2023. "A New Kind of Leaker: Spilling State Secrets to Impress Online Buddies." *The Washington Post*, April 15. https://www.washingtonpost.com/nation/2023/04/15/classified-documents-leak-discord/.

REFERENCES

Flegenheimer, M. 2018. "What Does 'Off the Record' Really Mean?" *New York Times*, August 2. https://www.nytimes.com/2018/08/02/reader-center/off-the-record-meaning.html.

Fox News. 2015. "76-Year-Old Woman Robbed, Punched Inside Omaha Church." Accessed March 1, 2024. https://www.foxnews.com/us/police-76-year-old-woman-robbed-punched-inside-omaha-church.

Franklin, Jonathan, and Emma Bowman. 2023. "Tyre Nichols' Death and the Release Of Body-Cam Video." *NPR*, January 28. https://www.npr.org/2023/01/28/1151504967/tyre-nichols-memphis-police-body-cam-video.

The Free Dictionary. n.d. "News Leaks." Accessed March 1, 2024. https://www.thefreedictionary.com/news+leak.

Freedom Forum. n.d. "Leaks and the Media." Accessed March 1, 2024. https://www.freedomforum.org/leaks-and-the-media/.

Fritsvold, Erik. n.d. "Police, Media Relations, and Social Media." *University of San Diego Online*. Accessed April 6, 2024. https://onlinedegrees.sandiego.edu/police-media-relations-and-social-media/.

Frye, William B. 2005. "A Qualitative Analysis of Sensationalism in Media." West Virginia University. Accessed March 1, 2024. https://researchrepository.wvu.edu/etd/3218/.

Gallo, Stephen. 2023. "Media Exclusives: How and When to Use Them." *Reputation Ink*, June 29. https://inksights.rep-ink.com/2023/06/media-exclusives-how-and-when-to-use-them/.

GroundTruth. n.d. "Designated Market Area (DMA)." Accessed March 8, 2024. https://www.groundtruth.com/glossary_term/what-are-designated-market-areas/.

Haislop, Tadd. 2020. "Colin Kaepernick Kneeling Timeline: How Protests During the National Anthem Started a Movement in the NFL." *The Sporting News*, September 13. https://www.sportingnews.com/us/nfl/news/colin-kaepernick-kneeling-protest-timeline/xktu6ka4diva1s5jxaylrcsse.

Hall, Kevin. 2020. "Mcclatchy Files Bankruptcy to Shed Costs of Print Legacy and Speed Shift to Digital." *McClatchy DC*, February 14. https://www.mcclatchydc.com/news/nation-world/national/article240139933.html#storylink=cpy.

Hayes, Dawaune. 2020. "Kenneth Jones Fatally Shot by Police According to Witness and Reports." *Noise Omaha*, November 21. https://www.noiseomaha.com/news-now/2020/11/20/kenneth-jones.

Henderson, Andrea Y. 2023. "9 Years After Michael Brown's Killing, Ferguson's Sacred Ground Evokes Calls for Progress." Saint Louis Public Radio, August 9. https://news.stlpublicradio.org/culture-history/2023-08-09/9-years-after-michael-browns-killing-fergusons-sacred-ground-evokes-calls-for-progress.

History.com. 2009. "Watergate Scandal." Last updated August 1, 2024. https://www.history.com/topics/1970s/watergate.

History.com. 2012. "Florida Teen, Trayvon Martin is Shot And Killed." Accessed April 6, 2024. https://www.history.com/this-day-in-history/florida-teen-trayvon-martin-is-shot-and-killed.

History.com. 2014. "Michael Brown Killed by Police In Ferguson, MO." Accessed April 6, 2024. https://www.history.com/this-day-in-history/michael-brown-killed-by-police-ferguson-mo.

The History Makers. n.d. "Reverend Al Sharpton." Accessed April 6, 2024. https://www.thehistorymakers.org/biography/reverend-al-sharpton.

Hoffenberg, Noah. 2022. "What's an Editorial? A Letter, And Column: The Parts That Make Up Our Papers." *Bennington Banner*, April 3. https://www.benningtonbanner.com/community-news/whats-an-editorial-a-letter-and-column-the-parts-that-make-up-our-papers/article_47e55ef2-903f-11ec-9676-c7c188cd010c.html.

Hutchinson, Bill. 2023. "Recent High-Profile Deaths Put Police Body Cameras in Focus." *ABC News*, March 5. https://abcnews.go.com/US/recent-high-profile-deaths-put-police-body-cameras/story?id=96848683.

International Association of Chiefs of Police (IACP). 2018. "Officer-Involved Shootings: A Guide for Law Enforcement Leaders." Accessed April 6, 2024. https://www.theiacp.org/sites/default/files/2019-05/Officer%20Involved%20Shooting%20Guidelines%202018.pdf

ipso. n.d. "What we do." Accessed March 1, 2024. https://www.ipso.co.uk/what-we-do/.

Keller, Chris L. 2011. "AP's Guidelines for 'Off the record', 'Background' and 'Deep Background'". *Chris Keller Blog*, August 1. https://blog.chrislkeller.com/aps-guidelines-for-off-the-record-background/

Kennedy, Brian, Alec Tyson, and Cary Funk. 2022b. "Americans Trust In Scientists and Other Groups Declines." Pew Research Center, February 15. https://www.pewresearch.org/science/2022/02/15/americans-trust-in-scientists-other-groups-declines/.

Kesslen, Ben. 2020. "Protests Erupt in Omaha After Police Fatally Shoot Black Man During Traffic Stop." *NBC News*, November 22. https://www.nbcnews.com/news/us-news/protests-erupt-omaha-after-police-fatally-shoot-black-man-during-n1248561.

KETV. 2013. "Police Call in Extra Internal Investigators for 33rd Seward Disturbance Investigation." *KETV.com*, March 23. https://www.ketv.com/article/police-call-in-extra-internal-investigators-for-33rd-seward-disturbance-investigation/7638557.

KETV. 2014. "Police Chief Holds News Conference on Shooting Death of 5-Year-Old Girl." *KETV.com*, January 15. https://www.ketv.com/article/police-chief-holds-news-conference-on-shooting-death-of-5-year-old-girl/7131191

KETV. 2015. "Woman Sneaks Into Henry Doorly Zoo, Is Bitten By Tiger." *KETV.com*, November 2. https://www.ketv.com/article/woman-sneaks-into-henry-doorly-zoo-is-bitten-by-tiger-1/7655946.

KETV. 2022. "Family of Man Killed by Police, Gather to Walk in Remembrance." *KETV.com*, June 5. https://www.ketv.com/article/family-of-man-killed-by-police-gather-to-walk-in-remembrance/40199656

KETV. 2023. "Omaha City Council Member, Police Officers Charged in Federal Indictments as Part of the PACE Investigation." *KETV.com*, April 21. https://www.ketv.com/article/omaha-multiple-indictments-arrests-federalinvestigation-pace-program/43669497.

KETV NewsWatch7. 2023. "Omaha Police Chief On Target Shooting." YouTube. Accessed August 21, 2024. https://www.youtube.com/watch?v=LWkVEAS82s0&ab_channel=KETVNewsWatch7.

Klinger, David. 2001. "Police Responses to Officer-Involved Shootings." *National Criminal Justice Reference Service*. Retrieved April 6, 2024. https://www.ojp.gov/ncjrs/virtual-library/abstracts/police-responses-officer-involved-shootings.

REFERENCES

KMTV News Omaha. (n.d.). "Actual COPS Television Show Press Conference." YouTube. Accessed August 21, 2024. https://youtu.be/pun2K52TO1s.

Korhonen, V. 2023. "Number of Law Enforcement Officers U.S. 2004-2022." Statista. Accessed January 15, 2024. https://www.statista.com/statistics/191694/number-of-law-enforcement-officers-in-the-us/.

Krbechek, Anjuli Sastry, and Karen Grigsby Bates. 2017. "When LA Erupted in Anger: A Look Back at the Rodney King Riots." *NPR*, April 26. https://www.npr.org/2017/04/26/524744989/when-la-erupted-in-anger-a-look-back-at-the-rodney-king-riots

Law Insider. n.d. "Traditional Media Definition." Accessed January 15, 2024. https://www.lawinsider.com/dictionary/traditional-media.

Law Officer. 2020. "Omaha Police Chief Rips the Media: 'You Never Ask Me How Our Officers Are Doing.'" Accessed March 4, 2024.

LeBlanc, Cathie, et al. 2017. *Introduction to Media Studies*. https://media.pressbooks.com/.

Lebron, Christopher J. 2018. *The Making of Black Lives Matter: A Brief History of an Idea*. Oxford University Press.

Levin, Sam. 2023. "'It Never Stops': Killings by US Police Reach Record High In 2022." *The Guardian*, January 6. https://www.theguardian.com/us-news/2023/jan/06/us-police-killings-record-number-2022.

Graham, Gordon. 2016. "Law Enforcement Response to Positional Asphyxia." *Lexipol*, January 26. https://www.lexipol.com/resources/todays-tips/law-enforcement-response-to-postional-asphyxia/.

Library of Congress. n.d. "Assassination of President Abraham Lincoln." Accessed August 21, 2024. https://www.loc.gov/collections/abraham-lincoln-papers/articles-and-essays/assassination-of-president-abraham-lincoln/.

Lorette, Kristie. 2024. "What Is a Media Market?" *Smart Capital Mind*, May 16. https://www.smartcapitalmind.com/what-is-a-media-market.htm.

Madrid, Pamela. 2023. "USC Study Reveals the Key Reason Why Fake News Spreads on Social Media." *USC Today*, January 2017. https://news.usc.edu/204782/usc-study-reveals-the-key-reason-why-fake-news-spreads-on-social-media/.

Mapping Police Violence. n.d. "Homepage." Accessed April 6, 2024. https://mappingpoliceviolence.org.

Marburger, David. n.d. "Reporter's Privilege Compendium." *Reporters Committee for Freedom of the Press*. Accessed August 21, 2024. https://www.rcfp.org/privilege-compendium/6th-circuit/#:~:text=Disclosure%20may%20be%20compelled%20where,a%20source%20may%20be%20compelled.

Media Council. n.d. "About Us - Ethics & Journalism." Accessed August 21, 2024. https://www.mediacouncil.ca/about-us-ethics-journalism/.

MediaTracks Communications. n.d. "Top 100 Media Markets." Accessed March 4, 2024. https://mediatracks.com/resources/top-100-media-markets/.

Motta & Motta LCC. n.d. "Our Attorneys." Accessed August 14, 2024. https://www.mottalawfirm.com/our-attorneys/

My Media Jobs. n.d. "2022–2023 DMA Market Rankings." Accessed August 21, 2024. https://mymediajobs.com/market-rankings.

Myers, Daniel J. 1997. "Racial Rioting in the 1960S: An Event History Analysis of Local Conditions." *American Sociological Review* 62 (1): 94–112. https://doi.org/10.2307/2657454.

NAACP. n.d. "Origins of Modern-Day Policing." Accessed April 6, 2024. https://naacp.org/find-resources/history-explained/origins-modern-day-policing.

Nalbandian, Mira. 2022. "The Big Six's Big Media Game." *Pathfinder*, May 9. https://pwestpathfinder.com/2022/05/09/the-big-sixs-big-media-game/.

National Action Network. n.d. "Search results for: Rev Sharpton police." Accessed April 6, 2024 https://nationalactionnetwork.net/?s=rev+sharpton+police.

New York Times. 2015. "South Carolina Officer is Charged with Murder of Walter Scott." *New York Times*, April 7. https://www.nytimes.com/2015/04/08/us/south-carolina-officer-is-charged-with-murder-in-black-mans-death.html.

New York Times. 2020. "George Floyd's Death and the Resulting Investigations." *New York Times*, May 31. https://www.nytimes.com/2020/05/31/us/george-floyd-investigation.html.

New York Times. 2023. "Editorial on Omaha's Policing and Community Response." *New York Times*, May 6. https://www.nytimes.com/2023/05/06/opinion/omaha-jacob-gardner-james-scurlock.html.

Nikolaev, Alexander G. 2009. "Images of War: Content Analysis of the Photo Coverage of the War in Kosovo." *Critical Sociology* 35 (1): 105–130. https://doi.org/10.1177/0896920508098659.

NYC.gov. n.d. "About NYPD." Accessed August 21, 2024. https://www.nyc.gov/site/nypd/about/about-nypd/about-nypd-landing.page.

O'Dowd, Peter, and Savannah Maher. 2019. "Native Activists Seek Justice Department's Help Investigating Indigenous Man's Death in Omaha." *WBUR*, March 12. https://www.wbur.org/hereandnow/2019/03/12/zachary-bearheels-mental-health-native-activists.

OED Online. 2022. "New Media Definition." *Oxford University Press*. https://www.oxfordlearnersdictionaries.com/us/definition/american_english/new-media.

Reichel, P. L. 1988. "Southern Slave Patrols: Transitional Police Type." *American Journal of Police* 7 (2): 51–77. https://www.ojp.gov/ncjrs/virtual-library/abstracts/southern-slave-patrols-transitional-police-type

Olzak, Susan, Suzanne Shanahan, and Elizabeth H. McEneaney. 1996. "Poverty, Segregation, and Race Riots: 1960 to 1993." *American Sociological Review* 61 (4): 590–613. https://doi.org/10.2307/2096395.

Omachonu, John O. 2023. "Reporter's Privilege." Free Speech Center, November 14. https://firstamendment.mtsu.edu/article/reporters-privilege/#:~:text=The%20idea%20behind%20reporter's%20privilege,matters%20of%20legitimate%20public%20importance

Omaha Police Department. n.d. "Incident Data Download." Accessed April 6, 2024. https://police.cityofomaha.org/crime-information/incident-data-download.

Omaha Police Policy and Procedure Manual. 2020. "Arrest and Control." .

Omaha Police Policy and Procedure Manual. 2024 . "BWC Scorecard." Accessed February 5, 2024. https://www.bwcscorecard.org/static/2016/policies/2016-05-26%20Omaha%20-%20BWC%20Policy.pdf.

REFERENCES

Omaha World Herald. 2016. "Editorial: Garcia Verdict Was the Result of Strong Work All Around." October 29. https://omaha.com/opinion/editorial-garcia-verdict-was-the-result-of-strong-work-all-around/article_65880f90-8bef-50ab-a065-d141919815b8.html.

Omaha World Herald. 2020. "Editorial: Act in Ways that Help Our Neighbors and Our City." Accessed March 3, 2024. https://omaha.com/opinion/editorial-act-in-ways-that-help-our-neighbors-and-our-city-in-this-chaotic-moment/article_f90a5597-155a-5669-8903-412162c42a92.html.

Omaha World Herald. 2023. "Monday Night Shooting – OPD Chief Provides Details." Accessed March 3, 2024. https://omaha.com/monday-night-shooting---opd-chief-provides-details/video_fee85bae-a132-11ed-8afd-83ad285e2622.html.

Oxford Learner's Dictionary. n.d. "Ally Definition." https://www.oxfordlearnersdictionaries.com/us/definition/american_english/ally_1.

Pal, Judy, Khadijah Carter, Eric Kowalczyk, and Christine Townsend. 2023. *Strategic Communications for Law Enforcement Executives*. Office of Community Oriented Policing Services.

Parrish, P. 1993. "Police and the Media." *FBI Law Enforcement Bulletin* 62 (9): 24.

PBS. 2015. "The LAPD Scandal." Accessed April 6, 2024. https://www.pbs.org/wgbh/pages/frontline/shows/lapd/scandal/cron.html.

PBS News. 2019. "Deadly Police Shootings Keep Happening: Data Could Be a Missing Piece." Accessed April 6, 2024. https://www.pbs.org/newshour/nation/deadly-police-shootings-keep-happening-data-could-be-a-missing-piece.

Perez, Juan Jr. 2013. "Cover-Up by Omaha Police Officers Alleged." *Omaha World Herald*, April 5. https://omaha.com/news/cover-up-by-omaha-police-officers-alleged/article_378089c1-7aed-55ba-b8a9-6ff4025498d4.html.

Pew Research Center. 2022. "Trust In America: Do Americans Trust the Police?" Accessed April 6, 2024. https://www.pewresearch.org/2022/01/05/trust-in-america-do-americans-trust-the-police/.

Phillips, Brad. 2014. "A Perfect Example of a Great Press Conference." *The Throughline Blog*. Throughline. September 2. https://www.throughlinegroup.com/2014/09/02/a-perfect-example-of-a-great-press-conference.

Pilger, Lori. 2022. "Defense Attorney Argues Garcia Should Face Resentencing Trial in Omaha Killings." *JournalStar*, November 29. https://journalstar.com/news/state-and-regional/nebraska/defense-attorney-argues-garcia-should-face-resentencing-trial-in-omaha-killings/article_22ba9df6-52b3-58cb-99c2-2a2a2bfbb0c3.html.

Police Violence Report. n.d. "Homepage." Accessed April 6 2024. https://policeviolencereport.org/.

PRLab. n.d. "Embargoed Press Release: Meaning, Examples, and How To Use." Accessed February 5, 2024. https://prlab.co/blog/embargoed-press-release-meaning-examples-and-how-to-use/.

Public Disclosure Commission. n.d. "Definition of Open Press Conference." Accessed February 5, 2024. https://www.pdc.wa.gov/rules-enforcement/guidelines-restrictions/definition-open-press-conference#:~:text=Cite%20as%20PDC%20Interpretation%20No,92%2D03&text=The%20official%20may%20or%20may,the%20ballot%20measure%20at%20issue.

The Reporters Committee for Freedom of the Press. n.d. "Journalists Jailed or Fined For Refusing to Identify Confidential Sources, as of 2019." Accessed February 15, 2024. https://www.rcfp.org/jailed-fined-journalists-confidential-sources/.

Reza, F. 2022. "Bias and Photographs: The Role of Media." Retrieved March 1, 2024.

Saad, Lydia. 2020. "Black Americans Want Police to Retain Local Presence." *Gallup News*, August 5. https://news.gallup.com/poll/316571/black-americans-police-retain-local-presence.aspx.

Schmidt, Samantha. 2017. "A Mentally Ill Man Died After Police Shocked Him 12 Times. The Chief Wants 2 Officers Fired." *The Washington Post*, June 12. https://www.washingtonpost.com/news/morning-mix/wp/2017/06/12/a-mentally-ill-man-died-after-police-shocked-him-12-times-the-chief-wants-2-officers-fired/.

Schrotenboer, B. 2023. "Kobe Bryant Family Gets Nearly $29 Million Settlement in Case Over Helicopter Crash Photos." *USA Today*, February 28. https://www.usatoday.com/story/sports/nba/2023/02/28/vanessa-bryant-kobe-bryant-crash-photos-settlement-county/11368845002/.

Schudel, Matt, Emily Davies, and Peter Hermann. 2021. "Charles Moose, Montgomery County Police Chief During 2002 D.C. Sniper Attacks, Dies at 68." *The Washington Post*, November 26. https://www.washingtonpost.com/obituaries/2021/11/26/charles-moose-dead/.

Serrano, Richard A. 1991. "Officers Claimed Self-Defense in Beating of King." *LA Times*, March 30. https://www.latimes.com/archives/la-xpm-1991-03-30-mn-850-story.html.

Shearer, Elisa. 2021. "More Than Eight-In-Ten Americans Get News from Digital Devices." *Pew Research Center*, January 12. https://www.pewresearch.org/short-reads/2021/01/12/more-than-eight-in-ten-americans-get-news-from-digital-devices/.

Society of Professional Journalists (SPJ). n.d. "Here's How to Share Information with Reputable News Media." Accessed March 1, 2024. https://www.spj.org/leak.asp.

SPUR. 2018. "Policy for the Use of T asers by San Francisco Police Officers." Accessed April 6, 2024. https://www.spur.org/voter-guide/2018-06/sf-prop-h-police-use-tasers.

Statista. 2024. "Number of People Killed by the Police in the United States from 2013 To 2024." Accessed April 6, 2024. https://www.statista.com/statistics/1362796/number-people-killed-police-us/.

Steppat, Desiree, Laia Castro Herrero, and Frank Esser. 2022. "Selective Exposure in Different Political Information Environments – How Media Fragmentation and Polarization Shape Congruent News Use." *European Journal of Communication* 37 (1): 82–102. https://doi.org/10.1177/02673231211012141.

Stoddard, M. 2023. "Audit Finds Omaha Schools Pension Plan Has $1 Billion-Plus Shortfall, 'Significant' Issues." *Omaha World Herald*, June 22. https://omaha.com/news/state-regional/government-politics/audit-finds-omaha-schools-pension-plan-has-1-billion-plus-shortfall-significant-issues/article_7747c050-1116-11ee-8827-d3233783a6ca.html.

Strate, Lance. n.d. "What Is Media Ecology? Three Definitions; An Overview of Media Ecology." Media Ecology Association. Accessed December 22, 2023. https://www.media-ecology.org/What-Is-Media-Ecology.

Suggs, Ernie. n.d. "Ferguson Brown FAQ." *Atlanta Journal Constitution*. Accessed April 6, 2024. https://www.ajc.com/news/ferguson-brown-faq/.

REFERENCES

Swasy, Alecia. 2015. "Setting or Chasing the Agenda: Who Controls the News? Keynote Report for the Associated Press/Donald W. Reynolds Journalism Institute." Retrieved from

The Technology and Social Change Project. n.d. "Media Ecosystems." *The Media Manipulation Casebook*. Accessed January 15, 2024. https://mediamanipulation.org/definitions/media-ecosystems.

United States Census Bureau. 2019. "QuickFacts: United States" and "QuickFacts: Omaha City, Nebraska." Accessed April 6, 2024. https://www.census.gov/quickfacts/fact/table/US,IPE120221 and https://www.census.gov/quickfacts/fact/table/omahacitynebraska/IPE120221.

United States Census Bureau. 2020. "2020 Census Results." Accessed September 6, 2024. https://www.census.gov/programs-surveys/decennial-census/decade/2020/2020-census-results.html.

United States Census Bureau. 2023. "Omaha, Nebraska." Accessed September 6, 2024. https://data.census.gov/profile/Omaha_city,_Nebraska?g=160XX00US3137000.

United States District Court. n.d. "Grand Juror Handbook." Accessed April 6, 2024. http://www.scd.uscourts.gov/Jury/grandjuror.asp.

University of Washington Library. n.d. "Savvy Info Consumers: Detecting Bias In The News." Accessed April 6, 2024. https://guides.lib.uw.edu/research/evaluate/bias.

University of Wisconsin–Green Bay. 2023. "Identifying Bias: Politics and the media." Accessed April 6, 2024. https://libguides.uwgb.edu/c.php?g=600365&p=4157309.

US Department of Justice. n.d. "FOIA.gov." Accessed April 6, 2024. https://www.foia.gov/faq.html.

US Department of Justice. 2016. *Collaborative reform initiative: An assessment of the San Francisco Police Department*. Accessed April 6, 2024. https://sfgov.org/policecommission/sites/default/files/Documents/PoliceDocuments/Transparency/DOJ_COPS%20CRI_SFPD%20OCT%202016%20Assessment.pdf.

US Department of Labor. n.d. "Occupational Safety and Health Administration: Whistleblower Protection Program." Accessed April 6, 2024. https://www.whistleblowers.gov/.

US Department of the Treasury. n.d. "Freedom of Information Act." Accessed April 6, 2024. https://home.treasury.gov/footer/freedom-of-information-act.

Vanacore, Rylan. 2021. "Sensationalism in Media." *Reporter*, November 12. https://reporter.rit.edu/news/sensationalism-media.

Vanderbilt Law School. 2021. "Police Arbitration." *Vanderbilt Law Review* 74 (4), May 28. https://vanderbiltlawreview.org/lawreview/2021/05/police-arbitration/

Vedantu. n.d. "Media." Accessed August 21, 2024. https://www.vedantu.com/civics/what-is-media.

Walker, Ezekiel J. 2023. "Omaha 360 Cuts Shootings by 50%, Other Cities to Follow." *The Black Wall Street Times*, February 22. https://theblackwallsttimes.com/2023/02/22/omaha-360-cuts-shootings-to-50-other-cities-to-follow/.

Wallace, Rodrick M., Mindy T. Fullilove, Robert E. Fullilove, and Deborah N. Wallace. 2007. "Collective Consciousness and Its Pathologies: Understanding the Failure of AIDS Control and Treatment in the United States." *Theoretical Biology and Medical Modelling* 4: 10. https://doi.org/10.1186/1742-4682-4-10

The Washington Post. 2022. "Police Shootings Database." Accessed April 6, 2024. https://www.washingtonpost.com/graphics/investigations/police-shootings-database/.

The Washington Post Live. 2023 (April 27). "Protecting Public Safety." YouTube. Accessed April 6, 2024. https://youtu.be/a-zfipEx77M.

Westervelt, Eric. 2023. "More People Are Getting Away with Murder. Unsolved Killings Reach a Record High." *NPR*, April 30. https://www.npr.org/2023/04/29/1172775448/people-murder-unsolved-killings-record-high.

WikiLeaks. n.d. "What is WikiLeaks?" Accessed April 6, 2024. https://wikileaks.org/What-is-WikiLeaks.html.

Wikipedia. n.d.(a) "Dennis Rader." Accessed August 14, 2024. https://en.wikipedia.org/wiki/Dennis_Rader.

Wikipedia. n.d.(b) "List of Serial Killers." Accessed August 13, 2024. https://en.wikipedia.org/wiki/List_of_serial_killers_in_the_United_States.

Withrow, Brian. 2023. "Racial & Identity Profiling Advisory Board 2022 Annual Report." Accessed April 6, 2024. https://porac.org/wp-content/uploads/PORAC-2022-RIPA-Report-Analysis_FINAL.pdf.

World Atlas. n.d. "How Many Serial Killers Are On the Loose Today?" Accessed September 6, 2024. https://www.worldatlas.com/crime/how-many-serial-killers-are-on-the-loose-today.html

World Population Review. (2023a). "California Cities by Population." Accessed April 6, 2024. https://worldpopulationreview.com/states/cities/california.

World Population Review. (2023b). "Omaha, Nebraska Population." Accessed April 6, 2024. https://worldpopulationreview.com/us-cities/omaha-ne-population.

Wu, Katherine J. 2019. "Bullets That Killed John F. Kennedy Immortalized as Digital Replicas." *Smithsonian Magazine*, December 9. https://www.smithsonianmag.com/smart-news/bullets-killed-kennedy-immortalized-digital-replicas-180973714/.

Yeung, Douglas. 2018. "Social Media as a Catalyst for Policy Action and Social Change for Health and Well-Being: Viewpoint." *Journal of Medical Internet Research* 20 (3): e94. doi: 10.2196/jmir.8508. PMID: 29555624; PMCID: PMC5881041.

Glossary

Active killer: A term used to describe an individual or individuals currently engaged in a violent and deadly attack, often within a confined area. **Chapter Six.**

Affinity reporting: A form of journalism where a reporter's personal preferences, affiliations, or biases influence their reporting, leading to imbalanced or biased coverage. **Chapter Nine.**

Ally: A state of formerly cooperating with another agency, or to combine resources for mutual benefit. The goals of a law enforcement agency and the media are distinct, so an ally relationship is inappropriate. **Chapter Four.**

Arbitration: The process of resolving disputes or conflicts through a neutral third party, often used in discipline cases involving law enforcement officers. **Chapter Five.**

Assumed standards: Fundamental and widely accepted elements or aspects within a particular field or profession. **Chapter Nine.**

Authorization for Use of Military Force (AUMF): A legal authorization, often granted by a government's legislative body, that allows the use of military force under specific circumstances. This term gained prominence in the context of discussions about military interventions and conflicts. **Chapter One.**

Banning a reporter: The process by which a law enforcement agency media restricts or denies a specific reporter's access to certain information, events, or sources due to concerns related to ethics, behavior, or credibility. **Chapter Nine.**

Black Lives Matter: A social justice movement advocating for the rights and equality of Black individuals and addressing police violence and systemic racism. **Chapter Three.**

Blog: An online platform or website where individuals or groups share their thoughts, ideas, and experiences on various topics, often in a personal or informal style. **Chapter Six.**

Body worn camera (BWC): A small camera worn by law enforcement officers on their uniform or equipment that records audio and video footage of their interactions with the public. BWCs are used to enhance transparency, accountability, and evidence collection. **Chapter Seven.**

CALEA: The Commission on Accreditation for Law Enforcement Agencies, a nonprofit organization that establishes professional standards for law enforcement agencies. **Chapter Three.**

Championship culture: An organizational environment within law enforcement agencies characterized by high standards, collaboration, commitment to excellence, and a strong sense of purpose. A championship culture emphasizes teamwork, continuous improvement, and dedication to achieving goals. Within a championship culture, the players hold each other accountable and don't wait for the coach to do it. In law enforcement agencies, the officers will hold each other accountable before commanders need to step in. **Chapter Seven.**

Civilian Press Information Officer (PIO): A civilian who represents the law enforcement agency with the press information office. **Chapter Four.**

Closing statement: A concluding address delivered at the end of a press conference, summarizing key points and reiterating essential messages. **Chapter Six.**

Collective consciousness: The shared beliefs, values, attitudes, and perceptions that characterize a group. **Chapter One.**

Court of public opinion: A metaphorical concept describing the collective judgment of a society regarding a particular issue, often formed through media coverage, social discourse, and public discussions rather than legal proceedings. **Chapter Eight.**

Credentialed reporters: Journalists and media personnel who have been officially authorized and granted access to attend a specific press conference or event. **Chapter Six.**

Crisis intervention training (CIT): A specialized training program designed to equip law enforcement officers with the skills needed to effectively interact with individuals in a mental crisis. This training focuses on de-escalation techniques, recognizing signs of mental illness, and fostering empathy and understanding. **Chapter Seven.**

Confidential informants: Individuals who provide information to law enforcement agencies, typically in exchange for protection or benefits, while maintaining their anonymity. **Chapter Ten.**

Confidential sources: Individuals who provide information to journalists with the understanding that their identity will be protected and not disclosed to the public. Confidential sources are essential for investigative reporting. **Chapter Ten.**

Counter source: An individual in the media who provides information to a law enforcement agency about stories that are being worked on. **Chapter Ten.**

Crisis intervention team (CIT): A specialized unit within law enforcement agencies consisting of personnel trained to handle crisis situations involving individuals with mental health issues or emotional distress. **Chapter Seven.**

Critical event: An incident or situation that requires immediate attention, often involving public safety, law enforcement actions, or major emergencies. **Chapter Five.**

Critical media strategy: A comprehensive and strategic plan developed by law enforcement agencies to effectively handle media interactions during critical events

GLOSSARY

and emergencies, ensuring accurate information dissemination and public perception. **Chapter Five.**

Critique by comparison: An analytical approach in which a subject or situation is evaluated by contrasting it with analogous cases, allowing for the identification of differences, similarities, strengths, and weaknesses. **Chapter Eight.**

Disproportionate: Refers to a lack of balance or fairness in the distribution of something. In this book, it refers to a situation where outcomes, such as police shootings, occur in an unequal manner. **Chapter Three.**

Disprove a negative: A process aimed at demonstrating that a negative assertion or claim is false or incorrect. This can be challenging, as it involves proving the nonexistence of something, which often requires a high burden of evidence. **Chapter Eight.**

Duty to intervene doctrine: A principle within law enforcement that mandates officers to intervene and prevent or stop another officer from using excessive force or engaging in wrongful actions while on duty. This doctrine underscores the responsibility of officers to ensure the safety and well-being of both citizens and their fellow officers. **Chapter Three.**

Early warning tracking system: A system implemented by law enforcement agencies to monitor and identify potential performance issues or red flags in officers' behavior. This system helps to proactively address concerns and provides opportunities for corrective action before issues escalate. **Chapter Seven.**

Editorial: Content produced by news organizations that express opinions, interpretations, or analysis of news events. **Chapter Five.**

Enemy: When a law enforcement agency has a desire to avoid the media in an acrimonious relationship. The media is an afterthought and a burden to the agency. **Chapter Four.**

Evaluate and adapt: A continuous improvement approach within law enforcement that involves regularly assessing policies, procedures, and practices to identify areas for enhancement. This mindset promotes adaptability and ensures that the agency remains responsive to changing circumstances. **Chapter Seven.**

Evaluation phase: The stage in a critical media strategy where the law enforcement agency evaluates the critical event and determines the mode or means of communicating with the press. **Chapter Five.**

Federal Communication Commission (FCC): An independent regulatory agency in the United States responsible for overseeing communication networks, including radio, television, cable, and telecommunications. The FCC's role encompasses regulating media ownership, content, spectrum allocation, and ensuring compliance with communication laws. **Chapter Nine.**

First Amendment: The first amendment to the United States Constitution, part of the Bill of Rights, guarantees fundamental rights, including freedom of speech, freedom of the press, freedom of religion, and the right to assemble peacefully. **Chapter Six.**

"Four Character Types of Leakers": A classification system categorizing individuals who leak information. The four types are Status Seeker, Mr. and Ms. Personal Gain, Vendetta Seeker, and Internal Terrorist. **Chapter Ten.**

Freedom of Information Act (FOIA): A federal law in the United States that grants individuals the right to access information held by federal government agencies. FOIA aims to promote transparency and accountability by allowing the public to request and receive government records. **Chapter Ten.**

Freedom of the press: A constitutional right that protects the freedom of media organizations and journalists to report news and information without censorship or undue interference by government or other entities. **Chapter Nine.**

Fugitive Unit: A specialized unit within law enforcement agencies focused on locating and apprehending individuals who are evading the law, such as suspects with outstanding warrants. **Chapter One.**

Full Taser deployment: Refers to the deployment of Tasers throughout the law enforcement agency. Full deployment can refer to all "street" officers being assigned a BWC. **Chapter Seven.**

General source: A broad term referring to a source that provides information, where the source may not be directly involved in the investigation but does work for the law enforcement agency. **Chapter Ten.**

George Floyd: An African American man whose 2020 death during an arrest in Minneapolis, Minnesota, sparked global protests and renewed discussions on racial justice. **Chapter Three.**

Great Conundrum: A complex challenge that involves balancing the principles of freedom of the press, which encourages open and unrestricted journalism, with the responsibility to maintain accuracy, fairness, and ethical standards in reporting, particularly in sensitive or controversial topics. **Chapter Nine.**

Gunfire funnel: The trajectory area of a fired round that is unimpeded. Being in this area poses a danger, as there is no cover. **Chapter One.**

Hands up phenomenon: A symbolic gesture involving raising one's hands in the air, often associated with surrender or submission. In the context of this book, the phenomenon refers to situations where a witness falsely claims a person's hands were up in the aftermath of an officer-involved shooting. **Chapter Eight.**

"If it bleeds, it leads": A phrase reflecting the media's tendency to prioritize and highlight sensational or violent stories. **Chapter Three.**

Individual monumental event: A personal event in an individual's life that holds profound meaning and has transformative effects. These events can include personal

GLOSSARY

achievements, life-changing experiences, or critical turning points that significantly shape the person's identity or trajectory. **Chapter One.**

Instant social media: Refers to the rapid dissemination of information through social media platforms in real time. Law enforcement agencies use instant social media to share updates, alerts, and important information with the public swiftly and efficiently. **Chapter Seven.**

Headline tilt: When headlines are misleading or designed to convey excitement, when the story is rather dull. **Chapter Nine.**

Internal terrorist: One of the four character types of leakers. Leakers with a disruptive agenda, seeking to undermine or cause chaos within an organization or institution. **Chapter Ten.**

International Association of Chiefs of Police (IACP): A professional organization that represents law enforcement leaders from around the world. The IACP offers resources, training, and advocacy to promote effective policing practices and collaboration among law enforcement agencies. **Chapter Seven.**

Law enforcement baseline media strategy: The foundation for the day-to-day media operations of a law enforcement agency. It is the minimum or starting point for handling all aspects of the media. **Chapter Four.**

Law enforcement critical media strategy: A plan of action for media communications when a crisis or critical event or time period is upon the law enforcement agency. **Chapter Four.**

Law enforcement source: A source within a law enforcement agency who provides information to the media or public, often related to ongoing investigations or personnel matters. **Chapter Five.**

Leaks: The unauthorized release or disclosure of confidential or sensitive information to the public through someone in the media. **Chapter Five.**

Lethal cover officer: An officer strategically positioned to provide protection and armed support during an operation or confrontation where lethal force might be required. The lethal cover officer is ready to respond if the situation escalates to a point where deadly force is necessary. **Chapter Seven.**

"Look at me" reporter: A term used to describe a journalist who prioritizes self-promotion, seeking attention or recognition for their reporting rather than emphasizing the story's importance or accuracy. **Chapter Nine.**

Machination possibility: Refers to the inclination to believe in and propagate theories suggesting hidden collaborations among individuals or groups in law enforcement, typically involving secretive actions, plots, or intentions by law enforcement officials. **Chapter Eight.**

Media ecology: The study of the media and how it affects the human environment through perception, understanding, and feelings. **Chapter One.**

Media ecosystem: The interconnected network of media outlets, platforms, and audiences that shape the dissemination and reception of information. **Chapter Three.**

Media impact: The influence and effects that media messages have on individuals, communities, and society. **Chapter Three.**

Media market: The geographical area in which media outlets serve a specific audience and advertisers target consumers. **Chapter Three**.

Media oversight hypocrisy: The phenomenon characterized by a perceived double standard where the media reports on the need for independent law enforcement oversight, yet the media has no independent oversight in America. **Chapter Nine.**

Media packet: A collection of documents and materials provided to journalists during a press conference, containing essential information, press releases, background data, and images. **Chapter Six.**

Media scroll: A banner at the bottom of the television that scrolls, alerting the public to a critical event or matter of public safety. **Chapter Four.**

Media self-rule: The media has no independent oversight in America; as such, the media sets their own rules. The media governs themselves by establishing ethical guidelines, codes of conduct, and standards for responsible journalism. Media self-rule can pose a problem for law enforcement agencies looking to contest an already written or aired story. **Chapter Nine.**

Media staging area: A designated location where media personnel gather to cover an event set up by the law enforcement agency. The staging area is closer to the crime scene than the public is allowed to go. The staging area is set up so the media have a designated location to report and receive briefings from the law enforcement agency. **Chapter One.**

Mock press conference: A practice session where participants simulate a real press conference to prepare for handling media interactions effectively. **Chapter Six.**

Mr. and Ms. Personal Gain: One of the four character types of leakers. Leakers who are primarily motivated by personal benefits, such as financial gain or career advancement. **Chapter Ten.**

New media: A term used to describe various digital communication sources used to spread information, such as the internet and social media. **Chapter Four.**

News embargo: An agreement between a news outlet and a source or agency to delay the release of specific information until a specified date and time. **Chapter Five.**

News exclusive: A news story or report provided exclusively to one news outlet, giving them the sole right to publish or broadcast the information. **Chapter Five**.

Next question approach: A method used by press conference hosts to acknowledge and move on to the next question when an inquiry wrongly becomes contentious. **Chapter Six.**

GLOSSARY

"Off the record": A phrase used in journalism to indicate that the information being shared is not intended for publication and should not be attributed to the source. **Chapter Five.**

Officer-Involved Investigations Team (OIIT): A specialized unit within the Omaha Police Department tasked with conducting thorough and impartial investigations into incidents involving officer-involved shootings or other in-custody deaths. **Chapter Seven.**

Officer-involved shooting (OIS): A term used to describe incidents where law enforcement officers discharge their firearms, resulting in injury or death. **Chapter Seven.**

OIS reduction cocktail: A strategic blend of approaches, tactics, and training methods employed by the Omaha Police Department to decrease the frequency of officer-involved shooting incidents. **Chapter Seven.**

On background: A term in journalism where the information provided can be used in the story but without directly attributing it to the source. **Chapter Eight.**

On-scene presser: A press conference held at the location of a critical event. **Chapter Six.**

Opening statement: An initial address delivered at the beginning of a press conference, setting the tone and outlining the key points to be discussed. **Chapter Six.**

Other police encounter deaths: This term refers to fatalities that occur during interactions between law enforcement officers and individuals, aside from officer-involved shootings. It encompasses deaths resulting from various causes such as physical force, medical conditions, or positional asphyxia. **Chapter Seven.**

Peer: A person who is equal to another in abilities, qualifications, age, background, and social status. Law enforcement and the press are separate and distinct but socially equal in status, so a peer relationship is appropriate. **Chapter Four.**

Photo lean: A term related to visual media, describing the selection and presentation of photographs that may convey a particular perspective or narrative, intentionally influencing the viewer's interpretation. **Chapter Eight.**

"Pick the headline" game: An interactive exercise where participants choose compelling headlines that capture the essence of a given story or press conference. **Chapter Six.**

Police media ecosystem: The specific framework within which law enforcement agencies interact with and respond to the media. **Chapter Three.**

Policing press conference (PPC): A specialized type of press conference conducted by law enforcement agencies to address matters related to critical events, criminal investigations, or emergency situations. **Chapter Six.**

Population certainty: A concept that asserts anytime there is a large collection of people, it is inevitable critical matters will arise for law enforcement to handle. It is not a matter of if, but when. **Chapter Three.**

Positional asphyxia: A potentially fatal condition that arises when an individual's body position restricts their ability to breathe. This can occur during physical restraint, leading to respiratory distress and, in extreme cases, death. **Chapter Seven.**

Presidential watch: When major news correspondents travel wherever the president goes, presumably so the press never misses a national moment involving the president. The press missed President Kennedy's assassination. **Chapter One.**

Press corps: A group of journalists who regularly cover a specific organization, event, or government body. **Chapter Five.**

Presser: An informal abbreviation for a press conference, where information is presented to the media and questions from reporters are answered. **Chapter Six.**

Press conference formula: A structured approach or framework used to organize and deliver information effectively during a press conference. **Chapter Six.**

Press Information Office: A department or unit responsible for managing media relations within a law enforcement agency, implementing a baseline media strategy and addressing the daily media concerns for the agency. **Chapters Three.**

Press Information Officer (PIO): An individual within a law enforcement agency responsible for communicating with the media and disseminating official information. **Chapters One.**

"Prove it to me": A psychological mindset wherein individuals require substantial evidence or proof before accepting or believing a statement, claim, or accusation. This mentality seeks concrete validation before acknowledging the validity of a situation. **Chapter Eight.**

Racial bias: The predisposition toward judgments, behaviors, or attitudes based on a person's race or ethnicity. This bias can result in unequal treatment and can influence decisions and actions, including those of law enforcement. **Chapter Eight.**

"Release the video" demands: This refers to calls from the public for law enforcement agencies to make available video footage of events, such as officer-involved shootings. **Chapter Eight.**

Reporter list: A roster of journalists and media representatives invited to attend a press conference or to cover a specific event. **Chapter Six.**

Retention gap mitigators: Strategies and techniques employed by law enforcement executives to shield problem officers from the public. The goal is to minimize the amount of contact the problem officer has with the public. **Chapter Seven.**

Rumor antagonist: An individual or entity that deliberately spreads false or misleading information (rumors) with the intent to provoke discord, confusion, or dissent among a group or community. **Chapter Eight.**

Selective coverage: The practice of choosing to report on certain events, topics, or issues while omitting or downplaying others. Selective coverage can influence public perceptions by highlighting specific aspects of a story. **Chapter Nine.**

GLOSSARY

Shield laws: Legal statutes or regulations that provide protection to journalists from being compelled to disclose their confidential sources or provide other information in legal proceedings. Shield laws vary by jurisdiction and aim to preserve press freedom while respecting legal processes. **Chapter Nine.**

"Show me the body": Expresses disbelief regarding a claim or assertion until tangible evidence, often in the form of a physical body or definitive proof, is presented. In law enforcement, it can also help provide closure for the families of victims. **Chapter Eight.**

Signature occurrence: A happening where everyone in society knows what occurred. It has received in-depth media coverage, but the collective consciousness of society has not been altered by the event. A signature occurrence is one step below a societal monumental event. **Chapter One.**

Societal monumental event: An occurrence so impactful it changes the course of history and the collective consciousness of a population. A societal monumental event is a defining moment for a country, state, or city and has historical significance. **Chapter One.**

Society of Professional Journalists (SPJ): A professional organization dedicated to promoting ethical journalism practices and fostering a commitment to accurate and unbiased reporting. The SPJ provides resources, guidelines, and support for journalists to uphold high standards of journalistic integrity. **Chapter Eight.**

Source close to the investigation: A term used in journalism to refer to individuals who have knowledge about an ongoing investigation but may not be directly involved in law enforcement. **Chapter Ten.**

Status seeker: One of the four-character types of leakers. A leaker motivated by the desire to enhance their reputation, visibility, or standing within an organization or community. **Chapter Ten.**

Straw purchase: A transaction in which an individual, who is legally eligible, purchases a firearm on behalf of someone else who is not legally allowed to make the purchase. **Chapter Eight.**

Suicide by cop: A tragic scenario in which an individual intentionally behaves in a threatening or aggressive manner toward law enforcement officers with the intention of provoking them to use deadly force. This term describes cases where individuals seek to end their own lives by causing the officers to use lethal force in response. **Chapter Two.**

Time line of events: A chronological sequence of key occurrences related to a particular event or situation. **Chapter Six.**

Time upon a law enforcement agency: A critical event that is lasting in duration, such as a pandemic or a prolonged serial killer investigation. **Chapter Five.**

Tip lines: A method for the populace to communicate with a law enforcement agency on important matters. Tip lines exist for mass shooters, Crime Stoppers, school bullying, and Amber Alerts for abducted children. **Chapter Four.**

Traditional media: The use of radio, television, or print to receive and report on the news. **Chapter Three.**

Training spectrum: Refers to the range of training programs and practices offered within a given field, which can vary in complexity and intensity. In the context of law enforcement, the training spectrum includes a diverse array of courses designed to equip officers with the necessary skills and knowledge for their roles. **Chapter Seven.**

Transition phase: The period in a critical media strategy when law enforcement shifts back to a baseline media strategy. **Chapter Five.**

Watchdog: A role often assumed by the media, where journalists scrutinize and monitor government actions and institutions. **Chapter Three.**

Whistleblower Protection Act: A US federal law that safeguards individuals who expose wrongdoing or misconduct within an organization, typically in the public interest. The act prohibits retaliation against whistleblowers for their disclosures. **Chapter Ten.**

"Walls have ears": A saying that suggests that even private conversations can be overheard or spread, emphasizing the need for caution and privacy. **Chapter Ten.**

Vendetta seeker: One of the four character types of leakers. Leakers driven by a desire to settle personal scores, seek revenge, or harm someone they perceive as an adversary. **Chapter Ten.**

Zapruder film: A famous 8mm amateur film captured by Abraham Zapruder on November 22, 1963, which documented the assassination of President John F. Kennedy in Dallas, Texas. The film is a key piece of evidence in understanding the events of that day. **Chapter One.**

About the Author

Chief Todd Schmaderer has distinguished himself as a pivotal figure in law enforcement, serving as the 32nd Chief of the Omaha Police Department (OPD) since August 2012. At the time of this book's publication, he stands as one of the longest-serving chiefs in the Major Cities Chiefs Association (MCCA), leading a department comprising 1200 employees, including 906 sworn officers.

Under his leadership, Omaha has witnessed significant advancements in public safety and police-community relations. Chief Schmaderer's tenure has seen a remarkable reduction in gun violence, with homicides reaching four-year stretches at 40-year lows and achieving an 80% clearance rate over the last decade. The department has also experienced a notable decrease in complaints against officers, a substantial increase in diversity reflective of the community, and a reduction in officer-involved shootings to their lowest levels. Notably, Omaha recorded no homicides for 120 days in 2019, went the first 133 days of 2023 without a homicide, and finished 2023 with a 100% homicide clearance rate.

Chief Schmaderer brings to this book an authoritative perspective, shaped by his extensive experience in law enforcement and reinforced by his substantial academic achievements in criminal justice. His educational journey includes a Bachelor of Science in Criminal Justice from the University of Nebraska at Omaha, followed by a Master of Science in the same field from the University of Cincinnati. Further augmenting his expertise, Chief Schmaderer is also an esteemed graduate of the Federal Bureau of Investigation (FBI) National Executive Institute. Together, these elements of his background synergize to solidify his role as a well-qualified expert in the subjects discussed in this text.

Throughout his career, Chief Schmaderer has been at the forefront of addressing major crimes and significant national policing events in Nebraska. His experiences range from managing citywide civil unrest and police corruption scandals to overseeing the arrests of two serial killers and navigating high-profile cases involving child deaths, over 350 murders, more than 50 officer-involved shootings, and high-profile in-custody deaths, including during the pandemic of 2020. He has pioneered OPD's media strategy, conducted nearly 100 press conferences, and has been featured in national media outlets such as Dateline NBC, CNN, Fox News and Washington Post Live.